INTERPRETING DISABILITY

A Qualitative Reader

Philip M. Ferguson
Dianne L. Ferguson
Steven J. Taylor

Editors

Teachers College, Columbia University
New York and London

Published by Teachers College Press, 1234 Amsterdam Avenue
New York, NY 10027

Library of Congress Cataloging-in-Publication Data

Interpreting disability : a qualitative reader / Philip M. Ferguson,
  Dianne L. Ferguson, Steven J. Taylor, editors.
      p.   cm.
  Includes bibliographical references and index.
  ISBN 0-8077-3122-6. — ISBN 0-8077-3121-8 (pbk.)
  1. Handicapped—United States.   I. Ferguson, Philip M.
II. Ferguson, Dianne. III. Taylor, Steven J., 1949- .
HV1553.I58   1992
362.4′0973—dc20   91-24973
                                                  CIP

ISBN 0-8077-3122-6
ISBN 0-8077-3121-8 (pbk.)

Printed on acid-free paper
Manufactured in the United States of America

99 98 97 96 95 94 93 92   8 7 6 5 4 3 2 1

CONTENTS

Conclusion: The Future of Interpretivism
             in Disability Studies

Philip M. Ferguson, Dianne L. Ferguson,
& Steven J. Taylor

ACKNOWLEDGMENTS

Creating a collection of research studies such as this simultaneously creates a collection of debts of gratitude owed to the many people who helped us along the way. This book would not have been possible without their help, patience, and cooperation.

As editors, we are perhaps most obviously indebted to all of the authors of the individual chapters. As a group, these contributors represent an excellent sample (purposeful, of course) of the growing population of interpretivist researchers in disability studies. We thank them for their research, certainly, but also for their responsiveness to all of our requests and comments throughout the assembly process for the book. We hope they approve of the final construction (social, of course). Seven of the chapters included here are revised versions of articles and reports originally published elsewhere. We thank these publishers for permission to reprint those contributions.

Brian Ellerbeck, our editor at Teachers College Press, patiently provided us with a combination of gentle encouragement and serious discussion. His unflagging interest in the project kept us going as more than one deadline passed and the task list still seemed depressingly long. His efforts improved the book in countless ways.

Mary Donegan and Cindy Colavita in Syracuse, and Linda Wicklund and Myrna Zitek in Eugene, helped produce multiple versions of multiple manuscripts. Their efficiency and expertise made the cross-country coordination of editorial tasks easier than we had any right to expect.

Our own research for this book was partially supported by the Office of Special Education and Rehabilitation Services, U.S. Department of Education (Grants No. G008715566 and H133B00003-90. However, all of the opinions expressed herein are solely those of the individual authors and editors, and no endorsement by OSERS is implied or intended.

INTRODUCTION
Interpretivism and Disability Studies

Philip M. Ferguson, Dianne L. Ferguson,
& Steven J. Taylor

This is a book of research stories. We realize that the juxtaposition of "research" and "stories" may seem odd, if not downright contradictory, to some people. In special education—indeed, in much of social science—we learn early on that research can come in reports, studies, evaluations, critiques, monographs, and maybe even summarized in an occasional review. But serious research has little to do with what we usually think of as stories. Research is scientific and objective; stories are artistic and subjective. Research is scrupulously neutral; stories are openly laden with values. Good research tries to follow a standardized procedure; good stories try not to repeat a familiar plot. Research makes the researchers as interchangeable as possible; narrators often become an important part of the stories they tell. Whether talking about disability or any other topic of social science, surely reporting research and telling stories are two very different activities.

We beg to differ. The origin of this book of readings resides in our shared conviction that despite this seeming disparity in purpose and function, the goals of research are perfectly compatible with the discovery of good stories. It depends on the perspective, world view, or paradigm one brings to the research endeavor. We have reached this conviction during our years of trying to convey the key elements of one such paradigm in interpretive research methods to college students in special education and related fields. The three of us have all tried many approaches and techniques to wean these students from their comfortable but restrictive reliance on the objectivist world view that underlies traditional quantitative research. Increasingly, we have come to believe that the best way for most of these students to gain a quick appreciation of the interpretivist paradigm as a valid approach to the study of social reality is to convince them of the value of telling stories.

There is an important distinction here, however. It is not just the stories themselves whose value the students must appreciate; the *telling* of the story is equally important. For it is only in "the telling" that both a speaker and an audience are implicitly included, and that is where interpretation comes in. We tell our stories to interpret our lives for other people. Upon hearing them, other people interpret our interpretations. All individuals have their own particular stories. However, it is your telling of your stories that best reveals how you really make sense of your world: which stories you choose to tell about your life; what words you use; to whom you tell your tales. In this dual sense, the research collected here illustrates the value of telling stories in the study of disability.

This is, then, a book *of*—not *on*—interpretivist research methods. Our aim as editors has been to exemplify rather than to explicate qualitative techniques. Although many of the individual contributions describe the methods used to collect and analyze data, the main purpose of the collection is not to provide a "how to" text for interpretive research. At this point, such a text would be redundant. There are now several introductory texts on the theory and practice of this variously labelled (interpretivist, qualitative, ethnographic, phenomenological, and so on) approach to research (Bogdan & Biklen, 1982; Glaser & Strauss, 1967; Goetz & LeCompte, 1984; Guba & Lincoln, 1989; Lincoln & Guba, 1985; Lofland & Lofland, 1984; Miles & Huberman, 1984; Strauss & Corbin, 1990; Taylor & Bogdan, 1984).

What many of these books on methods do not provide are examples of what that research might look like in its published forms. For students within the fields of special education, rehabilitation, disability studies, and related areas, we think it is also useful to demonstrate the range of issues on which interpretivist research has already contributed to an understanding of how people experience and portray disability in our society. Despite the growing use of this approach to research in special education, many of the best examples of interpretivist inquiry in the area of disability still come from outside the professional disciplines oriented toward therapy or training. Fields such as anthropology, sociology, and history all have established bodies of interpretive research on the nature and experience of disability. With this book, we have tried to address the need to make a sample of this widely dispersed research more readily accessible to students, researchers, and practitioners in special education and rehabilitation.

THE "DISCOVERY" OF INTERPRETIVE RESEARCH

Interpretivist research is not a new phenomenon. Within many specific fields of social sciences and the humanities there are long traditions of research that provide a rich history of narrative inquiry in its various forms. Over the last several years, however, a new awareness of—and tolerance for—this type of research seems to have pervaded areas of disability studies, such as special education, previously dominated by quantitative (e.g., surveys) and/or behavioral (e.g., single subject designs) research methods. Increasingly, in the main professional journals of the various specialties, one can find calls for the acceptance of qualitative research (Heshusius, 1989; Jacob, 1990; Odom & Shuster, 1986; Stainback & Stainback, 1984; Taylor, 1988) and an openness to value-based inquiry (Heshusius, 1982; Peck, 1991; Poplin, 1988; Skrtic, 1986). However, two important points arise about this newfound acceptability.

Methods and Paradigms

First, it is important to make a distinction here between paradigms of knowledge and reality, and methods of inquiry and analysis. Most of the growing tolerance for qualitative research in special education has been at the level of methods, not paradigms. The frustration of post-positivists with the failed strictures of logical positivism has led to increased flexibility in design and techniques. It has not led to a wholesale abandonment of the objectivist paradigm. In this narrow version of pluralistic research, qualitative methods are fine as long as they meet the same or similar standards of objectivist epistemology (e.g., validity and reliability) that apply to quantitative methods. What is less common as of yet in this emerging openness is an accommodation of research done within nonobjectivist world views or paradigms, with different standards of truth-claims and the justification of knowledge. The importance of distinguishing methods of inquiry from paradigms of knowledge has led an increasing number of researchers to prefer different terms for methodology and paradigms (Smith, 1989). Thus, qualitative and quantitative methods can both be used within objectivist or interpretivist paradigms (Guba & Lincoln, 1989).[1]

As the title of this book indicates, this is intended as an interpretivist reader in disability studies, not just a qualitative one. The studies reported here involve more than the addition of a few open-ended questions to an otherwise structured questionnaire. The observations conducted by the researchers represented here provide more than anecdotal supplements to more precise measurements of operationalized variables. The research collected here not only relies on qualitative methods to collect and analyze its data, but it also operates from within a broadly interpretivist world view. We have chosen work that in some way or other has made what others have called "the interpretive turn" (Rabinow & Sullivan, 1979).

Themes and Variations

It is important to recognize the distinction between interpretivist and objectivist paradigms. It is also important to recognize the abundance of distinctions within interpretivism itself. Interpretivism is not monolithic. There are many versions, many variations. Some of these differences occur over fairly esoteric matters of conceptual detail; others involve more basic disagreement over central tenets of ontology (the nature of existence) and epistemology (the nature of knowledge).

Proponents of the paradigm cannot even agree on what to call their world view. Naturalism, conventionalism, constructionism, and holism are all names that other scholars prefer for positions that resemble what we are calling interpretivism. In terms of methods usually associated with this paradigm, the labels can be even more confusing. Qualitative research, ethnography, ethnomethodology, naturalistic inquiry, and hermeneutics are all terms for different ways of gathering and analyzing information about the world that have evolved within what we call the interpretivist paradigm. Adherents of one or another of these schools would undoubtedly have chosen a different set of studies to illustrate the paradigm. Their points of emphasis would differ from ours. On some issues (for example, the potential compatibility of interpretivist and objectivist paradigms) there is sharp disagreement.

This diversity can be confusing to students familiar with a uniform set of rules and procedures: a *t*-test is a *t*-test is a *t*-test. However, the true inconsistency would come with an unvaried interpretivism. The diversity that exists simply betokens a resistance to standardization that is itself one of the hallmarks of interpretivist thinking. It is for this very reason that illustrations of the paradigm in practice can be as helpful as explanations of its principles and techniques.

CENTRAL TENETS OF INTERPRETIVISM OR "HEY, BROTHER, CAN YOU PARADIGM?"

Despite the variations in understanding and emphasis on exactly what interpretivism means, there are identifiable beliefs that loosely bind its supporters to one another. These beliefs represent a kind of conceptual confederation within which the various tribes of interpretivists can define their shared territory and negotiate their shifting boundaries. At the risk of alienating one tribe or another, we think it is important to give our own guide to interpretivist landmarks. The following four tenets may at least help to orient the reader who is exploring this paradigm for the first time.

Reality Is Created and Social

Interpretivists generally believe that in some sense reality is always a process of social construction. Reality is not a fixed or objective phenomenon. What is or is not "real" or "true" is a matter of social definition. People, as social actors, construct the reality or truth of a situation. The value of telling stories is that that is precisely how one discovers what the social constructions are. Indeed, what we mean by the term *story* is simply one person's, or one group's, social construction of "what happened."

In most cases, one of two structures of interpretation holds with regard to social construction. First, everyone often agrees so completely on a particular social construction that no one notices any longer that it is, in fact, a construction and not the actual thing or event. An example might be the accepted greeting behavior of smiling and waving a hand as someone approaches. Only when this behavior is interpreted as something other than a friendly hello are we reminded that meaning it as a greeting is a construction of our intentions, not an objective feature of our physical movements. The second situation is where one person's or group's particular social construction of an event or object holds sway over other people's constructions. In this situation there is not so much a consensus of interpretation as there is a dominance of one over others. Think of what it "meant" to be "female" about 20 years ago. There was a dominant social construction of what was and was not feminine or female, but this does not mean that there were not always many women who had very different interpretations and social constructions. It was just that no one ever asked them to tell their stories.

A Split Between Subject and Object Is Impossible

Once within the assumptions of the interpretivist paradigm it becomes misleading to think of it as subjective. At the heart of the interpretive paradigm is a fundamental challenge to the subjective/objective dualism embedded in Western culture. If everything is unavoidably "subjective," then the dichotomy itself becomes misleading. Indeed, such a dichotomy between subject and object, knower and known, is itself a construction of the objectivist paradigm, which is then forced upon the other paradigms as a way of defining them in words the objectivists will understand. The preferable way would be for objectivists to learn another language game: one where objectivity literally made no sense. In the interpretivist paradigm, to speak of choosing subjectivity is analogous to a fish discussing its choice of water over land.

A Split Between Fact and Value Is Impossible

This is the ethical corollary of the preceding tenet about subjectivism and objectivism. Facts are not only the products of social constructions;

their production never occurs in a moral vacuum. Many physical scientists recognize this better than social scientists. Regardless of whether they choose to do so, few of today's physicists would argue that working on the "Starwars" project (or the Strategic Defense Initiative) is a morally neutral action. Logical positivism holds that "you can't imply ought from is." Objective reality, in other words, has no inherent ethical implications. No accumulation of factual premises will ever justify a moral conclusion. Insofar as science is about the accumulation of facts, then morality has no place in the process. This contention is harder to make today because our century has seen the logical extreme of this approach to science in Hitler's Germany. Again, however, the point to note for the interpretivist paradigm is not simply to reverse the argument and contend that you can imply ought from is. Rather, the ethical stance of interpretivism is that you cannot separate facts and values at all. Facts do not simply imply values; they are values.

The Goal of Research Should Be Interpretive Understanding

The goal of research within the objectivist paradigm is to describe, predict, and control. Because of interpretivism's fundamental belief in the multiple realities of social construction, prediction and control become questionable. The linear approach of cause–effect, cause–effect is replaced by a much more holistic understanding of how things change over time. Instead of "describe, predict, and control," the goal of interpretivist research might better be described as "describe, interpret, and understand." Moreover, the understanding sought is a kind of empathic process whereby one tries to approximate the perspective of others. At least since the work of Max Weber, interpretivists have adopted the German word "Verstehen" to convey this deeper, fuller sense of understanding.

However, it is also important to note this emphasis of interpretivism on empathy and understanding is not simply an excuse for sloppy research. Interpretivist research is not simply the collection of poignant vignettes or supportive anecdotes: a kind of warm and fuzzy approach to research. Interpretive research, properly done, is just as systematic, just as rigorous, as the best statistical analyses one can find.

THE AIMS AND ORGANIZATION OF THE BOOK

Given this orientation to interpretivism generally, we need to say a final few words about the aims and organization of the book. We have already described the purpose of the book in general terms. What we want to do here is describe how we have tried to realize that purpose through the specific studies selected for inclusion in this reader, and how we have organized those studies.

Disability and Interpretivism

The book intends to go beyond a methodological purpose to illustrate the power of the interpretivist paradigm to reveal the experience and meaning of disability in our culture in richer terms than normally achieved. As Howard Becker has noted (1966/67), interpretivist research is particularly suited to giving voice to the "underdog" in society. The emphasis on created and intentional reality within interpretivism places an unavoidable focus on discovering the multiple perspectives of all the "players" within a social setting. To the extent that some perspectives have received less attention than others in our society, allowing those "underdog" perspectives to emerge should have some empowering effect. Certainly people with disabilities and their families have historically belonged to those groups of devalued people without much voice in what was done to and for them by more powerful groups within society.

Interpretivist research on people with disabilities is, therefore, unavoidably and intimately connected to the social status of those individuals. The very process itself of studying disability in this way instead of in more traditional ways is part of the outcome of how we understand the people to whom we apply the various handicapping labels. This does not mean, of course, that every interpretivist study on disability has to focus on the perspective of people with disabilities. Some interpretivist research (see Chapters 1 and 4, for example) has an indirectly empowering effect by revealing what is taken as objective reality as "simply" the perspective—the social construction—of relatively more powerful groups within a setting and culture. The recognition of "the medical model" (Gliedman & Roth, 1980) as but one way (although the dominant way) to understand disability has prepared the way for other perspectives to gather attention. Most important, this has meant taking the perspective of disabled people themselves more seriously.

Through this reasoning, it became clear to us in editing the book that it should be organized by content rather than by method; by what the research discovered about disability, rather than by how it made the discovery methodologically. Again this is a book *of* interpretive research *on* disability. If the readings contained here convince you of the value of interpretive research, but fail to deepen your understanding of the experience and portrayal of disability, then the book will not have done what we hoped. The research we chose fell into four basic contexts for experiencing disability. Each of these contexts will be described more fully in our introductory comments at the beginning of each part. Those introductions also include suggestions for further readings on that particular area of interpretive disability studies. We will only briefly identify the parts here.

Part I. Disability at the Edges of Life. The chapters in this part of the book
   share a focus on how infancy, old age, and social isolation affect the
   social meaning given to disability.
Part II. Disability and the Schools. This part is the closest in context to
   traditional special education research. The three chapters examine—at
   various levels of theory and critique—the changes occurring in our
   public schools for integrating students with disabilities.
Part III. Disability and the Community. The chapters here examine the differences between physical and social integration. As people with even the
   most severe disabilities move into the community, the awareness grows
   that social isolation can occur in even the most integrated of settings.
   The crusades for social integration have affected families as well as
   disabled people themselves.
Part IV. Disability and Culture. Perhaps the most pervasive, and yet the least
   recognized, context for disability is the cultural stew of images and
   stereotypes about disability that inevitably simmers on the back burner
   of everyone's consciousness as we make our way through life. This
   part presents some research into both negative and positive images of
   disability in our culture.

Qualitative Options

Despite our focus on content as the organizational framework for the book, we have not neglected the methodological purpose to provide a sampler of interpretivist research. Across all of these parts we have included as wide a range of research as possible. This has not been easy. The diversity within interpretivism creates many more options for the researcher than with the more standardized procedures of objectivist research. In addition to the choices of how to collect qualitative data, there are several other important categories of variation. No single book could hope to capture examples of all these variations. We have tried to include some that we think are particularly useful and/or important. There are at least three types of methodological differences that the reader should look for.

1. *Multiple methods of data collection.* There are three *main* ways in which
   most interpretivist research gathers its information. Participant observation involves the unstructured observations of research participants in
   naturalistic settings. Out of these observations come lengthy fieldnotes,

written by the researcher. Interviews of participants are a second major way for collecting information. These interviews are usually less structured and more open-ended and in depth than traditional interviews of quantitative techniques. Finally, there is the qualitative analysis of formal and informal documents (e.g., photographs, diaries, official policy statements). A specific qualitative study may call upon any or all of these techniques for data collection.

2. *Multiple research purposes and designs.* The reason for doing a particular qualitative study can also vary. In many situations the foremost goal of the research is to provide as rich or "thick" a descriptive account of a setting, group, or individual. In such instances, the descriptive case study is usually the design of choice. In other contexts where openly advocative purposes apply, the use of action research designs may be more appropriate (see Chapter 6, for example). Other purposes can lead to other design decisions involving life histories, program evaluations, or social criticism and policy analysis.

3. *Multiple presentation styles.* One of the most noticeable ways that reports of qualitative research can differ from more traditional quantitative research is in the actual written style and format of those reports. For example, many interpretivists find it impossible to pretend that they were unnoticed observers of the events they are analyzing. As a result, much interpretive research assumes a more prominent narrative voice as a natural part of the methodology. Writing styles in general within interpretivist research tend to be less formal and less structured. It is often hard for interpretive research to confine itself—even if it wanted to—to the rigid formats of many social science journals (introduction, methods, results, discussion). The selections chosen for this book represent some of the range of presentation style that is still fairly rare within special education and related fields.

The instant one begins to look beyond the narrow disciplinary boundaries of special education and rehabilitation for examples of interpretivist research on disability, one realizes how rich and lively the range of inquiry actually is. The studies contained in this collection can only suggest the variety of topics, research methods, and presentation styles that now exists in this type of disability research. It is clear that an interdisciplinary field of disability studies is now thriving. Although the field certainly includes more than just interpretive research, it is fair to claim that the flexibility of interpretivism has played a major role in allowing the multiple perspectives inherent in such an approach to disability to flourish together. We hope this reader bolsters that claim.

NOTE

1. Obviously, much more could be said about this distinction. Those who would like to read a fuller discussion could start with the recent book by Guba and Lincoln (1989, pp. 156–183) and an excellent article by Smith and Heshusius (1986). A defense of methodological compatibility of qualitative and quantitative techniques can be found in the "soft nosed logical positivism" (p. 19) described by Miles and Huberman (1984).

REFERENCES

Becker, H. S. (1966/67). Whose side are we on? *Social Problems, 14,* 239–247.

Bogdan, R. C., & Biklen, S. K. (1982). *Qualitative research for education: An introduction to theory and methods.* Boston: Allyn & Bacon.

Glaser, B. G., & Strauss, A. L. (1967). *The discovery of grounded theory: Strategies for qualitative research.* Chicago: Aldine.

Gliedman, J., & Roth, W. (1980). *The unexpected minority: Handicapped children in America.* New York: Harcourt Brace Jovanovich.

Goetz, J. P., & LeCompte, M. D. (1984). *Ethnography and qualitative design in educational research.* New York: Academic Press.

Guba, E. G., & Lincoln, Y. S. (1989). *Fourth generation evaluation.* Newbury Park, CA: Sage.

Heshusius, L. (1982). At the heart of the advocacy dilemma: A mechanistic world view. *Exceptional Children, 49,* 6–11.

Heshusius, L. (1989). The Newtonian mechanistic paradigm, special education, and contours of alternatives: An overview. *Journal of Learning Disabilities, 22,* 403–415.

Jacob, E. (1990). Alternative approaches for studying naturally occurring human behavior and thought in special education research. *The Journal of Special Education, 24,* 195–211.

Lincoln, Y. S., & Guba, E. G. (1985). *Naturalistic inquiry.* Beverly Hills, CA: Sage.

Lofland, J., & Lofland, L. H. (1984). *Analyzing social settings: A guide to qualitative observation and analysis* (2nd ed.). Belmont, CA: Wadsworth.

Miles, M. B., & Huberman, A. M. (1984). *Qualitative data analysis: A sourcebook of new methods.* Newbury Park, CA: Sage.

Odom, S. L., & Shuster, S. K. (1986). Naturalistic inquiry and the assessment of young handicapped children and their families. *Topics in Early Childhood Special Education, 6*(2), 68–82.

Peck, C. A. (1991). Linking values and science in social policy decisions affecting citizens with severe disabilities. In L. H. Meyer, C. A. Peck, & L. Brown (Eds.), *Critical issues in the lives of people with severe disabilities* (pp. 1–15). Baltimore: Paul H. Brookes.

Poplin, M. S. (1988). Holistic/constructivist principles of the teaching/learning process: Implications for the field of learning disabilities. *Journal of Learning Disabilities, 21*, 401–416.

Rabinow, P., & Sullivan, W. M. (1979). The interpretive turn: Emergence of an approach. In P. Rabinow & W. M. Sullivan (Eds.), *Interpretive social science: A reader* (pp. 1–21). Berkeley: University of California Press.

Skrtic, T. M. (1986). The crisis in special education knowledge: A perspective on perspective. *Focus on Exceptional Children, 18*(7), 1–16.

Smith, J. K. (1989). *The nature of social and educational inquiry: Empiricism versus interpretation.* Norwood, NJ: Ablex.

Smith, J. K., & Heshusius, L. (1986). Closing down the conversation: The end of the quantitative–qualitative debate among educational inquirers. *Educational Researcher, 15*(1), 4–12.

Stainback, S., & Stainback, W. (1984). Broadening the research perspective in special education. *Exceptional Children, 50*, 400–408.

Strauss, A. L., & Corbin, J. (1990). *Basics of qualitative research: Grounded theory procedures and techniques.* Newbury Park, CA: Sage.

Taylor, S. J. (1988). Preface to "Generations of Hope." *The Journal of The Association for Persons with Severe Handicaps, 13*, 175–176.

Taylor, S. J. & Bogdan, R. (1984). *Introduction to qualitative research methods: The search for meanings* (2nd ed.). New York: John Wiley.

Part I

DISABILITY AT THE EDGES OF LIFE

Life has many edges to it, some more visible than others. There are the temporal edges of birth and death, of course. These are probably the most familiar edges, if only because everyone crosses them. While few of us can remember our beginnings or predict our end, there are periods of our life course—early childhood and old age—that are closely associated with these endpoints. Other edges are less clearly marked, and most of us do not approach them. There are margins to our social and cultural life, for example, in addition to the temporal limits. In some cases, these social margins correspond with actual geographic locations reserved for those whom we decide to keep at the edge of the social map. Thus, we exile some "marginal" people to an isolated, "borderland" existence in prisons, mental hospitals, asylums, or other institutions. In other cases, the cultural edges have no distance from the time and place of our daily lives. We confront these edges in the extremes of wealth or poverty, religion, and morality that characterize some people on the fringes of "typical" behavior and beliefs. These edges run down the streets of our cities where homeless people congregate: as close to us as an extended arm, but usually a world away. The lines run through the welfare agencies and social work offices that guard these cultural borders. These edges are all around us, visible but unseen to the majority of mainstream culture.

Many people with disabilities spend their entire lives on some edge or other. Some of them are born with a precarious hold on life itself. Their lives begin—and sometimes quickly end—with a medical struggle. Others with disabilities have normal health but are physically marginalized through placement in institutions (mental hospitals, developmental centers, large nursing facilities). Finally, even if allowed to stay in our midst, many people with disabilities and their families live in a kind of cultural prison of constant poverty and social control.

Traditionally, the techniques and temperament of qualitative researchers have been especially well-suited to the study and understanding of people at the edges, the margins, the extremes of life. Many of the classics of urban ethnography and symbolic interactionist research focus on various groups of people located—by choice or by command—beyond the mainstream of white, middle class culture. Works such as *Street Corner Society* (Whyte, 1955) and *Tally's Corner* (Liebow, 1967) present thick descriptions of urban life among poor Italian and black males, respectively. The equally hidden culture of the extremely rich has also been studied (Domhoff, 1975). Richly detailed life histories allow readers to begin to see the world through the eyes of people with various socially constructed labels: transsexuals (Bogdan, 1974), drug dealers (Williams, 1989), juvenile delinquents (Shaw, 1966), and elderly women (Matthews, 1986).

As we mentioned in the introduction, this is one of the reasons that qualitative research is so valuable in disability studies: It gives voice to people who are often studied but seldom heard. The use of techniques such as participant observation, in-depth interviews, life histories, and document analysis permits the researcher to blur the edges that often separate people with disabilities from the rest of society. Qualitative research can gain access to levels of life or groups of people that are simply unavailable without the extended "time in the field" typical of participant observation and in-depth interviewing. The perspective of the unheard can emerge because qualitative research implicitly challenges the "hierarchy of credibility" (Becker, 1966/67) that gives progressively greater credence to those at the centers of power and society, those who are furthest from the edges of life.

Each of the chapters in this section illustrates this strength of qualitative research by focusing on the experiences of people with disabilities or their families who live on one or more of the boundaries we have mentioned. Together they illustrate how different techniques of gathering qualitative data and presenting the findings can serve effectively to portray the experiences and interpretations of these groups (and those who try to control these groups).

The first two chapters examine the interactions of parents of young children with professionals involved in providing services to both the parents and the children. In Chapter 1 Bogdan, Brown, and Foster examine the categories and interpretations that structure the interactions of staff and parents in neonatal intensive care units. Their careful analysis reveals how unofficial conceptual schemes (e.g., who are the "good" parents and the "bad" parents from the medical staff's point of view) can undermine even the best intentions at effective communication. This chapter also illustrates how qualitative study can explore the relevance of its findings for other settings and contexts. By "testing" their grounded theory in additional intensive care units, Bogdan et al. are able to speak directly to the issue of how "transferable" their results might be. Their speculation about the character of parent–professional communication in general suggests a variety of applications for their findings beyond the medical settings (classrooms, residential programs, therapy programs, and so on).

Chapter 2 by Janko also deals with parents of young children, but in a very different context of an intervention program for abused and neglected children. By definition, all the children in this program either have, or are at risk of developing, permanent disabilities from the abuse or neglect they have allegedly received. Janko presents a case study of one parent caught up in the accusations and interventions of a child protection agency's experimental support program. Again, the differences in how the parents and professionals view the events that bring them together are powerfully described. Janko's research uses the same combination of observations, interviews, and document analysis employed by Bogdan, Brown, and Foster. However, Janko presents her findings in a much more personal style that eschews much of the "invisible narrator" conventions of traditional academic research. The result is a narrative that conveys the shared experiences of the researcher and the participant in a much more direct and immediate language. This more personalized style of reporting qualitative research is becoming increasingly popular and acceptable.

In Chapter 3 Todis takes us to the other end of the life course in her study of an elderly couple who are both labelled mentally retarded. Todis uses a life history approach to let her two participants tell their stories. Again, however, despite the very different context and design for the research, this chapter, too, discovers the theme of formal services that are intended as supportive but are not always perceived that way by those receiving them. Grace's and Wilbur's lives together provide an interesting contribution to our understanding of the complexities of topics such as formal and informal support networks, independence and reliance, and emotional relationships in old age.

The final chapter in this part provides yet another style of presenting qualitative research. In this case, Chapter 4, by Taylor and Bogdan, might be referred to as an example of "meta-ethnography" (Noblit & Hare, 1988) or qualitative review, wherein multiple studies or reports are synthesized within an explicitly theoretical framework. The authors draw upon qualitative investigations of institutional life, done by themselves and others, to construct an organizational theory of how large, residential facilities for mentally retarded people continue to justify their existence in the face of shifting social attitudes about their appropriateness. The study illustrates how qualitative research can move beyond a purely "micro" focus on individual experiences to the "macro" level of social analysis and criticism. The chapter also shows how aggressively the institutions at the edges of life and culture resist efforts toward social change.

REFERENCES

Becker, H. S. (1966/67). Whose side are we on? *Social Problems, 14,* 239–247.
Bogdan, R. (1974). *Being different: The autobiography of Jane Fry.* New York: Wiley.
Domhoff, G. W. (1975). *The Bohemian Grove and other retreats.* New York: Random House.
Liebow, E. (1967). *Tally's corner.* Boston: Little, Brown.
Matthews, S. H. (1986). *Friendships through the life course: Oral biographies in old age.* Newbury Park, CA: Sage.
Noblit, G. W., & Hare, R. D. (1988). *Meta-ethnography: Synthesizing qualitative studies.* Newbury Park, CA: Sage.
Shaw, C. (1966). *The jack roller* (2nd ed.). Chicago: University of Chicago Press.
Whyte, W. F. (1955). *Street corner society.* Chicago: University of Chicago Press.
Williams, T. (1989). *The cocaine kids: The inside story of a teenage drug ring.* Reading, MA: Addison-Wesley.

SUGGESTED READINGS

Blatt, B., & Kaplan, F. (1974). *Christmas in purgatory.* Syracuse, NY: Human Policy Press.

This is a famous book within the field of mental retardation. It does not pretend to be "balanced" and "objective," just powerful and true. The book combines text and photographs to present a stark commentary on life in the "back wards" of large public institutions. Methodologically, the book is an example of action research that did help galvanize public opinion about the necessity to reform the social policies and practices that had allowed such extremes of neglect and abandonment to persist.

Bogdan, R., & Taylor, S. J. (1982). *Inside out: The social meaning of mental retardation.* Toronto: University of Toronto Press.

Using a life history approach, this book allows two individuals labelled mentally retarded to tell their own stories about growing up in institutions. The book illustrates the potential of qualitative techniques such as un-structured, in-depth interviewing to reveal the perspectives of disabled people themselves. Not incidentally, the book also presents a powerful account of how the category of mental retardation is socially constructed by the dominance of some perspectives over others.

Conrad, P., & Schneider, J. W. (1980). *Deviance and medicalization: From badness to sickness.* St. Louis, MO: C. V. Mosby.

The study of life at the cultural edges of society involves an area of sociology called deviance theory. While the concept of deviance extends to all types of behavior (criminal, sexual, and so forth), the categories of disability are prominent topics in the sociology of deviance. This book provides an excellent introduction to the understanding of deviance from an inter-pretivist (the authors call it "social interactionist") paradigm. The chapters on mental illness, learning disability, and child abuse are particularly relevant.

Goffman, E. (1961). *Asylums: Essays on the social situation of mental patients and other inmates.* Garden City, NY: Doubleday, Anchor Books.

This is an extremely influential study that helped reframe the social understanding of institutions and the people who live and work in them. Commonly used concepts in current sociological analysis, such as "total institution," are drawn from this work. Goffman's work does not discuss the details of his methodological techniques, but develops an insightful account of regimented, organizational control.

Guillemin, J. H., & Holmstrom, L. L. (1986). *Mixed blessings: Intensive care for newborns.* New York: Oxford University Press.

A carefully written ethnography of a newborn intensive care unit, this book demonstrates several interesting methodological components. First, it shows how qualitative and quantitative methods can be combined within a single study. Second, it employs a procedure of analytic induction by testing its initial descriptions in a purposefully selected sample of additional nursery settings. Finally, the book combines careful description with a concluding section of policy recommendations.

Gubrium, J. *Living and dying in Murray Manor.* New York: St. Martin's Press.

This is a moving account of how daily life gets organized and defined in one specific nursing home. The author used participant observation techniques to study all levels of staff and administration, as well as "the clientele" of the home. The author presents a somewhat different picture of institutional life than Goffman's, describing a complex social setting with elements of cheer and companionship as well as boredom and isolation.

Chapter 1

BE HONEST BUT NOT CRUEL
Staff/Parent Communication
on a Neonatal Unit

Robert Bogdan, Mary Alice Brown,
& Susan Bannerman Foster

The second time we visited an intensive care ward for infants (neonatal unit) we witnessed an event that foreshadowed the focus of the research reported here. A couple had come to visit their three-quarter-kilogram (26-ounce) critically ill, premature son. They were rural poor, in their early 20s, and had driven 80 miles that morning for the visit. They taped the carnation they bought at the hospital gift shop onto the heavy steel pole that held a heater over the open plastic box in which their child lay. Both stood near the child talking to each other and to the fragile infant, "You be home soon fella," the father said to his son. His mother added, "Everything's all ready for you." A nurse, standing within hearing distance, approached the couple and said, "Now, you have to be realistic, you have a very sick baby." That night the baby died. When the parents were told they were overpowered with grief. The mother said that the news took her completely by surprise. This story illustrates how instances of failed communication can exacerbate the already tragic circumstances that frequently exist in intensive care nurseries. The overwhelming importance of effective communication between staff and parents gradually became the focus of our field research study of neonatal units. Specifically, we became interested in developing an understanding of who talks to parents about their child's condition, what they say, and what parents hear.

What physicians tell patients (Cartwright, 1964, 1967; Waitzkin & Stoeckle, 1972) and parents of juvenile patients (Davis, 1960, 1963; Korsch, 1974; Skipper & Leonard, 1968) has been the subject of social

An earlier version of this chapter appeared in *Human Organization, 41*(1), 6–16, 1982. Reprinted by permission of The Society for Applied Anthropology.

science investigation for as long as there has been a social science of medicine (Parsons, 1967). Of special interest has been the communication of bad
news (McIntosh, 1979), of pending death (Rowe et al., 1978), of chronic
disease (Glaser & Strauss, 1965, 1968), and of disabling physical and
mental abnormalities (Jacobs, 1969; Taichert, 1975).

The study reported here lies within the symbolic interactionist tradition (Glaser & Strauss, 1965), which also has a long association with the
sociology of medicine (e.g., Becker, Geer, Hughes, & Strauss, 1961; Glaser
& Strauss, 1968; Strauss, Fagerhaugh, Suczek, & Wiener, 1985). We used
this approach to explore the specific patterns of communication that occur
when medical staff speak with or about parents of infants with a variety of
life threatening and potentially disabling conditions (Duff & Campbell,
1973; Jonsen & Lister, 1978). Researchers often study a topic like professional–parent communication as an isolated occurrence, that is, without an
understanding of the setting in which it occurs (e.g., Clyman, Sniderman,
Ballard, & Roth, 1979; Wiener, 1970). Our use of interactionist research
methods allows us to emphasize the context of communication on neonatal
units, stressing how the staff perceive the units and highlighting aspects of
the units that relate to staff–parent communication. We examine the staff's
way of categorizing infants, parents, and each other. In addition, we describe perspectives they have that relate to talking to parents about their
children. Then we introduce the parents' world—how they experience the
unit and what influences what they hear when the staff speak. We conclude
with a discussion of the implications of our findings for theory, method,
practice, and social policy.

SETTING AND PROCEDURES

The Neonatal Unit

High technology neonatal units became a part of the medical scene
during the 1970s. The particular units we are concerned with are part of
recently developed perinatal systems. They provide level III care, which
means they have the highest level of trained personnel, use the most sophisticated equipment, and treat the most seriously involved infants in the
regions they serve. They receive referrals from hospitals with level II and
level I units. Special transport teams using chartered planes carry some
patients over 100 miles. The units we have studied have a maximum
capacity of 35 to 65 infants each (600 to 1,200 patients per year) and
employ 80 to 100 full-time nurses, 3 to 6 full-time neonatologists, a large

number of technical and other staff, plus 6 to 10 house officers who serve the unit in conjunction with their medical training.

Most of the patients are premature infants, the smallest weighing as little as 500 grams (slightly over 1 pound). Others have life threatening birth defects. Approximately 15% of the infants die; some are so premature that they need prolonged treatment on which they may become dependent or which may cause them irreparable damage (blindness, brain tissue destruction, chronic lung conditions). While most of the children leave the unit to live relatively normal lives, these units are places where many are at high risk of being part of the next generation of mentally retarded and otherwise handicapped people.

The newcomer to a unit is struck by the pace of activity, the long, intense hours the staff works, the sophisticated technology, and the life and death struggle that is a regular part of the routine. As one spends time on these units, all of those factors, plus the awesome sight of tiny infants with a substantial portion of their bodies covered with tape, attached to respirators, oxygen dispensers, I.V.s, and monitors, under heaters and bilirubin lights, with monitors beeping warnings of heart arrest, soon become the details of everyday life.

Method and Procedures

The data reported were collected during a one-year period on—and with people related to—neonatal intensive care units in urban teaching hospitals. Our work began under the auspices of a funded service project in which physical therapists, educators, social workers, and other professionals acting in teams were to provide services to infants who were at high risk of becoming developmentally delayed. Service providers were to go into the homes of the infants who had been on the unit and involve parents in the "intervention." We were to give information to the teams about the fit between what they planned to do and the service system as we observed it in operation. It seemed important for them to understand what parents experienced on the unit and what parents understood about their children's conditions. Our interests soon expanded beyond the project, and our data collection was enlarged so that we could explore the broader issues presented here.

We started our research doing participant observation (Taylor & Bogdan, 1984) on the unit the project served. We visited for 4 months, 2 to 4 times a week for 1 to 3 hours, taking extensive fieldnotes after each visit. In conjunction with these observations we interviewed physicians, nurses, and parents, in addition to reviewing official documents. After the initial

4 months, we increased our interviews with parents but decreased our observations on the unit. In addition, we expanded our observations to three other units: one in a neighboring state, and two in other cities but in the same state as a project unit. Our purpose in these visits was to explore generalizability and enlarge our emerging model. The visits to the other units were only for a day each and consisted of interviews with key personnel as well as observations.

During our observations on the project unit we went on rounds, attended case conferences, sat in on orientation sessions for new staff, and observed day-to-day activities, including discussions between staff and parents about the condition of their children. (We observed similar activities on the other units but on a more limited basis.) We completed more than 40 tape-recorded interviews ranging from 35 minutes to 2 hours in length, plus the less formal interviews done in the course of our observations. Many of the professionals we talked to had worked or were trained on units other than those on which we observed. We questioned them about those units and concluded that they were substantially similar to the ones described in this chapter. What we report here has, in various drafts, been presented to, discussed with, and, where warranted, modified in response to reactions from professional staff on the units.

THE CONTEXT OF COMMUNICATION ON NEONATAL UNITS

Patients as Seen by the Staff

From the perspective of the staff on the neonatal units, babies are not just babies. Instead, any particular baby fits into a loose typology that is part of the staff's way of seeing things. Regardless of whether parents or staff initiate conversations with each other about a child's condition, the context and content of what is said in that conversation can be understood only by knowing where in the typology the staff are locating that particular patient.

Staff on the units studied share an informal classification system of their patients, with statuses identified by a special vocabulary. (Similar classification schemes, although less detailed, are noted in Becker et al., 1961, and Duff & Hollingshead, 1968.) Although there are differences in specific phrases used and other details, the classification schemes are consistent from hospital to hospital.

Figure 1.1 depicts the staff's conceptual scheme of patients. Words in quotes refer to those consistently used on the units. Those without quotes are our phrases. These represent categories that the staff do not have specific

Figure 1.1
Staff Perceptions of Patients

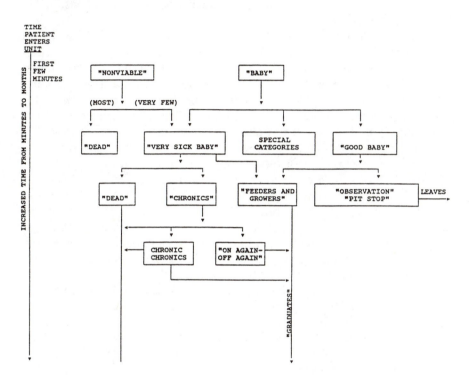

or consistent words for, but, as indicated by the way they talk ("Take a baby *like* this . . ." "This *kind* of infant . . .") and act (e.g., the amount of time spent discussing the baby at rounds), they do think of babies as belonging to. While all professional staff in all units studied use a scheme similar to the one presented, ours is an "ideal type" (in the Weberian sense) in that it neither captures perfectly nor seriously distorts any of the specific units' schemes. All staff on a particular unit do not see patients in exactly the same way. Nurses, for example, use a slightly different system than physicians, but on any unit staff have a general common vocabulary and scheme. While staff share the general typology, there may be disagreement as to what "type" any particular child is. As we will discuss, this can be a source of conflict over what is said and who talks to parents.

As Figure 1.1 suggests (see left-hand side), the classification system used by medical personnel is temporal. Those categories that are used early in the patient's career appear at the top of the diagram and those at the later stages appear progressively further down. As we will present in our discussion, the professional staff's classification system is related to timetables they hold regarding career patterns of patients on the unit (Davis, 1960; Roth, 1958).

During the first few minutes on the unit, the patient is classified as either "baby" or "nonviable." This judgment is made using a combination of gestation age, birth weight, Apgar scores, other tests and findings, and, in extreme cases, the extent and nature of apparent or assumed physical and mental abnormalities. While the staff of a particular unit has conventions for making such decisions, there is always an element of judgment. Conventions vary from unit to unit and over time. The size and gestation age of a patient considered viable have gone down drastically in recent years as a result of the development of technology and the growth of neonatology.

Nonviables, who are often referred to as "fetuses," may be placed in a special room or some other out-of-the-way place on the unit, and given no treatment.[1] Babies are treated, often using heroic means. Once a baby is on a particular treatment (e.g., a respirator), it is rarely withdrawn, although with consultation from parents, additional potential life-saving intervention may be withheld. Infants may be "no coded," which means there are orders not to use additional treatment if the patient arrests.

Often parents of nonviables arrive after the death and are told immediately of the event by the physician assigned to the child or by the highest ranking staff member present. (Sometimes parents are told that their child is nonviable, only to arrive and find the infant under treatment with the possibility of life reopened.) When the parents arrive before death, the attending officer, a house officer assigned to the child, or an available staff member discusses the condition with the parents, indicating that death is imminent and that the baby is not being treated. If the parent presses for treatment, there may be intervention. The great majority of nonviables are dead on arrival or die shortly after, but each unit has cases of the few who persevered and became "babies." Occasionally, a new arrival defined by some staff as baby is defined by other staff as nonviable. The latter staff will sometimes convey this pessimism by referring to the infant as a "fetus." These and other situations where there is disagreement are stressful for staff because they are expected to present a united front to parents. For the staff members who are critical of a treatment decision, not speaking to the parents about the matter may be difficult, especially if the staff member is a nurse who has come to know the parents.

During the first hours on the unit, most patients are given the status of baby. Some are placed in categories other than baby and nonviable during the first few minutes, but for most, more specific designations are held in abeyance until the patients have been observed, tested, and treated. During this period, parents are provided with general information about the condition of their child, with an explanation of how difficult it is to know anything specific at this early stage and that more will be known in time. Professional staff often use a specific amount of time in discussions with parents: "We will know more in 48 hours" or "in 72 hours."

The patient may remain an undifferentiated baby for a few minutes or a few days, but eventually moves into one of three categories: "very sick babies," "good babies," and "babies with special problems." This latter type includes infants with such problems as heart defects, hydrocephaly, spina bifida, undifferentiated gender, special syndromes, and other birth defects. They either leave the unit within a few days or join those with the status of very sick baby or good baby with a special anomaly. Certain special category babies (e.g., children with spina bifida) face the risk that exceptional procedures needed to keep them alive will be withheld. Special category babies are, more than any other type, put up for adoption or institutionalized. The most concentrated amount of time is spent talking to the parents who are involved in these decisions, and the way the child's condition is presented can be critical in formulating parents' thinking.

Good babies are babies judged not to be at high risk of dying but who need support and observation either because of birth-related trauma or because of prematurity. Often, they need to grow in order to reach the weight (4 to 5 pounds) required to be discharged from the unit. Good babies who are there for a day or less are called "observation babies" or "pit stops": Like race cars, they need only a quick check, some minor fixing, and they're on their way. As Figure 1.1 indicates, observation babies are not considered "graduates" of the unit. That designation is reserved for infants who spend longer periods of time on the unit.

Good babies who are not there just for observation are "feeders and growers." This phrase is used because the professional staff see them as basically healthy except for their low weight and minor problems. All they need to do is feed and grow before they graduate. There are a number of subcategories under feeder and grower. There are "3-hour babies" and "4-hour babies," these names deriving from the time between feedings. There are also "nipplers," babies that are beginning to take food by sucking. Other categories also contain such elaborate subdivisions.

Very sick babies are those the staff see as at high risk of dying. Most of these infants are of very low birth weight (1 kilogram or less) or have not spent enough time in utero to develop their lungs sufficiently to breathe on their own. Typically they are on respirators and oxygen and are dependent on other life support technology. Very sick babies may respond to treatment, be weaned from the machinery, and become feeders and growers. Other babies remain dependent on the life supporting devices and become known as "chronics." Chronics whose condition deteriorates or who remain at the same high level of technological support, we have referred to as chronic chronics, but the staff use a variety of epithets.[2] There are other babies under the heading of very sick babies whose reliance on life support technology fluctuates. At times they appear to be weaned, only to have a serious setback. A patient with this kind of pattern fluctuates between being chronic and being a feeder and grower. Any very sick baby can die or change to a good baby. Feeders and growers can, though it happens less often, change to very sick babies. The major thrust of the professional staff's work is to get patients to be feeders and growers.

A few patients from the chronic designation leave the unit while still using a minimal amount of life supporting devices, usually to go to a pediatric ward, but most who leave go through the feeder and grower route. Most of the ongoing communication between physicians and parents occurs in relation to new arrivals, very sick, chronic, chronic-chronic, and "on again–off again" babies. The long-term complications that may result from treatment, as well as disabilities, become of primary concern (and a topic of discussion) as chronic babies spend more time on the unit and as children are prepared to go home. Feeders and growers are moved to one end of a unit (or a separate room) and receive relatively little attention from physicians, with nurses being more active in parent communication and patient care.

Other factors related to how staff define patients are important in communication between staff and parents. Infants arrive on the unit through a number of routes. About 50% of the infants are transported from another hospital (the hospital of birth), while the other half are transferred from the delivery room of the hospital of which the unit is a part. Babies from other hospitals are called "transports," and those from within the hospital are called "our babies" or "from upstairs" or "from downstairs," depending on where the delivery room is located. Transports come with the special transport team and are not accompanied by parents, who, all through the patient's career, have less access to the patient and staff because of the distance between the hospital and their home. Babies from inside the hospital are rushed to the unit immediately after delivery. Wherever the baby comes from, the father often follows close behind. When involved, fathers typically visit and speak to unit staff first. While attending physicians often insist on talking to mothers either by phone or through visits to the maternity ward, fathers often convey information from the staff to the mother for the first few days and are most often the first person to explain the child's condition to the mother.

Who talks to the parents about the infant's condition and what is said depends on the different types of patients and where the patient is in his or her career on the unit. The designations and what they mean to the staff can be understood only within the timetables held for each status designation.

When a child first enters the unit, there is a tendency for physicians to talk to the parents and to say that "it is too early to tell." As time progresses, nurses play a greater part in communication, due to their greater access to parents and contact with babies. At certain times and with certain categories death dominates communication; at other times it is the child's future. It is easier to talk to parents about good babies than about chronic ones, and very problematic to talk about chronic chronics and on again–off agains. With feeders and growers the content of information centers on progress.

Parent Status as Seen by Staff

The typology of patients just presented is necessary to understand the context of who talks to parents about the condition of children and what is said. Patients are the subjects of professionals' diagnoses, prognoses, and treatments. But we have found that when the patient is a child, parents are assessed as well. On the basis of these assessments, judgments are made about who should talk to parents and what should be told regarding the child's condition and about parent participation in treatment. Physicians and nurses collect information from each other and from the parents and make judgments concerning what "type" parent they are dealing with. In encounters with parents, physicians and nurses "feel" parents out. Through observing them, hearing them talk, and, most important, assessing their reaction to information given, staff make judgments about what to say, how to say it, and who should do the talking. Staff indicate that "you have to talk to parents at their level." They adjust their explanations to a level that allows the parent to grasp what it is they are trying to convey, given what the staff judge to be the parent's intelligence, education, and emotional state.

Staff talk about three types of parents: "good parents," "not so good parents," and "troublemakers." While these terms are used, there is overlap in categories, disagreements as to which parents belong where, and changes in parents' status over time.

As we will discuss, what exactly is expected of a parent who is thought of as a good parent varies depending on the status of the child and the amount of time the child has spent on the unit. A good parent is defined as having a sufficient amount of these characteristics.

1. *"They understand."* As one physician put it when describing a good parent, "We communicate." Good parents ask questions the staff define as appropriate. They recognize the seriousness of the child's condition.

They are tolerant of not knowing the final outcome of the child's condition. Their knowledge of the baby's condition and treatment increases over time. They are grateful for the level of care available to them. They understand and conform to the unit's practices and schedule.

2. *"They care about the baby."* They visit regularly, touch the baby, phone and ask about his or her condition, and respond in what the staff deem as appropriate ways to good and bad news. The distance the parents live from the hospital is taken into account in judging whether the frequency of visits indicates concern. Some staff use the terminology of "bonding" to discuss this dimension of a good parent.

3. *"They show potential for giving the baby proper care if he or she leaves the hospital."* Babies who leave the unit are thought of as needing more care and more skilled care than typical babies. Good parents show they can provide the proper care in the proper environment.

Social class, age, and race are related to being a good parent, but they are not synonymous in the staff's minds. While some teenagers, inner-city blacks, and single parents are thought of as being good parents, most parents who are considered good are middle and upper class. The good parents are those that staff like to talk to the most. These parents are also free with their praise. They provide feedback concerning their understandings of how they and their child have been treated on the unit.

Not so good parents, some of whom are referred to as "doozies" or "one of those," are frustrating for the staff. The prototype of the not so good parent has characteristics that are the opposite of those of good parents.

1. *"They are like talking to a brick wall."* Staff see them as not having the ability or refusing to show that they understand the condition of their baby. Most often this means, according to staff, that the parents do not acknowledge the seriousness of their child's condition. This lack of communication is attributed to the parents and is thought of as stemming from one of two possible causes. The first is that the parent is too uneducated or unintelligent to understand. The second is that the parent is experiencing a psychological state termed "denial." Some staff use denial indiscriminately to refer to parents who do not see the condition of the child as they do. Others use it in reference to more specific parental behavior, and, as we shall discuss later, in relation to a stage model of parents experiencing the crisis of an intensive care infant. For whatever reason, these parents ask what the staff see as inappropriate questions (e.g., "When will my baby come home?" or "When will he be circum-

cised?" when the child is close to death). This type of parent is seen as not hearing when told of impending death or long-term complications the child may have.

2. *"They couldn't care less"* about the child. The parents rarely visit and do not call. When they do come, they stay a short time and do not touch or hold the child or in other ways show interest. Some staff have special concern about this dimension of the not so good parent because it is seen as the source of potential "failure to thrive" and "neglect cases."

3. *"They can't manage care."* These parents are seen as not having the skills, background, or resources (perhaps not even a home) to take care of the child. Staff typify one variety of not so good parents (teenagers) with the phrase, "They think they have a baby doll," often accompanied by "They don't know the first thing about taking care of a baby." Many nurses express special frustration with a parent exhibiting this dimension, because they see themselves giving one-on-one direct intensive care for long periods of time only to turn a child over to an environment in which inadequate care will be given.

Staff finds talking to not so good parents difficult. While repeated efforts may be made to "reach" them and while some change status to good parents, the frequency and length of contact decline after these parents have initial discussions with staff. Many not so good parents are poor, young, and culturally different from the staff.

There is a third category into which staff place parents—troublemakers. These are parents who pose special problems or make what the staff see as unreasonable demands. Some who fall into this category are good parents in that they understand, care, and are competent, but they are not satisfied with the treatment their child is receiving. For example, they do not feel that their child's life should be supported and are assertive in pursuing that point of view. Other parents are defined as overly critical or as "looking to sue." From the staff's perspective, these parents ask the same question to different staff in order to trip them up. Still others never seem to be satisfied. Rather than being grateful, they are always finding things wrong. Staff are extremely cautious in their communication with troublemakers.

According to staff, parents have to be understood in terms of their movement through the experience of having an intensive care baby. Some staff, borrowing from the professional literature on personal response to death or illness, think of parents as moving through specific stages in their response to the "crisis" (Culberg, 1972; Klaus & Kennell, 1976; Kubler-Ross, 1969). Some staff take the familiar five-stage model of adjustment popularized by Kubler-Ross for terminally ill patients and apply it unchanged to the parents they encounter. These staff describe parents as passing through the five stages sequentially—denial, anger, bargaining, depression, and acceptance—as they gradually come to grips with the fact that their newborn is not normal. It is important to point out that not all staff employ such an explicit stage model. Even those staff who do use the stage terminology are seldom rigid or purist in their use of the stages to evaluate individual parents. Perhaps the best way to describe the staff's use of the stage perspective is as a conceptual modifier of the basic typology of parents we just presented. That is, while staff tend to use the behaviors and reactions already mentioned as reasons to characterize parents as good, not so good, or troublemakers, they use the stage perspective to create some flexibility in their evaluations. Some parental behaviors, for example, are seen as typical for certain stages. It is when these behaviors are "excessive" of what the staff deem normal, or when the behaviors occur at a time that staff see as inappropriate, that they are used to classify parents into the not so good or troublesome categories. The stages modify the application of the basic typology, but do not change the categories of evaluation.

Regardless of how staff characterize parents, they almost always do so on very limited amounts and kinds of information. Most evaluations are based on limited knowledge, derived mainly from short observations, limited conversations, or secondhand reports of incidents and reactions. What is known is almost unavoidably episodic, with staff remaining fairly uninformed about the larger context and history of the perinatal experience in the lives of the parents.

This limited knowledge base does not result from any intentional neglect by the staff, but neither does it stop them from making their judgments and evaluations. As already mentioned, staff uniformly recognize the importance of communicating with parents. They regularly seek out parents to talk with, and phone parents of transport babies daily in the early stages of the patient's career. The units have open-door visiting policies for parents and grandparents, who can come to the unit any time, unannounced. They are encouraged to touch the baby and to call the unit as often as they want. In spite of this, and with some exceptions, staff and especially physicians spend relatively little time with parents. The priority is saving and mending the physical child. In general, staff know very little about what the parents are thinking and about their life outside the hospital.

Staff's Perspectives on Talking to Parents

To some extent, exactly what is said to parents and how it is phrased is a function of who is saying it. Staff have different styles that they have developed. Some say they picked up their approach during training or since being on the unit. People are seldom coached on what to say and how to approach parents—it is not a formal part of the training. Knowing how to talk to parents is seen as an art. As our discussion has suggested, some staff are defined as being better at it than others. Some, especially house staff, may define themselves as poor at communication and defer to others when they might normally be expected to talk. While some attending physicians are thought of as being better than others at communication, they are always expected to fulfill their parent-talking duties.

All staff would agree that they should be more systematic in their approach to parents. Some nurses in units where primary care is not followed advocate a primary care system, in which the infants are assigned to the same nurses week after week, as a way to have more consistent communication. Others suggest that increased communication between doctors and nurses regarding what is to be said to a parent in a particular case would improve the situation. While all agree that they should improve, they know that other aspects of their work are more pressing. Time is at a premium, and keeping the many babies alive and helping them become "feeders and growers" dominate their long workdays. In addition, the work they do on the patient as a physical being is more visible than conversations with parents. The medical work is subject to regular discussion and careful review at rounds and during case conferences. Conversations with parents often occur in private and, when heard, are not subject to critiquing as is their other work. In addition, the staff receive positive feedback from good parents, indicating they are successful in talking with parents. They can attribute the obviously poor communication with the not so good parents and the troublemakers to characteristics of the parents.

In the face of dismal odds, staff often try to find some glimmer of hope—both to justify their own efforts and to frame their interactions with the parents. Away from the parents, some staff raise questions about the value of keeping alive infants with very low birth weights and severe impairments. However, such reservations are countered by a shared history of surprising—even miraculous—cases. These unexpected successes create a fundamental staff perspective that "you can never really tell" how a child you are treating will turn out. Nurses keep scrapbooks and picture collections of children who are successful graduates. Parents of graduates visit the units and bring their children with them. One unit has a yearly get-together of ex-patients and their parents. The parents who return are visibly grateful, and the children are most often normal. They provide living testimony to the value of the staff's work. Frequently you hear, "This child was once less than 1,000 grams and look at her now."[3]

"You can never really tell" is an important theme in understanding what is said to parents as well. Staff tell stories of infants who were judged to be nonviable and put aside to die, only to live, and of children who had cerebral hemorrhages who grew to normal intelligence. While staff make judgments about who they think will live and who will die, and speak among themselves about babies who "will never go home," this is always tempered with a comment that suggests that although they may judge who will and who will not die, "you can never really tell." In conversations with parents, unless there is very clear evidence of impending death or clear diagnosis of impairment, "you can never really tell" dominates the tone of communication.

The fact that "you can never really tell" dominates communication with parents, rather than more pessimistic assessments, has to do with another understanding the staff share. That is, "Be honest, but not cruel." While there is variation in the degree to which staff are optimistic rather than pessimistic in what they tell parents about their child's condition (Clyman et al., 1979), there is general agreement that one should not take away hope from the parent. It is cruel to be "too negative"; the parent may withdraw from the infant and, if he or she were to live, irreversible damage might be done to the relationship. On the other hand, staff share the perspective that it is bad to surprise parents with bad news; it is important to foreshadow possible revelations and if there is a chance of death, there should be some prior warning. The staff sometimes soften bad news by suggesting that a child's temperament or disposition provides reason for hope. One father was told that although his child was very ill, the child was a "fighter." Another parent was told that her child was not a quitter and that the staff wasn't giving up. Despite these children's poor medical health, the families were encouraged not to give up hope.

Another part of "Be honest, but not cruel" is often not to burden the parent with too many of the problems that might be faced later in the child's career, not to be too pessimistic about the long-term prognosis. Some use the technique of normalizing the child's condition by saying something like, "I have seen children who were a lot worse than this who are now doing fine." On occasion some staff cite prognostic statistics, but statistics are generally thought to be inaccurate and to tend to mislead, as parents are prone to misinterpret the predictive potential for their child.

Another practice related to the perspective, "Be honest, but not cruel," is the use of euphemisms and less than direct phrases in discussing the child's condition. Such expressions as "You have a very sick baby," or "Your baby is very immature," or "Your baby has a tough going," are used at times instead of "We think your baby is going to die." "Developmentally de-layed" and "learning disability" are sometimes substituted for "mentally retarded." The use of euphemisms is in line with "Don't be cruel," as well as "you never can really tell."

The Parents' View

Space does not permit us to fully discuss the parents. Parents do not know the staff's typology of patients, parents, and staff, nor do they understand the staff's perspective and rules on talking to parents. For the staff, the units and interactions with parents are part of the routine of everyday life. For professionals, the unit is a place where they practice medicine; for parents, it is a place where *their child* is.

For most parents, the neonatal unit is initially an unknown world—"neonatology" and even "intensive care for infants" are words that they have never heard before the birth of their child. Similarly, some of the conditions that their child may have are completely outside their realm of experience. Further, many do not know the difference between an intern and a neonatologist. Parents process information they receive from the staff through the world as they understand it. What staff think they are communicating is often not what parents hear. For example, in a setting where death is a regular occurrence, "You have a very sick baby" may mean "Your baby is going to die," but in the context of parents' lives, it may mean their baby is going to be in the hospital a few extra days. Much of the parents' early activity on the unit as well as their state of mind is consumed with trying to understand what has happened and what it means. Not having a set of understandings to draw on often leaves them confused and without a repertoire of consistent behavior.

Of course, the relative levels of understanding and confusion reached by parents not only arise from their experiences in the nursery, but emerge from their own personal history that they bring to the nursery. This history varies greatly from family to family. They are disproportionately young and poor, but middle class and wealthy people are represented. Some had no prenatal care and kept the pending birth out of their minds until it happened. For others, the anticipated birth is the fulfillment of a dream. Some had no prior warning that the birth would be unusual or the baby would be at high risk of death or of being developmentally disabled. Others were seeing specialists because their pregnancy was known to be high risk. Some parents have had medical training; others do not know what the heart does. For some it is their first child; for others it is one of many. Some are married; others have no partner with whom to share the events. Some have recently lost jobs; others have just started a new business. For some, grandmothers will be looked to for guidance; for others, the clergy; for still others, specialists. Others will depend entirely on the staff of the unit. Only by knowing the details of the many worlds of parents prior to and surrounding the neonatal experience can we begin to understand how they experience the unit and what they hear when staff talk to them.

While what parents hear and understand is related to their world, their understanding is changed by the events of the birth and their experiences in and surrounding the unit. Mothers are often physically exhausted, if not unconscious, immediately after giving birth. Many do not understand where their baby has gone. Fathers (if present), on the other hand, are torn between being with their partners and following their babies. Many of the mothers are on maternity wards where other mothers have their babies close by. This intensifies their sorrow at not having their babies with them. The first visit to the unit can be traumatic. The sight of the babies with their medical paraphernalia and the number of people and intensity of activity can be overwhelming. Some parents put complete confidence in the doctors no matter what the doctors' status and do not ask many questions. They leave the particulars to the doctors. Others learn the details of the child's condition and consult with various people, taking an active role in monitoring doctors and carefully listening and interpreting what is said. It can be misleading to generalize about the stages parents go through in learning about the unit and their child. For some, having a child admitted to the unit may not be as traumatic an event as other events they may experience later—such as the realization of pending death or of permanent physical or mental disability.

Parents seek out information and receive it from a variety of sources in addition to the staff's words. They learn about the physical layout of the unit and what a move from one place to another means in relation to their child's condition. They pay attention to staff members' gestures and tone of voice, looking for unspoken information about the child's condition. They compare their child with others they have known and others on the unit. They talk to friends and relatives and make note of casual remarks made on the unit. In addition, they view the mass media with an eye to clues on how to understand their child. While for the majority the stay on the unit is less than a month, some stay up to a year. Parents of long-term patients often develop a detailed knowledge of the setting, read their child's charts, and get to know the staff well. While at first these parents think in terms of their child getting well soon, they change their timetable of their child's development and look for small signs of change. For some parents, particularly those of long-term patients, the experience on the unit seriously changes their relations with each other, with friends, and with family—it changes their lives. For some it is the start of a life of being the parent of a child with a disability. For the most part, parents leave the unit knowing their life has been changed but not knowing their child's condition, and in most cases not very aware of what the future might bring.

CONCLUSION

When we first asked the physicians what they told parents about their children's condition, they said, "We are completely honest." Similarly, during our first visits, when we asked nurses what they told parents, they said, "Everything." These phrases have a special and circumscribed meaning for those who work on neonatal units. Further, in our interviews with parents and through observations, we began to see the other side of staff–parent communication. What physicians and other hospital staff thought they said to parents was often not what parents heard. Our research was guided by the questions, Who talks to parents? What do they say? What do parents hear? Our presentation reveals that there are no simple answers to those questions. Only through a description of salient aspects of the setting can we begin to grasp the meaning, process, structure, and entangled communication in such a complex environment. We have described the rudiments of an elaborate communication system, one that operates on several levels and from many perspectives. The phrases, "Be honest" and "Tell everything," for example, take on distinct meanings depending on who is talking to whom, about whom, and under what conditions, and the nature of the information to be conveyed.

Neonatal units are more complex and intense than most other settings in which professionals talk to clients. The news that is to be communicated is unique too, but there are understandings to be derived that transcend the substantive focus of our description. For example, special education teachers, in a manner similar to that described in this chapter, often size up and type parents, and on that basis decide what to say and how and whether they will involve the parents in their child's educational program. Schools, like hospitals, develop conventions regarding who talks and what they say, and this affects what it is that parents hear. For parents seeking information, encounters with professionals in schools as well as hospitals are episodic and seldom with knowledge of the context from which professionals are operating. The way we have approached studying communication between professionals and parents has broad application and requires that we concentrate on seeing communication from the participants' point of view and that we understand the context of the setting in which communication takes place. Obtaining such information from a variety of settings will move us toward a grounded theory of professional–client communication.

We conclude this chapter with a reminder of the weakness in our research. It is particularly important to point it out, because our focus is a setting that is alive with human drama and saturated with ethical dilemmas. On such units, decisions are made concerning who should be treated.

Communication between staff and parents affects such decisions, but the social policy and culture that created the situation in which staff and parents find themselves also have to be studied. Neonatal units were, in part, the United States' answer to its embarrassing position among other nations in rates of infant mortality. Why a technological solution to the problem was embraced rather than one that emphasized prevention has to be understood. As we cannot ignore the society and culture that created these settings, we would also be remiss if we did not point out that what is occurring in these settings can have a profound effect on the future of the society of which they are a part. By decreasing the birth weight and gestation age, by changing definitions of what is "a baby," we are witnessing events that may transform definitions of life itself.

NOTES

1. We do not want to suggest that it is a daily occurrence on these units that severely deformed and brain damaged babies are left to die or that babies who might have lived are regularly not treated. The units we studied practice what some staff call "aggressive medicine." In fact some house staff and nurses are often critical of what they feel is "overly aggressive treatment."

2. Epithets used for chronic chronics vary from unit to unit. Such benign phrases as "sad case" and "never going home" are sometimes used, but "premie trash" is used by some staff on one unit. Other phrases are used for other categories. On one unit babies with severe problems are referred to as "trainwrecks." "Gork" is used on more than one unit to refer to infants who are severely neurologically impaired. Such terminology is generally not shared with outsiders and is never used around parents. Staff that do use such expressions explain the use by saying that work on such units is difficult and it is their way of venting frustration.

3. Staff feel that due to rapid changes in the field of neonatology, data on the outcomes of various birth weight intensive care infants are outdated.

REFERENCES

Becker, H. S., Geer, B., Hughes, E. C., & Strauss, A. (1961). *Boys in white: Student culture in medical school.* Chicago: University of Chicago Press.

Cartwright, A. (1964). *Human relations and hospital care.* London: Routledge and Kegan Paul.

Cartwright, A. (1967). *Patients and their doctors.* London: Routledge and Kegan Paul.

Clyman, R. I., Sniderman, S. H., Ballard, R. A., & Roth, R. S. (1979). What pediatricians say to mothers of sick newborns: An indirect evaluation of the counseling process. *Pediatrics, 63,* 719–723.

Culberg, J. (1972). Mental reactions of women to perinatal death. In N. Morris (Ed.), *Psychosomatic medicine in obstetrics and gynecology* (pp. 326–329). New York: S. Karger.

Davis, F. (1960). Uncertainty in medical prognosis, clinical and functional. *American Journal of Sociology, 66,* 41–47.

Davis, F. (1963). *Passage through crisis.* Indianapolis: Bobbs-Merrill.

Duff, R., & Hollingshead, A. (1968). *Sickness and society.* New York: Harper & Row.

Duff, R. S., & Campbell, A. G. M. (1973). Moral and ethical dilemmas in the special-care nursery. *New England Journal of Medicine, 289,* 890–894.

Glaser, B., & Strauss, A. (1965). *Awareness of dying.* Chicago: Aldine.

Glaser, B., & Strauss, A. (1968). *Time for dying.* Chicago: Aldine.

Jacobs, J. (1969). *The search for help: A study of the retarded child in the community.* New York: Brunner/Mazel.

Jonsen, A. R., & Lister, G. (1978). Newborn intensive care: The ethical problems. *Hastings Center Report, 8*(1), 15–18.

Klaus, M. H., & Kennell, J. H. (1976). *Maternal-infant bonding.* St. Louis: Mosby.

Korsch, B. M. (1974). The Armstrong lecture: Physicians, patients and decisions. *American Journal of the Diseases of Children, 127,* 328–332.

Kubler-Ross, E. (1969). *On death and dying.* New York: Macmillan.

McIntosh, J. (1979). *Communication and awareness in a cancer ward.* London: Croom Helm.

Parsons, T. (1967). *The social system.* Glencoe, IL: Free Press. (Originally published in 1951)

Roth, J. (1958). Ritual and magic in the control of contagion. In E. Jaco (Ed.), *Patients, physicians and illness* (pp. 229–234). New York: Free Press.

Rowe, J., Clyman, R. I., Green, C., Mikkelson, C., Haight, J., & Ataide, L. (1978). Follow-up of families who experience a perinatal death. *Pediatrics, 62,* 166–170.

Skipper, J. A., & Leonard, R. D. (1968). Children, stress and hospitalization. *Journal of Health and Social Behavior, 9,* 275–286.

Strauss, A., Fagerhaugh, S., Suczek, B., & Wiener, C. (1985). *The organization of medical work.* Chicago: University of Chicago Press.

Taichert, L. C. (1975). Parental denial as a factor in the management of the severely retarded child. (Discussion of two patients). *Clinical Pediatrics, 14*(7), 66–68.

Taylor, S. J., & Bogdan, R. (1984). *Introduction to qualitative research methods: The search for meanings* (2nd ed.). New York: John Wiley.

Waitzkin, H., & Stoeckle, J. D. (1972). The communication of information about illness. *Advances in Psychosomatic Medicine, 8,* 180–215.

Wiener, J. M. (1970). The attitudes of pediatricians toward the care of fatally ill children. *Journal of Pediatrics, 76,* 700–705.

Chapter 2

BEYOND HARM
A Case Study of the
Social Construction of Child Abuse

Susan Janko

What do the words "child abuse" mean? For most of us they are words that conjure up images of victimized children and deviant adults. They evoke sympathy for child victims and condemnation of adult abusers. Sensational stories are reported in newspapers and on television about ritualistic beatings and sexual abuse of young children. Agencies designed to protect children are criticized for allowing children to stay in abusive situations or for waiting until children have been abused before intervening. Simultaneously they are charged with violating the rights of parents accused of maltreating their children. Despite the increasing incidence of child maltreatment and increased public awareness, it is a problem surrounded by questions and misunderstandings. Popular portrayals of child maltreatment represent only partial truths about the problem (Pelton, 1981).

This chapter is about parents who maltreat their children. It is part of a larger study conducted in a program for maltreated children and their families. The program is offered collaboratively by a state child protective services agency and a nonprofit community agency. The purpose of the program, according to Georgia (all names have been changed), one of the program co-directors, is "to protect children and maintain families" in accordance with the mission of Child Protective Services (CPS).

APPROACHES TO THE STUDY OF NEGLECT AND ABUSE

The overriding purpose of this study was to learn how abuse and neglect were viewed by parents identified as having maltreated their children. The perspectives of parents are not easily accessible to professionals, and I consider their views to be valuable to those of us who think we are doing something about child maltreatment. This was my motivation for conducting this research, which lasted one year.

I used a qualitative field study approach that included three strategies outlined by Zelditch (1962): participant observations, interviews, and enumeration and sampling. During the first 4 months of the study, I conducted participant observations during weekly intervention sessions to gather information about the intervention setting and establish relationships with parents and program staff (Bogdan & Biklen, 1982). Participant observations were also useful for learning about specific incidents and reconstructing events (Zelditch, 1962). My daily observations were transcribed and coded in the form of fieldnotes each day after they were collected. As I reviewed them each evening, I was eager to start talking to parents in depth to get to the heart of things.

I started interviewing parents 2 months after I began participant observations, when I was familiar with the program and parents were willing to talk. In-depth, open-ended interviews provided access to parents' and staff members' views of experiences I had observed or heard about during participant observations (Taylor & Bogdan, 1984). I interviewed staff after parents to ensure that the direction of the study would be guided by parents' responses. My questions became more focused as I analyzed data when themes emerged and issues needed clarification. Interviews were, as Zelditch (1962) suggested, an efficient way to gain information about norms and status.

The third method I used, enumeration and sampling, was accomplished with a questionnaire that asked for information about demographics, child and family characteristics, and use of services. Data from the questionnaire are reported in the larger study. For this chapter, I reviewed publications about the legal and administrative framework of the state child protective services agency, program schedules, training materials, and evaluations. Parents and staff were consulted during data analysis and writing to check the accuracy, completeness, and representativeness of the data with the sources and to check the plausibility of my interpretations.

Field researchers need to "cultivate close relationships with one or two respected and knowledgeable people (key informants) in the early stages of research" to gain access to settings and inside information (Taylor & Bogdan, 1984). Staff members were willing—even eager—to talk, and several served as key informants. That was not so with parents. Although regarding parents as respected or knowledgeable was incongruous in a setting that served parents because they were "abusive," one parent, Ann, was articulate, seemed reliable, and was willing to talk. She became a key informant. Although 20 families were enrolled in the program and are represented to some degree, this chapter focuses primarily on Ann and her family.

The chapter chronicles how Ann became labelled "abusive" and entered the child welfare system. The sequence in which information is presented in the chapter parallels the way data were analyzed—events are described chronologically within categories. Descriptions are followed by explanations in the words of parents and staff about how they made sense of those events. The way I made sense of the data is incorporated in the last section, "Getting out of the System." The themes in this chapter emerged from data I collected from all families and staff. Ann's story will, I hope, illustrate the problem.

I first met Ann when I was observing in a classroom that included four of the 20 families enrolled in that 14-week session, together with staff from the program and CPS. Ann was a parent I had seen around the program during the first few months I conducted observations. Like other parents when the study began, she did not seem particularly friendly so I did not approach her except for an occasional greeting as we passed during intervention sessions. After several months of systematically recording weekly fieldnotes, I was familiar with schedules and activities, knew the staff and families by name, and recorded topics of their discussions during casual conversations, program planning, and debriefing meetings following intervention sessions. I had interviewed one parent and was eager to interview others, but parents kept their distance.

Ann was 29. She had fair skin and thick, dark hair that hung in waves beneath her shoulders. She usually wore worn but clean T-shirts and jeans, and looked well-scrubbed. She was tall, large boned, and athletic-looking, but frequently walked with shoulders hunched, arms folded across her chest, and a scowl that effectively maintained a distance and masked a quick sense of humor and intelligence that I imagined few people persevered long enough to discover. Ann had been accused of maltreating her 20-month-old son Ben—an accusation that dramatically affected her life and eventually brought her to the program.

The day Ann and I first talked, she came to the program alone and watched from the anteroom of a classroom while other parents played with and cared for their children. She had just come from a nearby hospital where Ben had been hospitalized the previous night for asthma and croup. I approached her, and she seemed appreciative to talk to someone. I was so delighted a parent would talk to me that I did not notice that Ann had neither family nor friends nearby despite her son's hospitalization.

Ann had not had sleep or food in a day so I offered to take her to lunch. She asked if she could smoke in my car, and when I hesitated she volunteered to drive instead. We went to a small cafe near the program that warm, sunny spring day and sat in her car while she ate a gourmet hamburger, periodically stopping to complain about the spicy Dijon mustard. We talked over an hour until she expressed concern about leaving Ben alone too long in the hospital.

After Ann told me about Ben, I asked her how she came to be involved with the program. I started interviews with parents with a question I thought would be broad enough to elicit a variety of responses about their relationships with the program. Ann's response was similar to the responses of all parents I eventually interviewed. Rather than talk about the program, she described the situation that led to her involvement with CPS. My initial fear that parents would not share information, or would convey only superficial details, quickly subsided as Ann began to talk. By the end of our first interview, my head was swimming with information and questions. Sorting out the details of her life took nine additional interviews and numerous informal conversations.

GETTING INTO THE SYSTEM

Being Reported to cps

Ann, her husband Mike, and Ben had recently moved from another state to be closer to Mike's family. Ann protested the move and was angry about being "in a place where [my husband] took me away from all my support, all my friends. He was just drinking, threatening me all the time, and threatening to take the baby." Ann described the situation prior to Ben's removal by CPS: "Mike dumped me and Ben off at his mom's and said if he did not get rid of me he would probably kill me." Drinking, drugs, and arguments were usual during their 4-year relationship.

During the 9 months since Ben's birth, Ann had periodic bouts of depression that escalated after their move and separation. "If people walked up behind me," she explained, "I just jumped, and I was shaking all the time." Concerned that her depression might not subside, Ann mentioned during a group counseling session that she was "afraid for herself and her son." Ann's counselor, assuming Ann meant she might hurt her son, reported what Ann had said to CPS. Child Protective Services did not formally respond at that time because an incident of abuse had not actually occurred.

After Mike left Ann and Ben, Mike's mother assumed responsibility for most of 9-month-old Ben's care. One Sunday, however, she left Ben in Ann's care while she attended church. Ann described what happened.

[My mother-in-law] just took over and I couldn't do anything with him. I couldn't feed—he wouldn't eat for me. He wouldn't do anything for me. So they just went to church that one day and left me there. I tried to feed him, and I let it go on for about a good 20 minutes before I, you know. And I tried feeding him, and he was spitting it all over me. So then I tried the bottle, cutting off the nipple. If you've ever been hit by a plastic bottle, it hurts, in the face. So we were sitting on the couch and he just threw himself back and hit me. And I just stood him up, and I just said, "Now, Ben, stop it." [Ann demonstrated how she held the baby upright and gave him an abrupt shake.] Then my mother-in-law came home and I was sitting there crying because it was the first time I had ever been aggressive with him. And it didn't hurt him. He stopped. I got his attention. He was in the crib crying and my mother-in-law came home, and I told her what happened.

Ann's counselor suggested she ask her doctor to prescribe medication for her nerves. During a visit with her physician, Ann, encouraged by her mother-in-law who accompanied her, told her doctor that she had shaken Ben. The physician reported the incident to CPS. Not long after, Ann's mother-in-law saw a counselor at the same mental health clinic, who compared notes and exchanged information with Ann's counselor. Ann's counselor again made a report to CPS. By that time, CPS had received three reports about Ann. Ann described what happened during her next counseling appointment: "They knew what was going to happen, and they kept me over at mental health, and they just went in and took him." Ann's voice softened: "I ended up in the psychiatric ward because I just had a breakdown."

Substantiating Abuse

When CPS receives reports of abuse or neglect, a caseworker interviews the children, parents, or both, depending on the situation and age of the children. If the caseworker believes the children are in imminent danger or are afraid to go home, the caseworker and a police officer remove them from their homes. Once removed, the children are placed in shelter homes for a period not longer than 30 days, after which they are transferred to foster homes. Although 30 days is the legal limit, temporary placements can take longer. The problem, Georgia the co-director explained, was constant shortages of approved foster care homes and the limited number of homes willing to accept multiple placements so that siblings could remain together.

Within 24 hours following the removal of children from their homes, a court hearing is held. Child Protective Services presents the circumstances of the children's removal to the court, and the judge determines whether the children will return to their parents or the state will retain custody. If the court rules in favor of the state, the judge orders a fact finding to occur within 30 days. A fact finding was likened by Georgia to a trial in which CPS proved they were "right and the parents did these bad things, or the parents proved they did not do these bad things. Or the parent could stipulate right there, and say, 'Yeah, I did this.'" Sometimes, Georgia said, fact findings take as long as 6 months. During that time, children remain in foster care homes, and many stay long after fact finding. According to CPS records, children remained in foster care a median 22 months and experienced a mean of 3.2 placements during that time.

In Ann's situation, Ben was placed in his grandmother's rather than his father's custody. However, the court permitted Mike to have unlimited visits with Ben and issued a restraining order that prevented Ann from seeing her son. One week after her admittance to a psychiatric hospital, Ann was released with a diagnosis of situational depression. No longer allowed to live at her mother-in-law's because Ben was there and with no place else to live, she moved into sheltered housing. Ann recalled those days: "I didn't do anything but go to work and come home, and cry and wish I had my baby."

A short time later, Ann and Mike reunited, but Ben remained with his grandmother. According to Ann, her CPS caseworker advised Mike to divorce her (which he eventually did) and warned him if he returned to Ann, CPS would place Ben in a permanent foster home. I asked Ann if she believed the caseworker really said that, and she replied that Mike maintained it was true. The caseworker denied saying it, and Ann did not know who was telling the truth. Nevertheless, to prevent CPS from discovering their reunion she and Mike decided to retrieve Ben and move to a new community. Mike's mother moved to the same town, called CPS in the first community, and reported that her son and daughter-in-law were living together with Ben.

Ann's caseworker warned the couple that CPS would make Ben a ward of the court—a statement Ann interpreted as meaning Ben would be taken from them. To prevent this from happening they decided to make another move. This time they decided to go to Ann's home state. When they arrived there, Mike called his lawyer and Ann's caseworker and was warned that a grand jury would convene in 3 days to indict them for custodial interference—a felony charge. Within 3 days they returned home.

After their return, Mike's drinking and Ann's difficulty coping with Ben continued. Ann and her mother-in-law, who was by that time "on Ann's side," read an article in a local newspaper about an intervention program for families involved with CPS. Ann called Isabelle, the program's other co-director, to ask if her family could attend. Unlike the majority of parents in the program, who were court-ordered to attend, Ann was what the staff called a "self-referral." In fact, it was almost a year since Ben had been removed, and Ann had never been formally charged by CPS.

> It's like a year down the line and they didn't even put me in front of the judge and charge me with child abuse. . . . But they sure made it sound like I was some big danger to my son and that I literally shook him so hard that—for something that got so blown out of proportion and sounded so terrible, no, they never brought me up on charges. . . . [The caseworker] finally admitted that she knew I never abused him.

When I asked why CPS had intervened, Ann told me, "Because he was at risk. . . . Because there were possibilities that he might be abused."

In Ann's case, and I suspect in many cases, it was impossible to know what really happened. Ann compared the situation with the way communication occurs in a children's game: "Have you ever played that game where you sit in a circle and one person says something, and it goes around a circle, and by the time it gets back to you it's totally not even what you said at all? That's what happened to me. But in a very serious matter."

The process of verifying abuse from circumstantial evidence—a process described by Elmer (1977) as "dubious at best"—seemed to be at issue with many parents. The following excerpt from an interview with Ann illustrates the complexity of many situations where abuse or neglect is suspected by CPS.

Susan: When I hear you talk about all the painful stuff that was going on when CPS got involved, it makes me think you really did need some kind of help at the time.

Ann: I was asking for help, but I didn't know where to go. I had only been in town for a month. But I don't think it was the right kind of help—to take my child, because that just made matters worse. I was on the verge of having an emotional breakdown, and when it happened, I had it for sure. Then while I was in treatment, I couldn't get anywhere, and I couldn't accomplish anything because I was so upset and I had all these upsetting phone calls. They just took the baby. . . . So, I didn't get any help. Yeah, I needed help and I could have got the help I needed, I think, and still kept my child. . . . That part I disagree with because I was asking for help, because I knew what was going on was wrong. . . . They think that's the way they helped me, was to take my child.

But to a degree, I agree because the situation was not good for him. But then to another degree, I mean, I self-reported. It wasn't like I was beating up on my kid and got reported from 15 different people. Okay, so it was kind of "iffy." Then I got blamed for the whole thing. And I'm a danger to my son, and I don't belong with my son, and all of a sudden if Mike is going to divorce me and file for full custody, then [CPS] will drop the case. . . . That I did not agree with, and I felt really railroaded.

Susan: Paint a different scenario. What would have been helpful to you at that time? What would have been a better way, not only for you, but for Ben and the whole family?

Ann: Well, I think personally that Ben should have gone into a foster home, been kept totally out of the picture. Because there was too much, with him being with his grandmother and then Mike having unlimited visitations and me having none, there was too much using Ben as a pawn. [Ann imitated Mike.] "If you don't do this, you won't see Ben again, and if you report me for breaking your finger, you won't see Ben again." I think he should have gone to a foster home, and then instead of totally focusing on me, I think since we were a family, the whole family should have been investigated as a family instead of singling me out and letting Mike have unlimited visitations. All he did was get drunk and cause more problems that way. I think since we were a family, it should have been dealt with as a family.

GETTING INTERVENTION

Slipping Through the Cracks

Substantiation of child maltreatment by CPS results in assignment of a caseworker who develops a service contract for parents. Service contracts contain a list of requirements parents must fulfill before children will be returned and cases closed. Fulfilling contracts does not guarantee the return of one's children or case closure, however. Service contracts might prescribe drug treatment programs, clean random UAs (no drugs or alcohol in urine samples), anger management classes, or on-time attendance for all parent–child visits. Service contracts are individually developed, but because CPS and the community have limited options for services, contracts among families are more alike than different. Moreover, services listed on contracts do not guarantee availability. For example, the high demand for drug and alcohol treatment programs and the corresponding shortage of placements resulted in families waiting months for services. After months of involvement with CPS, some families still did not know what service contracts were. Others "slipped through the cracks."

The Program

Most families enrolled in the program had been ordered to attend by the court. They were known by CPS as "difficult." Frequently their children were in foster care. They were families who had been in the system for long periods, sometimes several years, and had to be dealt with in one way or another—either by returning their children and closing their cases or by "permanent planning," that is, by legally obtaining permanent custody so the children could be adopted by other families. A few families self-referred. Because the waiting list for families was long, only self-referrals who were believed to be in greatest need were permitted to enroll.

Even for families who acknowledged problems, needed services were difficult to obtain. The system reacted to crises rather than preventing them, as this passage from an interview with Georgia illustrates.

> Sometimes people will ask for treatment, ask for help. I get phone calls from people who say, "Gee, I'd like to be in your parent training program. I have a lot of trouble with my children." They don't have an open case with CPS. They've just heard about parent training. And I say, "I'm sorry. Unfortunately, in order to be in this program you have to have an open case with CPS," and I refer them to other parent training programs in the community, but I don't know if there are many services out there that deal directly with the children. I think most of them are parent support groups, which are important and really good, but they don't always meet the need of this population. So, then we find out about them later on. Maybe a year later, or 6 months later, they will end up in the system because they needed help and they couldn't get it. So they end up in the system when they're court-ordered to attend parent training. And I would much prefer that they attend voluntarily rather than be court-ordered. I probably get, I would say on average, two of those phone calls a week.

Intervention offered by the program differed from most interventions available through CPS in that it involved families rather than parents alone. Sessions were held one day a week for 14 weeks in a community church away from CPS, on neutral territory. Those children who were in foster care were transported to the program, where they met their parents in cheerful preschool classrooms and in meeting rooms with large windows and comfortable sofas. This was in sharp contrast to the small, barren cubicles at CPS, where parents who were not enrolled in the program visited their children one hour a week under caseworker surveillance. In the program, parents practiced skills during play and caregiving activities that they learned during the initial didactic portion of training: nutrition, child development and safety, nonpunitive ways to manage their children's behavior, and problem-solving strategies.

Parents had positive comments about the program. Jean, a 22-year-old parent of five children who ranged in age from 1 to 8 years, commented about her interactions with her oldest daughter.

> She hasn't gotten a whipping since she's been home from foster care. I used to pull her around by the hair. I used to slug her. To me, I thought I had reason to do that. I thought she was being disrespectful. But since my parenting class, I've learned it's not disrespectful. They're voicing their opinions. They have reasons to feel like that. I feel like that sometimes too. And I just never understood that.

Pauline, a 19-year-old parent of a 3-year-old with special medical needs, described what she felt after completing the program.

> To me it's kind of like a guiding light through a tunnel. There are no lights in the tunnel. You don't know how to get out. It's like there's this light that shows you the way out. And once you get out, these heavy bricks that have been on you for so long are gone.

Ann's Experience

At first, Ann seemed uncomfortable in the program although she had requested enrollment. I recall seeing her with a dour expression, body bent forward, hovered over Ben, her arms extended as if to prevent some impending disaster. In the months that followed, Ann grew more relaxed with Ben both in and outside the program. She discovered she could be a competent parent.

One day Ann announced proudly that she had helped Isabelle arrange activities for the other families in the classroom and had even led her group in a song. She attended every session and enrolled Ben in a therapeutic preschool offered by the community program. Although problems at home with Mike's drinking and fighting continued and Ann was frustrated waiting for counseling to treat her chronic depression, she seemed to manage.

The first time I visited their two bedroom apartment, she gave a tour of her garden. She had cleared a small plot of land about 2 feet by 3 feet in front of her door and planted green beans, zinnias, and marigolds. She tended them daily, watering and weeding until a profusion of buds were waiting to blossom. Her worn but clean apartment had pictures on the walls, and Ben's toys were gathered in orderly piles. She talked of plans to paint the kitchen, hang blinds in the front window, and buy a screen door.

Ann's life changed abruptly throughout the year, as did the lives of most parents in the program. One afternoon a few weeks after our visit, I approached Ann as she stood in an alley behind the church with other parents. Lighting a cigarette, she told us in a low, monotone voice that her husband just spent his $300 paycheck on camping gear and left in his car. It was the sixth of the month and their apartment rent, television rent, and electricity bill were not paid.

Ann called Aid to Families with Dependent Children (AFDC) and learned she would have to wait 30 days from the date her husband left before she could receive welfare money. Since she had no money and knew no one from whom she could borrow, she gathered a few personal belongings and took them to her mother-in-law's garage sale where she earned $50 for food. She still needed money for rent and utilities. Whenever she saw a television repair truck drive by, she was "sure they were coming to repossess her TV." An eviction notice from her landlord was a prerequisite for receiving emergency rent funds. Another parent recommended Ann approach her landlord and explain the situation. She advised Ann to ask for an eviction notice rather than wait until she received one, "because by then the landlord has had it."

One morning while I was at work Ann called from the welfare office. She apologized immediately for calling, then asked if I would pick up her and Ben and drive them to the social security office. I asked for the address of the building, and she left to ask an employee. As I waited, I heard Ann speak to Ben in a gentle, firm voice, then in a raw, pleading voice, asking him not to hurt another child whose loud protests were followed by a chorus of squeals and cries.

When I arrived, Ann and Ben were waiting outside the one-story cement block government building. We loaded Ben's stroller in my car, situated Ben in the backseat, and fastened his safety belt. Dropping into the front seat, Ann told me a woman in the office had suggested she attend parenting classes. She hated her husband, she said, for what he was doing to her. That morning she had awakened too late to catch the bus to keep her welfare appointment, so with baby and stroller in tow, she hitchhiked to the welfare office. They could not take time to eat and chance missing the appointment. They had neither money nor time to eat out or catch a bus home before their next appointment—missed appointments might mean missed meals in the future.

Despite the difficulties resulting from her separation from Mike, I felt optimistic about Ann's future. Her intelligence was apparent from our conversations, and I reasoned that her middle class background gave her a boost over other parents in the program. However, like other parents in the program, she had continual struggles with money, depression, alcohol and drugs, and parenting. Ben's behavior seemed particularly trying after his father left.

Ann said her self-esteem and confidence started to improve when she began the program. Staff encouraged rather than criticized; they found things she was doing right so she did not feel stupid or inadequate. In contrast, Ann felt humiliated by CPS and resented "them." Ann believed the program helped in some ways, but as time passed she commented that the program could not help with most of her problems.

THE CONTEXTS OF ABUSE: FAMILIES AND SOCIETY

Ben was known as "Bam Bam" by teachers at the therapeutic preschool he attended. His constant activity demanded a great deal of energy from caregivers. Although he was a handsome child who loved socializing with adults and children, Ben's repertoire also included a number of behaviors not appreciated by others, including hitting, biting, screaming, and arching his back if someone attempted to pick him up when he did not want to move. I recall feeling my stomach tighten as I approached Ann's apartment to take her and Ben out for Thai food. I sighed with relief when we had finished dinner and no major accidents or incidents had occurred.

After dinner Ann asked if we could stop at the park. It was a pleasant spring evening so we stopped for about an hour to reward Ben's good behavior in the restaurant. Ann smiled and laughed as she pointed out Ben's skill at throwing a ball, swinging, and sliding. Ben, attempting to play basketball with some teenage boys, fearlessly chased the ball and crouched under the hoop to try and catch the ball as it spiraled toward him.

As we watched, Ann reminisced about her brief career on a girls' basketball team when she was a teenager. I felt pleased and hopeful hearing her memories of a normal childhood activity. As the sky grew darker we talked about leaving the park, hesitating because we knew Ben would not want to and would likely make us pay. We mapped out a strategy that involved a matter-of-fact statement to Ben that we were leaving, carrying him if necessary, and a quick getaway in the car. He surprised us as he had during dinner, and we had an uneventful trip home.

Back in the apartment, Ann changed Ben's diaper and, with her face a few inches from his, told him how much she loved him and gave him small kisses. He smiled at her as she tucked him in his crib and sang a lullaby. Afterward we talked for several hours about her childhood and family. Our candid conversation made me feel sad and cognizant of the real differences in our histories, despite our common economic background. After the interview, I wrote in my fieldnotes that I wondered whether, given her background, Ann would ever have a secure life or be able to provide a stable home for Ben.

Ann described her childhood as "average." She was adopted during infancy by a family who also adopted a second child. She remembered living in an "ordinary" home as a toddler, then moving to a home on a golf course as her father's business grew successful. Her parents traveled frequently, leaving Ann and her brother at home with live-in caregivers. She thought her family's changing economic situation roughly coincided with an onset of violence, but did not recall exactly how it started.

Incidents of physical abuse started when she was about 12. When Ann and her brother argued, her mother, she said, "couldn't control us, and that would make my dad mad. Then they'd start fighting, and he'd start hitting her." Ann stood between her parents and told her father, "Hit me, hit me," and he did. Ann described her father's behavior.

> He'd just go into these rages. Like, if he came home and me and my mom were arguing or something like that, he'd get really mad and start hitting. He hit with his fist sometimes. He used to wear those big skull men's rings, you know those colored rings with stones— and the stone would leave these little bruise marks on my arms. He used to take a belt to me most of the time. He'd start hitting me, and he couldn't stop. Just like with my mom, he'd start hitting her, and it took me screaming at him most of the time to stop. . . . I remember all sorts of incidents, like sitting at the dinner table and having a beer glass go flying across the table, with forks and knives flying across the table.

Ann attributed the violence in part to her mother, who "had a mouth on her . . . and just never knew when to quit." She described her mother as "caustic," and remembered spending time in her room feeling upset and angry, but feeling she had no one to go to for help. "I couldn't ever do anything," she explained, "because if I tried to tell her how I felt, you know, 'Don't talk back,' or, 'Don't be belligerent.' So I did a lot of acting out, a lot of acting out, because I couldn't get any good attention any other way, and I couldn't express how I was feeling." Ann provided examples of what she meant by "acting out."

> Punching walls and putting my hands through windows and punching people. And then when I turned to drugs, I turned it in on myself, and I was very self-destructive. Because I think when you

resort to putting a needle in your arm, that's the ultimate destructive behavior toward yourself.

At 13, Ann began using drugs and alcohol, and in her words has "done everything." During the following 3 years she began having trouble at school, ran away from home, and, with an acquaintance who was prostituting, had her first sexual experience, with a stranger on the streets from whom she contracted gonorrhea. At 16 she was placed by her parents in an institution for girls with problem behavior. Ann stayed in the institution for a year-and-a-half, where she broke windows with her fists and yanked hair from staff members' heads when they tried to restrain her.

Released from the institution when she was 18 and no longer welcome in her parents' home, Ann, having recently inherited $10,000 from her grandmother's estate, was on her own. She spent the entire sum of money in 8 months by buying heroin and crystal methamphetamine. She became pregnant by a man she described as a heroin junkie and had an abortion at her parents' insistence. At 19, out of money and resources, Ann moved in with a man 50 years her senior who gave her food, shelter, and drugs in exchange for sex.

Ann's life was a series of drugs, social programs, and brief relationships with men until her early 20s, when she married her first husband, and at 23 gave birth to a daughter. Ann and her husband abused drugs and alcohol, and Ann was accused of neglecting her infant daughter by CPS. When the child was 10 months of age, she was removed by CPS.

Ann maintained contact with her daughter until the child was 2, at which time she allowed her daughter to be adopted—a decision she described as "the right thing." I asked if she felt comfortable with her decision, and she answered:

Yes. Why shouldn't I? I loved that child enough to let her go to a home where there's no drinking, no smoking, no drugs. . . . So why should I feel bad? And even though people try to use that against me, I will not feel bad about it. Because there's one kid out of how many kids that got saved and got put in a good sound home.

She paused and lowered her voice, "Of course when they first took her from me I had a hard time with it. I tried to commit suicide three times."

A pattern of painful interactions with her family continued throughout Ann's life. I recall looking through Ann's family photo album as she pointed to pictures of people who were important in her life. I was struck that many of them were counselors, social workers, and professionals from agencies and institutions that had taken the place of Ann's family from the time she was 16.

Miscommunications between Ann and her family continue to the present. A short time before this study began, Ann's father died suddenly while on a trip outside the country with her mother. Ann's mother did not notify Ann until a month after his death because "there was nothing you could have done anyway." Ann wept as she told me about her last conversation with her father. It occurred during the time she and Mike were first enmeshed with CPS and had left the state with Ben.

> See, what was going on, it was me against my husband and Child Protective Services. I told my dad, "Yeah, I'm going to get custody, and I'm going to bring him home," and all that. In the meantime, Mike and I decided to get together, but we couldn't tell anybody because we didn't want Child Protective Services to know because if they would have known, they would have taken Ben from both of us.
>
> So I had to lie to my dad and tell him I was giving Mike custody. I couldn't trust my dad enough to tell him, because I was afraid he was going to tell Child Protective Services. I had to lie to him. And he was going, "Well, why all of a sudden?" because I was telling him how awful Mike was, and he's going, "What is going on? Now you're just going to give up and give him custody?" So he disowned me. He said he never wanted to talk to me again, and as far as he was concerned he didn't have a daughter, and as far as I should be concerned that I don't have a father. And that was our last conversation.

One time I asked Ann to paint a picture of her family. I expected to hear about Ben, Mike, and her current situation; instead she talked about her own parents.

Susan: If you could paint a picture of your family, what would it look like?

Ann: That's pretty easy. It is jet black, cloudy. I'm trying not to cry. I would draw a heart that's broken. And I would draw kids that are crying.

Susan: Who would the kids be?

Ann: Me. My brother. See, he always kissed ass. He was like momma's boy. Cause I was the oldest, so he could get away with murder, and I always got blamed for it. Cloudy, black, broken heart, and the kids crying. . . . And then you know I thought Mike's got a family, and I thought maybe I found a family. No, that would have been too easy. I have to have a neurotic mother-in-law, a gay brother-in-law, and they all are drunks. A drunk sister-in-law, a gay brother-in-law.

Ann's story echoes what professionals dealing with the aftermath of child maltreatment already know: Child maltreatment occurs in families with histories of maltreatment. Yet CPS removes children from their families and returns them to the same families without providing adequate treatment for parents or children. Ann was the exception. She self-referred to an intervention program that would address problems within family relationships.

Even when parent–child and family relationships are addressed by intervention, poverty is not. Child maltreatment does occur in families that are middle and upper income (evidence of this was provided by Ann's description of her childhood); however, the number of families living in poverty and involved with CPS is greatly disproportionate (Wolock & Horowitz, 1979). This may be due in part to the privacy afforded middle income families insulated by private residences, relying on their own personal and monetary resources, versus the visibility of families living in temporary shared housing or apartments with paper thin walls, relying on social services for medical care, food, and monthly income. People in poverty may be reported more often.

Still, most children identified as having been maltreated live in poverty and all that goes with it: small, unsafe places to live; no immunizations, vitamins, or checkups with a family doctor; inadequate diets; not enough quarters for phone calls, buses, or laundromats; no day care, trips to the zoo, or new school clothes. Poverty itself is detrimental to children without the compounding effects of maltreatment (Elmer, 1977).

In a country where two incomes are needed to support a family (Garbarino, 1988), it is not surprising that families identified as abusive are often headed by single mothers. Our nation is one of the few industrialized nations where children and their mothers are not entitled to basic health care (Miller, 1987) and where quality, available child care is becoming increasingly difficult to attain even for families with sufficient monetary resources.

Economically impoverished environments are also socially impoverished environments (Garbarino, 1990). Families struggling to meet basic needs may have little time, money, or energy left for their children. Families provide the context in which children grow. They are the constant in their children's lives. As a society, we cannot support children without supporting their families.

For Ann and other parents in the program, poverty and related issues compromised the parenting skills they acquired during intervention. Likewise, parents' performance of parenting skills in the program seemed to have little bearing on caseworkers' judgments and decisions regarding parents' abilities to parent outside the program.

GETTING OUT OF THE SYSTEM

Deciding When Cases Should Be Closed

How does the system decide when parents will provide safe environments for their children? Program co-director Georgia offered her impression of how CPS decided when parents were ready to resume parenting.

> How do parents get out of the Child Protective Service system and resume their lives? I think it's guess work. They're in this program. They have the opportunity to demonstrate [their abilities to parent] because they're here with the children. And we can record whether or not they can, in a controlled setting, adequately care for their children. Until the children are returned home, or have extended home visits, we can't assess whether or not they can maintain the skills and generalize them to the home environment. There's always a risk. There's no assessment out there, there's no way of knowing or predicting how children are going to do once they're returned to the home. If they're not in the parent training program, they have visits at the CPS office in the small rooms for an hour a week. And I think the caseworker sees whether or not parents attend and sees whether or not they go to their counseling appointments or their drug treatment appointments. That's basically it. Do they do what they're told to do? The compliant parents are the ones who get the results, regardless of what they can demonstrate with their children.

Co-director Isabelle expressed similar concerns. She talked about a mother referred to the program for intervention whose parental rights were terminated prior to completion of the 14-week session. The caseworker never observed the parent in the program and talked to Isabelle briefly over the phone only once about the mother's performance during intervention sessions. Although the parent never missed a session, was responsive to feedback from the staff, had positive reports for every session, and was working at a temporary job and looking for permanent work, the caseworker's concerns centered on the length of time it was taking the parent to find a permanent job and housing. Isabelle did not believe all evidence was considered by the caseworker making the decision to pursue termination of parental rights.

> I really had hope for this parent. I saw a lot of other [parents] that were a lot worse. So, again, there's that discrepancy between some people getting 3 years of chances—which I don't agree with, either

(I think that there has to be some kind of decision made for the child's sake)—and others getting the absolute minimum. And is that based on agency standards, or is that based on a law, or is that based on just the caseworker's whim? Sometimes I feel a lot of decisions are made based on the caseworker's whim, and that concerns me.

Whether or not parents were successful in regaining custody of their children, the process took a long time. The program began scheduling consecutive sessions for parents needing longer than 14 weeks—which was nearly all parents. Parents who stayed too long were another matter. When weeks stretched into years, the staff became discouraged with parents' lack of progress. Some parents did not acquire the skills necessary to exit the program, but they successfully completed CPS service contracts. This situation forced decisive action from CPS—action not always in the children's best interest. If parents showed up at the program, completed their service contracts, and did not do anything that warranted a report of maltreatment, their cases were sometimes closed and children returned, despite misgivings from program staff about the well-being of the children.

The causes and treatments of child maltreatment and reasons for the opening or closing of cases were rarely clear or certain. Every parent and staff member with whom I spoke believed actual incidences of maltreatment were just one of many reasons families became involved with CPS. Staff members mentioned family instability, parents' mental health, parents with disabilities, and lack of money, jobs, and clean, safe (or any) homes. Issues of welfare payments, sheltered housing, violent arguments, counseling and treatment program waiting lists, boyfriends in jail, problems with parents, and unpaid medical bills were inherent in every situation I observed. Getting one's CPS case closed hinged on much more than competent parenting skills.

Child maltreatment appeared to be viewed by some CPS staff from the narrow perspective of a parent harming a child. Sometimes that perspective broadened to include parent and child, or, in the case of the program, families. Karla, an interventionist in the program, talked about abuse in a broader context.

When I'm complaining about some issue, when a family's had a really hard time, when I'm angry because a child is homeless, or whatever, my brother will say in a very sarcastic tone, "Yes, but Karla, they're our most important resource." Lip service is basically what it is. There's one statistic that shoots the theory all to hell, that the bottom line is the best interest of the child: Children are the number one, fastest growing population of poor in the country.

That's abuse as a matter of public policy. That's the worst kind of abuse, it's the most insidious. . . . It makes it really hard for me to get angry at a parent. . . . You know, it's picking on the little guy, the defenseless guy, to go after parents when society allows a child to be living under those conditions.

Staff members of the program agreed that caseworkers were probably caring at one time, but impossible caseloads and a system designed to react to crises rather than prevent them seemed to create feelings of apathy symptomatic of dealing with seemingly unresolvable situations. Parents needing protracted, intensive support and services waited for treatment or received brief classes of questionable value while their children spent years in sequential foster care placements. Meier and Sloan (1984) noted that parents feel trapped in intervention programs that profess to strengthen parenting skills and reunite families but instead lead to relinquishment of parental rights as the goals of court-related services, child protective services, and therapeutic intervention services operate at cross-purposes.

Mismatches are common between many societal problems and policies designed to address them. Funding sources and policy makers want quick, easy solutions. Some well-intentioned professionals make promises in order to obtain funding, and begin to believe quick, easy solutions are possible. Others respond to agency standards aimed more toward efficient dispositions than effective outcomes. Policies that require quick, easy solutions perpetuate systems that view parents as "bad" and expect that legal intervention will make parents straighten up and child maltreatment disappear. But parents who maltreat children because of personal histories, drug or alcohol addictions, lack of competent parenting skills, or socioeconomic situations rather than malevolence will not become "good parents" by virtue of some agency simply pointing out to them that they are "bad parents" and taking their children away. The problems that bring families to CPS are too complicated and deeply rooted.

The Importance of Appearing Earnest

Did CPS caseworkers help parents deal with their problems? Some did, sometimes. Many parents, fearing possible repercussions, were not always honest with caseworkers about their problems. Ann professed trust for her second caseworker and advocated honest relationships. How could she, she asked, get help if she could not be honest about her problems? She expressed mistrust for her first caseworker, however, saying she feared telling the truth about her depression and her husband's drinking and violence because she thought CPS would take her child again. (Despite advocating honesty, one time she told me how she got clean UAs while using drugs.) Although she portrayed some parents in the program as angry and mistrustful, and who viewed the program as "stupid," Ann also talked with candor about parents' denial of maltreating their children.

> We all didn't get here because we didn't do anything. And you will hear people say, I didn't abuse my children. Well, something got you involved with Child Protective Services. You won't hear a lot of people admit that there's a potential for child abuse, or, "yes, I might have done it, but I didn't mean to do it." You don't hear that. You just hear denial, denial, denial. I'm willing to admit that there is a potential for abuse, you know, and there is a problem.

Counter to my expectations, every parent I interviewed eventually told me CPS should have intervened in their lives. Admitting a problem, however, did not mean help was forthcoming. Ann waited months for counseling and drug and alcohol treatment. Feeling desperate, she called her caseworker weekly from a pay phone to ask for services that were unavailable, even though they were court-ordered. Four months into the study, I asked Ann how she was going to get out of the system. She responded that unless she got some help, she never would. She recognized that unless she was honest about her problems, she would not get the help she needed, but as long as she was honest, CPS would "never see [her] as quite fit to parent."

EPILOGUE

Ann's ex-husband returned, and she enrolled in school to earn a nurse's aide certificate. Mike's drinking and violence escalated, so she and Ben left to live in temporary sheltered housing for battered women. Ann left school before graduation and, when the time she and Ben were permitted to live in the shelter ended, was forced to move into the only affordable apartment she could find.

The two moved to a second floor apartment in a part of town well known for drugs and crime. It was the kind of neighborhood where a child at play would seldom be watched by a friendly neighbor; residents rarely took pride in their surroundings, and few remained long enough to put down roots. I first visited the apartment a week before Christmas. Passing a man whose stare made me uneasy, I knocked on the door and watched the drapes pull aside a few inches as Ann peered out the side of the window, checking to see who was there before opening the door. I encountered a suffocating wall of hot air that radiated from a baseboard heater as the door opened, and Ann wrapped her arms around me for what seemed like minutes.

A sagging old double bed occupied a quarter of the living room, and a dresser with a rented television on it, a broken lounge chair, an end table and lamp, and Ben's toys piled in one corner occupied the rest. The living room constituted the entire apartment except for a bathroom, closet, and closet-size space without appliances that served as a kitchen. Tattered drapes hanging unevenly from the only window maintained privacy but also obstructed the daylight, making the apartment feel small and close.

Ben was asleep on the bed, so we sat carefully as Ann shared how difficult it was making ends meet. Mike was not helping with money, and the apartment was too small for raising a child, especially one as active as Ben. The apartment was not decorated for the holidays, but the program made certain that Ben received gifts from Santa. We spoke a short time and vowed to talk again after the holidays.

One evening two months later Ann called from her apartment, where she sat alone with an unopened bottle of wine. Ben was at a sitter's provided by her drug and alcohol treatment program so that she could attend evening meetings. She had had serious problems with Ben the previous 3 days. It was rainy and cold and they could not leave the apartment because Ben had been sick with asthma for the past 3-and-a-half months. "I'm afraid I'll hurt him," she said.

Ann relayed bits and pieces about the events troubling her. During a tantrum, Ben broke the handle of her friend's new car when he had taken them to lunch. Ann directed her friend to take them to the intervention program office, where she walked in and announced to staff members that she could not handle Ben and was going to leave him there.

Crying softly, she told me that she felt inadequate. She had hit Ben with her fists, but, she assured me, she hit him on his legs. "Oh, Ann," I said, "Don't hit your child." "I know," she said sounding frustrated. I asked if it helped to hit him, if he behaved better. "It doesn't help, and it's terrible to hear him, 'You hurt me, you hurt me.' I'll tell him, 'I'm sorry,' and he says, 'Thank you, Mama.'" She cried harder and said, "I'm just like my dad, and I know it, and I hate it."

I asked her if she had told Isabelle and she said yes. I later confirmed this when several staff members from the program told me about the same incident. "Crosschecking" or confirmation of information from multiple sources (Taylor & Bogdan, 1984) happened readily throughout the study as staff and parents frequently talked about each other. I was relieved that I would not have to file a report with CPS.

We talked about things to help reduce the stress and frustration she felt. She could not afford to attend school so that she could get a "decent job" because she would lose welfare money. She received $369 each month and spent $235 on rent—not enough left to orchestrate a move or pay more rent much less pay tuition. No matter what she tried "there was always a barrier." Several times she told me she felt afraid: "I think of dying too much . . . feeling like there's no way out."

When I hung up I thought, perhaps Ann is right. Perhaps there is no way out. There are strategies available to help parents acquire knowledge about parenting. Parents said the program did a good job of that. But the acquisition of parenting skills addressed only part of Ann's problems. Ann lived a monotonous stream of days in an apartment measuring 10 by 16 feet, feeling pain from teeth she could not afford to fix, caring for a child who had no space to play, receiving threats but no money from her ex-husband, while seeking constant medical attention for Ben, whose asthma was worsened by stressful situations. The parenting skills Ann demonstrated in the program were lost as her situation outside the program deteriorated.

But Ann's story differs greatly according to when it is written. Two months after Ann called me with an unopened bottle of wine, she completed 4 weeks of school toward her nurse's aide certificate. The program helped her find a resource to pay for her school. She scored four As, a B, and a C on her tests. She was surprised and proud that she could succeed in school after so many years.

Ann was taking medication for her depression and, because she doubled her dosage without consulting her physician, was having difficulty remaining awake and alert. Ben was seeing a play therapist because of his aggressive behavior. (Ann had bruises in the shape of Ben's teeth covering her forearms.) Yet the therapist, Ann reported, seemed more concerned about her than Ben because of the stress in her life.

Ann found an attorney through the phone book and planned to file for custody of Ben. She selected the attorney because the first visit was free. She does not seem concerned about the $750 attorney's fees, despite having to choose each month between food and diapers because she cannot afford both. The attorney accepts payments.

Ann seemed happier than at any other time during the past year, but I knew that by the time our next conversation occurred her life might have changed drastically. The changes in Ann's life were usually crises that brought her to a new agency or prolonged her association with a familiar agency. Eventually each agency or professional would tire of her or she would tire of them. Ann began relying on social service agencies when she was 16; after a while they became—or she came to see them—as her only resources.

Ann thinks that this time she is going to make it—get a good job and close her CPS case. I do not know if the beginning of Ann's story will predict the end. I hope not. Ann's journey has been long and torturous. If it is to end happily she will need some things not offered by CPS or intervention programs—things that make any of us happy or successful. She and her son will need food, medical care, and a safe, secure place to live, grow, and play. Perhaps with a job she will be able to obtain those things. Like all of us, she will need an occasional someone to lean on. Perhaps she will receive the kind of help that will enable her to be strong and independent enough to find support outside of social service systems.

REFERENCES

Bogdan, R., & Biklen, S. K. (1982). *Qualitative research for education: An introduction to theory and methods*. Boston: Allyn & Bacon.

Elmer, E. (1977). *Fragile families, troubled children*. Pittsburgh, PA: University of Pittsburgh Press.

Garbarino, J. (1988). *The future as if it really mattered*. Longmont, Co: Bookmakers Guild.

Garbarino, J. (1990). The human ecology of early risk. In S. J. Meisels & J. P. Shonkoff (Eds.), *Handbook of early childhood intervention* (pp. 78–96). Cambridge: Cambridge University Press.

Meier, J. H., & Sloan, M. P. (1984). The severely handicapped child and child abuse. In J. Blacher (Ed.), *Severely handicapped young children and their families* (pp. 247–272). Orlando, FL: Academic Press.

Miller, A. (1987). *Maternal health and infant survival*. Washington, DC: National Center for Clinical Infant Programs.

Pelton, L. H. (Ed.). (1981). *The social context of child abuse and neglect*. New York: Human Sciences Press.

Taylor, S. J., & Bogdan, R. (1984). *Introduction to qualitative research methods: The search for meanings* (2nd ed.). New York: John Wiley.

Wolock, I., & Horowitz, B. (1979). Child maltreatment and material deprivation among AFDC-recipient families. *Social Service Review*, *53*, 175–194.

Zelditch, M. (1962). Some methodological problems of field studies. *American Journal of Sociology*, *67*, 566–576.

Chapter 3

"NOBODY HELPS!"

Lack of Perceived Support in the Lives of Elderly People with Developmental Disabilities

Bonnie Todis

During the past 20 years, considerable research has focused on the link between social support and various aspects of physical and mental health. Lin, Simeone, Ensel, and Kuo (1979) define social support broadly as "support accessible to an individual through social ties to other individuals, groups and the larger community." A model developed earlier by Weiss (1974) increases the utility of this definition for research purposes by specifying the nature of the "social ties" through which support is conveyed. Weiss's model describes social support in terms of six functions or provisions that may be obtained from relationships with others (Cutrona & Russell, 1987). Two assistance-related provisions—guidance (advice or information) and reliable assistance (tangible assistance, or the knowledge that it is available if needed)—are applied to problem solving in conditions of stress. Four nonassistance-related provisions are not directly related to problem solving and provide beneficial effects during periods of both high and low stress. They include reassurance of worth (recognition of one's competence, skills, and value), attachment (emotional closeness), social integration (a sense of belonging to a group that shares similar interests, concerns, and activities), and opportunity for nurturance (the sense that others rely on one for their well-being).

For the general population, social support has been shown to have a role in health maintenance and disease etiology (Gottlieb, 1981, 1983; Pilisuk & Froland, 1978); in buffering stressful events and life strains (Cobb, 1976; Cohen & Wills, 1985; Dean & Lin, 1977; Gore, 1978); and in general adjustment and mental well-being (Gottlieb, 1981, 1983; Lin et al., 1979). In the field of gerontology, researchers have demonstrated that the elderly experience the benefits of social support listed above (Cutrona,

Russell, & Rose, 1986; Wan, 1982) as well as others, including lower chance of institutionalization (Palmore, 1976), more satisfactory recovery from illness (Finlayson, 1976), and greater life satisfaction (Larson, 1978; Lowenthal & Haven, 1968; Palmore, 1979). Likewise, a number of researchers in the field of developmental disabilities have highlighted the importance of social support for various aspects of successful adjustment of individuals with developmental disabilities who live in community settings (Edgerton, 1967; Edgerton & Bercovici, 1976; Koegel, 1982; Landesman-Dwyer & Berkson, 1984; Landesman-Dwyer, Berkson, & Romer, 1979; Mitchell-Kernan & Tucker, 1984; O'Connor, 1983; Seltzer, Seltzer, & Sherwood, 1982; Willer, Intagliata, & Wicks, 1981; Zetlin, 1986).

Despite this large body of research, however, no studies to date have specially investigated the function of social support for the burgeoning population of elderly persons who have developmental disabilities. Given the stressful life circumstances of many elderly persons with developmental disabilities (e.g, attrition of family support due to the deaths of parents and declining health of siblings, low income, and retirement), social support issues would be expected to be highly salient. A few studies that examine the quality of life of this population provide evidence that social support has a positive impact on this group (Edgerton, Bollinger, & Herr, 1984; Kennan, 1988) and, conversely, that lack of social support is a significant factor in negative well-being (Herr, 1983). This chapter takes a more detailed look at one of the questions related to the provision of social support to elderly persons who have developmental disabilities: how social support is perceived by that population and how those perceptions affect the way services are utilized or, perhaps more important, not utilized.

THE LIFE HISTORY METHOD

The respondents discussed in this chapter, Wilbur and Grace Winston (all names are pseudonyms), were two of six participants in a life history study designed to examine quality of life issues of older adults with developmental disabilities who live in community settings. Several factors make life history methodology the obvious choice for collecting data for such a study. In constructing a life history, a field researcher meets regularly over a period of several months—or longer—with the respondent for either an unstructured interview or a participant observation. In the interviews, topics of discussion are raised initially by the respondent. A topic's frequency of mention and duration in discourse and the respondent's affect while speaking on the topic are noted to ascertain its significance for the respondent. While this approach sometimes produces long periods of silence in the early interviews while the researcher waits for the respondent to bring up topics, it over-comes many of the problems associated with obtaining information from this group, including acquiescence (Sigelman, Budd, Spanhel, & Schoen-rock, 1981), social desirability (Edgerton, 1984), and tendency to select the last choice on either–or questions (Sigelman, Schoenrock et al., 1981).

In participant observations, a researcher often accompanies a respon-dent as he or she goes about the activities of daily life. This allows the researcher to strengthen rapport with the respondent, provides a context for incidents mentioned in the interviews, and helps the researcher determine the correspondence between what the respondents *say* they do and what the researcher *observes* them doing (Edgerton, 1984). The life history gradually emerges from experiencing daily events with the respondent and members of his or her support system, checking the researcher's perception of those events with the various participants in ongoing interviews, and placing this emic view of the respondent's current situation in the broad context of his or her entire life experience.

Qualitative methods are well-suited not only to the population but also to the topic addressed here, social support (Koegel, 1982, 1986). The fact that life history studies are longitudinal makes it possible to study one of the key features of support systems: the fact that the components of systems, as well as the needs the systems address, change over time. Another feature of life history research is that it views topics holistically, allowing support networks to be studied as systems in which the components constantly interact and balance each other.

In this study, I interviewed each of the two respondents every other week in sessions lasting about one hour. As the rapport between us grew, and I became familiar with the context of the respondents' lives, I often directed questions back toward topics that we had already discussed in order to clarify information or ascertain their relative importance to the respon-dents. In general, however, the content of the interviews was determined by Wilbur and Grace.

During the weeks between interview sessions, I spent time observing the daily routines of each respondent. This involved 2 to 3 hours a week (per respondent) of accompanying the respondents as they paid bills, went grocery shopping, attended senior citizens activity groups, went on walks, or had coffee with friends. Because the respondents are a married couple, they were involved together in many of the participant observations. How-ever, an effort was made to spend time with each of the respondents individually.

I also obtained data from sources other than the primary respondents, including each of their official files at the Developmental Disabilities Divi-sion office, relatives, current and former case managers, and former care providers. In addition, Grace and Wilbur were valuable sources of information about each other. Each of them often shared his or her perceptions of what the other person was thinking or reported on the spouse's private reactions to events. These reports sometimes related to events not mentioned by the spouse or conflicted with the spouse's account of the event and his or her reaction to it. In analyzing the data, I used these multiple perspectives provided by outside informants to supplement but not supplant data obtained directly from each of the primary respondents. The result is separate life histories of two people whose lives have rather recently become intertwined.

RESPONDENTS

Wilbur was born in 1917, in rural Missouri, "down around the Ozarks." At the time he participated in the life history study he was nearly 70 years old but looked much younger. Tall, strong, and wiry, he moves rather stiffly, both as a result of old injuries and because he is self-conscious in social situations. Although reserved and soft-spoken, once he starts talking about a topic of interest, Wilbur converses with ease and will "visit" for hours.

Wilbur was raised by his father's brother, a widower with two young sons, who married or at least assumed responsibility for his sister-in-law when Wilbur's father died. The mother soon left the family, however, and the three boys were raised by Wilbur's uncle as brothers. None of the boys attended school regularly. Instead they spent their days fishing and playing in nearby creeks. During the Depression, Wilbur, like other young men, took odd jobs on neighbors' farms and government jobs on road-building crews for which he was paid 30 cents an hour.

It was only when Wilbur's cousins left the area to join the army and find work elsewhere that their paths began to diverge. Until that time, any developmental disability that may have been noted had not resulted in his being treated differently. With the cousins' departure, however, Wilbur and his uncle were left on the family farm in increasing isolation and poverty. When the uncle died in 1972, Wilbur's cousin James returned to Missouri to dispose of the farm and take Wilbur back to Oregon with him. Not having seen Wilbur in 23 years, James was struck by the change in his cousin. He seemed confused, withdrawn, and frightened, not at all the clown and daredevil James remembered from his youth.

Once in Oregon, Wilbur lived with James and his wife Harriet, but Harriet soon found this arrangement unsatisfactory and another place had to be found for Wilbur. He lived in a succession of foster care homes, often with other residents who had recently been released from state institutions and whose deviant and sometimes violent behaviors Wilbur found disturbing. Other foster care homes were located so far from Wilbur's sheltered workshop that bus service was not available, and he spent 4 or 5 hours a day waiting for rides from his day care providers.

Finally, a young professor in the department of special education and his wife made an apartment in their basement available to Wilbur and another man with developmental disabilities. They provided not only a place to live but also training in independent living and social skills. Wilbur began to get around the community on the city bus, to go to and from work, to do his laundry and grocery shopping, and to visit Grace, a woman he met at the sheltered workshop.

Grace Hudson was born in 1929, 12 years after Wilbur. She is short and stout and looks younger than 60, but her physical condition is so poor that she behaves like someone much older, requiring assistance to negotiate stairs and to get out of soft chairs. Like Wilbur, Grace is shy in new social situations. However, while Wilbur remains reserved, Grace quickly "warms up" and becomes garrulous and animated.

Grace has lived most of her life in the Northwest city where she met Wilbur. One of three daughters in a family of eight children, she, like Wilbur, attended school only briefly. She remembers sitting at the back of the classroom and getting little attention from the teacher. Her parents, probably to the teacher's relief, soon decided she would be better off at home.

Grace does not have as many memories of her childhood as Wilbur does, perhaps because she was more isolated and her experience was less varied than his. Grace seldom left the house and, besides her parents and siblings, was acquainted with only a few long-time neighbors. Gradually, the other children married and left home, and Grace was left alone with her parents.

Sometime during early adulthood, Grace came to the attention of the formal social service network. Her parents began to rely on Supplemental Security Insurance (SSI) payments to offset the expense of maintaining Grace in their home, and she was employed at the sheltered workshop where she eventually met Wilbur. She also began to attend an activity center for adults with developmental disabilities, where she made her first friend, Mary Ann.

As her parents' health declined, Grace was called upon to do more of the household chores and sometimes was kept home from work to keep her mother company. An older brother lived next door and a younger brother moved his family into a trailer on the parents' acreage, allowing Grace to continue working and participating in her activities, including seeing Wilbur and Mary Ann.

In response to her new independence, and following the example set by her brothers and sisters, Grace began to talk about getting married. Her father gradually accepted the idea, but her mother remained adamantly opposed until her death in 1980. Grace and Wilbur were married a few months later. He was 62 and she was 50.

At first the couple lived in Wilbur's apartment, but when the professor and his wife had their first baby, other arrangements had to be made. About 6 months after the wedding, Grace's father died. Her youngest brother, Dick Hudson, and his wife Trudy moved into the parents' house, making their trailer available to Grace and Wilbur. Wilbur continued working at the sheltered workshop until mandatory retirement at age 65. Grace, however, quit work and stopped attending all her activities soon after she was married. In fact, until Esther French was assigned to be their case manager about 5 years after Grace and Wilbur were married, Grace seldom left the trailer and often stayed in bed for weeks at a time. Wilbur assumed responsibility for all household tasks and in his free time explored the city bus system or visited his cousin James.

Esther assigned a senior companion, Myra Fiori, to take them to a senior citizen activity center one morning a week and to spend another morning with them doing whatever activities they chose, usually paying bills, banking, shopping, or going out for lunch. Esther made it clear to Grace that she was required to accompany Wilbur and Myra on these excursions. The change in Grace was immediate and dramatic. Both Esther and Myra were impressed with how quickly she dropped her rather sullen, withdrawn demeanor and became talkative and animated. The change in Wilbur was slower. He never had been very comfortable in social situations, but he too became more relaxed and outgoing.

DESCRIPTION OF SOCIAL SUPPORT SYSTEM

Marriage

When asked how their lives had changed since their marriage, both Wilbur and Grace replied, independently, that they now have companionship that was lacking before. Wilbur also stated that if he had not married Grace, "There's no tellin'" where he would be living now, acknowledging that marriage provided a long-term solution to his housing problems. For Grace, getting married was a chance to assert herself, to improve her status, and to prove to herself and others that she was "just like everybody else." These factors, however, are less salient features of the relationship than the companionship and support Wilbur and Grace provide each other.

Many of the Winstons' interactions resemble those of any other married couple. In terms of Weiss's model, Wilbur amply provides the assistance-related provisions of guidance and reliable assistance to Grace, but she is unable to reciprocate. This imbalance may be compensated for by Wilbur's receiving a greater degree of satisfaction from the opportunity-for-nurturance provision—the sense that Grace relies on him for her well-being. The couple seems to meet each other's social support needs more than adequately for the three remaining nonassistance-related functions of social support in Weiss's (1974) model (reassurance of self-worth, attachment, and social integration). They discuss the events of the day with each other, consider how their actions will affect the other, and are careful not to commit to plans until they have conferred with the other partner; they take each other's perspective and defend each other in conflicts with family members.

However, to an outsider some features of mutual support seem to be lacking from this relationship; although the Winstons sometimes discuss an issue in private, most of their conversation concerns scheduling activities and shopping lists. They often guess at what the other is thinking, or find out through a third party, rather than ask each other directly. Because Grace lacks many independent living skills, the roles in the relationship have been divided disproportionately, with Wilbur assuming responsibility for money management, grocery shopping, cooking, and cleaning. Grace's main contribution to the relationship seems to be her extensive family ties, which are a source of both support and conflict for the couple.

In spite of the fact that the mechanisms by which support is provided may not be apparent to outsiders, the couple themselves find the relationship satisfying. Wilbur says, "It's somebody to be with all the time . . . talk and go on with her and this, that, and the other. . . . You can reason with her." For Grace, being married means, "I'm not alone, for one thing . . . I found the right one. Gonna stick with him, too!"

Family

Although three of Grace's brothers and their wives live in the same city as she and Wilbur, Dick and Trudy are the ones who are called upon, both by Grace and Wilbur and by social service personnel, for assistance. This is not entirely due to proximity, since Grace's oldest brother Calvin also lives next door to the trailer.

Dick and Trudy assumed a large part of the responsibility for Grace when they decided to move their trailer to help her care for the elderly Hudsons. After the parents' deaths, responsibility for Grace fell to them, in part because she and Wilbur were living in their trailer and they were the

Winstons' landlord, in part because Grace had gotten used to the idea that they would be there if she needed them, and in part because they were more willing than the other siblings to fill the primary support role. This role involves seeing to it that Grace and Wilbur have something to do on holidays and are included in other family celebrations, maintaining the trailer, and being available in case of emergencies. One of Grace's favorite, often-repeated stories is about the time Wilbur got sick with pneumonia and Trudy drove them both to the hospital. She stayed with Grace for several hours while Wilbur was admitted, helping her answer questions and fill out forms. When they got home, it was very late, and Trudy insisted that Dick turn on the porch light at the trailer before she would allow Grace to go in.

Before Esther became case manager, Trudy and Dick did their best to coordinate the Winstons' services, provide transportation, and help them manage their finances. Most of these tasks were undertaken by Trudy because she was home during the day with a young son and because Dick is illiterate and unable to cope with correspondence from the agencies. Trudy, on the other hand, has had a great deal of experience in this area. At least two of her sisters, one of her brothers, and perhaps her mother have developmental disabilities, some form of mental illness, or both. Several of these family members and assorted nieces and nephews live just a few houses away from Dick and Trudy and rely on her for help in dealing with agencies and sometimes for financial assistance.

Social Service Agencies

During the first 6 years of Grace and Wilbur's marriage, the couple "were put on the back burner" of the social service system. There was a restructuring of services, and Wilbur's and Grace's files were transferred twice, first from Adult and Family Services to Adult and Senior Services and then to Developmental Disabilities Division (DDD). Before DDD took over, case managers in Adult and Senior Services were burdened with many jobs, such as certifying homes, in addition to case management. They were overworked, and as a result between 1980 and 1986 Wilbur and Grace, who were higher functioning than many clients who had a supportive family, rarely saw a case manager except when a new one came out to get acquainted.

Although Trudy was all too familiar with the social service system, she had neither the skills, time, nor desire to manage her own family, her mother's and her siblings' problems, and the Winstons' affairs. She took Wilbur and Grace to medical appointments and to visit Wilbur's brother and tried to keep on top of the paperwork, but after 5 years of marriage, the Winstons' situation was bleak. Grace hardly ever left the trailer. In fact, she often stayed in bed and had gained a great deal of weight. Although Wilbur tried to stay active, Trudy thought he seemed depressed. Worst of all, their finances were in total disarray. Because Wilbur prefers to present store clerks with a large bill, rather than try to count out the correct amount in smaller bills, change and small bills had accumulated in the trailer. Dick became concerned that Wilbur and Grace would be targets for robbery and deposited the money in their account. This raised their balance above the maximum allowed by Social Security and their monthly payments were reduced. Trudy was unable to get the payment restored, both because she was confused by the paperwork and because she no longer had the time, having started working as a motel maid when her son entered public school.

Esther's first act as the Winstons' case manager was to take them to the Social Security office to get their full payment restored, and since then she has spent much of the time allotted to the Winstons' case coming up with ideas for them to spend money to keep their bank balance below the allowable limit. These ideas include traveling to see Grace's relatives in Washington state, buying new curtains for the trailer so that the old curtains could be returned to Trudy, buying Christmas presents for family members, providing the turkey for Grace's family's Thanksgiving dinner, taking Dick and Trudy out to eat, and hiring a housekeeper. An additional benefit of these activities was that they promoted interaction with, and goodwill toward, Grace's family.

Another of Esther's goals was to get the couple involved in activities in the community, which she accomplished by arranging for Myra to be their senior companion. Esther had some ideas for activities in which Myra could involve Wilbur and Grace, including the group at the senior citizens' center, but encouraged Myra to find other things for them to do, as her schedule permitted. Esther hoped that Myra would also be able to work with Grace on some skills like counting money and riding the bus alone. Myra says, "I tried that, but I didn't have good luck with it because if she doesn't want to do anything, you cannot budge her at that particular time."

Esther persisted in looking for ways to improve Grace's skills. There was growing concern from both family members and service personnel about how Grace would manage if Wilbur had to be hospitalized or died before her. Noting their age difference and Wilbur's several medical problems, Grace frequently mentioned this issue too, saying that if she didn't learn to manage money, buy and prepare food, and "keep the trailer up," "it would all be on my shoulders if something happened to Wilbur." She even acknowledged that she would "probably end up somewhere in a [nursing] home." This was a possibility she dreaded chiefly because it was the scenario her mother had predicted for Grace in her old age, assuming that she would never marry.

The family frequently reiterated to the Winstons the dire consequences of Grace's continued resistance to acquiring independent living skills, in an attempt to motivate her to apply herself to the task. Wilbur was quietly supportive of their efforts, helping Grace distinguish coins and bills and explaining how to use her bus pass, but he stopped short of applying any pressure for her to persist if she showed the slightest resistance.

At a time when Grace seemed receptive to instruction, which coincided with a time when Trudy and Dick became alarmed at the clutter that was accumulating in the trailer, Esther proposed to the Winstons that they hire a housekeeper. Carol began to come out once a week to clean and reorganize the trailer. At first Wilbur grumbled that he would have to get up early to find things, like coffee filters, that she might have moved, but since Carol's visits meant less work for him and less criticism from Dick and Trudy, Wilbur and Grace tolerated Carol's visits. After a few visits the trailer was clean and tidy, and Esther proposed that Carol spend the time working with Grace on cooking skills. At first Grace was enthusiastic and bragged about the meals she prepared while Wilbur sat and watched television for a change. But after about a month she flatly declared, "I don't wanna learn to cook no more." Everyone, including Wilbur, was baffled by this sudden change.

Wilbur, however, had his own list of complaints about Carol. She required them to buy food for the cooking lessons that they did not usually eat; her recipes made too much and the leftovers were wasted; her visits were scheduled at an inconvenient time; her insurance would not allow her to transport the Winstons in her car; and, worst of all, her services were not something they were entitled to, as he had thought, but were billed to the Winstons each month. Attempts to address these concerns and point out that they had adequate money to pay Carol were unavailing. The Winstons told Esther to tell Carol her services were no longer needed.

A few weeks later Myra came up with a plan to enroll the Winstons in classes offered through the community college for adults with developmental disabilities. Again, both Wilbur and Grace initially were enthusiastic. They knew many of the other students from the sheltered workshop they had attended before Wilbur retired. Wilbur was willing to give reading another try, and Grace told the instructor she would like to "learn money." However, when it became clear that transportation would not be provided by Myra because of schedule conflicts and that I was willing to accompany them on the bus only until they knew the route, they dropped the idea and did not attend a single class on their own.

Efforts to get Grace to have her hair washed at a local beauty shop succumbed to a similar fate. At first, when I drove her to her appointment or rode with her on the bus, Grace seemed delighted by the attention from the hairdresser and her improved appearance. When I told her I would be unable to go with her on a regular basis, she stopped having her hair washed until Esther ordered her to ride to the beauty shop on the bus with Wilbur every 2 weeks. She complied for a couple of months, then stopped going altogether, in spite of the fact that Esther reissued her directive and the hairdresser called her to ask where she had been.

Wilbur, as noted above, usually stays out of conflicts between Grace and members of the support system. He has on occasion, however, displayed his own form of passive resistance to efforts by social service personnel to "help" him. At Christmas time, he let it be known that the concept of gift giving was foreign to him and that he did not want to buy gifts for Trudy, Dick, and Grace. Esther insisted, however, pointing out that Dick and Trudy were hosting the holiday dinner and would be giving them a gift and that this was a good way to keep their bank balance under control. Wilbur reluctantly agreed to let Grace buy a small gift for his in-laws and selected a wallet for Grace. He never gave it to her, however, in spite of the fact that Grace gave him a shirt she had chosen for him.

With Esther actively campaigning to get the Winstons to prepare for the future, as well as coordinating their service, Trudy and Dick found they could devote less time and energy to helping Grace and Wilbur. Trudy had had several frustrating experiences with trying to teach Grace household skills and was relieved to turn the responsibility over to someone else. The Hudsons still maintained enough contact to be assured that there were no serious problems at the trailer, making casual inquiries about whether the Winstons received their checks, noticing when Myra's schedule changed, and monitoring the couple's health care needs without actually seeing to the details of how those needs were met. Sometimes Wilbur and Dick worked together on tasks like repairing Wilbur's bicycle, and Grace and Trudy still occasionally chatted about family members, but Esther's skillful case management clearly made it possible for the Hudsons to have much less interaction with Grace and Wilbur.

The Winstons' Perspectives

Both Wilbur and Grace independently praised Esther's effectiveness as case manager, which resulted, they believed, from her familiarity with their situation and her accessibility to them. Not only could they reach her easily by telephone, but she also regularly contacted them. As Grace put it, "Like Wilbur says, now, she keeps tabs of us. She keeps more tabs of us than the others did."

However, the lessening of contact with Dick and Trudy made possible by Esther's close attention was not viewed so positively. Wilbur was philosophical about the change, pointing out that Trudy had a job now and that she had a lot of "irons in the fire with her own family," but Grace was resentful that Trudy was no longer as available as she once had been and that the Hudsons frequently went out for the evening without letting the Winstons know where they were going. She frequently complained, "Trudy don't hardly do nothing for us no more." Grace expressed her resentment of Dick and Trudy's new independence by making an elaborate show of her disinterest in their activities. She delighted in "sneaking" away from the trailer and having Dick ask later where they had been. In reporting these episodes, she sniffed, "They don't tell us where they go. Why Trudy don't pay any attention to stuff over here. . . . They never tell us, and they go all the time, all hours of the day and night."

DISCUSSION

The Winstons' support system is a particularly good illustration of the two types of social support available to people with developmental disabilities who live in community settings: formal support through social service agencies and informal support provided by family and neighbors. Their experiences also point out an important feature of the support systems of elderly persons with developmental disabilities: the fact that as family members die, experience declining health, or simply grow tired of being responsible for the family member with developmental disabilities, social service agencies are called upon to provide more personal kinds of support.

Grace and Wilbur's marriage solved a host of support-related problems for their respective families. For Wilbur's family there was no more concern about his housing needs and a sharing of concern with the Hudsons about his general welfare. For the Hudsons, Grace's marriage to a "cosmetic genius," as Wilbur has been described, meant far less daily contact with Grace was required. Nevertheless, the Hudsons were more than willing to have Esther take over not only the paperwork required to ensure Grace and Wilbur's well-being, but also the mechanisms for delivering services to which they were entitled. Planning activities, providing transportation, preparing for the future, and much of daily problem solving all could be handled by Esther or people hired by her.

This expanded support network made available to the Winstons services and activities that they enjoyed greatly, and unarguably improved the quality of their life. However, when asked, "Who helps you do the things you need to get done?" Grace promptly and angrily replied, "*Nobody*! I and Wilbur work it out ourselves. We work together." This answer, as well as the resistance shown by both Grace and Wilbur to expand the types of support provided to them, was unexpected, given their initial enthusiasm for classes, training, and assistance, and the obvious improvements in their life circumstances resulting from Esther, Myra, and Carol's services.

These negative reactions arose because of what the Winstons actually experienced when responsibility for their support shifted from family to agencies. What had been support now became control (or at least the threat of control). The issue of control is at the heart of the contrast between formal and informal support systems. According to McKnight (1987), agencies are designed to *control* people; informal associations result from people acting through *consent*. Although agencies are constantly reorganizing themselves in an effort to provide what can be characterized as "care," such a managed system can only deliver service, not care. Care is a special relationship characterized by consent rather than control and therefore available only through informal, community channels (McKnight, 1987). A growing body of social support research bolsters this view, showing that a strong interaction exists between the type of social provision and its source (Constable & Russell, 1986; Cutrona, 1984, 1986; Russell, Altmaier, & Van Belzen, 1987). That is, certain types of social assistance are effective only if they come from the right person or group, and certain types of assistance are likely to be perceived as controlling and demanding rather than enabling when offered by people from dissimilar social backgrounds or life experiences (Coates & Wortman, 1980). According to Thoits (1986) effective support is most likely to come from "socially similar others" who have faced the same life circumstances.

The social networks of elderly persons with developmental disabilities are almost certain not to include many "socially similar others." Grace and Wilbur are atypical and fortunate in this regard, since they are married and able to provide each other effective emotional support. Perhaps what each finds supportive about the relationship is that the other is thoroughly familiar with the life circumstances that result from having developmental disabilities. The Winstons are also fortunate to have maintained contact with family members. However, through the years those ties have weakened as siblings have become occupied with their children, jobs, friends, and hobbies. Grace and Wilbur, like other elderly persons with developmental disabilities, have been denied opportunities now available to many mentally retarded children to form friendships in school and work settings with other individuals who are retarded. The friends that elderly persons may have met in workshops or community activities are seldom able to provide instrumental support or reliable information support, although they may be valued sources of social provisions that can be classified as socioemotional support (Turner, 1983).

In short, the effectiveness of the social support available to elderly persons with developmental disabilities is mitigated by the fact that much of it comes from sources that are perceived to lack the critical element of empathic understanding, the sharing of their effective experience imaginatively and vicariously (Thoits, 1986). The "services" offered Grace and Wilbur fail to take into account details of their daily lives that only careful listening and observation reveal: the fact that Wilbur is afraid to ride the bus after 3 P.M. because the traffic becomes heavy then; Wilbur's pride in his household management skills and his offense at the notion that he needs help in this area; his ambivalence about whether the term "handicapped" applies to him and whether he really "deserves" all these services, anyway. It is for reasons like these that Wilbur often resists and sometimes refuses what he perceives not as efforts to help, but attempts to control his and Grace's lives.

Grace's reasons for feeling unsupported and resisting certain services are slightly different. She not only resents the control, justified by concern about her future, exerted by members of the support system, but she also senses that the emphasis on self-improvement implies a lack of willingness to care for her. While she enjoys the concern, attention, and praise that accompany living skills instruction, it sometimes feels to her that acceptance by her family, Esther, and Myra is contingent on her continuing to become more self-sufficient.

An early definition of social support stressed its unconditional nature, calling it "the subjective feeling of belonging, of being accepted, of being loved, of being needed all for oneself and not for what one can do" (Moss, 1973). Grace seems to need to reassure herself, when too much attention is being focused on the new skills she is acquiring, that the people in her support network value her for herself and not just for what she can learn to do, which, incidentally, also makes their lives easier and their futures more carefree. Perhaps it is precisely this that Grace fears: by becoming more self-sufficient, she would be making it possible for her family to be free not to care about her anymore.

Support for this view comes from a conversation with Grace following a meeting with Esther, Dick, and Trudy regarding plans for her future. The meeting was called when Esther became aware that after Carol was dismissed Grace became almost obsessively concerned that she would be put in a nursing home if Wilbur died. After the meeting, Grace reported with relief, satisfaction, and even triumph, "I's to stay in the trailer if anything happens to Wilbur. . . . All the money and cooking and that'll all be on Esther and Trudy." She had succeeded in getting reassurance from her support providers that with Wilbur removed from her support network, responsibility for her well-being would not be "all on her shoulders" as she had previously feared. Her social network would, in fact, *increase* their provision of support to her to compensate for the loss of Wilbur's support.

Grace and Wilbur's situation is not unlike that of many other elderly people with developmental disabilities living in community settings. Their life histories show that simply having contact with agency representatives and family members and having access to activities and programs is not enough to ensure that older people with developmental disabilities will *feel* supported. As this population increases, there is a need to know more about how they perceive and use social support and about the interaction of support and provider. Thoits (1986) suggests that empathic understanding and perceived competence in the care provider can compensate for dissimilarities between provider and support recipient. Given the deficiencies of the informal support network of aging adults with developmental disabilities, there is a need to develop training to increase the empathic understanding provided by paid caregivers, as well as their expertise in case management, in order to ensure that what they provide is perceived as "care" as well as "service."

REFERENCES

Coates, D., & Wortman, C. B. (1980). Depression and maintenance and interpersonal control. In A. Baum & J. Singer (Eds.), *Advances in environmental psychology: Applications of personal control* (Vol. 2, pp. 149–182). Hillsdale, NJ: Erlbaum.

Cobb, S. (1976). Social support as a moderator of life stress. *Psychosomatic Medicine, 38*, 300–314.

Cohen, S., & Wills, T. A. (1985). Stress, social support, and the buffering hypothesis. *Psychological Bulletin, 98*, 310–357.

Constable, J. F., & Russell, D. (1986). The effect of social support and the work environment upon burnout among nurses. *Journal of Human Stress, 12*, 20–26.

Cutrona, C. E. (1984). Social support and stress in the transition to parenthood. *Journal of Abnormal Psychology, 91*, 378–390.

Cutrona, C. E. (1986). *Social support and depression among the elderly.* Paper presented at the midwinter meetings of Division 12 of the American Psychological Association, Melbourne, FL.

Cutrona, C. E., & Russell, D. W. (1987). The provisions of social relationships and adaptation to stress. *Advances in Personal Relationships, 1*, 37–67.

Cutrona, C. E., Russell, D. W., & Rose, J. (1986). Social support and adaptation to stress by the elderly. *Psychology and Aging, 1*, 47–54.

Dean, A., & Lin, N. (1977). The stress-buffering role of social support. *The Journal of Nervous and Mental Disease, 165*, 403–417.

Edgerton, R. B. (1967). *The cloak of competence: Stigma in the lives of the mentally retarded.* Berkeley: University of California Press.

Edgerton, R. B. (1984). The participant-observer approach to research in mental retardation. *American Journal of Mental Deficiency, 88,* 498–505.

Edgerton, R. B., & Bercovici, S. M. (1976). The cloak of competence: Years later. *American Journal of Mental Deficiency, 80,* 485–497.

Edgerton, R. B., Bollinger, M., & Herr, B. (1984). The cloak of competence: After two decades. *American Journal of Mental Deficiency, 88,* 345–351.

Finlayson, A. (1976). Social networks as coping resources. *Social Science and Medicine, 10,* 97–103.

Gore, S. (1978). The effect of social support in moderating the health consequences of unemployment. *Journal of Health and Social Behavior, 19,* 157–165.

Gottlieb, B. H. (Ed.). (1981). *Social networks and social support.* Beverly Hills, CA: Sage.

Gottlieb, B. H. (1983). *Social support strategies.* Beverly Hills, CA: Sage.

Herr, B. (1983). *Quality of life among aging mentally retarded persons.* Paper from the Mental Retardation Research Center, University of California.

Kennan, K. E. (1988). *R-62 life history report.* Eugene: University of Oregon, Research and Training Center in Mental Retardation.

Koegel, P. (1982). Rethinking support systems: A qualitative investigation into the nature of social support. (Doctoral dissertation, University of California, Los Angeles, 1982). *Dissertation Abstracts International, 43,* 1214A.

Koegel, P. (1986). Social support and individual adaptations: A diachronic perspective. In L. L. Langness & H. G. Levine (Eds.), *Culture and retardation* (pp. 127–153). Dordrecht, Holland: D. Reidel.

Landesman-Dwyer, S., & Berkson, G. (1984). Friendships and social behavior. In J. Wortis (Ed.), *Mental retardation and developmental disabilities:* Vol. 13, (pp. 129–154). New York: Plenum.

Landesman-Dwyer, S., Berkson, G., & Romer, D. (1979). Affiliation and friendship of mentally retarded residents in group homes. *American Journal of Mental Deficiency, 83,* 571–580.

Larson, R. (1978). Thirty years of research on the subjective well-being of older Americans. *Journal of Gerontology, 33,* 109–125.

Lin, N., Simeone, R. S., Ensel, W. M., & Kuo, W. (1979). Social support, stressful life events, and illness: A model and an empirical test. *Journal of Health and Social Behavior, 20,* 108–119.

Lowenthal, M. F., & Haven, E. (1968). Interaction and "adaptation": Intimacy as a critical variable. *American Sociological Review, 33,* 20–30.

McKnight, J. L. (1987). Regenerating community. *Social Policy, 17*(3), 54–58.

Mitchell-Kernan, C., & Tucker, M. B. (1984). The social structures of mildly mentally retarded Afro-Americans: Gender comparisons. In R. B. Edgerton (Ed.), *Lives in process: Mildly retarded adults in a large city* (pp. 173–192). Washington, DC: American Association on Mental Deficiency.

Moss, G. E. (1973). *Illness, immunity and social interaction.* New York: John Wiley.

O'Connor, G. (1983). Presidential address 1983: Social support of mentally retarded persons. *Mental Retardation, 21,* 187–196.

Palmore, E. (1976). Total chance of institutionalization among the aged. *The Gerontologist, 16,* 504–507.

Palmore, E. (1979). Predictors of successful aging. *The Gerontologist, 19,* 427–431.

Pilisuk, M., & Froland, C. (1978). Kinship, social networks, social support and health. *Social Science and Medicine, 12B,* 273–280.

Russell, D., Altmaier, E., & Van Belzen, D. (1987). Job-related stress, social support, and burnout among classroom teachers. *Journal of Applied Psychology, 72,* 269–274.

Seltzer, M. M., Seltzer, G. B., & Sherwood, C. C. (1982). Comparison of community adjustment of older vs. younger mentally retarded adults. *American Journal of Mental Deficiency, 84,* 9–13.

Sigelman, C. K., Budd, E. C., Spanhel, C. L., & Schoenrock, C. J. (1981). When in doubt, say yes: Acquiescence in interviews with mentally retarded persons. *Mental Retardation, 19,* 53–58.

Sigelman, C. K., Schoenrock, C. J., Winer, J. L., Spanhel, C. L., Hromas, S. G., Martin, P. W., Budd, E. C., & Bensberg, G. J. (1981). Issues in interviewing mentally retarded persons: An empirical study. In R. Bruininks, C. E. Meyers, B. B. Sigford, & K. C. Lakin (Eds.), *Deinstitutionalization and community adjustment of mentally retarded people* (Monograph No. 4, pp. 114–129). Washington, DC: American Association on Mental Deficiency.

Thoits, P. A. (1986). Social support as coping assistance. *Journal of Consulting and Clinical Psychology, 54,* 416–423.

Turner, J. L. (1983). Workshop society: Ethnographic observations in a work setting for retarded adults. In K. Kernan, M. Begab, & R. Edgerton (Eds.), *Environments and behavior: The adaptations of mentally retarded persons* (pp. 147–171). Baltimore: University Park Press.

Wan, T. T. H. (1982). Factors affecting use of health services. In Lexington Books (Eds.), *Stressful life events, social-support networks, and gerontological health: A prospective study* (pp. 97–113). Lexington, MA: D. C. Heath.

Weiss, R. (1974). The provisions of social relationships. In Z. Rubin (Ed.), *Doing unto others* (pp. 17–26). Englewood Cliffs, NJ: Prentice-Hall.

Willer, B., Intagliata, J., & Wicks, N. (1981). Return of retarded adults to natural families: Issues and results. In R. Bruininks, C. E. Meyers, B. B. Sigford, & K. C. Lakin (Eds.), *Deinstitutionalization and community adjustment of mentally retarded people* (Monograph No. 4, pp. 207–216). Washington, DC: American Association on Mental Deficiency.

Zetlin, A. G. (1986). Mentally retarded adults and their siblings. *American Journal of Mental Deficiency, 91,* 217–225.

Chapter 4

DEFENDING ILLUSIONS
The Institution's Struggle for Survival

Steven J. Taylor & Robert Bogdan

By definition, all organizations have goals and formal structures. In the Weberian (1947) tradition, scientists have until recently emphasized the instruments of formal organization. Formal organizations have been conceptualized as rational structures oriented toward the pursuit of stated goals (Blau & Scott, 1962; Etzioni, 1961). Blau and Scott (1962), for example, define an organization as a social unit composed of people working together to accomplish common ends. When viewed from this perspective goals define the purpose of an organization, while normal structures represent the rational means used to accomplish those goals.

Increasingly, however, sociologists and anthropologists have begun to direct attention to the symbolic nature of organizational goals and formal structures (Bittner, 1974; Jacobs, 1969; Kamens, 1977; Meyer & Rowan, 1977). Organizational goals justify the existence of an organization and provide members with meaning for their activities (Jacobs, 1969). Formal structures represent a means of displaying organizational responsibility and rationality (Meyer & Rowan, 1977). For us, organizational goals and structures act as legitimating myths that are used to gain the support of external public groups on which organizations depend for their survival. For instance, the goals and formal structures of universities are designed to legitimate the idea that students have acquired the necessary educational experiences to perform certain roles in society (Kamens, 1977).

Every organization faces the possibility that its legitimating myths may be shattered. Shadows fall between what organizations say they do and what they actually do—between their espoused goals and everyday practices. Studies of human-service organizations reveal a great discrepancy between formal myth and actual reality; mental hospitals do not treat (Goffman, 1961), nursing homes do not comfort (Gubrium, 1975), reform

---

An earlier version of this chapter appeared in *Human Organization*, *39*, 209–218, 1980.

schools do not reform (Platt, 1969), drug centers do not rehabilitate (Roth, 1971), and job training programs do not train (Scott, 1969).

This chapter deals with a type of organization that is engaged in a struggle for survival: institutions—formerly called "state schools," now variously referred to as "developmental centers" or "training schools"—for people labelled "mentally retarded." As used in this chapter, "institution" means a total institution in Goffman's (1961) sense.

Of interest here is how organizational standard bearers (institutional professionals and officials holding administrative positions) manage the visible discrepancy between goals and practices. The subjects of our study include persons with the titles of director (superintendent), assistant director, business officer, chief of service (mid-level administrator), and team leader (lower-level administrator).

In *Asylums*, Goffman (1961) described the rigid distinction between institutional staff and inmates. What Goffman did not discuss is the ambivalence and even hostility between different levels of staff—ward staff, or attendants, on the one hand and institutional officers on the other. Officials share certain elements that distinguish them from other levels of staff; their work does not involve direct day-to-day contact with residents; their professional identities and careers are concerned with work with people (Goffman, 1961); they have been schooled in an ideology of service to humanity; and, as the name "standard bearers" suggests, they represent the organization in relations with the outside world.

To be sure, institutional professionals and administrators may differ from each other according to their responsibilities and positions in the hierarchy. However, we are interested in their common perspectives and reactions to the outside world. Also, while we do not maintain that these common perspectives and reactions are shared by all standard bearers, we do take the position that they characterize the dominant views of those we have studied. Finally, we do not claim that these dominant views originated with these standard bearers. Many of the perspectives described in this chapter have been handed down from one generation of institutional officials to another.

This study uses qualitative methods and analytical procedures (Bogdan & Taylor, 1975). A major source of data is extensive participant observation at four northeastern institutions (pseudonymously referred to as Central, Cornerstone, Eastern, and Empire Developmental Centers) that we and student observers conducted between 1970 and 1977. Three of these institutions are located in one state, and the fourth in another; three are old facilities, established at the turn of the century, while the fourth is a relatively new institution, constructed in the 1970s; three are located in small towns, and the fourth in an urban area. At the time we studied them, these institutions ranged in size from slightly over 250 residents to approximately 3,300.

We have also used participant observation data collected by student observers at seven additional institutions located in the first-mentioned state. Like Eastern, Empire, Cornerstone, and Central, these facilities vary widely in size, age, and geographical area. While these data have enabled us to generalize our findings, we have not based any conclusions solely on data collected by others.

In addition, one of us, using a participant observation approach, visited 11 other institutions in five other states: one in a third northeastern state; one in a western state; two in a midwestern state; three in a southern state; and four in a mid-Atlantic state. Three of these institutions were toured in 1979, while eight were toured in 1980.

All of the participant observations, whether conducted by ourselves or others, focused on ward life at these 11 institutions (Bogdan, Taylor, De Grandpre, & Haynes, 1974; Taylor, 1977/1978). However, semi-formal interviews were conducted with at least one, and usually several, high-ranking officials at each institution. Also, we or the student observers toured the institutions with officials before observing ward life. At several institutions, we reported our findings to institutional officials at the conclusion of our observations. At Empire, for example, we met with the administrative staff to discuss the observations of 15 graduate-student observers, each of whom spent 6 full days living at the institution. Of course, on these occasions, we carefully recorded officials' reactions to our findings and observations.

We drew upon three other sources of data. First, there were written documents and materials: brochures, policy statements, memoranda, statistical data, and institutional newsletters. On some occasions, we obtained administrators' written reactions to outside criticism. A second source of data was public information, for example, court records and newspaper articles. For institutions for which our sole source of data was public information, we have not attempted to conceal the names of the facilities. Finally, we spent time with administrators and professionals at annual professional conventions, social gatherings, and other meetings. Often these contacts provided our best sources of data on administrators' perspectives.

The remainder of the chapter is devoted to how institutional standard bearers develop a world view as well as practical strategies to manage the discrepancy between their goals and their accomplishments. First, we show how a new set of legitimating myths has been developed to justify the existence of institutions. Second, we consider how institutional administrators manage relations with the outside world. Third, we describe the accounts and defenses used by standard bearers when faced with outside criticism.

THE SYMBOLIC TRANSFORMATION OF INSTITUTIONS

Traditionally, one or more of three legitimating myths have been used to justify the existence of institutions for mentally retarded people (Kanner, 1964; Rosen, Clark, & Kivitz, 1976; Sarason & Doris, 1959; Wolfensberger, 1975). First, as the names "state school" and "training center" suggest, these institutions have been designated as education and training centers for people who are mildly or moderately retarded. Education and training have been defined less in terms of academic instruction than moral discipline and hard work, including caring for the severely disabled residents of the institution. Second, institutions have found legitimacy in providing custodial care for individuals labelled as severely and profoundly retarded and/or multiply handicapped. Some institutions were founded as custodial asylums or infirmaries for the nonambulatory. For instance, Empire was founded in the late 1800s as the "Empire State Custodial Asylum for Unteachable Idiots." All institutions, regardless of why they were originally established, eventually developed custodial departments for the care of the severely disabled. Finally, institutions for people with mental retardation have been justified as agencies of social control. Spurred by the eugenics movement around the turn of the century, many institutions were founded to segregate retarded people, especially the "high-grade feebleminded," and thereby prevent the distribution of allegedly defective genes associated with crimes, feeblemindedness, and degeneracy throughout the population. Thus, Central Developmental Center was established as "Central State Custodial Asylum for Feebleminded Women of Child-Bearing Age" during the latter part of the nineteenth century.

In the modern (post World War II) period, institutions have had as legitimating myths the education of the more mildly retarded and the custodial care of the more severely disabled. With the waning of the eugenics movement in the 1920s, social control gradually ceased to serve as a legitimating myth for state schools for the retarded. By the end of World War II, professionals and institutional officials were eager to disassociate themselves from the logical extension of the eugenic policies of Nazi Germany.

Until recently, the modern institution found legitimacy in presenting itself as a place in which the retarded were given benign care and treatment. Critics, however, have shattered this image of the institution. As public exposés, scholarly studies, court evidence, and professional critiques have ably demonstrated, institutions have provided neither education nor humane care. Rather than educate, institutions debilitate; rather than provide care, they abuse. Some critics, in increasing numbers, go further than pointing to a discrepancy between goals and conditions; they suggest that the institution, by its nature, is inconsistent with humanitarian, educational, or therapeutic goals.

What is occurring at present is a symbolic transformation of developmental centers for mentally retarded people, in response to attacks from the larger society. The old goals, formal structures, and vocabularies no longer serve to legitimate the existence of institutions to external publics or to institutional officials themselves. The old legitimating myths are being discarded and new ones created. Not surprisingly, the new legitimating myths conform to current ideologies in the field of mental retardation and to the vocabularies used by institutional critics.

The facilities in this study are in the process of changing their goals, structures, and vocabularies along the lines of what has been termed the "developmental model" (Wolfensberger, 1972, 1975). This trend is epitomized by the renaming of Willowbrook State School, in New York (an infamous facility exposed in the 1960s and 1970s for its atrocious living conditions), to Staten Island Developmental Center. None of the institutions in the study has accomplished a perfect symbolic transformation. Old structures and vocabularies persist to some extent.

Some institutions have progressed further than others in creating new legitimating myths. An institution's relations with the outside world seem important in influencing the extent to which it has developed new goals, structures, and vocabularies. Thus, institutions routinely exposed to outside criticism, whether from courts, reporters, professionals, or parents, seem more likely to subscribe to a developmental model. Those located in remote areas are more likely to cling to the elements of a traditional medical or custodial model. However, our data do not warrant a simple linear explanation. What is important is that all the institutions are moving in the same direction.

Institutional Goals

Many of the institutions in this study were originally called asylums. Sometime after the turn of the century they were retitled state schools or state hospitals. In the 1970s, many institutions were renamed developmental centers, regional centers, or education and training centers. The state in which Empire, Central, and Cornerstone are located recently renamed all its institutions as developmental centers.

During the early 1970s, institutional goals were phrased in terms of education and custodial care. An official bulletin disseminated by Empire Developmental Center around 1972 reads:

> Empire Developmental Center, responsible for the care and treatment of
> the mentally retarded, is one of several Developmental Centers in the

Department of Mental Hygiene of (State). . . . Some of the aims of the School are: (1) To care for those residents who are unable to help themselves; (2) To help those who are able to be accepted back into the community as useful citizens; and (3) To teach each resident to become as self-sufficient as possible.

By the mid- to late 1970s, many institutions had developed a new set of goals emphasizing residents' potential for growth and development. A statement prepared by the administration of Central Developmental Center presents the goals of children's service in the following manner:

The objective of the Children's Habilitation Service will be to promote optimum realization of each individual's potential for successful and satisfying adjustment to his environment, adaptation to others in his environment, and contribution to society.

Cornerstone Developmental Center, one of the more "progressive" institutions in the study, adopted the goal of normalization in the mid-1970s. One official policy statement declares that the goal is "to promote programs both within the facility and in the community which adhere as closely as possible to the principles of normalization." Another publication defined Cornerstone's philosophy as "normalization—the concept of providing an environment and programs that will enable a handicapped person to function in ways considered to be within the acceptable norms for his society." By the end of the 1970s, the agency responsible for operating institutions in this state had adopted the goal of normalization for all its facilities.

Institutional Structures

As Meyer and Rowan (1977) state, organizations structurally reflect the social reality constructed by their goals. Traditionally, asylums or state schools were organized as a rigid medical hierarchy. Governing the institutions were the medical officers or superintendents. Ward service supervisors, usually nurses, occupied the next level in the institutional pecking order. Attendants occupied the bottom rungs of the organization. Teachers and other professionals held staff positions and lacked line authority.

The modern institution is in the process of being reorganized. According to the formal organization of the institution, authority and responsibility are being decentralized. Elements of the hierarchy remain. There is a director, an assistant director, chiefs of service (in charge of children services or adult services), team leaders, unit coordinators, and direct care staff.

Typically, administrative positions are staffed by professionals with backgrounds in psychology, education, or management. But, according to the formal structure, day-to-day decision making follows a team approach or "unitization" (Sluyter, 1976). As one optimistic administrator put it, "Our new philosophy is unitization. Service will revolve around the patient and the patient won't live in a way that is simply convenient for the staff." Another standard bearer explained what the team approach would mean at his institution:

> The psychologist could diagnose problems and prescribe services and directions. The social worker could use the community setting to place these men wisely in community activities. The guidance counselors could steer the residents' everyday rocky ship. The physician and nurse could administer medical problems. The school teacher could prepare him basically for his educational needs when he goes into the community. The speech therapist could improve his expressive and receptive speech and language abilities. Finally, the attendants could follow up the recommendations of any professional consultant rather than babysit.

Another recent trend at institutions is the proliferation of policies governing almost every aspect of residents' care. This reflects an increased emphasis on displaying rationality and responsibility to the outside world as well as the requirements of federal Medicaid standards. Thus, at all institutions, there are policies concerning the reporting of incidents, abuse, the use of restraints, positioning techniques for nonambulatory residents, housekeeping procedures, the preparation of meals, and so on. In addition, all institutionalized residents have "treatment plans" or "individual habilitation plans," which contain a statement of therapeutic goals, means to accomplish those goals, and objective measures of progress.

Ironically, our data provide some evidence to suggest that, if anything, decision making became *more* centralized at institutions during the 1970s. In the past, attendants made decisions regarding the use of restraints or isolation. Today, physicians must certify that such practices are "in the resident's best interests." Further, treatment teams and individual staff avoid making potentially controversial decisions concerning residents' care or ward practices, leaving high-ranking officials with the responsibility of making these decisions.

Institutional Vocabularies

Nowhere is the symbolic transformation of institutions more evident than in institutional vocabularies (Meyer & Rowan, 1977). As noted, the names of the facilities and titles of staff have been changed to present a new image of institutions. In similar fashion, inmates are no longer called "patients," but "residents" or "clients." Buildings and living units have been renamed to reflect current ideological thrusts. At Eastern, custodial buildings have been redesignated "living and learning units." Another institution refers to its wards as "halfway houses." On the wards ("units") mundane activities and traditional practices carry new names. For example, at one facility "motivation training" refers to coloring with crayons and listening to music. Figure 4.1 contrasts the traditional institutional legitimating myths—goals, formal structures, and vocabulary—with the new developmental legitimating myths created in recent years. Again, not all institutions have incorporated all of the elements of the new legitimating myths.

Although recent changes in the goals, structures, and vocabulary of institutions communicate a concern with providing individualized and normalized care for residents, these changes are to be seen as symbolic, rather than real. These facilities *are* total institutions. For residents, daily life is routinized and regimented.

MANAGING RELATIONS WITH THE OUTSIDE WORLD

One of the consequences of institutional exposés, court suits, and public critiques has been to open the operations of a closed organization to the view of all. It is common knowledge these days that institutions are "bad" places. Nearly everyone associated with mental retardation has seen, in newspapers, in magazines, or on the news, pictures of squalid institutional conditions.

Institutional standard bearers, like administrators in all organizations, actively manage outsiders' impressions of their facilities by presenting fronts consistent with organizational goals (Goffman 1959, 1961). This is not new. What is new is that the events of the 1960s and 1970s (exposés, public scrutiny, lawsuits, militant parents, and so on) have demanded increasingly sophisticated impression management techniques. Institutions can no longer automatically deny access to members of the outside world.

It would be misleading to suggest that the typical official consciously manipulates or lies to outsiders. Administrators and professionals approach their work by highlighting the positive features of their institutions and downplaying the negative features. They organize their work so as to be more familiar with those parts of the institution that more closely approximate the therapeutic ideal than with those in which blatant abuse occurs. As Roth (1971) notes of professionals in public hospitals, institution officials tend not to be knowledgeable about the day-to-day happenings on the

Figure 4.1
The Symbolic Transformation of Institutions: Goals, Structures, Vocabularies

	Traditional Model	"Developmental" Model
Goals	Custodial care, education	Normalization, habilitation
Formal Structure	Rigid, medically dominated hierarchy; policies vaguely formulated; practices governed largely by custom, tradition	Team approach, unitization; all aspects of institution and resident care governed by written policies
Vocabulary		
Facility name	State school, hospital	Developmental center, regional center, education & training center
Staff titles	Superintendent Supervisor Ward charge Attendant, aide	Director Chief of service, team leader Unit coordinator Therapy aide, mental hygiene assistant, advocate
Living quarters	Ward Custodial ward Punishment ward	Unit, halfway house Living and learning unit Special treatment unit, behavior shaping unit

Figure 4.1 (*continued*)

Inmate titles	Patients	Residents, clients
	High grade, low grade	Mildly, moderately,
	Moron, idiot, imbecile	severely, profoundly retarded
		Developmentally disabled
Practices	Straightjackets, camisoles	Restraining devices
	Tripping	Toileting
	Isolation	Time-out
	Activities referred to by descriptive names, e.g., going for walks, coloring	Motivation training, recreation therapy

wards and to spend their time physically isolated in administrative enclaves. They may seldom, if ever, visit the back wards (this is a common complaint among institutional attendants). Thus, to a large extent, institutional standard bearers may believe in the reality they create for outsiders.

Institutions use many standard public-relations techniques in dealing with the outside. Many up-to-date institutions employ a public-relations specialist for precisely this purpose. Officials write and distribute various literature outlining institutional goals and philosophy as well as the wide range of services that are supposed to be available to residents. Institutional literature paints a blissful picture of institutional life. A brochure distributed by Central Developmental Center contained these words:

> It has been said that no man is an island. Neither is this Institution, nor the people in it. For many it is a bridge—a bridge from an aimless and isolated life in the community to useful and integrated membership in society. For others, it is a haven—offering the kind of care, protection and nurturing which are necessary to foster the blossoming of a delicate plant. For none is it a dungeon of oblivion and neglect, walled up against the rest of the world. Rather it is a place of devotion and dedication which draws upon the good will, resources and services of society and, in turn, contributes to the benefit of welfare of that same society. Yes . . . "This is Central Developmental Center."

Similarly, institutions issue press releases announcing special events—field days, picnics, staff recognition awards, the visit of a celebrity. In 1976, one institution sent out a press release to announce the renaming of its buildings along bicentennial lines, for instance, "Independence Hall." Another institution sponsored a widely publicized poster contest at a local high school, with the theme "At [our institution], we care."

Officials make regular public appearances to promote the preferred image of the institution. These include speaking engagements before community groups as well as appearances on local radio and television talk shows. One institution's director writes guest editorials for a large urban newspaper. In addition, institutions often operate booths at community gatherings as vehicles to distribute literature.

Institutions receive regular requests from outside groups and individuals to visit or tour the facilities. Officials use a variety of strategies to deal with these situations. They may deny access to certain outsiders (university students or unaffiliated individuals) by invoking the "rhetoric of rights"; that is, by using their obligation to respect residents' rights to privacy and confidentiality as a means of keeping conditions hidden from public view. However, it is difficult to deny access to certain persons—parents, attorneys, advocacy groups, elected officials, and other influential persons—for to do so is to run the risk of the appearance of a cover-up.

Goffman's (1959) distinction between front regions and back regions provides a useful point of departure for understanding how institutional officials manage the impressions of outsiders. The front regions—those most visible to outsiders—give the appearance of benign, idyllic retreat where residents receive appropriate care and treatment. Thus, the grounds of most institutions are filled with tall trees, meticulously groomed gardens, and stately buildings. The administrative building is likely to be an old Victorian or colonial structure, with carefully polished woodwork and floors.

Institutions sometimes have special rooms set aside for visits between residents and family members. As Goffman (1961) notes, the decor and furnishing of these rooms more closely approximate outside standards than residents' actual living quarters. Staff will usher unexpected visitors to these rooms to "protect the privacy of other residents" or "allow you to be alone with your child." Whether or not institutions maintain visiting rooms, staff expect family members to give notice prior to visits. This enables staff to dress residents in normal, as opposed to "state issue," clothing and to make sure they are properly showered or shaven, as opposed to having an unkempt appearance.

Institutions may sponsor an open house for members of the community. These tend to be highly staged affairs during which outsiders are taken to model programs, shown the newest equipment and facilities, and introduced to the "institutional characters"—a woman 101 years old, a man who paints pictures, a child with an exotic disease. An "open house" is never truly open to the point of making back regions—living units, especially those for more severely disabled residents—accessible to outsiders. In fact, an open house may consist of nothing more than staff presentations. At one institution, officials show slides of selected living units during these occasions.

Some institutions do provide tours to interested community groups. All institutions give tours to influential persons. Officials discourage tours on weekends, since institutions are characterized by an utter lack of structured activity at these times; if possible, officials will avoid taking outsiders to typical living units, especially the back wards (so called because custodial units have historically been located the farthest from the administration building).

In preparation for visits by important outsiders, the staff will scrub the floors, place new bedspreads on the beds, mount decorations on the walls, and make special efforts to keep residents clean and dressed. On one Empire ward, the staff maintained a supply of stuffed animals that were placed on residents' beds immediately before a tour and removed and put away immediately afterward.

Institutional tour guides define (Scott & Lyman, 1968) and predefine (Hewitt & Stokes, 1975) outsiders' experiences and observations at the institutions. The typical tour begins with a brief discussion of the philosophy of the institution, the nature of its clients, its financial and other hardships, and its progress over the years. During the tour, guides tell visitors what to see and how to interpret it. They usually have ready-made interpretations for the absence of programming or any form of meaningful activity: Visitors "just miss" or "come too early" to observe the programs offered to residents, or they happen to visit on a "school holiday" or "our therapist's day off."

An organization's legitimating myths will structure its standard bearers' accounts for its activities. For example, business executives have ready-made explanations for making excessive profits; prison officials, at least those subscribing to retribution goals, have ready-made explanations for imposing hardships on inmates; military officers have ready-made explanations for taking lives. Institutional officials tend to provide differing accounts for abusive or dehumanizing conditions, according to whether they subscribe to a traditional custodial model of services or a new developmental model. Of course, since most training schools are in the process of symbolic transformation, different officials at a single institution may offer accounts reflecting either traditional or new legitimating myths. Similarly, a single official may offer a different type of account at different times or in different situations.

What distinguishes officials' accounts is whether they involve a denial or admission of the harmfulness of conditions or practices. If, on the one hand, an institution is characterized by traditional legitimating myths, its officials will be inclined to suggest that conditions are not harmful or that they are inevitable. If, on the other hand, the institution is presented as being based on a developmental model, its officials will tend to admit to the harmfulness of conditions, but also provide detailed rationales or excuses for why they exist. *Any* official may deny the existence of certain conditions or events. However, critics are usually able to document at least some of their charges, so this defense is of limited usefulness.

Denial of Harm

Officials may account for dehumanizing conditions by attributing them to the nature of their population. As one official commented during a tour, "Conditions are bad here, but what can you expect with severely retarded, acting-out residents?" This is similar to what Sykes and Matza (1957) refer to as "denial of the victim" and Ryan (1972) calls "blaming the victim."

Historically, institutions never aspired to provide anything more to severely retarded and multiply disabled people than pure custodial care—feeding them, supervising them, and cleaning up after them. Officials who cling to traditional perspectives will deny that the lot of more severely disabled residents can be improved. If the wards smell and are unclean, this will be accounted for by the presumed inability of residents to be toilet trained; if residents rock, bang their heads, remove their clothes, and abuse themselves or each other, this will be explained by inherent characteristics of the severely mentally retarded. This line of defense is epitomized by Nelson Rockefeller's account for dehumanizing conditions at Willowbrook, offered in response to a question asked during Senate hearings on his confirmation as vice-president in 1974: "It is very difficult to get people to devote their lives to take care of a human being while really in full fact it is no more than a vegetable" (U.S. Senate, 1974, p. 139).

One way to deny the harmfulness of institutions is to provide examples of abusive and dehumanizing conditions in noninstitutional settings. Some officials claim that even if institutional conditions are not good, they provide better care than mentally retarded individuals can receive elsewhere. In the words of one administrator, "There will always be a need for institutions . . . as long as we have serious problems like the severely and profoundly retarded. This is the best treatment that some of the kids will ever get." Officials can provide countless examples of abuse and exploitation in group homes, foster families, and even residents' own families. Thus, one explained, "As for this institution, this is the best thing for some of these kids. They are fed, kept warm, and clothed. For some of them this would not have happened because some come from unbelievable home situations."

Officials may also defend their institutions by condemning their critics (Sykes & Matza, 1957). As one standard bearer stated, "People are always criticizing institutions and how they are run and even whether they should exist. Yet they offer no alternatives or solutions." When officials use this defense, they are suggesting that critics are naive or misguided in believing that conditions could be otherwise. In short, outsiders "don't know what it's really like." Some officials go farther by accusing critics of serving their own self-interests. As they put it, politicians are after votes, reporters are after hot stories, lawyers are after a fast buck, academicians are trying to build their reputations, and parents are attempting to alleviate their own guilt. By condemning their condemners, officials try to get their institutions off the hook.

Any official may use denial as a defense. At any institution, some officials will blame the victim, discredit families and community alternatives, and at least privately question the motives of critics. But this line of defense is inconsistent with current legitimating myths and ideologies. One cannot subscribe to the developmental model, on the one hand, and deny residents' potential for development, on the other. Nor can abuses in noninstitutional settings or the motives of critics excuse officials' failure to provide programming or even a safe living environment for the persons under their care. Increasingly, officials account for abusive conditions not by asserting their inevitability, but by attributing them to circumstances beyond the institution's or their own control.

Denial of Responsibility

One pervasive belief among institutional officials is that society (the general public and elected officials) has never provided them with the resources and funds to accomplish their goals. They defend the institution and themselves by pointing the finger of blame elsewhere. One administrator accounted for his institution's problems as follows: "Money is the problem. We have to work within the budget. But we need more employees and some up-to-date, modern, fireproof facilities." Another official expressed the point more directly: "The public complains, but there is nothing more that can be done if people aren't willing to help and we cannot get more funds."

A corollary of this belief is that institutional conditions have improved over the past and will continue to improve as the public provides greater resources with which to accomplish the institution's noble ends. Officials point to declining populations and increased staffing to demonstrate that things have improved. One Empire administrator stated, "There have been many improvements. In 1965 there were 4,300 residents and we have reduced that number greatly and we've hired many more employees." Eastern's director, a relatively new administrator, explained, "You'll find that this institution is probably unlike any other you've ever been to. We've gone through a lot of changes over the past couple years." And a Central standard bearer had this to say: "I've worked here 25 years and I've seen a great many improvements. Of course, everything isn't perfect yet." Institutional officials may also compare their institutions with others to show that conditions are not as bad as they could be. Thus, a deputy director at Eastern admitted that his institution was a "hole," but added, "It's the best institution in the state."

Institutional officials, admitting that their facilities are overcrowded and that more mildly retarded persons should not be institutionalized, increasingly blame the "community" for their problems. Thus, neighborhoods may be blamed for not accepting people labelled as mentally retarded: "If the community isn't willing to accept these people, there's not much we can do." Parents and community agencies may be blamed for exerting pressure on the institution to accept more residents than it can accommodate. An official at a midwestern institution offered this explanation for the failure of his institution to place people in the community.

> The residents ought to be served in training programs in the community. However, these facilities do not exist and thus demands for the use of the institution continue from parents and community agencies. . . . We do have an ongoing deinstitutionalization program, but we can only deinstitutionalize to the point that community facilities are available.

By locating responsibility for the institution's problems with the public, legislators, community agencies, parents, and others, officials can maintain their belief in the institution's legitimating myths and avoid organizational and personal responsibility for abusive and dehumanizing conditions. Their institutions are good, even if they are bad.

The Rhetoric of Rights

Earlier, we discussed how the rhetoric of rights—specifically, residents' rights to privacy and confidentiality—may be used to keep the institution's operations hidden from public view. Officials may also invoke residents' rights in accounting for certain practices and conditions.

The rhetoric of rights may be used either to attack mandated changes or to justify benign neglect. An example of the former is found in officials' response to recent laws prohibiting institutional peonage. One administrator commented, "We used to have them doing all kinds of work, and they liked it. It made them feel important. We can't let them work anymore, so they have to sit around all day doing nothing."

As a justification of current practices, the rhetoric of rights may be used to account for a failure to provide residents with programming or encourage them to act in socially appropriate ways. At one institution, administrators justified the lack of programming for one profoundly retarded, nonverbal resident on the grounds that he refused to participate in recreational activities. At a midwestern facility, an official offered this account for residents being naked in ward dayrooms: "If we talk about rights, maybe one should have the right to be naked in one's personal environment." This official justified the dressing of residents in nonnormalizing clothing on the same grounds: "We try to provide residents clothing which is 'normal' but some prefer to wear clothing which may appear 'baggy' and inappropriate—which is frequently their choice." The rhetoric of rights is most often used to justify childlike decorations in adults wards and childlike possessions (toys or stuffed animals) for adults. Officials are likely to claim that retarded adults want childlike decorations and possessions, even though no attempt is made to provide them with age-appropriate objects. The rhetoric of rights goes hand in hand with the new legitimating myths of institutions.

The Protection of Policies

One reason for the proliferation of institutional policies is to create the appearance of bureaucratic efficiency and rationality. Another is to avoid organizational and administrative responsibility for the actions of direct-care staff.

As noted earlier, institutional officials issue policies covering almost every aspect of resident care. Policies prohibit physical or psychological abuse; policies define when and how residents may be restrained or placed in isolation; policies specify procedures for reporting accidents and injuries; policies call for the implementation of ward programs. When their institutions are characterized as being abusive or repressive, officials respond by holding up written policies as a way of getting the organization and themselves off the hook. One midwestern official countered charges that residents were secluded in locked dormitories during the day by stating, "This is not policy." Similarly, the director of a western institution responded to a legal aid organization's charges that physical restraints were used excessively, for staff convenience, and as punishment, by sending the attorneys the institution's policies on physical restraint and behavior modification.

By using policies as a means of defense, administrators create a definition of abuse as idiosyncratic and uncontrollable. Abuse is presented as a consequence of the failings of attendants. One official explained, "We try to teach our attendants. . . . It isn't easy since we're dealing with human beings with all their weaknesses." Another official, speaking at a professional convention, claimed that administrators have no control over attendants' actions: "I'll tell you what the problem with the institution is. It's those damn civil service regulations and all that civil rights crap. We can't get rid of anyone. We have to give them a hearing. . . . If we could start firing people, we wouldn't have abuse."

Officials may account for a lack of ward programming in the same manner. For some, attendants are rather backward folks: "You have to remember that most of them have not graduated high school and have no experience at all. It's one of the bad points about the institution." For others, attendants just do not care: "Those wards are really bad places. The attendants don't really care about the kids. . . . They spend their time on other things rather than on the kids."

To blame attendants for the institution's problems is to destroy staff morale and create hostility between higher and lower levels of staff. Perhaps for this reason, most officials make frequent public testimonials to the dedication of most attendants and, at least in public statements, blame abuse and policy violations on "a few rotten apples in the barrel." One administrator elaborated on this theme:

I have some bad seeds in my department as I'm sure you'll find in every organization. I cannot do anything about them because they are smart enough not to get caught. The union has strict rules that protect the bad worker. I will stand up for one of my good workers any time. If we see something wrong we will write it up and take it to the director's office.

Attendants, for their part, complain that "higher-ups" impose unrealistic expectations on them and use them as scapegoats for conditions beyond their control (Bogdan et al., 1974; Taylor, 1977/1978).

CONCLUSION

There are two general conclusions to be drawn from this study. The first has to do with the survival of total institutions for people with mental retardation. As we have argued, institutions have adopted a new image and new legitimating myths in response to external forces for change. And institutional officials have developed increasingly sophisticated strategies and defenses to deal with the outside world.

We cannot predict whether total institutions will be successful in their struggle for organizational survival. But we can say that the battle will hinge on their ability to maintain legitimacy among important external publics. While direct observation of institutional life reveals a wide discrepancy between goals and practices, the new legitimating myths uphold the image of the institution as a benign, therapeutic setting serving humanitarian ends. Further, as the current furor over institutional abuse and dehumanization dies down, it is possible for total institutions to cloak themselves in the legitimating myths of the past. The institutional model first gained widespread acceptance during the eugenics movement around the turn of the century. Renewed social science interest in the biological bases of behavior and the inheritability of intelligence clearly does not bode well for mentally retarded citizens. Whatever the case, the institution's struggle for survival will continue to take a symbolic form.

The second conclusion relates to institutional officials and professionals—those we have referred to as organizational standard bearers. These officials are not alone in facing criticism from without. On the contrary, their lot is shared by professionals in a wide range of service organizations accused of harming those they purport to help (Biklen, 1975; Blatt, 1970; Lasch, 1978; Piven & Cloward, 1971; Ryan, 1972; Scott, 1969; Szasz, 1970). What is the impact on human beings who are trained in professional schools to serve the "less fortunate" and then graduate to positions in the labor force in which their activities have a detrimental effect? The officials in our study may signal the coming of a crisis for professionals working in human services. Professionals make a large investment in time and training to get to the positions they occupy. With declining job possibilities and career alternatives, it is difficult to leave positions in which they are unable to carry out their service orientation—to help people. As their flawed rationales become transparent, the trap they find themselves in may be one of the significant problems this generation will have to face. Their crisis may be one of the prices to be paid for confronting our human service system directly and liberating its clients.

EPILOGUE, 1991

STEVEN J. TAYLOR

It has now been over 10 years since "Defending Illusions" was first published. Since the populations of public institutions for people with mental retardation declined steadily throughout the 1980s, it is reasonable to ask how the institutions are faring today in their struggle for survival.

In the fall of 1990, I took a class of students to visit "Central Developmental Center," described in this chapter, for a tour of its programs and facilities. Our tour was conducted by a high-ranking official at the institution. Early on in the tour, we were informed that Central Developmental Center is scheduled for closure. "Empire Developmental Center" as well as several others in this state have already been pronounced closed in line with national deinstitutionalization trends.

Our tour guide gave us impressive statistics on the number of persons who have been moved from the institution to community programs and explained that the remaining "individuals" (as she put it: "We don't call them clients or residents anymore; we call them individuals") would move to the community by next spring.

The first stop on the tour was a "day treatment center" located in a large building in the middle of the institution's spacious grounds. When the institution is officially closed, this will become a "community-based program." After a brief visit to an older building that will be evacuated, the class was taken to some newly constructed "community residences." As the tour guide explained, "We call them homes, because they're homes just like yours and mine." The "community residences" or "homes" were eight identical 12-bed facilities constructed on the grounds of the institution. Empire constructed similar "community residences" on its grounds. The tour guide assured us that life in these "homes" was no different than life at similar 12-bed facilities spread throughout the outlying area.

So, a decade later institutions still cling to life. But the nature of the struggle has changed. Institutional officials seldom defend their institutions today. They have adopted the vocabulary of their critics and symbolically transformed the institutions into "community-based programs" and "homes."

REFERENCES

Biklen, D. (1975). *Let our children go.* Syracuse: Human Policy Press.

Bittner, E. (1974). The concept of organization. In R. Turner (Ed.), *Ethnomethodology* (pp. 69–81). Baltimore: Penguin.

Blatt, B. (1970). *Exodus from pandemonium.* Boston: Allyn & Bacon.

Blau, P., & Scott, R. (1962). *Formal organizations.* San Francisco: Chandler.

Bogdan, R., & Taylor, S. (1975). *Introduction to qualitative research methods.* New York: John Wiley.

Bogdan, R., Taylor, S., De Grandpre, B., & Haynes, S. (1974). Let them eat programs: Attendants' perspectives and programming on wards in state schools. *Journal of Health and Social Behavior, 15,* 142–151.

Etzioni, A. (1961). *A comparative analysis of complex organizations.* New York: Free Press.

Goffman, E. (1959). *The presentation of self in everyday life.* Garden City, NY: Doubleday, Anchor Books.

Goffman, E. (1961). *Asylums: Essays on the social situation of mental patients and other inmates.* Garden City, NY: Doubleday, Anchor Books.

Gubrium, J. (1975). *Living and dying in Murray Manor.* New York: St. Martin's Press.

Hewitt, J. P., & Stokes, R. (1975). Disclaimers. *American Sociological Review, 40,* 1–11.

Jacobs, J. (1969). Symbolic bureaucracy: A case study of a social welfare agency. *Social Forces, 47,* 413–422.

Kamens, D. H. (1977). Legitimating myths and educational organization. *American Sociological Review, 42,* 208–219.

Kanner, L. (1964). *A history of the care and study of the mentally retarded.* Springfield, IL: Charles C. Thomas.

Lasch, C. (1978). *Haven in a heartless world.* New York: Basic Books.

Meyer, J. W., & Rowan, B. (1977). Institutionalized organizations: Formal structure as myth and ceremony. *American Journal of Sociology, 83,* 340–363.

Piven, F. F., & Cloward, R. (1971). *Regulating the poor: The functions of public welfare.* New York: Random House.

Platt, A. M. (1969). *The child savers.* Chicago: University of Chicago Press.

Rosen, M. G., Clark, R., & Kivitz, M. S. (Eds.). (1976). *The history of mental retardation* (Vols. I–II). Baltimore: University Park Press.

Roth, J. (1971). The public hospital: Refuge for damaged humans. In S. Wallace (Ed.), *Total institutions* (pp. 55–67). Rutgers, NJ: Transaction Books.

Ryan, W. (1972). *Blaming the victim.* New York: Vintage.

Sarason, S. B., & Doris, J. (1959). *Psychological problems in mental deficiency.* New York: Harper & Row.

Scott, M. B., & Lyman, S. (1968). Accounts. *American Sociological Review, 33,* 46–62.

Scott, R. A. (1969). *The making of blind men.* New York: Russell Sage Foundation.

Sluyter, G. V. (1976). The unit management system. *Mental Retardation, 14*(3), 14–16.

Sykes, G. M., & Matza, D. (1957). Techniques of neutralization: A theory of delinquency. *American Sociological Review, 22*, 664–670.

Szasz, T. (1970). *Ideology and insanity.* Garden City, NY: Doubleday.

Taylor, S. J. (1978). The custodians: Attendants and their work at state institutions for the mentally retarded (Doctoral dissertation, Syracuse University, 1977). *Dissertation Abstracts International, 39*, 1145A–1146A.

U.S. Senate. (1974). *Hearings before the Committee on Rules and Administration on the nomination of Nelson A. Rockefeller of New York to be Vice President of the United States.* Washington, DC: U.S. Government Printing Office.

Weber, M. (1947). *The theory of social and economic organization.* New York: Oxford University Press.

Wolfensberger, W. (1972). *Normalization.* Toronto: National Institute on Mental Retardation.

Wolfensberger, W. (1975). *The origin and nature of our institutional models.* Syracuse: Human Policy Press.

Part II

DISABILITY AND
THE SCHOOLS

Schools may be unique among our culture's social institutions in their role as repository of all our social ills, frustrations, and most unyielding debates. At least since the beginnings of compulsory education in the late 1800s, they have been tugged and stretched by successive, often competing, social demands. Perhaps the greatest social tug-of-war has been over the fundamental reason for education. Should schools strive to inculcate our nation's children with a love of knowledge and learning or is there primarily a much more fundamental charge to fill the ranks of our nation's work force?

The mixed messages to students that result from these steady tensions have been the subject of a strong, if relatively recent, history of qualitative research in education. Many such studies have sought to explore the various dynamics of the competing social forces that converge on schools, affecting their operations in "hidden" and unexpected ways. The differential treatment and schooling experiences accorded to students of various social classes has been one theme of such studies (e.g., Anyon, 1981; Rist, 1970; Willis, 1977); race (Rist, 1978) and gender (Anyon, 1984; McRobbie, 1978) are two similar themes.

A second strand of qualitative research in education focuses more on the experiences of teachers and other school adults. Examples include Wolcott's (1973) ethnographic study of the life of a school principal; Lortie's (1975) classic study of the life and careers of teachers; Blase's (1988) political analysis and Biklen's (1983) more feminist analysis, *Teaching as an Occupation for Women*; and a growing genre of studies of the socialization experiences of neophyte teachers (Blase & Greenfield, 1982; Bullough, 1989; Ryan, 1980). This last seems to be leading naturally to discussions about the use of an interpretivist perspective, and its methodological tools, in the preparation of teachers (Beyer, Feinberg, Pagano, & Whitson, 1989; Gitlin & Teitelbaum, 1983). Although these different examples employ the methodological tools of qualitative research in quite different ways, all are grounded in the words, experiences, and interpretations of schools' laborers.

An emerging strand of inquiry in education explores the use of qualitative research by teachers, sometimes alone and sometimes in collaboration with more traditional university researchers (e.g., Miller, 1990). Interest in this view of teachers as qualitative researchers has recently been the occasion of a methods textbook written directly for use by teachers in the field (Hitchcock & Hughes, 1989).

There is a much smaller tradition of qualitative research that concerns disability in schools, especially in the United States, perhaps because disability has often been a casualty of broader educational debates. Indeed, it is only in the past two decades that all students with disabilities have been required to comply with the provisions of compulsory education. However, this dearth may be better explained by special education's reliance on a traditional quantitative and behavioral approach to educational research. During the late 1960s and the 1970s when issues in education generally seemed to demand the tools of interpretivist analysis, special education experienced a renewed commitment to behavioral explanations of teaching and learning as the most useful constructs for developing educational experiences of students with increasingly severe and complicated disabilities.

The three chapters in this part sample very different uses of qualitative research to explore three different examples of disability in schools. Chapter 5, by Higgins, illustrates how qualitative research can serve as the basis for advancing recommendations for broader reforms of policy and practice. In this case the arguments and recommendations for including deaf students in public schools with hearing students also illustrate how some examples of qualitative research can move beyond the presentation of description to a frankly evaluative and prescriptive presentation to the extent that the research base becomes the backdrop for the policy agenda.

Chapter 6, by Davis and D. Ferguson, is an example of the kind of collaborative research becoming more common in other arenas of education. This chapter also illustrates that what follows from collaborative practice is the need to develop more dialogical presentation styles. The presentation illustrates the collaborative nature not just of the data collection, but also of the analysis and writing in the way the authors' voices alternate in a responsive pattern.

Chapter 7, by P. Ferguson, is the most traditional example of the three in qualitative research terms. This case study uses thick description to immerse the reader in the details of one classroom and the efforts of one teacher to integrate students with autism into a high school. In so doing, the chapter nicely portrays how physical proximity alone does not accomplish the more subtle and complicated social inclusion called for in Chapter 5 and illustrated in the accounts of John's and Gail's experiences in Chapter 6. Although the research for this chapter was completed several years ago, we include it here because we think it still speaks to today's discussions about integration and inclusion, as well as many teachers' experiences.

REFERENCES

Anyon, J. (1981). Social class and school knowledge. *Curriculum Inquiry, 11,* 3–42.

Anyon, J. (1984). Intersections of gender and class: Accommodation and resistance by working-class and affluent females to contradictory sex-role ideologies. *Journal of Education, 166,* 25–48.

Beyer, L. E., Feinberg, W., Pagano, J., & Whitson, J. A. (1989). *Preparing teachers as professionals: The role of educational studies and other liberal disciplines.* New York: Teachers College Press.

Biklen, S. K. (1983). *Teaching as an occupation for women: A case study of an elementary school.* Syracuse: Education Designs Group.

Blase, J. J. (1988). The everyday political perspective of teachers: Vulnerability and conservatism. *Qualitative Studies in Education, 1,* 125–142.

Blase, J. J., & Greenfield, W. (1982). On the meaning of being a high school teacher: The beginning years. *High School Journal, 65,* 263–271.

Bullough, R. V. (1989). *First-year teacher: A case study.* New York: Teachers College Press.

Gitlin, A., & Teitelbaum, K. (1983). Linking theory and practice: The use of ethnographic methodology by prospective teachers. *Journal of Education for Teaching, 9,* 225–234.

Hitchcock, G., & Hughes, D. (1989). *Research and the teacher: A qualitative introduction to school-based research.* New York: Routledge and Kegan Paul.

Lortie, D. C. (1975). *School teacher.* Chicago: University of Chicago Press.

McRobbie, A. (1978). Working class girls and the culture of femininity. In Women's Studies Group (Eds.), *Women take issue* (pp. 96–108). London: Hutchinson.

Miller, J. (1990). *Creating spaces and finding voices: Teachers collaborating for empowerment.* Albany: State University of New York Press.

Rist, R. (1970). Student social class and teacher expectations: The self-fulfilling prophecy in ghetto education. *Harvard Educational Review, 40,* 411–451.

Rist, R. (1978). *The invisible children: School integration in American society.* Cambridge, MA: Harvard University Press.

Ryan, K. (1980). *Biting the apple: Accounts of first-year teachers.* New York: Longman.

Willis, P. (1977). *Learning to labour: How working class kids get working class jobs.* Farnborough, England: Saxon House.

Wolcott, H. F. (1973). *The man in the principal's office: An ethnography.* New York: Holt, Rinehart and Winston.

SUGGESTED READINGS

Barton, L., & Tomlinson, S. (Eds.). (1984). *Special education and social interests.* New York: Nichols.

This anthology allows an interesting comparison between studies conducted from two different sociological perspectives. Half of the chapters adopt what the editors call a "structural-functional" perspective that illustrates what sociologists call "macro-level" analysis. The other half use a broadly qualitative approach (the editors refer to a "phenomenological" perspective). All chapters focus on the complexities of educational integration of students with disabilities.

Biklen, D. (1985). *Achieving the complete school: Strategies for effective mainstreaming.* New York: Teachers College Press.

Based on an extensive set of case studies of successful examples of integrated education, this book shows how interpretive research can move beyond thick description of individual cases to evaluative recommendations for improvements in policy and practice.

Ferguson, D. L. (1987). *Curriculum decision making for students with severe handicaps: Policy and practice.* New York: Teachers College Press.

Ferguson uses both participant observation and in-depth interviewing to analyze how teachers think about their jobs, their classrooms, and the students with whom they work. The book discusses how the teachers interact with the structural and attitudinal influences at work in special education systems, to construct a set of categories and concepts for their own understanding of "severe handicap."

Hemwall, M. K. (1984). Ethnography as evaluation: Hearing-impaired students in the mainstream. In D. M. Fetterman (Ed.), *Ethnography in educational evaluation* (pp. 133–152). Beverly Hills, CA: Sage.

A good example of qualitative methods used as part of a program evaluation project. The article works at two levels. It reports the context and results of the research itself, and also reflects on the process of using qualitative techniques for pragmatically oriented processes like program evaluation.

Mehan, H., Hertweck, A., & Meihls, L. (1986). *Handicapping the handicapped: Decision making in students' educational careers.* Stanford, CA: Stanford University Press.

This book reports the results of extended field work focusing on how students in one particular school system move into the special education maze through formal procedures and classification systems. The specific methods of the authors illustrate a type of qualitative research called ethnomethodology.

Murray-Seegert, C. (1989). *Nasty girls, thugs, and humans like us: Social relations between severely disabled and nondisabled students in high school.* Baltimore: Paul H. Brookes.

Together with the Ferguson book mentioned earlier, this book shows how two broadly interpretive studies of a similar setting and context (severely disabled high school students and their classrooms) can still result in very different results in both presentation styles and substantive findings. Murray-Seegert also provides, as does Ferguson, a helpful account of her methodological decisions in designing and conducting the research.

Chapter 5

WORKING AT MAINSTREAMING

Paul C. Higgins

Mainstreaming does not succeed "naturally," on its own (Biklen, 1985, p. x). It is a much greater challenge than most of us realize. To meet that challenge, to make mainstreaming succeed, many participants must do various kinds of work well. Based on several years of investigating and thinking about how we educate together deaf and hearing youth, I have developed some ideas about mainstreaming and what participants do when mainstreaming (Higgins, 1990). In this chapter I briefly describe my investigation, discuss the challenge of mainstreaming, introduce the concept of work within organizations, and explore several important kinds of mainstreaming efforts.

Many of the specifics of my discussion concern educating together deaf and hearing youth. However, this challenge is similar to the challenge of educating together diverse groups of young people—those with and without educationally significant impairments and those of different races and ethnicities. Therefore, I take from and speak to that larger challenge. (At times I will make the connection to the larger challenge explicit. Often I leave it to the reader to see how my discussion applies to his or her concerns.) In doing so, I also speak to how we can develop understanding about what matters to us.

RESEARCHING MAINSTREAMING

While many social observers seek objectivity, striving to be detached and neutral, I believe our best understanding of social life develops out of our personal involvement and/or commitment (Higgins & Johnson, 1988). While we do not need to participate in special education, nor do we need to be disabled, in order to develop useful understanding; our research is likely to be very sterile if it is only paid labor.

My concern with mainstreaming is personal. My parents are deaf. They both taught deaf youth and adults, my father for more than 50 years. Years ago I taught for one year at a state residential school for deaf children before I began graduate school. My wife has also taught at a state school for deaf children and for more than a decade in two different mainstream programs. I have come to know many of the deaf children she has taught and to learn a great deal about the challenges she and the many other participants face. Out of those experiences, I developed a more focused examination of mainstreaming.

During two school years I observed in the elementary, middle, and high school mainstream programs for deaf youth operated by a local school district to serve a multidistrict area. These were day-class programs in which deaf youth were educated in a combination of self-contained and mainstream classes. I observed in both types of classes, on the playground, and in the cafeteria. I talked with principals, administrators, and teachers in the self-contained and the mainstream classes; other staff; parents; and students (primarily deaf youth). I experienced misunderstandings with participants and tried to resolve them. I held long-distance telephone conversations with an administrator from a program in another state where my wife previously worked. I talked in person with another administrator of a mainstream program in the same state as the program I intensely observed. After developing and revising many of my ideas, I talked with an administrator of a nationally recognized mainstream program on the west coast. That program seemed to fit well within the ideas I had developed. And, of course, I read about other programs throughout the country and abroad. This brief description does not capture the complexity of my investigation. But even if a lengthier one could, I am not certain how useful that would be.

Many investigators believe that the proper method necessarily produces the appropriate results. While methodology does matter, it does not guarantee understanding (Stewart & Tucker, 1983). In all my work (e.g., Higgins, 1980, 1985), field research has ultimately provided me the opportunity to think about and explore my concerns, as well as to record my observations of what people were doing.

Therefore, I suggest a different criterion for deciding the merit of a scholarly work. Does it enable people to do their own work more successfully, to respond more effectively to their concerns? Merit does not reside within the methodology or within the pages of a report. Instead, merit arises from use, which may vary greatly from user to user. I suggest that the same criterion can be used by mainstream participants in evaluating the strategies they use to do mainstreaming.

THE CHALLENGES OF MAINSTREAMING

Mainstreaming is a "goal, indeed a value, we decide to pursue or reject on the basis of what we want our society to look like" (Biklen, 1985, p. 3). It proclaims that we want a society in which those with and without disabilities live and learn together, in which those with and without disabilities recognize their common humanity while acknowledging and appreciating their distinctiveness. However, while mainstreaming may aspire to a vision of a just society, much mainstreaming falls short. Mainstreaming deaf youth is particularly controversial. As one hearing impaired educator told an advocate for deaf people:

> You know the old sign for mainstreaming: two S-hands palms down opening to a "stream" outward from the body. The one we use now starts the old way but then becomes the sign for "oppressed."
> What does that signify? It signifies the hearing kids pushing a deaf kid down. (Greenberg, 1986, p. 3)

Many critics argue that mainstreaming oppresses deaf youth. Instead of integrating deaf and hearing students, mainstream programs "dump" a handful of deaf children of different ages, abilities, and needs into a self-contained class, set within a much larger school of hearing students. Without adequately trained staff, the deaf students are poorly served. Few hearing students (or staff) learn to sign. Because their hearing parents often do not learn to sign well, deaf children are also isolated at home. Deaf youth are separated from a signing community and a deaf community, both of which are found within residential schools, the historical backbone of the education of deaf children. Thus, the least physically restrictive environment is the most socially isolating environment for deaf youth. The most severe critics find mainstreaming another attempt by misguided hearing people to deny the validity of deafness (Higgins, 1990; Lane, 1987).

Two opposing views of deaf people have guided the education of deaf youth for the past 150 years. To Alexander Graham Bell and his philosophical descendants, deaf people were defective. Bell "found weakness and danger" in "human variety," "deviance" instead of mere differences (Lane, 1984, p. 340). The aim of Bell and his descendants has always been to make deaf people as much like hearing people as possible (Higgins, 1980). Thus, he championed educating deaf children among hearing youth and teaching them to speak and to speechread. He criticized residential schools for deaf children, reunions of former students, deaf teachers of deaf students, organizations of deaf people, periodicals and newspapers by and for deaf people, their "gesture" language, and other arrangements that he believed fostered a community of deaf people separate from hearing people. He criticized these arrangements because he feared that they constituted the

elements necessary to compel deaf-mutes to select as their partners in life
persons who are familiar with the gesture language. This practically limits
their selection to deaf-mutes and to hearing persons related to deaf-mutes.
They do select such partners in marriages, and a certain portion of their
children inherit their physical defect. We are on the way therefore towards
the formation of a deaf variety of the human race. Time alone is necessary
to accomplish the result. (Bell, 1883, p. 44)

Bell's fears were widely circulated, discussed, rebutted, and erroneously
reported. They became part of the concern about "defective" people and
how best to deal with them that swept the country in the late 1800s and
early 1900s (Lane, 1984, pp. 358–361; Rothman, 1971; Wolfensberger,
1975).

Others, deaf and hearing, have emphasized that deafness is part of the
diversity of humanity. Laurent Clerc, the pioneering deaf educator of deaf
students in the 1800s, saw "strength in human variety" (Lane, 1984,
p. 340). He and others, many of whom are critics of mainstreaming today,
knew that there was dignity in being deaf, not in spite of being deaf. They
understood that the handicapism of hearing people like Bell, which denied
the validity of being deaf and of signing, not primarily the hearing impairment, limited deaf people (Bogdan & Biklen, 1977). Deaf people lived rich
lives within deaf communities (Gannon, 1981; Higgins, 1980) and would
among hearing people when the latter "remove[d] the handicap by accepting deaf culture and language" (Lane, 1984, p. 340).

Admittedly, much mainstreaming today falls short of the promise
(Gliedman & Roth, 1980). However, it need not be oppressive. It can be
successful. Deaf children and others with disabilities can and do learn well in
the mainstream (Biklen, 1985, 1988; Higgins, 1990). If we commit ourselves to mainstreaming, it will make sense—educational, social, and moral
sense (Higgins, 1990). When done well, mainstreaming combats the oppressive attitudes and arrangements—the handicapism—that limit those
with disabilities far more than their impairments do (Bogdan & Biklen,
1977). Like racial desegregation, mainstreaming can be part of our commitment to a just society.

[Desegregation] involves a vision of the ideal pluralist society. . . . [It is a]
necessary means of teaching different races and ethnicities how to live and
prosper with each other. School desegregation need not—must not—
"bleach" blacks and browns to look and think like Anglo-Saxons. . . . Its
goal is for blacks, browns, and Anglos to respect each other's autonomy,
appreciate their mutual diversity, and welcome their mutual ties. (Hochschild, 1984, pp. 189–190)

Mainstreaming holds a similar vision. To achieve it, though, many participants must perform well in many different areas.

MAINSTREAMING WORK

The basis for my analysis of mainstreaming work grew in part out of my reading about medical work in hospitals. It served as a conceptual foundation for making sense of mainstreaming. I have often found making analogies to other realms of social life a useful means for making sense of my concerns. Sometimes those analogies become metaphorical frameworks for my own investigations. Therefore, I will briefly discuss medical work before turning to mainstreaming.

When we think of a hospital, we think of medical care, which doctors and nurses provide. We also realize that technicians, medical assistants, administrators, dieticians, and other hospital employees do various kinds of work, some of which we recognize as significant for patients' experiences, and much of which we do not. Even the central aspect of hospital work—medical work—involves more than we imagine.

Anselm Strauss and his colleagues (1985) have explored the social organization of medical work in hospitals. They have identified a variety of work done by staff, patients, and patients' families. Machine work—the production, tending, and utilization of often very sophisticated machines—is becoming increasingly important. Safety work—the bundle of activities designed to ensure patients' clinical safety in the hospital and beyond—is of paramount importance. The maintenance of sterile environments is one example of safety work. Comfort work—what might be called the giving of tender loving care—is important, though it may receive less attention from staff, to the discomfort of patients. Because medical staff perform their work on, to, and with people who can and do respond, sentimental work must be performed, though at times it may be performed badly. Trust must be established, patients need to be assisted to keep their composure, offenses by thoughtless staff must be rectified, and the like. Mistakes are made by participants, which must then be corrected—error work. All of this work, and more, needs to be coordinated so that it meshes smoothly together as the patient's illness is managed. Articulation work has that aim, for which the main physician and the head nurse often have primary responsibility.

Whether recognized or appreciated by staff, patients do various kinds of medical work, too. When patients monitor how they are feeling and report their assessments to staff, they often do very important work. Many people, not just paid medical staff, perform the array of hospital medical work necessary to successfully serve patients.

Mainstreaming is similarly complex (Biklen, 1985). Through diverse kinds of work done by many participants, mainstreaming is accomplished. Mainstreaming work is the set of activities that enable youth with and without educationally significant handicaps to be educated together. Staff, students, parents, and others do mainstreaming work. They may do it well or badly. They may consciously attend to it or do it without realizing it. Much of it is overlooked, and all of it must be improved. Mainstreaming work is interactional in a double sense. Through interactions with others, participants do mainstreaming work; in doing it well, participants enhance the present and future interactions of one another.

Much more than mainstreaming work takes place within mainstream programs. Much of the routine planning, supervising, scheduling, procuring supplies and staff, coordinating, generating resources, counseling, maintenance, teaching, and many other kinds of work have little to do with mainstreaming. Some of this work parallels medical work in hospitals. Participants do machine work—tending, maintaining, modifying, and using various devices, such as hearing aids, phonic ears, catheters, wheelchairs, communication devices, and life support systems. They comfort one another, not just students. They manage one another's sentiments, handle errors, and so much more.

A focus on mainstreaming work is important. It suggests to us that mainstreaming will succeed only through sustained effort. Perhaps more important, it encourages us to not individualize what is a social undertaking. Too often we point to traits of individuals to explain why we do what we do, or we blame our setbacks on the shortcomings of people. We individualize what is social. For example, educators typically mainstream deaf students with less severe impairments, a later onset of hearing loss, and more intelligible speech (and other characteristics). Instead of unthinkingly "dumping" deaf children into mainstream programs and classes, they often make placement decisions in part on the individual characteristics of deaf youth that seem to increase the chances of success (Higgins, 1990). However, to understand mainstreaming and to make it succeed, we need to use a broader focus. We must include the social arrangements and practices that make up mainstreaming and at times let us down.

To focus on individual characteristics is conservative (Stewart & Reynolds, 1985). To the extent that we cannot change individual traits, we are discouraged from changing present conditions. To continue the above example, what seems to be a reasonable educational practice in mainstreaming deaf students actually limits our commitment to changing greatly our educational arrangements and practices so that more deaf and hearing children can live and learn together well. However, when we realize that our procedures and practices matter, then we can change them to increase and improve mainstreaming. The appropriate question about mainstreaming, then, is not, "Does it work?" but "How can we make it work?" (Biklen, 1985, p. 1).

I briefly explore five kinds of mainstreaming work (see Higgins, 1990, for an extended discussion). These kinds of work—placement, enhancement, relations, identity, and monitoring—are important for educating together youth with and without educationally significant impairments. The work is interrelated; efforts in one area support or obstruct efforts in another. Further, participants' specific activities and strategies may address simultaneously the goals of several of these efforts.

Much of the following discussion will be couched explicitly in terms of mainstreaming deaf students. The ties to educating together diverse youth will often be obvious, but not always and not with the necessary particulars needed for meeting those differing challenges.

Placement Work

Through placement we put together and apart deaf and hearing youth (and others). We place mainstream programs in schools, staff and deaf students in the programs, and deaf students into specific classes and activities. We even assign students seats in mainstream classrooms. When done well, placement work proclaims that deaf students (and others) are integral members of their schools. It creates organizational opportunities for deaf and hearing youth (and staff, parents, and other participants) to interact meaningfully and learn successfully.

Placement shares certain essential goals with efforts directed at racial and ethnic desegregation in schools (Hawley et al., 1983). It aims to achieve continuity, a critical mass, and a clear commitment to integration. When mainstream programs remain in a school instead of being moved often, and when deaf and hearing students from a school graduate to the same advanced school, then continuity has been achieved. Continuity provides the opportunity for participants to come to know each other, which may take years.

A critical mass of deaf students is important, perhaps more so than for youth with other educationally significant impairments. A critical mass enables educators to group deaf children appropriately (in self-contained classes, as needed) and to provide the necessary staff, services, and equipment. It also increases the potential for deaf and hearing students to develop more successful relations and for deaf youth to become part of a signing community and a deaf community should they choose to do so. For example, in one rural mainstream program, a teacher who had been a speech therapist in a local hospital, but had no background in teaching deaf children, and whose self-professed signing skills were "not very good," taught four deaf children whose ages ranged from 4 to 12 (Brant, 1986/1987).

The principle of "natural proportions," in which students with a particular disability attend school in the same proportion as their disability exists within the general population (Biklen, 1985, p. 58), seems a less useful guide for mainstreaming deaf children. Deafness is a low-incidence impairment. Less than two-tenths of 1% of the school-age population is deaf (Schein & Delk, 1974, p. 28). If the principle of natural proportions is applied to an elementary school of 500 students, the mainstream program would contain one deaf student. Such isolation is one of the charges critics lodge against mainstreaming deaf children. While no one knows exactly what percentage would create a critical mass of deaf youth, the advice that any particular racial or ethnic group should constitute at least 15 to 20% of the student population and perhaps as much as one-third might be a useful guide (Crain, Mahard, & Narot, 1982; Hawley et al., 1983; Willie, 1978). Program placement should not disperse deaf youth; it should assemble them. Pairing residential schools for the deaf with nearby public schools, developing regional or multidistrict mainstream programs, establishing mainstream programs in smaller schools, or developing smaller clusters or units within a larger school (Hawley et al., 1983) can begin to develop a critical mass of deaf students.

Finally, careful placement work can demonstrate a commitment to integration. Permanence and substantial numbers demonstrate that commitment. So too can location and the extent of mainstreaming. Putting a self-contained class of deaf students in a mobile unit at the rear of the school building, shifting the self-contained classrooms from year to year, or putting deaf children in a separate lab group in a mainstream science class does not demonstrate a commitment to integration. Stably locating self-contained classrooms in ordinary places and grouping deaf and hearing students in smaller teams within mainstream classes does. Mainstreaming only or primarily those deaf youth who are thought to be "easiest" to mainstream because of less severe impairments or well-developed academic skills individualizes what is a social matter. This kind of individualistic approach to placement also undermines a "radical" commitment to integration, which is needed if mainstreaming is to succeed (Biklen, 1985). Placement involves more than physically putting people in places. It also includes modifying educational arrangements so that people can meaningfully participate together.

Imagine, for example, an 8-year-old deaf student who is typically called "low verbal." The youth reads and writes English extremely poorly and does not sign fluently. Given present placement practices, many educators (if they didn't place the youth at a residential school) would conclude that they should not mainstream this child, except perhaps for physical education and other nonacademic activities. At the same time, imagine that second-grade classes are studying about the community throughout the school year. What about the possibility that (with other kinds of mainstreaming work) the "low-verbal" deaf student could participate in skits in which the second graders dramatize how they and others would interact with people in their community, such as police officers, nurses, clerks, and others? Perhaps making these skits silent pantomimes would add to the challenge for the hearing children and enable the deaf child to participate more successfully. Such changes in practices can more successfully bring together deaf and hearing youth.

Not only are placements important, but so too are our practices for making placements. Placement practices can enable participants to become meaningfully involved and can demonstrate that mainstreamed students are integral members of their school. To the extent that all concerned parties are involved in making placement decisions, the importance of mainstreamed students to the school community is affirmed. However, when special education teachers tell, but do not meaningfully discuss with, parents of deaf children upcoming educational plans; when special education teachers inform, but do not consult with, mainstream teachers about placement; and when principals and guidance counselors assign deaf students to classes after the scheduling of hearing students has been completed, placement practices do not include all the participants. They exclude them. Continued consultation among prepared, competent parties is needed if placements are to be successful. This consultation takes a great deal of work, which I do not explore here.

Enhancement Work

Because mainstreaming is so challenging and complex, most programs will fall short in some way. Instead of abandoning mainstreaming as some suggest, however, a second kind of work can enhance the program's ability to educate together deaf and hearing students. Mainstream programs succeed when competent participants use effective organizational procedures. Enhancement aims to improve participants' ability to succeed in mainstreaming.

For example, when a mainstream program for elementary school deaf children moved to a new building due to crowding at its former school, administrators and staff tried to prepare participants for the change. During the spring before the move to the new site, deaf children, their parents, and their teachers visited the new school, and staff from the school that was soon to mainstream the deaf children visited the present program. During the summer sign language classes were offered so that, as the principal noted, teachers at the school to which the mainstream program was moving would at least be able to sign "Hi" to the deaf children. Such preparation was a modest start.

Enhancement is necessary in mainstream programs. When programs are first established, participants must be prepared. However, enhancement is important even in long-standing programs. Students, staff, and parents come and go. Circumstances change. Mainstream participants cannot become competent on their own. At the same time, the resources supplied by the education agency may be insufficient. Instead, by procuring supplies, services, positions, and personnel, participants can complement what the education agency presently provides.

Mainstreaming deaf youth necessitates enhancing the abilities of hearing students and staff, as well as the families of the deaf children, to communicate with deaf students. While this is not the only goal, it must be a main goal, and it is the one I take up here. Let me mention some ways that programs are working toward that goal or might try to do so.

Mainstream programs can assist parents of deaf children and other family members to become competent signers. The programs can offer instruction themselves or might refer interested families to community sign language classes. A lending library might be developed that included sign language tapes and video players. Consideration should be given to assisting families in attending summer learning vacations or intensive sign language instruction, which may be offered at residential schools for deaf students or at Gallaudet University and other universities for the deaf. However, offering sign language instruction will not be sufficient. Mainstream programs must also work to help families of deaf children to develop a commitment to learn to sign. Enlisting other parents to provide support for those who have yet to make a commitment, involving the deaf community as advocates for the parents' deaf children and "coaches" for the parents (coaching them in deafness), arranging transportation, providing child care, and the like may all be needed. And programs must begin to build that commitment as soon as possible. Delay typically creates difficulties.

Mainstream programs also have to enable hearing staff (which includes more than teachers) and students to learn to sign. Mainstreaming is not merely a means to enable deaf youth and others with educationally significant impairments to become used to doing the best they can in a nondisabled world. Instead, it is a means for enlarging our world to encompass all.

To be successful, signing instruction should be a routine, integral feature of the school. The well-meant suggestion that a class in "language arts can include an assignment to learn and practice sign language" (Stain-back & Stainback, 1985, p. 62) reflects a profound misunderstanding of signing and of the work needed to enhance participants' skills. Instead, the local education administration needs to support signing instruction. School leaders can demonstrate their commitment through their own participation in learning to sign. Continuing, convenient signing instruction for all members of the school community is needed.

Signing instruction for hearing staff works best when it is institutional-ized and offered regularly, not only when a mainstream program is first established. Administrators might reduce staff duties while they take sign-ing courses (e.g., even one less bus or recess duty per teacher). With the cooperation of a local college, the courses might satisfy recertification requirements. The local education administration might consider subsidiz-ing some or all of the cost of the courses, or increasing the salary of staff who take signing instruction (or who reach various levels of proficiency). Principals, of course, can enhance the success of the school becoming bilingual if they take the lead by learning to communicate with all their students. Such efforts and arrangements will help staff communicate with all the students in their schools, if not equally well with all. Some teachers may even become skilled enough to conduct their mainstream classes without an interpreter.

Similarly, signing instruction for hearing students becomes an essential component of a mainstream program. Sign choirs and clubs that involve deaf and hearing youth can be useful, particularly when they are comple-mented by other mainstreaming efforts. Where possible, a course in signing may become an elective for junior high and high school students or suffi-cient to meet foreign language requirements, as is the case in some states. Signing instruction is most successful when begun with elementary and kindergarten students.

Sign choirs are a common vehicle, but school-wide instruction is also needed. To provide that may take many instructors (though in-school television could be used where available). Interpreters, aides, older deaf students (at the elementary school or a nearby junior high or high school), older hearing students and mainstream staff who have learned to sign, and community volunteers, especially deaf citizens, could instruct hearing stu-dents from the beginning of their school careers. Fifteen minutes of instruc-tion each day, starting in kindergarten, would increase greatly the ability of hearing students to "talk" with deaf students. If time could not be made during the school day (though I believe it can be, which makes the instruc-tion integral to the complete school), then before-school instruction might be feasible. Often, students arrive early with little to do. A mainstream school for deaf students should be a signing school.

Enhancement also aims to procure needed resources. While it is reasonable to expect education agencies to support mainstreaming as they support other schooling components, they may not be able to provide all that could be helpful. Sustained advocacy, sometimes for many years, by supporters may eventually convince administrators to supply new resources, such as another interpreter position. Parents can not only advocate with administrators, but can form alliances with educators who can then advocate their own superiors (Biklen, 1985). By contacting the educators' superiors about a particular issue, parents demonstrate to those superiors that others beyond the educators are concerned. "Pushy parents can be a real plus." By drawing on the resources of the community, such as deaf citizens, or developing alternatives to the routine organizational procedures, such as increasing the signing skills of an aide so he or she can become an interpreter (when interpreters cannot be obtained), mainstream programs can complement what education agencies routinely provide. Enhancement increases the capacity of mainstream participants to educate together children with and without disabilities.

Relational Work

Physical integration is not the point of mainstreaming. Successful interaction is. While deaf and hearing children (and adults) must be together to interact, placing them together is not enough. Relational (and other mainstreaming) work seeks to enable participants to develop satisfying relationships. Participants become friends, respected colleagues, casual acquaintances, and even "just another person" in the school. When done well, relational work creates social integration.

However, mainstream programs can isolate youth with disabilities, especially the deaf, as well as their "special education" staff and parents. Instead of becoming integral members of the school, they remain outsiders. For example, one young deaf woman who encountered difficulties when mainstreamed in high school and subsequently started a support group for other mainstreamed deaf teenagers noted:

> They [the deaf members of the support group] don't have many hearing friends. I was surprised because many members of the group are very popular with other deaf people . . . but in the hearing high school, they don't have many friends. I thought I was the only one. I kept my feelings to myself, but when I heard all the other people, I let my feelings out. We find that we have many things in common in the frustrations. . . . For example, like if I want to try to communicate with hearing people, my voice sounds funny. I am very awkward and shy. I have good speech, but

sometimes it sounds funny. Hearing people look at me and kind of walk off to their friends and I feel bad. The same thing happens with other members of the group. We try to talk to hearing people, but they turn off. . . . They have their own world, they don't want to get involved with the deaf world. (Foster, 1987, pp. 15–16)

Similarly, nondisabled students, in this case the hearing, may be outsiders to the world of deaf students. Effective placement and enhancement begin to combat that potential isolation. An array of relational strategies can as well. I mention four of many that I have identified: socializing, serving, personalizing relations, and including.

Participating in pleasant exchanges strengthens relations among participants; seclusion does not. In a mainstream program for deaf students observed by others, the deaf education teachers were less integrated than the deaf youth. Their "segregation inhibit[ed the deaf students'] integration" (Biklen, 1985, p. 42). Among the many reasons for the segregation was their lack of socializing. The deaf education teachers always stayed in their own area of the school and ate lunch together. In the programs I observed, the deaf education staff (and to a lesser extent the deaf students) socialized with their hearing counterparts. Eating lunch with hearing staff (perhaps in a carpeted, uncrowded self-contained classroom), casual chats throughout the school day, invitations to others to participate in a holiday party in the self-contained classroom, an interpreter telling a mainstream teacher how much she enjoyed the teacher's class, making and sending get well cards to custodians and other staff who are sick, and other civilities made relations more cordial. Of course, the responsibility for cordial relations must be shared by all participants; but the recognition and support of that mutual responsibility require their own kind of work.

By serving their school, students with special education needs and their staff combat the unjust perception that they are a burden. Interpreters in a mainstream program for deaf youth routinely monitored the classes in which they interpreted when the teachers were called away. Staff may become coaches or sponsors of extracurricular activities (Biklen, 1985). An aide in one mainstream program that I observed helped a physical education teacher mend gym shorts and refereed volleyball games. Mainstreamed deaf students can help raise funds for their school alongside their fellow hearing students. Serving is done not for ingratiation, but for integration. It can show one's commitment to be an integral member of the school.

Through personalizing relations, mainstream participants become individuals instead of "one of those." When a consultant shows central office administrators things made by deaf children in the mainstream, the administrators learn about the students behind the statistics. When staff and hearing students learn to sign to deaf students, relations become less superficial. When stigmatizing labels, such as "learning disabled class," are replaced by neutral names, such as "Mrs. Smith's class," relations become more individualized (Biklen, 1985; Longmore, 1985). When mainstream teachers, interpreters, and hearing students make sure the mainstreamed deaf students know the names of their hearing classmates and which hearing student is speaking during class, then hearing children become more personal to deaf students. Personalizing relations provides opportunities for participants to move beyond categories to people.

When students with disabilities, their special education staff, and their parents are included in the life of the school, relations become stronger. When mainstream teachers pause after asking a question so that deaf students have a chance to respond—since a good interpreter is often a few words behind the teacher's speaking (Cokely, 1986)—they are trying to include all their students. When deaf youth go to and participate in assemblies like other students, they are being included. When special education staff have similar duties as other staff, their inclusion integrates them. When parents of special education students are made welcome at parent–teacher association meetings, a sense of belonging can develop. Various members of the school community also include one another when hearing youth and school staff go with deaf students on a field trip or participate in activities in a self-contained class. Reciprocal inclusion is more likely to succeed. With these four and other strategies, participants can enable one another to develop more successful relations.

Identity Work

Often we stigmatize people with disabilities (Bogdan & Biklen, 1977; Goffman, 1963). Too often we expect those we encounter, whether in school or elsewhere, to

> walk normally, speak intelligently, not to be sight or hearing impaired, have the usual level of physical stamina, and be able to follow the train of a normal conversation with relative ease. Any alteration in these attributes leads [many of us] . . . to define these individuals in less than positive terms. (Lindesmith, Strauss, & Denzin, 1975, p. 535)

In our eyes, they are flawed, discredited. They are not equally worthy people, perhaps not even people at all.

As a consequence of the effects of stigma, deaf youth, like others with disabilities, may be ambivalent (Higgins, 1980). While they seek to affirm themselves, others denigrate them. Deaf children may embrace themselves, but they may also discredit themselves. They may be uncertain about who they are and with whom they belong. Having perhaps little contact with deaf adults, they may actually wonder if they will be deaf when they grow up.

Parents of children with disabilities often have similar concerns. Who are their children and who will they become (Featherstone, 1980)? Most parents of deaf children are hearing (especially parents of mainstreamed deaf youth). Having little, if any, experience with deaf adults, believing that their dreams for their children have been destroyed, not knowing what awaits their children, wishing their children to be as "normal" as possible, not knowing how to decide among competing communication and education philosophies, inadequately communicating with their children, and having other family and additional responsibilities, parents of deaf children are often bewildered.

Through identity work, mainstream participants strive to create more satisfying, less stigmatizing identities for deaf youth, their parents, and the "deaf education" program in the mainstream school. They challenge the stigmatized identities of deaf students, create a proud deaf identity for the children and their parents, and promote the program.

Mainstream participants need to confront the stigmatizing actions of others: the hearing student who makes fun of sign language, the staff member who innocently asks whether a deaf middle school student who has come for an eye exam knows the alphabet, the mainstream teacher who with misguided sympathy inflates the grade of a deaf student. With little planning, if any, mainstream participants respond to demeaning actions (Biklen, 1985). Staff may admonish offending parties, particularly students, or positively characterize deafness or the deaf student who has been insulted. Deaf youth sometimes retaliate with equally offensive characterizations, but can be supported by a teacher's suggestion to ask more subtly using sign why the now bewildered hearing student is being rude.

These quick responses are not sufficient, however, because alone they do not create sustained, systematic challenges to stigmatization. Positive, anticipatory responses are needed as well.

By "breaking out," mainstream participants enable hearing students, staff, and parents to encounter deaf students performing competently and, perhaps more important, being ordinary people. The limiting labels no longer confine them. When a mainstreamed deaf student tells her classmates that she likes to tease her interpreter, her classmates glimpse that she is just like them. When deaf children participate in a school-wide talent show, they show hearing students that you may not need to hear to have rhythm. Small cooperative work groups provide opportunities for hearing students to see the (deaf) children behind the labels. Opportunities for students to "break out" of their stigmatized identities need to be a routine part of school life; otherwise it can become an exhibition, with deaf youth on display in the school's "sideshow" (Bogdan, 1988).

Routine, competent participation in mainstream schools, by both staff members and community members who are deaf, also challenges the stigmatization of deafness. Participation as staff members, guest speakers (who may not necessarily talk about their deafness), volunteers, and so on, emphasizes the multiple roles all people can serve. If mainstream schools are to educate our diverse children, then adults who participate in the schools should also reflect the diversity of the community.

Identity work not only challenges the stigmatization of deafness, but it also enables deaf youth (and their parents) to be proud of themselves (or their children) as deaf people, and to develop ties to the deaf community if they choose to do so. Enabling deaf children to socialize among themselves inside and outside of school, providing opportunities for them to know deaf adults, and incorporating deafness into the educational curriculum for deaf students can encourage them to develop a deaf identity and a solidarity with other deaf people. For example, a state-wide festival for secondary school deaf students enables them to become acquainted and realize that a larger deaf world awaits them. Studying deaf heritage, using stories about deaf characters to teach reading, and studying sign language just as other students study their language all serve to incorporate deafness into the education of deaf youth. Our curricula for all our students should reflect their diversity.

Promoting the deaf education program strengthens the identity of the participants; strengthening the identity of the deaf students enhances the reputation of the program. For example, sign choirs not only challenge the stigmatization of deaf students, but in bringing positive publicity to the sponsoring school, they enhance the identity of the mainstream program. When a consultant makes certain that her superiors know of the accomplishments of the mainstreamed deaf students, the administrators see the entire program more positively. We are known by the groups to which we belong. Improving the image of the groups in which people participate improves participants' identities as well. Through identity work, we transform into valued diversity what is too often taken to be a defect.

Monitoring Work

Regular monitoring from multiple perspectives can greatly enhance the success of mainstreaming (Biklen, 1985). Mainstreaming is complex, controversial, and difficult to achieve. Indeed, it seems that only by attempting it will we ever completely understand what it means to be successful.

Monitoring provides the information that will allow ongoing improvement and growth in what we understand about mainstreaming and in how well we are able to accomplish it. Monitoring generates the information to show skeptics that mainstreaming can succeed, to inform the indifferent that improvement is needed, and to assist the committed in making mainstreaming work.

It is important for participants from all perspectives to contribute to the monitoring efforts: parents of deaf children, mainstream staff, deaf and hearing students, administrators, support staff, and deaf education teachers. They do so formally through IEP conferences and audits. As with desegregation, however (Hawley et al., 1983), mainstream participants can also institute other forms of ongoing, school-wide monitoring, such as a faculty subcommittee that regularly reports to the faculty or a task force of students, staff, parents, and community citizens.

Participants also monitor informally. When staff chat with one another about mainstreaming efforts and activities, teachers and parents call one another, aides observe interaction among students at recess, students tell their teachers how they are doing in the mainstream, teachers observe interpreters in an assembly, and principals drop into a classroom, they are all monitoring the program. Monitoring work is most successful when participants take full advantage of the wealth of opportunities that their routine activities provide for generating information.

Participants sometimes monitor reactively, responding to the reports of others, or they may initiate their own, proactive monitoring. For example, after hearing about difficulties in a mainstream classroom, special education teachers/consultants might check for themselves. Reactive monitoring is rarely completely satisfactory. When participants who are removed from a particular mainstream setting rely exclusively on the reports of those directly involved, too often the reports may be complaints. People tend not to "trouble" others until trouble has developed. Thus, reactive monitoring may often embroil participants in situations where blame becomes the focus. Further, difficulties can grow larger (and less manageable) when participants depend too much on reactive monitoring.

Proactive monitoring complements reactive observing. It enables participants to notice difficulties before they escalate and to identify successes as well as problems. When parents of deaf youth observe in their children's schools and classes and contact their children's teachers, when deaf education staff observe in mainstream settings, when principals regularly participate in mainstream encounters, and when local education agency administrators routinely inquire about and observe mainstreaming, they monitor more actively.

Typically school members monitor by focusing on the individual progress of deaf students or others with educationally significant impairments. However, to do only that individualizes what is a social matter. Participants also must monitor the arrangements and procedures of their program. For example: What relational work is being attempted to enable deaf and hearing elementary school children to play together at recess? Who is involved and how? What are the results of those efforts? What are the present strategies for assisting hearing staff to learn to sign? Are they effective? These and other organizational concerns are also appropriate foci of monitoring work.

Too often monitoring focuses on shortcomings and problems. As in much reactive monitoring, only when a problem develops are others informed. Focusing primarily on shortcomings may strain relations among participants. Instead, participants should try to focus on successes as well, demonstrating that mainstreaming can succeed, and providing encouragement for each other. For example, teachers and principals in the mainstream program I observed contacted the parents of deaf students with news of their children's accomplishments, not only their difficulties. No doubt, they and other educators could do much more of that. Focusing on successes enables participants to develop positive relations with one another rather than being only the bearer or recipient of bad news.

One potential problem of this kind of proactive monitoring is that privacy becomes threatened. Participants, especially deaf students, may feel that what they do is known by too many in the school. Knowledge about them is not compartmentalized, not limited to the people and the setting involved. To the extent that mainstreaming becomes an integral component of a complete school, however, issues of privacy become less problematic. Guidance counselors will be able to "talk" with deaf youth about their problems instead of relying on an interpreter; so too may mainstream teachers. Mainstream teachers will directly contact their deaf students' parents instead of asking for advice from the deaf education teachers. When a principal punishes a deaf student, it may be done without a "go-between." Deaf students may still complain that too many people know too much about them, but their complaints will be no greater than those of any other student striving to grow independent of adults while also taking for granted the adults' support.

CONCLUSION

Mainstreaming aspires to a vision of a just society. Deaf and hearing children (and those with and without educationally significant impairments) can and should live and learn together—and apart. Critics charge, on the other hand, that mainstreaming oppresses deaf youth. It does not educate them well. It isolates them among hearing people at school and at home, and separates them from a community of deaf people.

The critics are right—but they are wrong, too. There are great risks in mainstreaming. Done poorly, it can be oppressive. But done well, it can be liberating. Many deaf youth do learn in the mainstream, become friends with hearing youth, and develop a proud deaf identity. Their world grows larger. Hearing participants, like the deaf, grow in their understanding of, and their abilities to live with, diverse people. But we can and should demand much more of ourselves.

Several decades ago it did not seem possible to desegregate our schools. Although we have not yet succeeded, we have come much further than many imagine.

> When fully and carefully carried out, mandatory desegregation reduces racial isolation, enhances minority achievement, improves race relations, promotes educational quality, opens new opportunities, and maintains community support. . . . Desegregation can teach students to respect, understand, and even like people different from themselves, and it pre-pares them for life in an increasingly multiracial nation. It can give parents more knowledge of and influence over their children's schools. (Hoch-schild, 1984, p. 177)

If desegregation can work, then why not mainstreaming? Through the kinds of work I have briefly explored here, we can achieve the vision of a just society to which mainstreaming aspires. The tremendous improve-ments in many countries' treatment of its disabled citizens in the past decades gives us hope (Meyerson, 1988). Now, we need courage and commitment.

Our research must also be informed by courage and commitment. Impersonal, seemingly objective investigations often produce sterile, con-servative results. Research that only attempts to describe our present arrangements, not to challenge them, may serve to maintain the inequities. Our task is to participate in the construction of a social world in which diverse people may live fully, together and apart, as they wish. To do so, our social investigations cannot be aimed at capturing absolute truth. There are too many competing visions for that. Instead, it must be aimed at developing understandings that help us for the moment transcend the pres-ent competing perspectives and practices. Our research must be aimed at enabling us to meet our challenges more successfully.

REFERENCES

Bell, A. G. (1883). *Upon the formation of a deaf variety of the human race.* Presented to the National Academy of Sciences, New Haven, CT.

Biklen, D. (1985). *Achieving the complete school: Strategies for effective mainstreaming.* New York: Teachers College Press.

Biklen, D. (1988). The myth of clinical judgment. *Journal of Social Issues, 44,* 127–140.

Bogdan, R. (1988). *Freak show: Presenting human oddities for amusement and profit.* Chicago: University of Chicago Press.

Bogdan, R., & Biklen, D. (1977). Handicapism. *Social Policy, 7*(4), 14–19.

Brant, W. A. (1987). The quality of interaction severely and profoundly hearing handicapped children encounter in rural public school programs in South Carolina (Doctoral dissertation, University of South Carolina, 1986). *Dissertation Abstracts International, 47,* 2993A.

Cokely, D. (1986). The effects of lag time on interpreter errors. *Sign Language Studies, 53,* 341–375.

Crain, R. L., Mahard, R. E., & Narot, R. E. (1982). *Making desegregation work: How schools create social climates.* Cambridge, MA: Ballinger.

Featherstone, H. (1980). *A difference in the family: Life with a disabled child.* New York: Basic Books.

Foster, S. (1987). *Life in the mainstream: Reflections of deaf college freshmen on their experiences in the mainstreamed high school.* Presented at the conference of American Instructors of the Deaf, Santa Fe, NM.

Gannon, J. R. (1981). *Deaf heritage: A narrative history of deaf America.* Silver Spring, MD: National Association of the Deaf.

Gliedman, J., & Roth, W. (1980). *The unexpected minority: Handicapped children in America.* New York: Harcourt, Brace, Jovanovich.

Goffman, E. (1963). *Stigma: Notes on the management of spoiled identity.* Englewood Cliffs, NJ: Prentice-Hall.

Greenberg, J. (1986). Unrealized promises: Reflections on PL 94–142 and the education of deaf children. *Gallaudet Today, 16,* 3–10.

Hawley, W. D., Crain, R. L., Rossell, C. H., Smylie, M. A., Fernandez, R. R., Schofield, J. W., Tompkins, R., Trent, W. T., & Zlotnik, M. S. (1983). *Strategies for effective desegregation: Lessons from research.* Lexington, MA: D. C. Heath.

Higgins, P. C. (1980). *Outsiders in a hearing world: A sociology of deafness.* Beverly Hills, CA: Sage.

Higgins, P. C. (1985). *The rehabilitation detectives: Doing human service work.* Beverly Hills, CA: Sage.

Higgins, P. C. (1990). *The challenge of educating together deaf and hearing youth: Making mainstreaming work.* Springfield, IL: Charles C. Thomas.

Higgins, P. C., & Johnson, J. M. (Eds.). (1988). *Personal sociology.* New York: Praeger.

Hochschild, J. L. (1984). *The new American dilemma: Liberal democracy and school desegregation.* New Haven, CT: Yale University Press.

Lane, H. (1984). *When the mind hears: A history of the deaf.* New York: Random House.

Lane, H. (1987). Mainstreaming of deaf children—from bad to worse. *The Deaf American, 38,* 15.

Lindesmith, A. R., Strauss, A. L., & Denzin, N. K. (1975). *Social psychology.* Hinsdale, IL: Dryden Press.

Longmore, P. K. (1985). A note on language and social identity of disabled people. *American Behavioral Scientist, 28,* 419-423.

Meyerson, L. (1988). The social psychology of physical disability: 1948-1988. *Journal of Social Issues, 44,* 173-188.

Rothman, D. J. (1971). *The discovery of the asylum: Social order and disorder in the new republic.* Boston: Little, Brown.

Schein, J. D., & Delk, Jr., M. T. (1974). *The deaf population of the United States.* Silver Spring, MD: National Association of the Deaf.

Stainback, S., & Stainback, W. (1985). *Integration of students with severe handicaps into regular schools.* Reston, VA: The Council for Exceptional Children.

Stewart, R. L., & Reynolds, L. T. (1985). The biologizing of the individual and the naturalization of the social. *Humanity and Society, 9,* 159-167.

Stewart, R. L., & Tucker, C. W. (1983). *Research for what? Notes on Mead's pragmatic theory of truth.* Unpublished manuscript.

Strauss, A., Fagerhaugh, S., Suczek, B., & Wiener, C. (1985). *Social organization of medical work.* Chicago: University of Chicago Press.

Willie, C. V. (1978). *The sociology of urban education: Desegregation and integration.* Lexington, MA: D. C. Heath.

Wolfensberger, W. (1975). *The origin and nature of our institutional models.* Syracuse: Human Policy Press.

Chapter 6

"TRYING SOMETHING COMPLETELY DIFFERENT"

Report of a Collaborative Research Venture

Christy Davis & Dianne L. Ferguson

As educational researchers explore their growing interest in alternative research methodologies (e.g., Beyer, Feinberg, Pagano, & Whitson, 1989; Fosnot, 1989; Guba & Lincoln, 1989; Heshusius, 1989), there is a renewed focus on the role of teachers as researchers (Cochran-Smith & Lytle, 1990; Duckworth, 1986; Hitchcock & Hughes, 1989; Kyle & Hovda, 1987). In various ways these authors argue that the very nature of teaching requires teachers to engage in inquiry and experimentation (Schön, 1983, 1987; Shulman, 1987; Sykes, 1983). Some further argue that educational research should become better grounded in the inquiry of practice and oriented more toward informing than toward prescribing practice (Fenstermacher, 1978).

While there continue to be examples and discussion in the literature of teacher research as "action research" (Ebbutt, 1985; Kyle & Hovda, 1987; Richards, 1987), some emerging examples argue for a shared research responsibility between teachers and collaborating university faculty (Miller, 1990). This chapter is an example of both of these ways of thinking about teachers as researchers. It reports the results of a collaborative research effort between a teacher (Davis) of students with mild disabilities and a professor of special education (Ferguson). The project spanned an entire year and occurred in two stages—a teacher-managed action research stage, and a collaborative analysis and discovery stage. We have organized the chapter to mirror this chronology. First, Christy Davis describes the action research phase of the project, which was conducted in a middle school in Powell, Wyoming. In the middle section Dianne Ferguson describes what occasioned the collaborative research effort and the events and decisions that led to the preparation of this chapter. In the concluding section we present our joint thoughts about both the results and the process of the research.

THE ACTION RESEARCH PHASE

A Need for Change

The fall of 1987 promised to involve change for many at Powell Middle School. Individualized education plan (IEP) meetings had resulted in placement of a larger than usual number of resource students in regular academic classes. At the same time, the district's Director of Pupil Services initiated a new program to shift resource rooms for grades 6–12 from a self-contained to an itinerant model over the next 3 years. Roughly 30 of Powell's 420 students in grades 6–8 were scheduled to receive itinerant resource room assistance in one or more academic subjects.

Since Powell Middle School is not very large, only one teacher is available at each grade level to teach each academic subject. In the past, many of the students labelled learning disabled struggled with their academic class placements. These students frequently failed despite getting help from resource room teachers whenever either they or their teacher requested it. We resource teachers might go into a class and read tests to them, or take notes so a student could listen more closely during special activities. Most of the time, however, our "help" was delivered only on a sporadic, "as needed" basis. It was not planful, systematic, or regular.

It also seemed to me that much of our resource help was ineffective because it focused primarily on helping students "patch up" assignments just enough to get by in class the next day. The students seemed to learn dependence rather than independence from our resource support. They continued to lack the skills to identify and manage day-to-day problems. At the same time, I tended to view the classroom teacher as one of the major barriers to student success. When I visited their classrooms, I always sought to discover what they were doing that impeded the students' success and figure out how to change these teachers so that my learning disabled students would succeed more consistently. Frustrations ran high for all concerned. I could see that meeting the needs of both the students and the classroom teachers required some changes, but I left school in the spring of 1987 not at all sure of what those changes might be.

A New Approach

After spending the summer taking courses toward my masters degree in special education, I returned with a fuzzy, but clearing, image of what the upcoming changes might entail. Certainly the details still eluded me, but I was clear about one important shift in focus. In the past I had tried to ease students' participation in their regular academic classes by changing how the teacher responded to and worked with "my" learning disabled students. In previous years such efforts had never succeeded to my satisfaction. Students still struggled to "get by" with whatever "quick fix" help I could supply during resource study hall. The teachers seemed uniformly resistant to my efforts to reform their teaching practices. My previous difficulties and the new ideas I encountered in one of my courses led me over the summer to a new way of thinking about my role. My new focus, I had decided over the summer, would not be to change the teacher, but to shift my attention and efforts to the students. I decided to coach students to recognize, interpret, and respond to their regular class surroundings with strategies that would give them a feeling of power or influence to succeed despite their learning disabilities and independent of my "help."

The Action Research Context

Two of my students, John, age 13, and Gail, age 12 (not their real names), were assigned to Mr. Blackwell's grade 7 social studies class. Indeed, John and Gail had been strongly recommended for this class by the grade 6 social studies teacher, Mr. Martin. Even after Mr. Blackwell carefully described his own demands, Mr. Martin encouraged the inclusion of John and Gail. Although he had experience with other disabled students, Mr. Martin singled out John and Gail, I believe, not only because they had been successful (managing Cs and Bs throughout the year), but because they were personable and outgoing and had good social relationships with peers in the class.

I knew John and Gail well. John had a reading deficit. He had a tough time decoding words, although his spelling and writing were pretty good. He always seemed to understand what he heard, but if he had to read material, he struggled, slowly, missing key vocabulary words. Gail, on the other hand, had difficulty understanding information she heard or read. While she could read what she encountered in a typical grade-level text, she stumbled over new vocabulary and had difficulty making sense out of what she read. She was also a weak speller and had difficulty expressing herself clearly in writing. Both when writing and speaking, her ideas tended to be disjointed—not well pulled together—unlike John, whose speaking and writing usually presented well-organized ideas.

Despite these learning difficulties, I thought of both John and Gail as fairly unique among my students. They both had pretty healthy self-images and felt fairly confident of their abilities. They had proven to themselves that they could succeed in classes outside the resource room, at least with some help. They also tended to be more expressive—joining in groups and having more friends outside of the other special education students.

Fall 1987—The First Month

Mr. Blackwell's period 4 social studies class had 24 students, including John and Gail. As the term began Mr. Blackwell reminded me of his plan to apply the same expectations to John and Gail as to all the other students. He wanted to discover how John and Gail managed the course materials and instruction without modifications. My own plan was to analyze Mr. Blackwell's class, providing support to John and Gail, as well as other students in need, along the way. In time, I hoped to discover ways to help John and Gail meet Mr. Blackwell's demands without my help. Initially I explained my role to Mr. Blackwell this way:

> My role is simply to come as pretty much another student, sit at a desk in the back of the classroom and take notes. When you give time for students to work I will certainly be available to circulate about the room and help anybody who needs help. My goal is to be in your class daily at the beginning of the year, to take notes, observe, and make sure that I know what is happening so that when John and Gail come to my tutorial class, I can support them on the kinds of things you are requiring them to do. By the end of the school year I do not expect to be in the classroom daily because, I hope, the students will be more able to be on their own by then.

Within the first week I realized that my initial support to John and Gail should consist of what I eventually called "help yourself" strategies. Like any other teacher, Mr. Blackwell operated his class in some predictable ways that students needed to quickly learn to anticipate. For example, he always began class promptly with a series of quick, one-time-only instructions for tasks to be completed while he took attendance. "Get out paper and pencil, look over your notes, and get ready to answer the questions on page 23." If a student was not alert enough to catch these critical bits of information, he or she might well have an unsuccessful day.

My first weeks of observation identified a variety of Blackwell-specific signals, routines, and expectations. I learned, for example, that he

Routinely lectured from the same location in the classroom

Rarely circulated through the room, even when students were working independently

Regularly praised students who were prepared enough to volunteer answers to his questions

Provided an objectives sheet for each unit that included the information students needed to learn in order to pass the unit test

Taught units of varying lengths depending on the mix of resources (like filmstrips) available to him

Required shorter and less frequent homework assignments for longer units (5–6 weeks) than for 2–3 week units

These specific teacher practices provided topics for my tutorial discussions with John and Gail over the term. Together we discussed how John and Gail might deal with Mr. Blackwell's rules, signals, routines, and expectations by developing both "how to" and "help yourself" strategies.

"How to" strategies

"How to" strategies generally involved me teaching John and Gail various new ways to get and stay organized, be prepared for class, and gather information. Unlike my previous efforts, however, this time I depended on John and Gail to select the study skills strategies they thought would work best for them. This emphasis on letting the *students* define what would work sometimes created some interesting discussions and negotiations. We did not always agree on what might work, but my new focus required me to try to give at least as much consideration to the students' points of view as to my own.

Both John and Gail needed help getting organized. During our tutorials, I taught them how to keep an assignment record, organize their notebook, plan when to do assignments, and better manage their time. Once they understood a strategy, both freely adapted it according to their own preference. For example, John preferred to incorporate his assignment record with a weekly calendar that fit on a single sheet of paper, thus reducing the bulk he carried from class to class. Gail, on the other hand, opted to use a small spiral assignment book kept in the front of her three-ring binder.

Both used the assignment record as a tool for planning time lines. Daily we evaluated assignments to decide which needed to be completed at school—where they could receive additional help—and which they could handle independently at home. We also used the assignment record to break apart big assignments with longer time lines into small, or more manageable, assignments.

While John and Gail both quickly adopted the logic of an assignment record to their benefit and preferences, they did not as readily follow my advice on keeping notebooks and paper organized. Although they both accepted the strategy of arranging their notebook by subjects, they resisted keeping their completed work in their notebook—preferring instead to store finished work in their textbooks. Using the assignment to mark the page from which the assignment came may have helped them find the page more easily during class, but after each lost a paper or two, they became convinced of the risks of the practice and each found a way to keep assignments in a separate section of their notebook.

Another set of "how to" strategies we generated together helped John and Gail more efficiently and effectively prepare for class. They both learned to identify key words and use them to write answers to questions. Abbreviations to speed expression and minimize spelling errors; new skills at using tables of contents, indices, and glossaries; the atlas, almanacs, and encyclopedias all helped them become more able to volunteer responses to at least some of Mr. Blackwell's questions.

Other resource room teachers may well have tried to instruct their students in such familiar study and organizational skills. I had myself. What made this year different was that I tried to teach these skills to John and Gail only when *they* were able to define a current and pressing need for them. My attention to the students' understanding of their needs also led us to develop the second category of skills and techniques—"help yourself" strategies.

"Help yourself" strategies

Both John and Gail understood that their personal limitations prevented the complete independence in Mr. Blackwell's class that they sought. Yet they still wanted freedom from the *special education* teacher. At the beginning of the year both John and Gail asked me not to "bother" them in Mr. Blackwell's class. They explained their fear that peers would identify them as special education students if they associated with me.

While I respected their desire for dignity and independence, I realized that they would also need some personal strategies that would allow them to manage the various demands of a variety of teachers. I agreed to limit my contact with them, avoiding stigma, we hoped, in exchange for their open discussion with me during tutorials of the problems they encountered and how they were trying to solve them. Our discussions were far ranging, as illustrated by this partial list.

Where should I sit so I can "get" what Mr. Blackwell wants me to but still be with my friends?
What should I do if I don't understand something so the other students don't think I'm dumb?
How can I ask for help without seeming too dumb to my friends?
Should I let Mr. Blackwell know what I have trouble with?
How do I "buy time" when I'm not prepared?
What should I do if I don't know an answer?

How do I work in a group and still cover up my weaknesses?
What should I do when I get home and can't figure out an assignment?
How can I use the other students for help and for what kinds of help?

Our discussions led John and Gail to develop some workable personal "rules." I resisted attempting to change their decisions, even if I thought another strategy might work better, in favor of letting them test their own decisions. Like "how to" strategies, "help yourself" strategies required the three of us to figure out ways for John and Gail to handle situations they encountered in regular class in whatever way felt most comfortable to them. When their strategies failed, I guided them to create new ones; but not all failed. For example, they each developed their own strategies for where to sit and how to ask for help.

John decided to sit in the back of the classroom with his buddies. He claimed he listened and understood better when he didn't have to watch the teacher. Gail, however, decided to sit in the front near Mr. Blackwell's typical lecturing spot. Not only did she feel this location would help her better see the pictures and maps he used, but she also figured that Mr. Blackwell liked students who sat in the front of the room and paid attention to him. She did decide to join her friends during group activities.

Getting help was a bit harder for both of them. Gail felt comfortable asking for help to spell words, to have directions repeated, or to locate elusive answers in the text, regardless of whether the help came from Mr. Blackwell or me. John, on the other hand, "had an image to maintain" with his buddies and resisted any teacher helping him in front of his friends. John's system worked like this:

> I'll raise my hand for help, but if Mr. Blackwell heads my way, I'll put my hand down or tell him I figured out the answer. I don't mind asking you for help; so when you are near my desk, I'll raise my hand. But don't talk too loud when you come over to help me. I will mark words and ask when you come near my desk. Sometimes I will listen to the guys in my group and they will say words I can't read. [As a last resort] if everyone is real busy, I can ask them to slow down a minute and spell a word for me.

As the year progressed, we all evaluated the effectiveness of the "getting help" strategies. Gail's strategies didn't change significantly. She began to hesitate less to ask Mr. Blackwell for help, deciding that if he took time to help her he would better understand her ideas. John, on the other hand, modified his approach considerably. He began to realize that each of his buddies had their own troubles with spelling and reading, sometimes calling *them* "dumb" during our tutorials. Gradually he began to risk asking Mr. Blackwell for help during class. If teased by a friend, his quick retorts— "Well, *you* spell it for me" or "You don't know either"—ended the challenge.

"Putting our heads together" strategies

While John and Gail could be successful strategists on their own, we all discovered that together we generated more and better solutions faster. In the process, I also developed a strategy. John and Gail entered tutorial class each morning eager with comments about Mr. Blackwell's class and how things were going. My listening skills quickly improved, hearing even the subtle criticisms and fragile satisfactions. Sometimes I found it difficult to refrain from identifying "the problem" they were facing. I resisted, however, in favor of helping them "find" the problem for themselves. In the process, I learned to better appreciate *their* problems from *their* perspective. As John repeatedly reminded me, I was not the one sitting in Mr. Blackwell's class every day trying to do the assigned work! In the end, this saved me a good deal of time. As I became more skillful at understanding the social studies class experience from the students' points of view, I was able to offer better suggestions. I also generally affirmed my change in approach.

Our joint problem solving gradually developed its own criterion. We tried to create strategies that allowed John and Gail to meet Mr. Blackwell's expectations while also allowing them to control as many of the factors affecting their success as possible. An example from Gail's experience on a group assignment nicely illustrates this "rule."

Gail decided she had a problem with a group assignment. During class her friends tended to chat and visit while Gail worked, joining in on the chatter only occasionally. This disproportionate contribution to the group task required extra out-of-class time from Gail to complete the assignment on time. When her friends asked for answers so they could also turn in papers on time, Gail decided she had a problem. Gail wanted her friends to change. She explained in our tutorial sessions that she wanted to share the work more equally, but did not want to jeopardize her relationships. John suggested a direct approach, advising Gail to tell her friends that she was "tired of doing all the work and if they didn't start doing more she would ask to work with other kids." Gail, however, sought more harmony. She did not want to risk either her friends' feelings or their friendship, but she did think Mr. Blackwell ought to be apprised. She asked me to explain the situation to him.

Instead, I wanted Gail to arrive at a solution that she could implement without my intervention. I guided her to identify her outcome: the group would divide the assignment and share their answers. With encouragement she also generated possible strategies: (1) tell the friends to do more of the work, (2) find a new group, (3) work alone, or (4) tell Mr. Blackwell about the situation.

Gail considered the implications. She didn't want to lose or antagonize her friends. Finding a new group would just involve more people in the problem. Working alone meant more work and less time with friends. Telling Mr. Blackwell might mean giving up control of the situation.

In the end Gail decided to talk to Mr. Blackwell. Although I offered to gently pave the way by bringing his attention to the group, Gail opted for independent action. She asked Mr. Blackwell to talk to the group during class, while emphasizing her desire to continue as a group member.

Mr. Blackwell followed through. That day he watched Gail's group work. Before class ended, he talked directly to the group about his observations, which confirmed Gail's experience. He also outlined some specific solutions the group could employ to share responsibilities. What I liked about the outcome was that Gail had learned to share responsibility for resolving a problem with someone other than the "special" person designated to do so. The experience enabled both Gail and Mr. Blackwell to take action that brought about useful change. I was not needed.

Some of our strategies involved not just accommodating John's and Gail's weaknesses, but also exploiting for their benefit some of the unique features of Mr. Blackwell's style of teaching. For example, since it always seemed better to take a chance to answer in Mr. Blackwell's class than not to answer at all, we developed ways for John and Gail to figure out probable answers even when they were not sure. During the unit on South America, for example, a question might be to name three exports from a particular country. Frequently some student would supply one export, but not all three. John and Gail practiced coming up with other examples in the same category, or checking other countries they had prepared for the same day for examples in the same category, and so on.

Routines and Novelties

By the end of the first month, John, Gail, and I had established the pattern of ongoing support and planning that carried us through the year. Tutorial class continued to provide the context for developing "how to" and "help yourself" strategies, which we created to build on the students' strengths. For instance, Gail's strength was getting material written down, even if not always accurately spelled. During class, then, her key strategy was to focus not so much on absorbing information, but on writing it down to absorb later. John, on the other hand, found the mechanics of writing laborious. Extensive note-taking tended to distract him from the content, so his key strategy was to listen and absorb as much as possible during class. I continued to attend Mr. Blackwell's class, but as John and Gail became more adept at using their strategies, my participation became one of providing general assistance to all the students.

We also developed a new set of strategies to respond to Mr. Blackwell's variations in routine. Mr. Blackwell's units, for example, varied widely in length, from 2–3 weeks to as much as 6 weeks. Shorter units meant longer daily assignments and required more class and home time to complete them. Longer units required less frequent and shorter out-of-class assignments, but also tended to involve more use of audiovisual (AV) and reference materials.

These changes in routine demanded new strategies. Longer units using AV materials forced us to develop new approaches for completing worksheet assignments, including previewing worksheets to identify key words, writing out key words to organize note-taking, and dividing up the questions and sharing answers during tutorial class the next day. Shorter units, with their longer class and home assignments, required both John and Gail to rely on more in-class strategies for making sure they completely understood the teacher's directions.

As the year progressed, John and Gail began to create and use new strategies, as demanded by changes in Mr. Blackwell's routine, without my assistance. The more success they experienced, the more confidence they gained. Indeed, by the end of the year, both expressed a desire to try more regular education classes in eighth grade.

Student-Negotiated IEPs

I was not fully prepared for the student empowerment that resulted from my action research. The previous year Gail had attended her annual IEP meeting, but participated only passively, nodding her head when necessary and briefly agreeing, "Yeah, that's okay with me." John had not attended his meeting. This spring Gail announced that both she and her mother would attend the IEP meeting "to review and plan" for next year. John informed me of his intention not only to attend, but to participate, saying he believed he ought to "have a say" in what classes he ended up taking in eighth grade. Once John and Gail established the trend, three more students joined the "movement."

Although I was taken a bit aback at their assertiveness, I realized on reflection that their newfound power to influence and change features of a classroom environment might suggest to them that they could have similar influence in other arenas that affected their school lives. The IEP meeting seemed the next logical step from their point of view. What they did not realize, however, was how different IEP meetings might be from social studies class.

I began meeting with John, Gail, and three seventh grade students to help them plan their participation in the upcoming IEP meetings. Their initial concerns were quite familiar. They complained about not being routinely invited to participate, questioned the presence of so many adults, and admitted feeling awkward talking to adults about their needs and preferences. One student feared that "I'm just a kid. No one cares what I have to say." Another cynically queried, "You [adults] already have your minds made up so why should I tell you what I think?"

Although expressed differently by each, the message was clear. John felt, "I'm not dumb. I know what classes I want to take better than you." Gail admitted that it might be "good to listen to what everyone in the meeting says," but "I can tell you what I want. I know you have some ideas, and so does my mom, but I have some too. I think we can all get what we want."

As the students and I began to plan their participation in more detail, I was again surprised at the students' agendas. Both John and Gail wanted to propose full involvement in the standard curriculum classes. John explained with feeling, "I want to go to all regular classes. I'm not dumb. I got A or B in social studies all year. I should get to take any classes I want. I don't want to take that stupid tutor class, or whatever it's called. I want to take shop and stuff. I'm smart. I can do it." Gail, although more circumspect, wanted the same. "I have talked to my mom and dad. They have some ideas about what I should take, but I have some ideas and they are not the same. I want to take all regular classes, even in science. I know that I will have to work hard, but I did it this year. If I have to give up something, that's all right. I want to have a tutorial class thing, or whatever you call it. That has really helped me. Could I have two of them?"

Our preparations included helping the students understand the IEP process, identify and defend their own priorities, and develop strategies for participation that would help express their wishes and get them met. They group practiced their presentations and observed a mock IEP meeting.

In the end, three of the students actively participated in their IEP meetings, each with some level of success. Gail's experience was perhaps the most successful example. She began by explaining to the group what she perceived as her strengths and then outlined the strategies she had developed and used to improve her success. She negotiated firmly with team members so that one of her important priorities—taking grade 8 science—ended up on the IEP.

I did not always agree with the students' choices or rationales, and I sometimes "lost" in the final negotiation. Any frustration I felt about my own diminished power was mitigated by my satisfaction with the students' newly found power. By that point, however, I suspect I might have been the only one who appreciated my role in that shift in power balance. In their newfound assertiveness, the students seemed to have completely forgotten about my role in helping them secure their power. I found the experience both humbling and rewarding.

THE COLLABORATIVE RESEARCH PHASE

One of the challenges of university teaching is that too often we cannot judge its impact, and only rarely learn of its more distant ripple effects. In this case, one of the "ripples" returned to my office a summer after taking a foundations course in disability studies. Christy Davis sat down in my office and related how "something about the course" sparked a period of reflection that returned her to the resource room students ready to try "something completely different." She continued, describing her action research effort, though she did not then describe it as action research.

As the story unfolded the purpose of her visit became clearer. She had carefully collected information throughout the year—notes, student products, records of conversations with students, her own reflections—but she wanted help writing up her project as research. Her immediate need was to submit a master's thesis. What captured my interest, however, was that the thesis seemed a secondary objective for her. Her more pressing interest was to make better sense of what had happened and figure out how to build on the experience. The need to complete the master's thesis, and a leave from her school for the fall term, provided the opportunity.

I was intrigued by the opportunity to discover more about what had been "completely different" for Christy during the school year just ended. I entered the project hoping to learn not only what she had tried, but what had happened for her as well as for her students, and, perhaps most important, *why* she thought things had occurred as they did.

From the beginning I anticipated that my involvement in the project would also be "completely different." I expected to be more of a participant in how our conversations unfolded as compared with some of my other experiences with interpretivist research. I planned to first discover Christy's understanding of the experience and then construct a line of inquiry that would pose questions "at the leading edge" of her thinking, as Grennon (cited in Fosnot, 1989) has described such investigatory interactions. In so doing, I hoped we would both arrive at a deeper understanding of not only what Christy's experiment had accomplished, but how she might continue her investigation.

Our collaborative research method involved extended conversations in the form of retrospective and reflective interviews. Using the open-ended interviewing techniques of qualitative research, I helped Christy recollect and reflect on her experience. Each interview was taped and reviewed, with sections transcribed and coded by Christy between meetings. Our 1- to 2-hour conversations generated 3- to 4-hour work sessions where Christy analyzed our conversations by color-coding her emerging explanations. Subsequent interviews generally began with Christy's report of her analysis efforts. Later, all the tapes were transcribed and used to assist in the preparation of this chapter.

Our collaborative effort to discover and explain the meaning of one teacher's experiment in program improvement involved three broad kinds of discussions: data generating discussions, reflection and discovery discussions, and presentation of findings discussions. Quite naturally, early interviews were dominated more by data generation and reflection, while later interviews began to focus more on presentation of findings and writing. However, all three types of discussions occurred throughout the summer and fall.

Data generating discussions not only provided me with much needed information about the school, students, and activities Christy experienced, but they also assisted Christy to discover additional information. For example, chronological questioning about the first week, first month, second month eventually led Christy to organize her writing similarly. This detailed reconstruction of events also helped Christy realize that it really took only a month to discover "what the game was" in the social studies classroom, allowing her to begin strategizing with John and Gail in earnest.

Our presentation of findings discussions explored various concepts from Christy's readings that might help her frame her emerging explanations. It required one full afternoon, for example, to explore the notions of "advocacy," "self-advocacy," "self-help," "empowerment," and "enablement" and how they might apply to Christy's experiences.

It was the reflection and discovery discussions, however, that proved the most exciting for both of us. As I listened I could hear Christy making the "sense" out of her experience that would help her design even more ambitious experiments. Indeed, my task became one of trying to anticipate the path of her thinking and offer her the concepts and metaphors around which her thinking might crystallize. In the process, I too discovered a good deal about one teacher and how she came to understand and make changes in her work. Since then I have used the discoveries in my teaching and to support other collaborative research projects with other teachers. I will return in the concluding section to both my discoveries and the directions in which they are leading me. First, however, I will illustrate, with two examples, how our reflection and discovery discussions produced changes in interpretation and discovery of meaning.

Describing the "Something Different"

During our first interview Christy described her intentions at the beginning of the fall this way:

> The idea of "empowerment"—enabling kids or people to do for themselves—was foremost in my mind. It was only a little seed trying to germinate in real dry soil; trying to figure out what it means when you enable somebody to do something. . . . The idea of changing meant that by January, for sure by May, the thing that I could judge change by was that I would not be in the regular classroom on a daily basis providing direct support.

Her plan for accomplishing this still only partially understood goal was similarly unclear. An early description revealed more about what she was changing from than what she was changing to.

> I would observe the classroom first of all and try to find out what kinds of things were happening in the class that the kids needed to understand in order to be successful. That was my first priority [and something] I had never done before. Before I always viewed the teachers as "my enemy" [and tried to discover] what they were doing that made the kid unsuccessful so I could change them.

A later interview helped her elaborate on how, as she explained to the social studies teacher, she would be able to be less present in the classroom by the end of the year.

> Because . . . things [will] have happened throughout the year to make those kids more independent—more able to be on their own. . . . It seemed apparent to me that the kids needed to learn what signals are in the environment, learn how to interpret those signals, and respond to that information in a way that was best for them.

Still later, she was able to explain the "something completely different" more fully as a shift in focus from "fixing" students (or teachers) to helping students find strategies to meet classroom demands despite their learning difficulties.

I've tried ["fixing"] for 8 years and I haven't seen a fixed kid leave my room yet. . . . That's probably why I responded in the way I did to class last summer and why I went back and tried something different—because I haven't seen anybody walk out of my room fixed. . . . We're not really ignoring the [student's] deficit, we're looking at approaching the deficit from a different standpoint—how we can compensate for that deficit. Is it possible that by building that compensation strategy [the students] begin to look at the problem in a different way and maybe understand it?

Toward the end of our conversations, she was much more specific about what she needed to do in order to achieve the "enablement" that she had been able to only incompletely describe at the beginning.

Not only do you have to have the student evaluate the effectiveness of the strategy that was tried—to tell you it worked or didn't work—you also have to have the teacher doing the same thing. Therefore, it becomes absolutely imperative that you have in your mind clearly what you are trying to accomplish. You also need to be sure to listen to what [the others] are telling you, that you should be evaluating. You need to be listening to what they are saying, and thinking about what is being accomplished. [By] keeping that in mind all the time, you know whether you are getting there or not. As soon as you start noticing that things are changing, it may be time to change to a different strategy or move on to . . . something else.

Negotiating Teacher Roles

The second example of growing understanding and changing interpretations involved the roles and relationship Christy shared with the social studies teacher. She had decided at the beginning of the year not to try to make the teacher change in favor of helping the students accommodate his demands, including those idiosyncratic ones that she might disagree with. She began by trying to find a way to personally manage her natural inclination to critique.

As I observed I was reshaping my thoughts about the teacher. "Hmm," I thought, "this guy's got a lot of good teaching practices that really can be worked with. It's not all bad. There are some things that I don't like, but that's not that important." . . . It suddenly became apparent to me that they were things that really bugged me more than they bothered him. And, that if he walked into my classroom, he would probably see things that I did that really bugged him that didn't bother me at all.

Despite this realization, she went on to report her inability to resist trying to change how the teacher prepared the unit objective sheet that he handed out as a study guide at the beginning of each unit.

I realized that if the kids knew exactly that information, they could easily "ace the test." . . . Unfortunately, his sheet was just too compressed. There was so much information that they needed to know and there was not space to write information on it at all. . . . So one of the first meetings that we had I went to him and said, "You've really outlined well the kinds of things that you're asking kids to know. Have you ever considered expanding that sheet so that there actually is space for kids to write their answers?" "Oh, that's a great idea!" he said, "Why don't you do that?"

I really didn't want to get involved in that role at all, but it was so important to me that I said, "Well, I'll give it a try." . . . His priority was that it all had to fit on one sheet of paper, [but] he didn't care if it was legal size or standard size. So I went down and played on the copy machine and, sure enough, I could enlarge it. He said if I figured it out to go ahead and run copies. I offered to come up and show him, but he said "No, no, no. I trust your judgment. Go ahead and copy." So, here I am running off 150 copies for all his classes. He thought it was wonderful. Used it. Never did it on his own. I stopped doing it after that and I realized I was upset because I thought it was a great idea. Why didn't he take it? He liked it! Then later, I had to chuckle because it was one of those things that for me was terribly important [but] it didn't bother him that it wasn't arranged in a fashion that was easy for kids to [use]. It no longer became an issue for me to try to go in and change the teacher.

Understanding these roles and relationships proved to be one of the more difficult and painful topics in our discussions. What I appreciated about the collaborative relationship Christy and I had developed was that neither of us resisted this difficult topic. During our third or fourth interview Christy reported being excited because she was beginning "to clarify some ideas."

So, it's more an equal exchange as opposed to that unequal exchange. I get the impression from the literature that we're looking at regular classroom teachers as being less equipped to handle these special ed kids we filter in to them. Therefore, they need our help as opposed to needing our support.

However, she discovered in subsequent interviews that some ways of supporting, while satisfying to the teacher, were less satisfying to her. She was indeed "not there to tell the teacher what he needed to change," but found that as a consequence she became his "classroom assistant." She did stop making copies of his unit objectives sheet, but found that her role, when she examined it from the students' perspective, was not to "teach" but to "help." Although her help expanded beyond her special education charges, she never took a turn in the "usual lecture spot." She realized that the experiment's success for her students seemed to have been purchased at the cost of her own professional identity and satisfaction.

Later, when preparing this manuscript, we talked more directly about these more personal exchanges. Christy reported that although parts of our talks "made me uncomfortable," transcribing those exchanges helped her to "resolve the conflict" by allowing her to attach different meanings to the experience. Indeed, it eventually allowed her to "identify how I fit" in the school and among the faculty in a fresh way. This altered perspective itself has led to new investigative efforts, but that is a story for another time.

CONCLUDING REMARKS

Certainly what we have reported here is a collaboration. What may be less clear is why we describe this collaboration as a *research* collaboration. Indeed, some readers might challenge our label, suggesting that our account better describes an instructional relationship, albeit one more characterized by the intimacy of mentoring than the distance of most university teaching. During preparation of this chapter, we discussed this issue directly and repeatedly. How was our activity "research" activity? What evidence is there from our notes and transcripts that something more than teaching and learning was occurring, since, we were sure, *that* was certainly occurring? Separately we agreed to write a description of our reactions to those meetings during the summer and fall and then meet to discuss the issues again.

Christy's narrative did not describe her as a student, or even a learner, but more in the role of an architect. "You gave me words to 'hang things' on. . . . Our meetings allowed me to explore my own ideas—to work through my own thoughts." Still, Christy approached the meetings with both anticipation and apprehension.

Our conversations often made me uncomfortable. I knew you would ask me probing questions that I would find confusing. I knew you would throw out thoughts that I would not be able to respond to. Still, I looked forward to our meetings knowing that I was working with a university professor who valued my ideas and wanted to help me direct my learning.

We both noticed how often Christy described Dianne's role as "helping me find catch phrases for things," "giving me words and ideas to organize my thinking," "helping me find patterns." The entire experience was about "making sense and moving on from there."

Dianne's recollections revealed that she also approached the meetings with mixed feelings. On the one hand, she was excited by the opportunity to watch Christy "make sense out of the school experiment."

I really enjoyed watching you figure things out. Each time you came, your thinking was in a different place. You had found new ways to think about and talk about not just what had happened, but what you wanted to do when you returned. I felt it was my job to give you the concepts and metaphors that would "work" for you.

As a university professor, however, she also worried about being too directive, "feeding you ideas and influencing too much how you came to interpret your experiences in that classroom."

In the end, what served to reassure us both about the research nature of our collaboration is what we both accomplished as a consequence. Christy described achieving a "new clarity" about her teaching that "went beyond attaching meaning." Indeed, she now views all her teaching as a kind of research. Her professional goals are now more likely to describe things she means "to figure out," sometimes with a systematic inquiry, and sometimes more informally.

Dianne used the experience to expand her own teaching and writing about teacher work. This has led to the development of a collaborative research strategy (Ferguson, in press) that is itself being studied more formally. It has also led to at least one other collaborative research project now being completed (Ferguson & Juniper, 1990).

Our collaborative relationship also serves to keep pulling Christy back to the university setting. Although she speaks of this pull with some bemusement, we both believe that it is a kind of evidence of the research nature of our collaboration. We plan to begin a new research venture in the near future. As with the one reported here, Christy will bring the topic and much of the data, while Dianne will provide the opportunity and structure for finding a broader insight. We have decided to focus on understanding the relationships of shared responsibility that develop, and might develop, between teachers trained originally as special educators and their general education colleagues. Christy will keep daily journal notes, augmented by some weekly reflections, which she will regularly mail to Dianne. Twice a month Dianne will call to discuss the journal notes, and the resulting collaborative conversation will be recorded for transcription and later analysis. We believe this new venture will help us further develop and understand the nature of this kind of collaborative research. Despite a certain humility about what we have not yet discovered about the power of such research relationships, we believe our experience illustrates what are certainly several key features.

First, the research responsibility is shared, but not equally in all aspects. It is the teacher member of the team who provides the occasion and much of the raw data, though the reflection and discovery discussions generate a good deal more. The professor member of the team seems to take more initial responsibility for generating possible explanations, but only initial responsibility. It is as if the teacher needs the "different way of thinking" that university professors are accustomed to in order to release her from the reflective restrictions of her setting. In our case, it is also the professor who has assumed the heavier responsibility for editing and polishing our written products. We expect this too is more a function of our different work habits than a reflection of any individual ability.

Second, the research purpose is also shared. We entered both projects trying to "figure out" and "make sense" of what had happened, is happening, and might happen in a middle school in Powell, Wyoming. We both realized that Christy's first efforts at action research had not been as well-supported or grounded in technique as either of us might have wished. Still, she was as systematic in her collection and analysis of data as experience and a certain intuitive research sense allowed her to be. We expect that subsequent efforts will reflect her growing abilities as an individual researcher and that, similarly, our joint efforts will benefit from our developing collaborative skills. Still, neither of us ever doubted that something quite interesting and provocative had occurred for both the teacher and her students. We both brought different information, research skills, and long-term interests to our initial venture, but we were clear from the beginning where our collaboration needed to lead: to achieving a rich enough understanding of what was occurring to permit improvement, elaboration, and growth for all the research participants.

Third, each collaborator used the results of the research effort both collaboratively and independently. We have prepared this summary together as a kind of closing chapter to our first collaborative research effort;

but each of us also used the experience and the results to pursue our own independent teaching and research agendas. Somehow we find this aspect most satisfying, and perhaps most important. The collaboration, quite naturally we think, supported both of us to pursue avenues of work that we each, separately, found most important and valuable. That our reflective paths seem to be crossing once again in a new collaborative research venture seems to us the best evidence both that our efforts are indeed *research* and that it is *collaborative.*

REFERENCES

Beyer, L. E., Feinberg, W., Pagano, J., & Whitson, J. A. (1989). *Preparing teachers as professionals: The role of educational studies and other liberal disciplines.* New York: Teachers College Press.

Cochran-Smith, M., & Lytle, S. L. (1990). Research on teaching or teacher research: The issues that divide. *Educational Researcher, 19*(2), 2–11.

Duckworth, E. (1986). Teaching as research. *Harvard Educational Review, 56,* 481–495.

Duckworth, E. (1987). *"The having of wonderful ideas" and other essays in teaching and learning.* New York: Teachers College Press.

Ebbutt, D. (1985). Educational action research: Some general concerns and specific quibbles. In R. G. Burgess (Ed.), *Issues in educational research: Qualitative methods* (pp. 152–176). Philadelphia, PA: Falmer Press.

Fenstermacher, G. (1978). A philosophical consideration of recent research on teacher effectiveness. In L. S. Shulman (Ed.), *Review of research in education* (Vol. 6, pp. 157–185). Itasca, IL: Peacock.

Ferguson, D. L. (in press). Teacher work groups: Getting a little help from your friends. *Teaching Exceptional Children.*

Ferguson, D. L., & Juniper, L. (1990). *A data-based programming approach for students with the most severe disabilities: An applied case study report.* Eugene: University of Oregon, Specialized Training Program.

Fosnot, C. T. (1989). *Inquiring teachers, inquiring learners: A constructivist approach for teaching.* New York: Teachers College Press.

Guba, E. G., & Lincoln, Y. S. (1989). *Fourth generation evaluation.* Newbury Park, CA: Sage.

Heshusius, L. (1989). The Newtonian mechanistic paradigm, special education, and contours of alternatives: An overview. *Journal of Learning Disabilities, 22,* 403–415.

Hitchcock, G., & Hughes, D. (1989). *Research and the teacher: A qualitative introduction to school-based research.* London: Routledge and Kegan Paul.

Kyle, D. W., & Hovda, R. A. (1987). Teachers as action researchers: A discussion of developmental, organizational and policy issues. *Peabody Journal of Education, 64*(2), 80–95.

Miller, J. L. (1990). *Creating spaces and finding voices: Teachers collaborating for empowerment*. Albany: State University of New York Press.

Richards, M. (1987). A teacher's action research study: The "bums" of 8 H. *Peabody Journal of Education, 64*(2), 65–79.

Schön, D. (1983). *The reflective practitioner*. New York: Basic Books.

Schön, D. (1987). *Educating reflective practitioners: Toward a new design for teaching and learning in the professions*. San Francisco: Jossey-Bass.

Shulman, L. S. (1987). Knowledge and teaching: Foundations of the new reform. *Harvard Educational Review, 57*, 1–22.

Sykes, Gary. (1983). Contradictions, ironies, and promises unfulfilled: A contemporary account of the status of teaching. *Phi Delta Kappan, 65*(2), 87–93.

Chapter 7

THE PUZZLE OF INCLUSION
A Case Study of Autistic Students in the Life of One High School

Philip M. Ferguson

As puzzles go, it is a large one. Matt works on it intently. He stands at a table in the back of the classroom and shifts his weight, back and forth, from one leg to the other. Occasionally he mumbles something inaudibly. The box lid with a fall landscape pictured on it leans against the wall at the back of the table. In front of the lid it looks as though the same picture had fallen, shattered into hundreds of cardboard shards. Oranges, yellows, browns, all of the autumnal hues seem splotched about on odd-shaped pieces of curves and knobs.

Matt stares at the just begun jigsaw puzzle. He picks up one piece and turns it quickly round and round with his fingers. His actions seem to speak with an eloquent ambivalence that he cannot say in words. I find myself imagining his internal conversation: "It must fit together. The piece belongs somewhere. Or is my persistence misplaced? I've fit so few together so far. But I have fit a few. I found a corner there, and several pieces of sky. More will come."

As I watch his silent struggle, I find myself thinking more about Matt. He is one of six students in the class. All are labelled as severely autistic. How do they fit together? There are over a thousand other students at the high school attended by Matt and his classmates. Where and how do they hook up with Matt? Then there are Matt's teacher, the principal, and the rest of the faculty. How do they color Matt's life? Are all of the pieces there? How much of Matt's puzzle has been finished? And where the hell is the picture on the box lid showing what it should look like when done?

Perhaps I have belabored the puzzle analogy. It suggests to me a useful perspective, however, for understanding how the integration of Matt and his classmates is and is not working. This class of six severely autistic teenagers is new to Lancaster High School this year. (Names and places have all been changed.) It is the first time that students as severely cognitively disabled as

Matt have attended Lancaster. Throughout my observations of this class and interviews with those associated with it, the one persistent theme was "We're not finished here, yet." Conclusions were tentative. Progress was juxtaposed with new and remaining problems. Remembering how things had been before was common. There was a sense of incompleteness about the class and its integration into the flow of the high school. The incompleteness appeared more basic than the normal efforts to fine tune a program while maintaining its current structure and organization. Agreement on the final goal was not clearly present. No one seemed sure they were all working on the same puzzle.

All of this makes an evaluation of Matt's class more difficult. The deficiencies in the nature and degree of integrated programming for Matt and the others are easily discovered. Mel, the class' teacher, quickly acknowledges them. But a snapshot judgment of the program's success or failure is too limited. The transitional, groping character of the program makes the history, the process, and the future as important as the details of Matt's day at the time I observed. How the people at Lancaster High are solving the puzzle is more informative than how much of the solution they have found.

PIECES OF THE PUZZLE:
THE STUDENTS AND TEACHERS

You need a feeling for who Matt, his classmates, and his teachers are before their past and future can be appreciated. This requires more than a one-paragraph description of the class. You cannot ask the students how they feel about their new school, or the typical students who sometimes stare at them in the halls, or the new requirements and risks. You cannot ask because they cannot say. But you can imagine how it must be puzzling for them, too.

Occasionally, as I watched the students—in the lunchroom, a shop class, or just walking down the long corridors at Lancaster—I would be reminded that it was not inanimate shapes that adults were moving about to see who fit where. These puzzle pieces were fitting themselves in, finding room for their own odd behavioral bumps and curves. We never just "mainstream." We mainstream students, people. They need to be seen and felt as helping to find their own solutions.

Mel and John, the classroom aide, are important too, of course. Both are short, unassuming men. And the class depends on them for much of its tone and structure. Their planning and performance at the high school have been crucial to the program's success. But they will speak for themselves when I describe the history of the class.

The six students in class range between 14 and 17 years old. All the students have been taught by Mel for several years (last year was an exception). He knows firsthand how each of them has changed. Mel describes his students as being in the lower half of the functional range for autistic children in general.

> It's a pretty low functioning class. I've certainly worked with kids labelled autistic who were much higher functioning. Lorna is the highest functioning student in this class. If there is such a thing as an average autistic kid, then Lorna would probably be at that level.

Lorna is a tall buxom black girl with a toothy smile almost always on her face. Although she says very little spontaneously, she seems to understand almost everything said to her. Along with Matt, she is the most independent and observant of the students. During the times I observed, for instance, Lorna was the only student to come over to me and say "Hi." It was only once, and in the middle of gym class, but it was the only verbal communication any of the students initiated with me.

Lorna often finishes the work samples used in class with time to spare. On such occasions her favorite activity is listening to music on the record player at the front of the room. She will go to the phonograph, choose an album, and put it on, all independently. Occasionally Mel has to remind her to put the needle down. Mel laughingly mentioned how they are trying to broaden Lorna's taste in music. She would customarily sort through a stack of 10 or 12 albums and always choose the same one: The Platters. While I was there, Lorna's taste, to Mel's relief, expanded to include the "Shaft" movie music.

Lorna does have some noticeable autistic behaviors. One hand is often at her ear, and she will rock while making quiet noises. Her smile has that frozen quality of an expression unchanged regardless of the situation.

Almost 18, Matt is the oldest member of the class. He is a good-sized (5'10" or so), well-built, handsome fellow. In many ways his overt behavior is the least bizarre or noticeably different in the class. Matt is a hard worker to the point of compulsiveness. He becomes noticeably bothered if asked to switch activities for some reason before a task is completed. Matt is also the only student who still lives in an institution, a source of no small irritation to Mel.

> You want to see what an institution can do to a capable person? Matt's a perfect example. He is so reluctant to do things spontaneously. He's learned *not* to do *anything* unless told. Sometimes he'll want to do something so badly, and it will be something perfectly

harmless like stopping in the hall for a drink of water, but instead of just doing it he'll get agitated and look for me or John. Or in class he might start rocking, but never call out for attention. He'll just sit there and get frustrated until one of us notices. It's really a shame. He's such a reliable and capable kid. It's almost like you have to force him to enjoy himself.

If given the direction, Matt can go independently anywhere he needs to in the school. Mel, for example, often gives Matt the key to the classroom and lets him go back early from lunch. It's not a short walk. As with Lorna, Matt understands almost everything said to him. He also has some good expressive language, but speaks so softly that you can barely hear him. With his skills, ability to observe and imitate, and generally reticent behavior, Matt has been the easiest student for Mel to integrate into several typical classes.

Bob is a tall skinny boy who is 16 years old. He is perhaps the quietest in the class, in terms of making sounds. Bob's face is usually expressionless. He has few of the odd perseverative hand movements of some of the other students. Bob counts out loud with a slow, deliberate speech that needs to be cued often. Unlike Lorna and Matt, Bob does not seem to have any sight word skills. And Bob is less adept than Lorna and Matt at learning from models.

An example of the comparative learning rates occurred once while I was watching the class in the weight training room. More on a whim than anything else, John decided to try to get Matt and Bob to jump rope. John modeled how and then had the two boys try. After a few false starts, Matt was making slow but successful efforts at swinging the rope around and timing his jump. Bob, on the other hand, was less successful: not jumping, forgetting to swing the rope, and other mishaps.

One envisioned Matt being able to jump rope fairly soon if the task was worked on. For Bob the complexity of the action seemed much more baffling. One sensed that several much more structured steps would need to be established first. But, while it would take longer, learning the skill still seemed possible.

Fred is the only student who still demonstrates any aggressive behavior. The behavior is episodic in nature, but is more troublesome because the incidents occur most often outside the classroom. Mel was working hard during my visits to isolate the incidents so as to better determine what precipitated them.

I should not exaggerate this. Fred is not a large boy, even for 14. And the episodes in question consist mainly of striking out, kicking, or hitting, but not with vicious or really dangerous force. As Mel described it:

Actually, you see worse stuff in the halls here every day. People beating on each other. And that's between friends. The trouble is Fred isn't selective about whom he strikes out at, when he does it. It's more dangerous for him, really, in that he might pick the wrong person some time.

Fred does all right, usually, as long as he and his hands are both kept occupied. When he is "tuning out," as John referred to it, Fred is calm but flicks his fingers in front of his eyes and chuckles. If not reminded by John or Mel, Fred often walks down the halls this way. He stares at his fingers, laughs, and seems oblivious to where he is going, but seldom runs into anyone even when the halls are crowded.

Fred has some of the best expressive language skills, but often does not use them well. What speech therapists call "pragmatic speech" is where Fred falters. You can hear him at his desk carrying on an elaborate, articulate conversation, but completely irrelevant to the time and place. "Go to bed and be quiet. Goddamn it, go to bed." At other times, in the cafeteria line for one, Fred can tell the server what food he wants, respond to questions, and do it all in very understandable speech. In short, Fred is probably the most unpredictable of the students.

Danielle and Josh are the two lowest functioning students in the class. They are both 14 but are even smaller than Fred. Their desks are the only two in the class that are placed close together. While the other four students often work independently on the assembly of tasks, Josh and Danielle usually need Mel or John with them to keep them working on their less complicated jobs.

Perhaps because I remembered similar feelings of my own as a teacher, I think I detected a slightly greater pride and pleasure in Mel with the progress made by Josh and Danielle over the years he has known them. The sense is not that Josh's and Danielle's relative status has changed to surpass the other students. Rather, it is the teacher's instinct that "With these two, the small gains are even more cherished." One's work with them, and their own efforts, are even more crucial, not less so, because of the starting point.

One afternoon, after Danielle had missed her bus, leaving Mel to take her home on his own, he recounted their history together.

When I first got her she was straight out of Troy [a large, infamous state institution for the retarded] and it was incredible. It was literally like a wild animal in a cage. She never stood still. She was constantly running around the room, screaming, pulling huge clumps of her hair out. No communication at all, no toileting skills, no eye contact, no eating skills. [This was about 7 years ago.]

Mel told of a similar if less dramatic change in Josh. It was after a scene in class where Josh had spit on the floor and been taken by Mel through an elaborate clean-up procedure.

> You have to understand what Josh's behavior used to be like. Three things characterized his acting out. He would take his shoes off, scratch, and spit. Now we have him down to just spitting. So there really has been a lot of progress. Sometimes he'll go 2 or 3 days straight without spitting at all.

Now, Danielle lives with a foster family and is a slender attractive girl who is eager to please. And Josh, who has always lived at home, is usually mild mannered, as Mel says. A little whining sometimes, but no real resistance unless the situation is new or unpleasant (e.g., barber's clippers). With both, only remnants of the former wild behavior can still be seen.

Mel and John communicate with Danielle with signs. I counted around five or six that Danielle used regularly. She understands 15 or 20. She is happy, curious, and occasionally manipulative. Mel frets sometimes that the skills Danielle has are not used at home as much as they could be. "She spends a lot of time just watching TV, pulling her hair, and sucking her thumb." But Mel also feels that the setting is an incomparable improvement over Danielle's institutional life. He works with the foster mother in a low pressure way.

Josh's mother has been much more involved over the years. Mel's concern, in fact, is that she may be at the point where a break is necessary. There are several other children at home, and the fatigue of years of attention to Josh's needs and demands is beginning to crush instead of just erode the mother's energy. Josh is now spending weekends at a group home near his family. He is scheduled for a full-time switch in the near future.

In class, Josh is the moper, the sad sack. He moves slowly, droopy-eyed, through the activities. Almost any physical activity is viewed with disdain by Josh. Mel and John push him to exert himself. When allowed as a reward, Josh likes most of all to play with a set of keys, quietly entranced with their jangling and shapes. Mel says, "At least I have him 'self-stimming' for something I want, rather than for just anything."

THE HISTORY

Students are not the only people who change and develop over time. So do teachers. Even administrators. And the programs that all three of these groups are associated with have stories to tell as well. At least, the good ones do. The history of how Matt's class came to be at Lancaster is also vital to understanding its problems and its strengths. What has happened to Mel and the students over the past 5 years and what happened at Lancaster High before they arrived constitute a large part of this puzzle.

"Discovering" Autism

Six years ago there were no students like Matt and Lorna, much less Josh and Danielle, at Lancaster. There were no such students at any public school in town. Mel and several of his current students were just beginning their relationship in the local ARC (Association for Retarded Citizens) school. Mel talked with me at length about how the changes started. He tells the story better than I could.

> It started at the ARC in 1975. What happened was that I and several other teachers at the school who had what you would now call TMR [trainable mentally retarded] classes repeatedly told the administration that we each had one or two kids who showed autistic characteristics. Usually we had 10 or 12 kids in each class, and the autistic kids just weren't benefitting from being in that large a group. So we got together and got some parents together and put a little pressure on the administration, and also on the county, because that was where the money came from.
>
> Well, they got the class set and asked me if I would be the teacher. I didn't know anything about autism then but I said, "OK, I'll try it." I thought maybe we could start off and get somewhere with it. Unfortunately, the psychologist they had hired to help start the program left before September. So come fall, I was really groping. I kept pushing the ARC to fill the position, to get someone in there with me who had some experience with autistic kids. Finally they got Danny.

Danny is an important person in the development of the class. Both he and Mel came over to the public school system later. Danny remains a consultant for Mel's class as a school psychologist. He visits the class one morning a week, and Mel still uses him for support and advice. Their working relationship seems much closer than that regularly seen between a teacher and the school psychologist.

Danny does not look or talk like a typical school psychologist. He has long hair and a full unkempt black beard. His attire tends to be very casual, running toward flannel shirts and blue jeans or cords. He is a very political person. When I asked him what he would look for if he were hiring a new

teacher for disabled kids, he answered, "Ideology first." Danny sees education as, most important, a part of a larger political philosophy.

Mel described how his association with Danny began.

> The ARC didn't want to hire Danny because of the way he looked.
> But I was on the interview committee and said, "Look, if this guy
> has some of the answers that we need, then don't worry about what
> he looks like. Close your eyes and hire him." So it worked out well.
> Danny was able to give me the structure I needed. When I look back
> on it now, it wasn't much at all. But it helped us to get through the
> first year and then we built on that. I guess the big thing we did that
> year was to toilet train all the kids.

Making the Jump to Public School

Mel's program, with several of the same students he has now as well as
others, continued at the private, segregated ARC school for 3 years. Mel
tried to refer some of the students out to their home districts but kept
getting rejections. The program was the "dumping ground" for the severely autistic kids, and the separate school districts kept refusing the
referrals because they lacked any programs for those students.

Danny and Mel finally approached the big city school district with
the proposal to start a public school program. To Mel's surprise, the
school district was receptive to the idea. He attributes the receptivity,
ironically, to the pressure created by another private, but integrated, program for autistic children that had started the year after his class. The
school, called Koinonia, was affiliated with the university in the city and at
that time had, to Mel's mind, students from a different, more educated
middle class background. Equally important, the Koinonia school only
went up to age 7 or 8. After that, other programs would have to be found
for the children attending the school. Mel gave me his perception of what
happened.

> The thing was, the parents of the class over at ARC were not very
> vocal. Except for Josh's mother, they were pretty much people who
> were having a real hard time making ends meet. They just didn't
> have it all together. And they weren't the kind of people who were
> going to go out and push for services. But over at Koinonia you had
> a group of parents who were really gung ho. People who were
> really going to push to see that their kids got the right kind of pro-
> gram after they left Koinonia. Well, I think the district was really in-
> timidated by the Koinonia model of full integration, and by these

parents who weren't going to take no for an answer. So I think they decided, "Well, before we go whole hog with this model, let's get a self-contained class started first."

Of course, as with most programs in this district, it was thrown together at the last minute. They hired Danny in July and me in August 1978. We quickly got our act together and just moved the class over to John Davis [an elementary school].

Mel and Danny made efforts over the next 2 years at John Davis School to decrease gradually the amount of segregation their self-contained class still had. The classroom was moved nearer the higher grade rooms after first being among the lower ones. Four of the six students now with Mel at Lancaster were in this class at Davis. So even then, the students were too old to be in an elementary school. But, as Danny put it, "We were trying to infiltrate a building, to get more and more acceptance."

The 1979–80 school year saw another big change for Mel and for the school. Given the history, it is relevant to understanding Mel's style and procedure. And it is not without irony. Mel tells it.

See in '79 was when they brought the Koinonia model over to John Davis. The only trouble was that the teacher who came over from Koinonia, too, had some real problems. She had no trouble with the special kids, well, nothing she couldn't have dealt with. But she couldn't handle the regular street-wise kids. Koinonia had typical kids, but they weren't typical kids. At least not the typical kids you get mixed in at John Davis. The kids just really intimidated her and sort of took over the class. It was sad. She had pictured herself in that sort of role and it just didn't work out. She had to leave just for her own mental health.

So anyway, the principals asked me to take over this integrated class. It was a big change because I had never worked with regular kids before. So anyway, I knew what was going on in the class, because I had been in there to observe. I went in with a real tough guy attitude to regain control of the class. And I was at least able to make it go for a year.

Lancaster at Last: A Matter of Principal

One can easily imagine Mel having stayed with the integrated class. It was a model program, one of the first of its kind in the country. And Mel had made it go for a year. But the development of the self-contained class was also continuing.

Against the background of the previous 5 years, it is easier to appreciate Danny's and Mel's efforts to get the class established at Lancaster at last. It also becomes increasingly clear how despite a soft-spoken, pragmatic style, Mel is able to discern and use the politics of a situation if he thinks it will help put more of the puzzle together.

The proposals for a self-contained class of severely autistic students at Lancaster were made in the spring of 1980. Mel and Danny had seen major progress in school district services to autistic children over the previous 3 years. Indeed, they had been active participants in that process. The move to Lancaster was seen as a natural and needed continuation of the process.

However, events at Lancaster had also changed during the recent past. As with most public high schools in America's cities, Lancaster had gone through a period of dramatic transformation during the 2 decades preceding my case study (the 1960s and 1970s), repeatedly punctuated by specific incidents and crises of racial, economic, and educational origins. It is within this larger history that the evolution of special education at Lancaster occurred. A rich and detailed account of those years at Lancaster (Grant, 1988) has provided a useful perspective of this larger context. Grant's book includes a discussion of how special education at Lancaster participated in the tumultuous events of that era. Without going into the level of detail and complexity available there, it may still be useful to briefly describe the pattern of expansion in special education at Lancaster as background for the collaboration of the "regular" staff with Mel and the special education administrators.

In common with most schools over the past 5 years, Lancaster has been fighting an increasingly difficult battle against declining enrollment. And at the same time as the total enrollment decreased, the percentage of black students from lower-income families increased. High academic achievement of students, a former priority in which the school took pride, has of necessity been replaced by pressure to serve the different needs of a different type of student. Discipline, vocational training, remedial classes, racial tolerance, and balance became the new focus of Lancaster High. It has been a vicious circle. Lancaster's staff and faculty want to maintain or regain an image of academic quality so as not to lose more students from professional, upwardly mobile families to private schools and suburbs. But the school must also serve an expanding nonacademic student population, if just to maintain tranquility.

In the face of this situation, the principal at Lancaster, Hank Belsky, has viewed special education students as one way of stabilizing his population base. As he said to one interviewer, "To put it bluntly, I need bodies. . . . If students are desirable, the other principals will fight over giving them up. Special education provided me with a choice because principals don't fight for the handicapped, at least not yet." Belsky also had other, more humanitarian instincts, of course. But the numbers game had to be played. As a result, approximately 80 of Lancaster's 1,100 students are now labelled as handicapped.

But there have been problems, too. As an administrator, Belsky is concerned that his school be seen as "one that works," one whose programs are successful. Yet, in his dealings with the central office special education staff, Belsky feels he has not been supported. He has taken on special classes only to have promised staff and services pulled out from under him. As a result, Belsky was reluctant when the proposal to move the autistic students was first made to him. Mel's description of the events is, again, clearer than mine would be.

> Well, I was on the planning committee last year that worked on the move over here. And Belsky's first reaction was "No way, I don't want those kids here." I think in his heart he's really sensitive to special ed kids. But in the past he's been burned by the special ed department. He's taken programs that he thought they were going to back, and then they didn't. So I think he was taking a little bit different approach, like a bargaining position, just to make sure that they followed through on their commitments.

Danny was somewhat less charitable in his assessment of Belsky's initial opposition.

> We finally had to go to Freund [the superintendent] and he more or less ordered Belsky to take the class. Of course, now he seems to be 100% behind us. He's really a success-oriented guy and doesn't want problems in his school. The program hasn't caused him any problems so now he's a big supporter.

Even with the class set to go into Lancaster in September, the concern and maneuvering did not stop. The styles and attitudes of Mel and Belsky became even more important. It was the coloring of the puzzle pieces now, not the shapes, that had to match. Again, I will let Mel tell the story.

> I know that they were having trouble finding a teacher for this class. I know two or three people had turned down the job, and I was really worried about it. The class was coming over here and every- thing was all set. There was just no teacher. I thought, if they put

a new teacher in there, or transfer someone who doesn't want to come, the program is going to fall apart. You have to know Belsky. He's a real tough character. If things don't go right he just blows his top. He's got the special ed administrators all really intimidated. They're all scared of him. You know, he just comes on real strong, no tact, just blows doors down. But he gets results.

Anyway, the middle of the summer, the idea hits me—"Why don't I go over there?" I knew Belsky and had worked for him before as a soccer coach. I thought I could get along with him. And I felt that the kids needed somebody who had some experience teaching them. So I decided to do it, but I had to set it up right.

First, I checked out a friend of mine who taught at Koinonia to see if he would consider taking my integrated class at John Davis School. He said "Yeah," so then I mentioned to Tunney [the director of special education programming for the district] that I would be willing to go over to Lancaster if he could find someone to fill the bill at John Davis. Well, he just kind of panicked and then after a few minutes I said, "Oh, maybe I know someone." Anyway, it all worked out and so by August I knew I was coming over here to Lancaster. And I'm pleased with the move.

SORTING OUT THE PROBLEMS

To say the least, Lancaster High did not roll out the red carpet for Mel, John (he moved over from John Davis, too), and the six autistic students. There was a history at Lancaster that all of them had to contend with. There was their own history from which they could learn. For Mel, the move to Lancaster was the fourth new program in 6 years, the third new building. He almost seemed like a pitcher who never got past the first inning, but never gave up any runs either.

Making It Stick

When I began my observations of Matt's class, the second semester was about one month old. The time since September had seen some new problems arise and some old ones continue. It had also seen some progress. The faculty and staff, the regular students, and the class curriculum all presented different issues that needed to be addressed if the program was to have the success that Belsky demanded and Mel sought. Some of the more persistent problems of the past year are described below.

Fear of the unfamiliar

The faculty, for the most part, knew nothing about autism. The questions would be put to Mel and Danny, "Are they dangerous?" "Can they talk?" "What's wrong with them in the first place?" "Why do they look at their fingers?" "What can we be expected to do with them?"

But at least when questions are asked, they can be answered. The other side of this problem for Mel was that teachers were not asking him enough questions. They were not reporting things that bothered them. One specific example of this involved Josh. Josh had never been in a setting where the men wore ties and coats. Josh quickly became fascinated and would stop male teachers in the hall to "check out their labels," as Mel referred to it. He would lift their ties and look under the coats, but to Mel the teachers seemed to take it in stride. It was only by accident, at a party, that Mel found out that the behavior was causing quite a lot of comment among the faculty.

> Jeez, I didn't realize everyone was that concerned about it. I got right on it, and we ended it right away, by having Josh keep his hands in his pockets. But it upset me. I want people to tell me right away about those things so I can nip them in the bud.

Dumping

A more stubborn problem mentioned to me by several teachers was a more generalized resentment at having special ed students "dumped" into their classes. It was a problem from Lancaster's history, not Mel's, but one that he now had to deal with. As the shop teacher explained it, "Some of the students have just shown up in class and it might be a week or a month—whenever I finally asked—before I would find out that the kid was EMR [Educably Mentally Retarded] or something. The communication has often been totally at my initiative or just nonexistent." The home economics teacher spoke of similar experiences in the past. "The special ed students were just scheduled in, two or three together, and no one told us what their problems were. And then we would have all kinds of discipline problems and wouldn't understand why."

Courtesy stigma

A third complaint voiced by some of the teachers mirrors the dilemma of Lancaster as a whole. Those teachers in subjects most commonly chosen for mainstreaming feared that the "brighter" students were not taking the class as a result. Again the home economics teacher:

> I feel bad that more and more of the academically inclined kids are staying away from home economics. And sometimes I feel it's because they see the special ed kids in my classes. I think maybe they say, "Well, I don't belong in that class; it has special ed kids in it." It's frustrating.

Student acceptance

The typical students have presented different problems. Two overlapping groups of students have surprised Mel by their negative reactions to his students: blacks and below average students. Mel remembered the first few months at Lancaster with a sort of bemused relief that the worst seemed over. "When we first got here, last fall, and we would walk down the hall, it was funny. The crowd would just part in front of us. Everyone would just back up against the walls." While I saw for myself that this extreme reaction had largely disappeared, other problems still troubled Mel.

> Here it's been just the opposite from John Davis. At Davis the students who were having some problems or were more disadvantaged really liked working with my kids. The sharper students couldn't have cared less. Here at Lancaster it's the high achievers who are most interested, and the low achievers who don't want anything to do with us. Maybe it's some kind of adolescent peer pressure.
>   And the reaction of the black students has bothered me too. They react very differently from the white students. I don't know why—maybe they are just more open about it. But when one of my kids touches them or something, they might jump away. I even had a couple of them scream, "Eek, he touched me," and that kind of stuff. It has nothing to do with the color of the kid that's touching them. If Danielle or Lorna [the two black students in Mel's class] walk up to a black girl, she will probably still back away. It's better than it was. We try to deal with it on an individual basis. John [who is also black] has gotten some track girls to come in the room at least, but they don't stay very long.

One student who would fall into the high achiever category and who had volunteered in Mel's class, verified that the general student reaction was less than perfect. However, she found it to be worse for the milder handicapped.

They just ignore the autistic kids, or maybe back off and stare. It's the retarded kids who really get brutalized. There's one girl who is always running around crying because they tease her, and another guy whom the students lead on without him knowing they are making fun of him. It seems like the ones who are retarded get it the worst.

Progress and Tactics

Fortunately, the problems have lessened. The picture should not be given of an intolerant faculty and a mean spirited student body. I will discuss below some specific efforts made by Mel and John. But my observations and interviews revealed a school that seemed at least tolerant of the autistic students. The faculty I talked with who had Matt or Lorna in their classes reported satisfaction with the way things had gone. If they were not "experts" on autistic behavior yet, they at least trusted Mel's and John's judgments about who was appropriate for a particular class and who was not.

The general students are not yet beating down Mel's door to volunteer. However, extreme reactions toward the autistic students seem to be the exception rather than the rule now. As one student put it in speaking of the disabled students in general: "I don't see any reason why they shouldn't be here. You might get your toes run over by someone in a wheelchair, but other than that there's no big problem."

Mel, too, has sensed the increased acceptance.

At the beginning, no one knew me or knew the kids. But as time went by and they saw us in the halls and met me and John, they've come not to think much of us, and some of them have shown real interest. The acceptance—or at least the tolerance—has really come around, I think. We've still got a ways to go, but I think we've made real progress this year.

PUTTING THE PIECES TOGETHER: SOME CORNERS OF INCLUSION

What integration and acceptance there is of the autistic students at Lancaster today is not the result of any one person's efforts. No single person is to blame for the great deal that remains undone. What exists has evolved rather than erupted. And the process is continuing. Nonetheless, some specific examples of partial success need to be mentioned.

Mel's and John's Integration

As the teacher and the classroom aide, Mel and John needed to include themselves—as well as the students—in the life of Lancaster. They set about accomplishing this with several specific strategies.

Extracurricular involvement with regular students

Both Mel and John helped coach this year. Mel was the soccer coach for the junior varsity team and John was an assistant track coach. These activities have had great advantages for a more rapid acceptance by both faculty and students. Both Mel and John know many more students than would have been possible otherwise. They are known to the students in a wholly different context than as teachers of disabled kids. The administration appreciates the assistance with athletics, and a favorable relationship has been furthered in that area. The assistant principal gave me his assessment: "Mel has really made himself a part of the faculty. Just another teacher. The soccer coaching helped that, I think." The fact that Mel sees it as "a great diversion" is not insignificant either.

Providing information

In addition to a 45-minute inservice session for the teachers, Mel has gone out of his way to find opportunities to talk to classes of students about autism. Two student volunteers in Mel's class came out of an advanced psychology class to which Mel had spoken. On another occasion Mel talked about autism before several sections of a freshman English class, as part of a unit the students were doing on note-taking.

Besides these are all the informal occasions—in the teachers' lounge, after school, in the lunchroom—when a question can be asked and answered individually. The attitude of openness and eagerness to answer questions has been useful and appreciated by the other faculty.

Finding the path of least resistance

Danny describes Mel's technique for infiltrating a new building as one of "working very hard, but quietly, to break down the doors without alienating people." An example of this is Mel's acceptance of a home economics class for Matt and Lorna that has all disabled kids in it. It is a new program at Lancaster this year. The home economics teachers had been very distressed by what they saw as "dumping" disabled kids into their classes. This new class was the solution they wanted to try. Mel's comment to me was, "It's not really integrated but that's how the teacher wanted to do it. So I went along."

On another occasion Mel explained his basic approach to such situations.

> I look for soft spots. I tell myself, "Just keep it real cool and low key. Just take one step at a time." Because there is no way six kids could come in and upset a school with a thousand plus students. That's just not going to happen. If there's a choice that has to be made, then the six kids will be gone.

Use of generic services

This might seem to be a fairly obvious action to take when integrating disabled students. Mel and John certainly look for ways to do this. An ironic discovery by Mel this year is that because many of the materials ordered for the class were not provided by the special education department, he has been forced to exploit the resources of the high school even more creatively than he might have otherwise. Mel is now skeptical about seeking much special help. Instead he would prefer consultants to come in and advise him on how to adapt the existing services at the school to his children's needs. Shop, home economics, the weight room, the swimming pool, and vocational education are all services that Mel hopes to use even more.

The Students' Integration

It must be stated first that Matt and his classmates spend most of their time apart from typical students, in a self-contained class. Only Matt and Lorna now go out for any classes. And only Matt's shop class is a truly integrated setting. (An integrated gym class was being started for both Matt and Lorna at the end of my time at Lancaster.) Nonetheless, the degree of integration accomplished by Matt and the others is not negligible.

Individual mainstreaming

Five mornings a week, Matt goes to a shop class with John. It is a regular class and it seems to be working well. The shop teacher is pleased. In fact, she reported to me that Matt presented fewer problems than did the more mildly handicapped students. The same is true for the home economics teacher. She has both Matt and Lorna in her class, assisted by Mel.

Two factors contribute to the success of what mainstreaming has occurred. First, Mel or John accompany their students to the classes they attend. The material presented is adapted by them to be appropriate for Matt or Lorna. Flash cards are used for home economics vocabulary. Demonstration is used in shop class. Above all, Mel communicates with the regular classroom teacher before the student arrives and maintains communication about how things are going.

Besides this support, a second factor, which cannot be denied, is that it is precisely because Lorna and Matt are more severely handicapped that their presence is less disruptive. Neither of them talks or is actively disruptive. As long as the teacher can rely on Mel and John to communicate with and supervise their students, the teacher is in fact less "burdened" by the autistic students than by other students who are talking out, requiring attention, and unassisted. This supports the premise that successful integration is in many ways more easily begun with severely disabled students, despite the fact that the opposite direction is the one most often used.

Large-group integration

The settings in this category include the lunchroom, the weight room, and the hallways. All six of the students are in these settings, usually together, alongside typical students. The stress has been on reducing the bizarre behaviors of the students in these situations as well as encouraging as much independence as possible. The six have reached the point where they can navigate the corridors fairly independently, especially Matt, Lorna, and Bob. At least the students do not march together. Mel has tried to promote further interaction by telling staff and students not to ignore his students if one of them is doing something inappropriate.

The cafeteria staff seem especially good at requiring Mel's students to indicate their desires, but at the same time not allowing them to delay significantly other students in line. Some students will now tell Bob or Fred to stop if they see one of them picking up garbage off the floor. Mel has found that if he asks a student to help out for a minute, he is seldom refused.

There is still too much clustering. All the students sit together at lunch, for example, even though someone surveying a crowded lunchroom would be hard pressed to pick out the table of autistic kids. All the students, boys and girls, go to the weight room together, although such groups are usually separated by sex. But a start has been made. And Matt and his classmates seem thoroughly to enjoy the casual turmoil of the normal high school.

Peer tutoring

Mel's shower training routine for his students is an example of integration because he used student volunteers to assist him with Danielle. The two students would accompany Danielle to the locker room, help her out of her clothes and into a swimsuit, help her get dressed again later, and follow her back to class. Not a lot. Just two typical students and Danielle, and for a relatively brief time. But the two students learned that they could communicate with Danielle, that they could teach her to do things and that she had different moods just as they did.

Danny described what he hoped the two girls got out of the shower training volunteer work.

> They are at least more comfortable. And when they are someplace else with some other kids, and someone's badmouthing our kids, I have a feeling that they would feel pretty bad at least, and might speak up and say something. The attitudes change slowly, even unconsciously at first. But at least the chances of them putting these kids down will be reduced. We need to have a lot more students go through that kind of experience.

THE FUTURE

The last section of the puzzle, a rather large section, has not been filled in yet. Indeed, the form and content of the final solution are far from clear. There are plenty of problems that have to be resolved.

One of the reasons for the success so far of the limited classroom integration of Matt and Lorna is the degree of support that Mel and John have provided to the regular teachers. One of them is with Matt and Lorna whenever a regular classroom is used. This has created an atmosphere of trust and interaction between Mel and the regular teachers. But Mel and John can only be in one place at a time. If the integration of the severely autistic students into the regular high school classes is to expand, one of two things will have to occur. Either the regular teachers will have to work with Mel's students without individual classroom support, or more people will be needed to provide that support.

To go very far in the first direction risks undermining the basis of the successful experiences so far. The result of the lack of support historically at Lancaster can be seen in the form of the new home economics class there. The absence of more systematic integration of disabled students who have been at Lancaster longer and whose handicap is milder than that of Mel's students reminds one of Belsky's complaint of lack of support from the special education department. It also suggests an absence of creative solutions to that lack of personnel by the staff already in place at Lancaster.

In the other direction lies the financial reality that more funded positions for classroom assistance are not likely to come flooding down from the central school district offices. One possible way around this is an increased use of peer tutors as support persons in integrated settings. One of the two student volunteers used by Mel this year suggested this as a solution.

> I'm on the Superintendent's council, and we had a session on the handicapped. I suggested that they use students who are interested in special ed as a way to get workers in the class, and they would get credit for it. With the cutbacks and having fewer aides, it might help that way too.

Questions of quality and continuity arise with the use of typical students in this manner, of course, but it is an idea that Mel has thought of too. Indeed, such a use of students might be more productive than having them "tripping over each other," as Mel put it, if they were all in his classroom at once.

Perhaps another option in thinking about this support problem is that many of the older autistic students should be integrated more into the community than into classes within the school building. At this point in Matt's life is it more important that he get into an integrated art class or learn how to ride on an integrated city bus; buy food in an integrated grocery store; or wash dishes, clean test tubes, and assemble parts in an integrated job setting? Supervision would still be needed, but the pool of people available for such a function, and the possible arrangements for accomplishing it, would be enlarged.

At the same time as reducing the pressures for integration in the building itself, such a community curriculum would also address a main concern Mel currently has about the quality of the prevocational and vocational curriculum. Mel envisions a "transitional class" of older autistic students such as Matt, Lorna, and Bob, who would spend at least half of each day away from the school. Job skills, leisure skills, and daily living skills could all be worked on away from the high school setting. Such a curriculum is not unusual now for many unlabelled students at Lancaster.

Vocational curriculum is currently perhaps the weakest part of Mel's program. It is a problem Mel worries about as much as increased integration. The two areas are not unrelated, of course. One of the big programming dilemmas of the future will be whether to train Matt and the others for the kinds of sheltered workshop jobs that exist in the community (although only after being on a long waiting list) or to train them for more integrated jobs that do not exist but would be more meaningful. Matt clearly has most of the skills needed for the kind of segregated, dead-end assembly jobs common to most workshops. The question is could Matt not just as well be trained to work in a local hospital sterilizing instruments, a local restaurant busing tables, or a local grocery store stocking shelves? I think he could. But would there be a job for him when he left Mel's class? Is it part of Mel's job, or Belsky's, to create those employment opportunities? If not, whose job is it? How this dilemma is solved in the next 5 years will go far in deciding what Matt's puzzle finally looks like.

A final area of concern to several people at Lancaster was summarized for me in a conversation with the vice principal: "There is going to be a revolt of gifted and even just above average kids and their parents about the school focusing on the lower third of the student population in terms of services. It's already happening and it will get worse."

The description of the recent past at Lancaster told of a tension between how the school has to see itself and how it would like to. The changing population has put the high school through a transition of character that is still not completed. Should the school strive for academic excellence when most of its students just need a job? Should it become a technical school whose students can fix a car but may have trouble reading a book? Or will it end up having neither academic quality nor vocational relevance by trying to have both?

The statement by the vice principal about the coming revolt was uttered as much in support as in warning of such a backlash. It illustrated for me the split personality I observed in the school's administration and staff. There seems to be an organizational ambivalence at Lancaster toward its disabled students. The ambivalence is analogous to Matt's as he confronted the jigsaw puzzle. There is no formative vision at Lancaster of how it wants to treat its handicapped students. There is serious doubt among some that services to disabled students should be expanded at all. The danger exists that the puzzle will be left undone, judged not to be worth the effort. That judgment is not shared by Mel or Danny, certainly. Right now it is a judgment only vaguely formed and often unsaid. Nonetheless, it is there.

There are two ways to solve a jigsaw puzzle. In the first, one goes from piece to piece, noting the shapes, finding two that fit, then finding a third, and so on. Little reference is made to what the final result will look like. If you put enough pieces together, the final product will emerge. In a sense this is how the history and progress and tactics of Lancaster High and Mel's class have proceeded. One step has led to the next. Events seemed to coincide nicely. People were not looking for a final picture to guide them. Or, if they looked, they seldom told each other what they saw.

The second way to solve a puzzle is by constantly keeping in mind the picture that is to be reproduced. Pieces are sought that match a particular detail of content and color in the desired image. The pieces gain their meaning only as part of the goal pursued, not as individual shapes. The future of Mel and his students at Lancaster requires a shift to this latter approach. An agreement will have to be reached at some point soon on just what the final goal is.

Of course, little of this question of approach is of any moment for Matt. He just keeps working on the puzzle. When I left Mel's class for the last time, Matt was still working on it. He had a long way to go. But he is compulsive about these things. I hope, with some help along the way, that Matt finishes the puzzle. I hope everything will finally fit together for him.

METHODOLOGICAL EPILOGUE

This case study was originally completed as one part of a much larger study of integration and mainstreaming of students with handicaps (Bogdan & Barnes, 1979; Bogdan & Kugelmass, 1984). I gathered the data over a period of about 4 months in the fall and winter of the 1981–82 school year. During that time I interviewed more than 15 adults with various connections to the autistic students at Lancaster High. These individuals included teachers (from both regular and special education), administrators, and support staff (classroom aides, cafeteria workers, custodial personnel). In Mel's case, there were multiple interviews done over the course of the study. In addition, I interviewed five students without disabilities who either participated in the class as "peer tutors" or had some other contact with the students with disabilities. Because of the limited verbal skills of the students in Mel's class, I did not conduct formal interviews with any of them. I did have short, informal conversations with several of the students when I was there doing observations.

The observations themselves usually lasted between 1 and 2 hours. Initially, these visits occurred once or twice a week across a variety of settings and times. Gradually the visits became less frequent and were interspersed with the interviews. All of the fieldnotes and interview transcripts were coded and analyzed with standard qualitative techniques (Taylor & Bogdan, 1984).

As with any case study, issues of relevance arise for what I found at Lancaster. Lincoln and Guba (1984) refer to this general topic as "transferability" to distinguish it from the analogous but distinct concerns of quantitative research with "reliability." No matter how accurate or trustworthy my description of Mel's class and Lancaster High School is, it is fair to ask just how well that account transfers to different settings and different times.

Relevance to other settings and times is always a question for case studies. Given all the specific history and context of events and personalities at Lancaster High, and lacking other examples with which to compare and synthesize my findings, how can I assume that Lancaster is in any way "typical" of other high schools or of other efforts to integrate students with autism. My answer, of course, is that I make no such assumption. Moreover, I challenge the notion that any other high school is any more typical. Each high school (every educational setting of any kind, for that matter) has its own set of unique events and specific personalities that interact with larger social forces and structures to construct its own pattern of understanding itself. Case studies are intended to reveal those patterns in as rich detail as possible. This does not mean that generalizations are impossible or even undesirable. Rather it simply places most of the responsibility for generalization to other settings on the readers themselves who know those other settings best. It is my responsibility as the writer to provide a thick enough description for the readers to make such judgments and comparisons.

My favorite response to this issue of relevance comes from Harry Wolcott. A respected anthropologist of education, Wolcott is perhaps best known for his detailed case study of the life and times of a single school administrator: *The man in the principal's office: An ethnography* (1973/1984). Wolcott reports being challenged as to the generalizability of his findings with variations on the same question: "What can we learn from a study of just *one* principal?" He says he finally recognized the obvious answer: "All we can!" (Wolcott, 1990, p. 68). The same answer could apply to the lessons of any case study, including that presented here.

REFERENCES

Bogdan, R., & Barnes, E. (1979). *A qualitative-sociological study of mainstreaming: National Institute of Education proposal*. Unpublished manuscript, Syracuse University, Center on Human Policy.

Bogdan, R., & Kugelmass, J. (1984). Case studies of mainstreaming: A symbolic interactionist approach to special schooling. In L. Barton & S. Tomlinson (Eds.), *Special education and social interests* (pp. 173–191). New York: Nichols.

Grant, G. (1988). *The world we created at Hamilton High*. Cambridge, MA: Harvard University Press.

Lincoln, Y. S., & Guba, E. G. (1984). *Naturalistic inquiry*. Newbury Park, CA: Sage.

Taylor, S. J., & Bogdan, R. (1984). *Introduction to qualitative research methods: The search for meanings* (2nd ed.). New York: John Wiley.

Wolcott, H. F. (1984). *The man in the principal's office: An ethnography* (rev. ed.). New York: Holt, Rinehart and Winston. (Original work published in 1973)

Wolcott, H. F. (1990). Making a study "more ethnographic." *Journal of Contemporary Ethnography, 19*, 44–72.

Part III

DISABILITY AND THE COMMUNITY

In special education and disability studies, interpretivist research first made its mark in the study of "total institutions" (Goffman, 1961). It is only more recently that researchers have turned to qualitative methods to study the lives of people with disabilities in noninstitutional settings. Despite its comparative newness as an area of focus, however, the study of disability and community life has already made significant contributions to the interpretivist understanding of the disability experience. The chapters contained in this part demonstrate the range and quality of these contributions. Before introducing the chapters, let us quickly review some of the major themes that have emerged from the study of disability and the community, and see how they fit with the larger interpretivist perspective on disability in general.

First of all, even outside the regimentation of institutional settings, disability is still a learned social role. Like other forms of social deviance (Becker, 1963), disability can be viewed not as an objective physical or mental condition, but as a role into which people are placed. As Scott (1969) argues in his classic study of blind people:

> The various attitudes and patterns of behavior that characterize people who are blind are not inherent in their condition but, rather, are acquired through ordinary processes of social learning. Thus, there is nothing inherent in the condition of blindness that requires a person to be docile, dependent, melancholy, or helpless; nor is there anything about it that should lead him to become independent or assertive. Blind men are made, and by the same processes of socialization that have made us all. (p. 14)

Since disability is a social role, labelling someone as disabled creates a self-fulfilling prophecy. People with disabilities are rewarded for behavior that conforms to social expectations associated with the disability role and punished for behavior that departs from these expectations (Bogdan & Taylor, 1982; Mercer, 1973).

Second, people with disabilities are outsiders in a nondisabled world. Because disabilities can interfere with normal social interaction (Davis, 1964; Higgins, 1980; Scott, 1969), people with disabilities are set apart from the nondisabled and may be defined solely in terms of their disabling conditions. Higgins (1980) writes:

> In a world where sounds are vitally important, deaf people are outsiders. They are also outsiders in a more profound sense. That world of sounds has been created and is dominated by those who hear. Thus, the deaf are outsiders in a world which is largely controlled by the hearing. (p. 17)

Third, people with disabilities experience stigma. In sociological and anthropological terms, a stigma is not merely a difference, but a characteristic that deeply discredits a person's moral character (Goffman, 1963). Research has documented the stigma associated with deafness (Higgins, 1980), epilepsy (Schneider & Conrad, 1983), chronic facial pain (Lennon, Link, Marbach, & Dohrenwend, 1989), mental retardation (Bogdan & Taylor, 1982; Edgerton, 1967), mental illness (Scheff, 1966), and physical disabilities (Davis, 1964). Edgerton (1967), who has provided one of the clearest analyses of stigma among people with disabilities, states: "The label of mental retardation not only serves as a humiliating, frustrating, and discrediting stigma in the conduct of one's life in the community, but it also serves to lower one's self-esteem to such a nadir of worthlessness that the life of the person is scarcely worth living" (p. 145).

Fourth, agencies and organizations designed to treat or care for people with disabilities create or reinforce behavior that further distances people with disabilities from the broader community. While institutions represent the most extreme example of this, community-based organizations and programs also may assist in socialization to the disability role and enmesh people with disabilities in a subculture with its own set of prescribed behavior (Scott, 1969). In a study of community programs, Bercovici (1983) writes:

> Many dehospitalized mentally retarded persons are not, and do not perceive themselves to be, living in the normal community, contrary to the assumptions that are generally held. The data indicate that these persons may be seen, instead, as inhabitants of a physically segregated and perhaps culturally distinct social system. (p. 138)

While the predominant themes in the qualitative study of disability and community revolve around the exclusion, rejection, and stigmatization of people with disabilities, recent research has begun to examine situations in which people with disabilities are accepted and included by nondisabled people. Groce's (1985) *Everyone Here Spoke Sign Language* is a striking example of a study of a community in which people with a demonstrable disability, deafness, were not rejected or stigmatized by other community members. In this anthropological/historical account of Martha's Vineyard in Massachusetts, Groce documents how the community unself-consciously accepted deaf people as full-fledged, undifferentiated members. Bogdan and Taylor (see Chapter 13, as well as Bogdan & Taylor, 1987; Taylor & Bogdan, 1989) have also studied how nondisabled community members form accepting relationships with people with severe mental and multiple disabilities. This brings us to the three chapters contained in this part of the book.

These chapters draw on different qualitative research methods and look at different aspects of disability and the community. Chapter 8, by Groce, is an historical account of a mildly retarded man, Millard Fillmore Hathaway, living in a small New England community around the turn of the century. Constructed from interviews with older townspeople who remembered Millard Fillmore, Groce examines the role he played in community life and discusses the meaning of this role. As Groce makes clear, by understanding the experiences of individuals with disabilities, we understand better the nature of our communities.

In Chapter 9 Goode contrasts outsider ("etic") and insider ("emic") versions of the identity of Bobby, a middle-aged man with Down Syndrome. According to Goode, an outsider's perspective on Bobby would emphasize his deficiencies and incompetence. Through interviews and videotaped observations, Goode shows how his own definition of Bobby's competence was transformed by attempting to adopt an insider's perspective on Bobby. Thus, people with disabilities can be viewed as incompetent from one perspective, but as competent when viewed on their own terms.

Chapter 10, by Phillips, is based on interviews with people with physical disabilities and looks at their definitions of success. Phillips shows how the disability rights movement, with its emphasis on disability as social minority status, has provided people with disabilities with an ideology that enables them to reject socially imposed definitions of disability. Thus, Phillips's chapter is consistent with the growing number of studies presenting a nondeterministic view of labelling and stigmatization.

As these chapters suggest, the study of disability and the community is complex. We need more studies of the experiences of people with disabilities in different communities and situations.

REFERENCES

Becker, H. S. (1963). *Outsiders: Studies in the sociology of deviance.* New York: Free Press.

Bercovici, S. (1983). *Barriers to normalization: The restrictive management of retarded persons.* Baltimore: University Park Press.

Bogdan, R., & Taylor, S. J. (1982). *Inside out: The social meaning of mental retardation.* Toronto: University of Toronto Press.

Bogdan, R., & Taylor, S. J. (1987). Toward a sociology of acceptance: The other side of the study of deviance. *Social Policy, 18*(2), 34–39.

Davis, F. (1964). Deviance disavowal: The management of strained interaction by the visibly handicapped. In H. S. Becker (Ed.), *The other side: Perspectives on deviance* (pp. 119–138). New York: Free Press.

Edgerton, R. B. (1967). *The cloak of competence: Stigma in the lives of the mentally retarded.* Berkeley: University of California Press.

Goffman, E. (1961). *Asylums: Essays on the social situation of mental patients and other inmates.* Garden City, NY: Doubleday, Anchor Books.

Goffman, E. (1963). *Stigma: Notes on the management of spoiled identity.* Englewood Cliffs, NJ: Prentice-Hall.

Groce, N. E. (1985). *Everyone here spoke sign language: Hereditary deafness on Martha's Vineyard.* Cambridge, MA: Harvard University Press.

Higgins, P. C. (1980). *Outsiders in a hearing world: A sociology of deafness.* Beverly Hills, CA: Sage.

Lennon, M. C., Link, B. G., Marbach, J. J., & Dohrenwend, B. P. (1989). The stigma of chronic facial pain and its impact on social relationships. *Social Problems, 36,* 117–134.

Mercer, J. (1973). *Labeling the mentally retarded.* Berkeley: University of California Press.

Scheff, T. (1966). *Being mentally ill.* Chicago: Aldine.

Schneider, J. W., & Conrad, P. (1983). *Having epilepsy: The experience and control of illness.* Philadelphia: Temple University Press.

Scott, R. A. (1969). *The making of blind men.* New York: Russell Sage Foundation.

Taylor, S. J., & Bogdan, R. (1989). On accepting relationships between people with mental retardation and non-disabled people: Towards an understanding of acceptance. *Disability, Handicap & Society, 4*(2), 21–36.

SUGGESTED READING

Edgerton, R. B. (1967). *The cloak of competence: Stigma in the lives of the mentally retarded.* Berkeley: University of California Press.

This book describes the community experiences of ex-residents of Pacific State Hospital in California. The cloak of competence provides the clearest analysis of stigma among people with mental retardation and examines how ex-residents of the institution manage this stigma in their daily lives.

Estroff, S. E. (1981). *Making it crazy: An ethnography of psychiatric clients in an American community.* Berkeley: University of California Press.

This book looks in depth at the experiences of clients in a community treatment program for people labelled as mentally ill. Estroff shows how "being crazy" becomes a means of survival for many people, both financially and psychologically. The book also raises some interesting ethical dilemmas about field work relationships and degrees of participation when doing interpretivist research.

Goffman, E. (1963). *Stigma: Notes on the management of spoiled identity.*
Englewood Cliffs, NJ: Prentice-Hall.

> In this influential sociological classic, Goffman presents a theory of stigma experienced by people labelled as deviant, including people with disabilities. Goffman examines how stigmatized people deal with their "spoiled identities" in relations with "normals."

Groce, N. E. (1985). *Everyone here spoke sign language: Hereditary deafness on Martha's Vineyard.* Cambridge, MA: Harvard University Press.

> This is an historical/anthropological study of how deaf people on Martha's Vineyard were integrated fully into the life of the community and were not defined as handicapped by other community members. Groce shows clearly that disability is a social construct and that the meaning of disabilities like deafness can vary dramatically from culture to culture.

Higgins, P. C. (1980). *Outsiders in a hearing world: A sociology of deafness.* Beverly Hills, CA: Sage.

> Drawing on interviews and his personal experiences, Higgins examines how deaf people are outsiders in the hearing world. The book addresses membership in the deaf community, stigma, and encounters between people with hearing impairments and hearing people. Higgins incorporates some of the findings in this book into policy recommendations for integrated education of deaf children in Chapter 5 in Part II.

Schneider, J. W., & Conrad, P. (1983). *Having epilepsy: The experience and control of illness.* Philadelphia: Temple University Press.

> This book looks at epilepsy from inside the experience. Schneider and Conrad explore how people with epilepsy define and relate to family members and the medical profession and how they contend with the stigma associated with epilepsy.

Scott, R. A. (1969). *The making of blind men.* New York: Russell Sage Foundation.

> This book discusses how blindness is a learned social role into which people with visual impairments are socialized. Scott demonstrates how agencies for the blind actually encourage attitudes and behavior that distance people with blindness from nondisabled people.

Chapter 8

"THE TOWN FOOL"
An Oral History of a Mentally Retarded Individual in Small Town Society

Nora Groce

This chapter is a detailed examination of the life of one man, Millard Fillmore Hathaway, a mildly retarded individual who lived in the village of Job's Harbor in the later part of the nineteenth and early years of the twentieth century.[1]

Western literature is replete with references to people who were considered to be mentally retarded, authors often giving passing mention to "the town fool" or "the village idiot." What was life actually like for such an individual? No one person's life can be wholly representative of an entire group, for each individual is unique. Yet I feel that a detailed examination of one life may provide insight into the larger question of how mentally retarded individuals are perceived in societies other than our own.

The data to be presented are an outgrowth of my ongoing research on the cross-cultural role of disabled people in noninstitutional settings (Groce, 1985). I did not set out to conduct a study of Millard Fillmore per se, for I was unaware of his existence when the study was initiated. Rather, it began as a study of the role of several disabled individuals who had lived in Job's Harbor in more recent times. Very little appeared in the town records about these people, so I contacted older members of the community who remembered the people I had initially identified as being of particular interest and began to collect some oral history about them.

It was during the collection of these oral histories that Millard Fillmore Hathaway's name began to come up with great regularity. "Oh yes," people would say, "and then there was always Millard Fillmore." He seemed to rank as a local character. The stories told about him were related with a considerable amount of amusement. They were never malicious, but

An earlier version of this chapter was published by the Wenner-Gren Foundation Working Papers in Anthropology, 1986.

everyone made it quite clear that there was something considered unusual about Millard Fillmore. Finally I began to ask my informants specifically about him—why his behavior was unusual, why his actions were thought to be so funny. By all accounts, the answer was that Millard Fillmore was "slow"; "feebleminded" was the local term most regularly applied. "He was not one of the intellectual lights of this community," one of my informants tactfully noted. "He wasn't too bright," another informant told me. A third mentioned, "Sometimes he wasn't all there." Yet another summed up what seems to have been the general community attitude, when he stated, "Well, he was Millard, and you made allowances for that." Millard Fillmore, according to all of them, was considered the town fool.

Job's Harbor is virtually identical to many of the small towns that line the rocky coast of New England. Founded in the 1640s by a handful of families whose descendants still make up the bulk of the town's population, Job's Harbor has changed little over the years. The inhabitants of the Harbor have always been fishermen, most combining fishing with subsistence farming, a few gaining their livelihoods from farming alone.

Before fishing declined and better jobs enticed many away, Job's Harbor was a busy, prosperous place. Its population had reached nearly 1,200 by the close of the Victorian era. Old photographs show neatly kept clapboard houses behind white picket fences arranged around the town green. There is a harbor lined with boats, a new brick town hall, and rising above all else the white wooden steeple of the old Methodist Church, which could be seen far out to sea.

Millard Fillmore Hathaway was born in Job's Harbor in the summer of 1858 and died there 62 years later. Although he shared a common Yankee heritage and participated in many aspects of community life, his life differed from that of his fellow townspeople in one important aspect. Millard Fillmore Hathaway was mentally retarded.

According to those who still remember Millard Fillmore, the role he played in Job's Harbor was that of "the town fool" or "the village idiot." Although this brief biography will focus on Millard Fillmore as a unique individual, it is also intended as a broader examination of mental retardation in a small American community. It is important to keep in mind that throughout history, retarded individuals have not existed apart from the rest of society. For this reason, in addition to the actual physical or psychosocial factors that may be the root cause of mental retardation in the individual, mental retardation is, in a very real sense, a sociocultural phenomenon. Nevertheless, little more than passing reference is usually given to this large group of human beings. Relatively little is known about retarded persons outside of institutional settings in our own society, and even less is known about retarded individuals in other cultures.

Many writers, as Edgerton (1970) has insightfully noted, have held a tacit assumption that "simple people" must have fared better long ago and/or far away when life was so much less complicated than it is for us in the latter part of the twentieth century. This concept is, of course, simplistic at best. As Edgerton emphasizes, no human society is simple, and no human society seems to exist in which some line is not drawn within the community between those who are considered to have an average adequate amount of intelligence and those who, for whatever reasons, it is believed do not.

Nevertheless, the simple people/simple society equation continues to be very much alive. This assumption is of particular concern today for, especially in the past 10 years, social policies have been changing under the direction of politicians who have adopted the position that "things were better back then" as an accurate assessment of how our society actually functioned. Back in "the good old days" in small town U.S.A., we are told, people used to take care of each other; now, we are advised, communities must again learn to take care of their own. It is assumed that the actual requirements of the needy, a class into which many mentally retarded individuals fall, can best be judged on a local rather than national level.

What is needed is more information. The life of Millard Fillmore Hathaway clearly shows that the life of a retarded person in a small town was far more complicated than our current nostalgia would indicate. In much the same manner as current politicians and social administrators, villagers today talk in an idealized fashion about the world they once knew—a world where everybody cared about each other and where someone like Millard Fillmore Hathaway would always be "looked after," well-liked, and respected. In many ways, there is no doubt that Millard Fillmore's life was richer for having been part of a small town society. But Millard Fillmore Hathaway froze to death one night in the chicken coop he called home precisely *because* the society in which he lived, the self-reliant small town that many regard so highly, was at least in his case unable to provide the help that he needed but would not request. It is hoped that the questions raised here by Millard Fillmore's life, and death, will lead us into a more critical examination of the complexity of life for mentally retarded individuals in the larger society.

A SKETCH OF MILLARD FILLMORE'S LIFE HISTORY

Perhaps the most logical place to begin is with the factual history of the life and death of Millard Fillmore Hathaway, as far as it is known. Born in 1858 and named after the then recent President of the United States, he was the third son in a large family whose ancestors first arrived in Job's Harbor 200 years earlier. His father was a fisherman, as were his fathers before him. Of Millard's six brothers, all would make their livings on the water, and his one sister would become a fisherman's wife.

We can only speculate about what his childhood was like. Children's lives rarely entered local oral history, and Millard's was no exception. His daily round of existence was no doubt little different from that of his siblings. His family was not particularly well-to-do, so children were expected to help out. Millard's play would have been frequently interrupted so he could help with chores in and around the house or down at the dock.

Millard's parents and siblings were all of average intelligence and no near relative is known to have been considered mentally retarded. It is not known when Millard's family recognized that he was not as mentally alert as his siblings, although several elderly family members recall stories suggesting that he may have taken slightly longer to learn to walk and talk than did his brothers and sister. These stories do not indicate that he was significantly delayed.

Whatever concerns his family may have had about his development, it was probably not until he began to attend school that his problem became obvious to those outside his immediate family.

As it did for most village children, school began for Millard at the age of six, in the local one-room schoolhouse. By all accounts, his schooling was not particularly successful. While most of the school records themselves no longer exist, it is known that he had considerable trouble, repeating almost every grade. Although he was able to write his name, whether he was ever able to read is questionable given some of the subsequent stories about him. In a small town, many are aware of students who do exceptionally well and exceptionally poorly. Millard Fillmore fell into the latter category. The labelling process had begun.

Exactly what Millard Fillmore's problem was is not known. Other than his being by local accounts "feebleminded," there were no associated physical problems. Of course, none of the standardized intelligence tests had yet been developed, but on the basis of the descriptions provided by his fellow villagers, we would probably consider him to have been mildly mentally retarded.

School for Millard ended at the age of 10, several years earlier than was considered usual for boys at the time. The average age at which school ended for the rest of the boys in Job's Harbor was 14. If he was perceived as being "different" from others when he left school, that difference became more glaringly obvious with each passing year as his childhood companions went on to marry, raise families, and establish lives of their own. Millard Fillmore never would.

Even as a teenager Millard began to act—and, for reasons to be discussed later, was permitted to act—distinctly differently from other boys his age. Less was demanded of him, particularly where work and responsibility were concerned.

He did not seem to have the patience to deal with the increasingly rigorous chores that were expected of him as he grew in strength and agility. It was not simply the fact that he lacked the initiative to undertake new tasks and to demonstrate an independence from his family that marked him as different from his age mates. Routine chores were often left undone.

In fact, unlike his siblings, Millard seemed reluctant to engage in hard work and effectively avoided it as often as he could. It was not that he was physically incapable of working. Of medium height, broad shouldered, and impressively strong, there were few tasks that he was unable to perform. Rather, Millard simply did not seem to relish the idea of working and would "wander off."

It should not be assumed that Millard's unwillingness to work was necessarily typical of a retarded person in Yankee society. Indeed, there were two other individuals in Job's Harbor who lived in roughly the same time period as Millard, both also considered to be mentally retarded, whose lives were quite different. The first lived at home and worked at odd jobs around town. This man had a reputation as a "hard worker" and was regularly referred to by my informants as "a good citizen," a description that obviously reflected the genuine respect local villagers accorded him. The second man, probably more seriously retarded, was less able to function on his own, but helped out around his parents' home and would occasionally add to the family income by digging a bucket of clams or mowing someone's lawn. He apparently took a great deal of time to do each task and often left things partially done, but everyone gave him a good deal of credit for trying.

That Millard was so dissimilar to these other retarded individuals should come as no surprise. There is no reason to assume that because one is retarded he or she should necessarily share personality traits with other retarded members of the society. Prevailing social attitudes toward individuals with a particular disability do not alone shape personality. Differences in family reactions to the retarded person in their midst, differences in social class, education, and life history all have an effect.

To say that Millard Fillmore did not work does not mean that he was inactive. Indeed, he was rarely still. Millard loved to travel, to wander around the countryside, and it is for that that he is still best remembered today.

To call him a wanderer is not an exaggeration. He would often walk out the door and be gone for days. As one informant remarked, "Time and tide meant nothing to him." Nominally, at least, for most of his life Millard lived with his parents. His siblings married one by one and established their own households, where he was always welcomed. In later years, as his parents aged, he spent an increasing amount of time with his siblings, especially his two oldest brothers. His clothes and his few personal possessions were scattered among all their houses.

Millard, however, preferred the great outdoors to any of his relatives' houses and spent most of his time and energy simply wandering. "I remember," his cousin told me, "his brother would ask him to do something, like feed the horse. Well, he'd go out, but you wouldn't see him again for two weeks. When he took a notion to go, he went."

Most often, Millard would be seen walking along the dusty roads that connected the isolated houses and fishermen's cottages to Job's Harbor. He was familiar with every road and path for miles around and never became lost. He apparently walked simply for the joy of walking and to "be out and among people." There was no set destination involved: "Lots of times, you'd pick him up, give him a ride, and he'd turn right around and start walking back the other way." Nor was there any particular logic or order to where he went: "Maybe you wouldn't see him for a month and then, all of a sudden, he'd just come out of the clear sky."

It was not unusual for him to cover 20 miles in a day. Frequently he would go even further. Often his travels would take him to villages far beyond the little world of Job's Harbor. At George's Inlet, 10 miles south of Job's Harbor, or Enos' Cove, 8 miles to the east, people still remember Millard Fillmore—they called him "the fool from Job's Harbor."

As he walked he sang, bellowing out Methodist gospel hymns at the top of his lungs. He seems to have had a virtually inexhaustible supply of songs—he would sing only gospel songs—and his voice is reported to have been quite good. Almost everyone who remembered Millard talked about his singing. It was usually the first topic people brought up when they began to talk about him, mentioning it long before they would mention the fact that he was mentally retarded. As one gentleman recalled:

> On white, frosty nights he'd start out of the house, come down to
> the general store here to get some chewing tobacco. He'd start sing-
> ing, hollering at the top of his lungs. He'd sing all the way down
> and all the way back, hymn after hymn. On cold night air, boy,
> would that sound travel. But ask for anything else, he didn't know.

Indeed, many older villagers speak of Millard's singing with a good deal of nostalgia. "I can hear him singing now," one woman told me. "It was one of the things that made this town such a pleasant place."

More often than not, wandering far from home, Millard found himself miles away when meal time rolled around or night began to fall. He would never ask for a place to stay, although people would frequently find him in their barns or houses. One man recalled:

> My father went into the barn one morning and he knew there'd been someone in the barn since he'd shut it up at night and the door wasn't fully shut. He went in and in the haymound, full of hay, he noticed there were these feet sticking straight up in the air. "Millard, is that you?" he said. And of course, it was.

Another remembered:

> And then, one other place he went and the lady got up, he came into the house after daylight came, and she got up and went downstairs, and he was in the bathroom combing his hair. She'd just come from away, married a local fellow, so she'd never heard nor seen Millard before. Nearly scared her to death. Yet he was harmless.

And someone else added: "And he'd go around, perhaps he'd sleep in our barn tonight, you know, and he'd sleep in somebody else's barn tomorrow night. That's the way he lived."

Villagers seem to have been less than enthusiastic about having him stay overnight in their homes or barns. No one was afraid of him—he was widely known, considered to be harmless, and was a great favorite among village children. Still, many worried that his visits would become regular if he could count on a place to stay.

Moreover, in a poor, hard-working community, hospitality can go only so far, particularly when an able-bodied man winds up on one's doorstep. Because he was physically able, few villagers were willing to give Millard a regular handout with no strings attached. Usually, villagers asked Millard to do some chore in exchange for a plate of food or a place to stay the night:

> I can remember him. He came in one time and stopped and asked for a handout. My mother gave it to him and when he was done, he said, "Can I do anything for you?" And she said, "Well, there's some wood out there that my son was going to chop, maybe you can chop it for him." Which he did.

Millard himself apparently felt obligated to volunteer to do some work in exchange for his meals, although opinion varies as to how hard he worked in this exchange. A relative recalled, "If they'd give him a dinner, he would go out and cut wood all afternoon to pay for it," while another woman remembered:

> He'd come, he'd arrive in the morning and he would come into my aunt's house and she would give him a cup of coffee and breakfast. Then she'd say, "Now you go out and bring me some wood." Fill up the fire box, you know. And he would. He would bring in one armful and the next armful, he'd be gone.

What Millard's parents and siblings thought of his behavior is unclear. They certainly would have preferred that he stay home, but they found they had very little control over him. As his niece remembers, her father, Millard's oldest brother, was more or less resigned to his behavior. "Well, it was no use to get upset, he never got in any trouble." If Millard was gone for over a week, generally his father or one of his brothers would go out looking for him, or at least pass the word along through the neighbors that he should come home. This often proved ineffective, but occasionally it worked and was certainly worth a try. Sooner or later, usually in a week or two, Millard would show up at his parents' house or on the doorstep of one of his brothers or his sister. After several days, or perhaps a week, he would be back on the road again.

People often looked forward to Millard's visits, not only because he did some chores or because they enjoyed his company, although some did, but also because he brought with him information that was appreciated in the small farmhouses and fishing shacks at which he stopped—news and gossip, particularly gossip. Wandering in and out of people's houses, Millard was well aware of some of the more private aspects of people's lives and was not always adept at deciding what to discreetly leave out when talking with neighbors. In fact, several of my informants remember that their parents were always glad to see Millard appear over the top of the hill for they knew he brought with him, more often than not, information on people they had been wondering about for weeks.

> He'd come round to my mother's and he'd been round to her sister's. He'd tell her all about it, you know, just to get in. It was all right. He'd go on and on about the neighbors. If you'd want to find anything out, just ask him about somebody and he'd go and find out and come back again. It kept him busy. Of course, you had to be careful about what he might overhear in your house or it would be all over the village.

MILLARD'S STATUS AS THE TOWN FOOL

While villagers recall Millard as "the wanderer" or "the singer," in fact, the largest number of stories still told about him concern his status as the town fool. At issue is not simply the fact that Millard was not as mentally alert as others in the community. Rather it is that Millard's lack of intelligence, and as a result, his lack of social adroitness, was considered to be a constant source of amusement. When asked what she remembered about Millard, for example, one of my informants replied, "Well, everything funny. He was supposed to be weak-minded, you know." Men sitting around the stove at the general store, women visiting each other to borrow a quart of milk or a needle, children walking to school would tell stories about Millard and laugh.

Some of these stories concerned situations Millard had brought upon himself. For example, a story known to almost everyone in town concerned the time he wandered into a barn seeking shelter from a storm and crawled into what he assumed to be the local butcher's wagon to take a nap. Waking up several hours later, he realized he was lying in the town hearse, assumed that he had died, and panicked. It is said that he ran 3 or 4 miles before someone could catch up with him and calm him down. A local wag made up a poem about the event, which was circulated widely in typewritten form.

Because he was oblivious to some of the niceties of social convention, the honesty of his statements or the directness of his actions often caused comment and amusement.

> He went over to Frank Brown's, and I guess he cut wood, did a few chores, and then they'd feed him. And by golly, they said, this day—they always had baked beans and brown bread, and they said Millard Fillmore'd ate about 12 plates of beans, baked beans and brown bread. Then he says to Frank's wife, "Gracey," he says, "your beans are very good, but your brown bread is kinda hard."

Or:

> One time, he went into Rose's house over in Enos' Cove, and her mother had just made a big pan of baking powder biscuits. And Millard said, "Them biscuits smell good!" And Rose's mother said, "Will you have one or two?" Millard says, "Why I'd be glad to." He finished the whole panful. He had an enormous appetite.

Millard's comments on such things as national politics, particularly in those cases where he obviously could have benefitted by some background information, were considered especially funny.

I remember hearing about the time there was this discussion in the general store—all the men would go there in the evening and hang around. The discussion turned to the fact that General Grant had just died. "That's too bad," Millard Fillmore said, "I guess they'll have to get another general."

While Millard seemed perfectly able to get himself into difficult situations, a good many of the stories told concern his reactions to situations into which others intentionally maneuvered him. Villagers admitted that they would occasionally tease or "josh" him. Teasing and playing tricks on each other went on regularly among almost all the adults in town to a certain extent, but Millard Fillmore was apparently the continual butt of pranks. While several informants insisted that Millard was not picked on any more than anyone else, one man summed up what seems to have been the actual situation by volunteering the remark, "Oh sure, he was teased just the same as everyone else, long as that anybody else was feebleminded."

For example, the teenage boys at the Methodist Church had a good time when Millard attended meetings.

We had church, prayer meeting service they called it, Sunday evenings. He'd [Millard Fillmore] come to church and the minister, who should have known better than to ask it, he'd say, "Does anybody have a favorite hymn?" We always had our fingers in the hymn books, we'd say Number 75, "God Will Take Care of You," or "Jesus, Lover of My Soul," to get him to sing. Familiar hymns. He'd stand with his book [he more frequently held the book wrong side up than right side up], and he'd pump it out, drown 'em out. He always ended right on the dot and knew every word in those hymns. He bellowed out, drown out the organ, drown out everybody else. I don't think they liked us boys to do it—we did it to be funny. I got the Devil when I got home. [Laughs] "What'd you give that song for?" Especially my sister: "What'd you give that number for, you knew he'd sing that loud." Well, of course I did.

Nor was this teasing restricted to adolescent boys; grown men would also join in.

Millard Fillmore, he used to get into what was the paper store and in the back was a pool room down near where the hardware store is now. Mr. Blair used to run the pool room, ran the store. In those days, tobacco brands like BL and Grant would come in cartons and instead of taking them and dumping them, they'd stack 'em up along the wall to decorate the place. Well, Millard, he used to sing songs, like "Roll, Jordan, Roll," or any of those hymns. The boys would get him to start singing and would get him backed up to the wall where those cartons were. One of the boys'd hit the stack of cartons when Millard reached a high note and they'd all fall down. Then old man Blair would get mad, run back to the back room, and drive Millard out by throwing coal at him and yelling, "Get the . . . , get the . . . ." He never figured out the boys were at fault, and they never told him.

Or:

Well, I remember, he used to come up here and the men used to raise the dickens with him. He would come to church, I remember one time he came to church and the men, some of them were standing around outside the belfry, just before services started. He walked into the church, and as he walked in, one of the men near the doorway gave him a good kick in the pants. Millard sang out, "God damn you!" The whole congregation, all them women and children and all were sitting there, the church was packed. Everyone heard him.

Because everyone in the village knew that Millard did not like to work hard, to get him working was considered a source of great fun.

I had four brothers and there were several of us out chopping wood one day. We burned wood in those days, of course. And Millard came along. He told us we didn't know how to saw and chop wood the right way. So we said, "Well, Millard, show us, will ya." So he showed us how and he did the whole of it while we watched him. He's showing us how 'cause we kept saying we couldn't, we didn't learn very quickly. Mother gave us heck for it, but I heard her and dad laughing about it after we'd gone to bed.

In another instance, it was the local Baptist minister that put him to work.

You know, they used to cut with scythes and Reverend Benjamin Jackson, lived over by the cove, I guess he might of took Millard Fillmore in from time to time and feed him. Then he'd get him out cutting grass. Of course, they'd cut acres with scythes and Benjamin'd get Millard Fillmore in front of him and by God, he'd swing and swing. Millard Fillmore had to keep going because he was afraid that if he'd stop, he'd get his head cut off. I can hear him now, hollering like the Devil to Reverend Jackson, "Slow down, slow down!"

Interestingly, in these stories, Millard Fillmore was not always the victim. If being the town fool left one open to teasing, being "one upped" by the town fool was considered to be even funnier—except by the person actually put in that position.

> He'd go up to the Coast Guard station there and they'd feed him, you know. Gosh, they had great grub up there. Well, one time, Jessie, who worked up there, as Millard was leaving, he says, "Well, goodbye Mr. Hathaway," and added something like, "Hard luck to you." "Same to yourself," Millard replied real politely.

> I remember Millard Fillmore with Anna in the Post Office one time. He was very blunt and she should of known better. She was a bright woman, but queer, acted funny. She saw Millard out there, and she said, "Why hello, Mr. Hathaway," the office was full of people, "How are you, Mr. Hathaway?" Now she wasn't that sociable—I don't know what'd got into her. He said, "Not very good." "Why what's the matter, Mr. Hathaway?" "Well, lately, I've had indigestion, constipation, and the piles." She'd asked a question, she'd got an answer. Well, that was a hit in the Post Office.

Millard may have received a good deal of teasing, but there were some social bounds that were not crossed. He was never physically harmed, nor were most people overly rude or cruel to him. For one thing, Millard was able to take care of himself to some degree.

> They used to talk to him, kid him along, you know. He didn't mind being kidded as long as you wasn't being sassy. If you were sassy, he'd tell you off. We never was, because we, I was a young man at the time, and, well, he was much, much older. He was a likeable old man.

Or as another informant stated:

> There was always some who'd tease him or something like that, but not too bad. With Millard Fillmore, oh, sometimes we used to raise the Devil with him, yes, I guess that's true. He wouldn't get too upset, not as a rule. Once in a while he'd get a little hot and people'd lay off. He was big and awfully strong.

Not everyone teased Millard. Members of his immediate family insisted that he be left alone, although they certainly heard stories around town about him, and within the family, told many stories about him with considerable amusement. A number of people felt that Millard was simply an unfortunate man and, as one woman phrased it, "It would be unkind to be anything less than Christian to him." Most of the actual teasing was left to men and boys, although if they got too carried away, someone, usually within their ranks, would call a halt, saying something such as, "Well, that's enough now." It should be noted that while a number of people in town said that they never teased Millard, everyone in town knew the same group of stories about him. This strongly indicates that while some refrained from teasing him themselves, most villagers listened with interest when these stories were told and retold. That many of those I spoke with could recall these tales with such accuracy after 50 years indicates how widely circulated and frequently repeated they must have been.

There were several reasons why actions toward Millard Fillmore were kept within bounds. For one thing, mental retardation in this society was considered to be something that could occasionally happen in any family. Physical or mental disability was not seen in Yankee society to be a sign that a particular individual or his or her family had transgressed, unlike in some societies, where an individual's disability is believed to be a punishment for previous sins (Groce, 1985).

Just as important, there were also very few people in town who were not in some way connected to Millard Fillmore by that intricate network that bound together all the members of this small village. If not related by blood or marriage to Millard, most villagers were friends with, lived near, or worked beside one of his many siblings. Individuals who might have been inclined to be rough toward Millard would have been held accountable by his brothers or sister. But it was not simply a case of having to account to Millard's immediate family that dictated community practices. A largely implicit, but nonetheless significant, community reality was that if you treated Millard too harshly, if the jokes or comments took too cruel a turn, the person or persons involved would themselves lose face in the eyes of the community. Past a certain point, taking advantage of Millard or having fun at his expense was socially unacceptable. Indeed, villagers often judged each other and outsiders by their actions toward Millard.

For example, a summer person once violated an unspoken code in hiring Millard, assuming he could be taken advantage of.

Someone asked him to move a trunk one time and he had to help load it and he went to this hotel and he helped lug it upstairs and the man, he was here on vacation, this man passed him 10 cents. I don't know what Millard said to him, but he made it clear that he didn't think that was enough. I think that was pretty mean myself. That summer person thought, you know, that he'd take advantage of him.

Such conduct was not restricted to summer people.

Someone said to him one day, "If you cut up this wood for me, why I'll give you something to eat." Well, he did it, and well, of course, I blame him in a way, but they put some cookies on a plate and some of those cookies were awfully old, awfully hard. I don't think that was good, myself, I don't approve of that. But Millard was clever enough to know what they'd done, so he felt over all the cookies before he ate one and he kept the soft ones, ate those.

The fact that villagers expected everyone to behave with a certain amount of decency toward Millard cannot be accounted for simply as the charitable or the proper thing to do. In fact, most villagers were genuinely fond of Millard; they had watched him grow up and knew him well, and although they may have considered his ways a bit strange, he was very much part of their world.

Millard occupied a specific role in the small village of Job's Harbor. As one informant told me, "He was the local fool, you know. Every town used to have one." He lived in many ways on the periphery of this society. He accomplished none of the things expected of a grown man, and he was oblivious to many of the finer social graces that allowed one to move smoothly in social situations. Nonetheless, he was included and actively participated in many aspects of community life. He readily joined in discussions, regularly attended church and local meetings, was invited to parties and weddings, and showed up at funerals. If his mental retardation left him less able at reasoning than his neighbors, he nevertheless shared most of the customs and adhered to most of the social values and constraints as other members of his society. In the end, this proved fatal.

MILLARD'S DEATH

Periodically, Millard refused to live with his family. His mother died in 1906 and his father in 1911, but his brothers' houses and that of his sister were always open to him. With growing frequency, however, Millard would move out into a nearby barn or outbuilding for several weeks or months after a family disagreement. After some time, his siblings would eventually convince him to move back. They were obviously aware of the fact that he was becoming less able to adequately feed, clothe, and house himself as he grew older, and they worried about him. Urging him to join them was the only thing they could do—it was impossible to *make* him do anything. It was not simply that he was stubborn, although by all accounts he was quite stubborn. Rather the problem lay in the basic concept of self-sufficiency, a cornerstone of Yankee society.

Traditionally, adults in Yankee society were considered to be independent, responsible individuals by the very nature of their adult status. To imply to any man or woman that he or she was not wise or responsible enough to take adequate care of him- or herself was virtually a direct insult. For those who obviously did not have enough reason to manage their own affairs, such as children, the seriously mentally ill, and some of those whose mental retardation was more severe than Millard's, it was considered acceptable to make decisions on their behalf. But Millard did not fall into this category. In this fiercely independent society, Millard was considered to be limited, but capable of taking care of himself in most day-to-day situations. As his niece told me, "He had so little, how could we say it was not enough? He was proud of what he could do."

An aging Millard had established himself in a chicken coop just beyond the cove in the late summer of 1921. Chances are that he had not eaten well for months, and informants remember that the coop shook every time the wind blew. While everyone in town was aware that Millard, in his bid to maintain some semblance of adult status by living independently of his siblings, was, in fact, not adequately fed, clothed, or housed, there was little they were able to do about it. While many villagers were happy to give him an occasional handout, no one outside his immediate family wanted the ongoing responsibility. A logical solution would have been to offer Millard Fillmore some form of regular assistance, so that he might have enough money to afford a decent place to live and an adequate amount of food. But to help Millard Fillmore, they would have had to make him a recipient of town funds. And to receive public assistance, to be "on the town," was considered perhaps the most disgraceful thing that could happen to a person or family.

The prevailing attitude was that public assistance was money that was being taken directly out of one's neighbor's pocket because, for whatever reasons, the recipient had failed in that most fundamental of all responsibilities in this society, the responsibility to be independent and self-sufficient.

Presumably, only the town selectmen, the officials actually in charge of town funds, knew who was receiving public assistance. But in actual fact, everyone knew. Usually no one said anything directly to the recipient of this assistance, but a very real stigma existed and affected that individual's relationship with practically every other member of the community. As one woman told me:

Oh my, no, nobody ever denounced them. No, no. I remember that
there was one man, who, oh, he was tremendous in size, he weighed
nearly 300 pounds and he was "on the town." They didn't put
anybody's name down that had aid, but in the town report it said
"one very large pair of pants" as one of the expenditures. [Laughs]
No name. Everybody knew who it was, but no name.

It is significant that most of my informants knew who was "on the
town," what the circumstances were that led to them being there, and for
approximately how long they had been on these rolls. They knew all this
despite the fact that these records were supposedly confidential and are still
not open to the general public. The majority of individuals listed on the
town public assistance rolls over the years were people who were both frail
and elderly, widows with several children, or those who were severely
disabled. While some of these individuals had no close relatives in the area
on whom to rely, many had already depleted the resources of their extended
families before requesting help from the broader community. Almost invariably, the disgrace of being on the public assistance rolls extended
beyond the individual to the larger extended family group. Consequently,
public assistance was seen as the very last resort.

Data gathered during this study indicate that those individuals who
eventually wound up on the town public assistance rolls often suffered for
years, with barely adequate housing, clothing, or food, before requesting
help. Often it seems it was only when an individual's health gave out as a
result of poor nutrition, inadequate housing, and overwork, that the person
would consent to be added to the rolls. While villagers today recall with
pride how "in the good old days," people took care of their own, in fact the
data I have gathered from Job's Harbor, the surrounding communities, and
other areas of small town New England seem to indicate that those who
were in need often suffered for years rather than request help from their
neighbors.

Millard Fillmore was undoubtedly aware of this prejudice. While at least
one neighbor urged him to apply for a little assistance, if only in the winters
when the part-time chores he would do for pocket money all but disappeared, Millard refused absolutely. "He was not," he told my informant,
"willing to take charity." "Thank goodness he was just an old bachelor," he
told another person. "The chicken coop was mansion enough for him."

This negative community attitude toward those receiving public assistance has changed slowly over the years. The change, at least in Job's
Harbor, seems to have come about in the 1930s as a result of the restructuring of local, state, and federal policies. During the Depression, under the
Roosevelt Administration, public assistance increasingly came from sources

outside the immediate community. Local people in Job's Harbor thought and still think little of this change in policy. It took away their highly valued sense of complete self-sufficiency. As one elderly informant explained, it was the beginning of the world "going to pot," adding, "It was Roosevelt that caused all these problems."

In fact, what happened seems to have been that those truly in need who previously would not have sought public assistance were willing to do so when they could apply for help outside their immediate community. Spared the public disgrace of begging for help from neighbors, for the first time many of those who lived on the margin came forward to request assistance from what was perceived to be an anonymous source. Public assistance from outside the local community was not and is not considered to be "free" money, nor was it thought of as something to be squandered or wasted. But it was help, often sorely needed, that could be obtained without a serious loss of face within one's home town. Shifting the burden of public assistance from local to state and national agencies may have increased the number of people on public assistance rolls, but it seems probable that it also eliminated a great deal of unnecessary human suffering.

This change in attitude, however, came too late to help Millard Fillmore Hathaway. One cold night in late January 1921, a blizzard came in off the water and the snow fell so heavily that people could barely see past their doorsteps. Millard, curled up in his chicken coop, his feet sticking out the door because it was too small a structure for him to fit in comfortably, could do nothing to keep warm. Several days later, his brother and a friend stopped by to see why Millard Fillmore had not been around town. The funeral was 3 days later. The church was packed.

DISCUSSION

There is one voice missing here and that is Millard Fillmore's. What he thought about himself and his community are things about which we can only speculate. It seems that Millard felt that he was a full and active participant in the world in which he lived. At times, he apparently referred to himself as "just an old bachelor" and he took pains to explain to at least one of my informants that it was his failure to marry that allowed him to carry on his rather unusual lifestyle. It must have been obvious to him that other bachelors in the community behaved differently, but he seemed pleased enough with this explanation to use it regularly. It is difficult if not impossible to believe that from time to time he was not confronted with the fact that he was thought to be "feebleminded." Whether he ever accepted that designation is not known.

If we cannot gain an insight into what Millard thought about himself and his role in his world, this short study of his life nonetheless raises several points that I believe merit consideration. In modern American society, mental retardation is often a category in which one is placed on the basis of an intelligence test score. Such tests were, of course, unavailable during Hathaway's lifetime. Even today, test scores tell us relatively little about the person being tested (Gould, 1981). Moreover, as a number of studies have shown that an individual can move in and out of the group labelled as mildly mentally retarded on the basis of test scores, where do we draw the line? Where did the people in Job's Harbor draw the line such that Millard Fillmore Hathaway fell below it? A working definition of mental retardation would seem more useful than one that relies on absolute numbers.

In attempting to determine what constitutes mental retardation in our society and in others, a more flexible criterion is in order. A person may be considered mentally retarded, I suggest, when because of restricted intellectual capacity his day-to-day ability to function in his community does not live up to the common expectations of the community at large, in keeping with that individual's age, sex, social class, and level of education. Although better known for quantifiable definitions of mental retardation, Binet and Simon (1916) long ago provided us with a very good working *social* definition of retardation when they wrote:

> It seems to us that in intelligence there is a fundamental faculty . . . the alteration or lack of which is of the utmost importance for practical life. This faculty is judgement, otherwise called good sense, practical sense, initiative, the faculty of adapting one's self to circumstances. To judge well, or comprehend well, to reason well, these are essential activities of intelligence. (pp. 42–43)

On the basis of this definition, the community in which Millard Fillmore lived considered him to be mentally retarded. Although he was able to judge, comprehend, and reason, he was not able to do these things well, or at least well enough, in the eyes of the people of Job's Harbor.

As an adult he could perform most simple and some complex tasks. He was more than able to carry on a conversation—indeed, he enjoyed talking with others—but he had trouble with complicated ideas. "If you asked him a civil question, he'd give you a civil answer," one villager remembered, but he often missed cues, innuendoes, and double entendres, in short, most of the subtleties that, though difficult to define, prove the dividing factor between marginal and full participation in daily interactions. He was considered to be, and felt himself to be, responsible for his actions, but in some social situations and in emergencies he had difficulty coming to what the society felt to be a correct decision and implementing it. Initiating tasks and regulating his own schedule were operations he was rarely called on to perform and may have been beyond him. These attributes seem to have been sufficiently below the norm for people to have been acutely aware of them.

Millard's reluctance to work may not have been initially related to his retardation, but ultimately the fact that he was retarded meant that people tolerated this behavior. If he had not been considered mentally retarded, it is likely that his parents and siblings would have pressured him to do more to help the family unit. If he consistently refused, most probably he eventually would have been asked to leave home or ultimately have been disinherited. It is not surprising that he did not marry. In a community that valued hard work, no local woman would consider as an eligible marriage partner a man who was not a hard worker.

What is significant in the case of Millard Fillmore is that he was permitted to violate the expected norms because he was viewed as mentally retarded. This was not done out of any widely held community belief that a retarded person was necessarily incapable of being a responsible working member of the community—indeed, as we have seen, two other mentally retarded villagers behaved quite differently. Rather, it seems to be that when someone such as Millard Fillmore decided to violate community expectations or could not fulfill them, there were simply few social sanctions that could be imposed on him. He was not particularly interested in moving out of his parents' home, nor did he ever seem to be interested in getting married. Ridicule and sarcasm more often than not were lost on him. While some villagers had little to do with Millard Fillmore because of his dislike of work, the overriding local opinion seems to have been that Millard was simply "feebleminded" and, hence, could not be blamed.

It should also be kept in mind that the fact that Millard Fillmore was mentally retarded does not alone explain why he was designated as "the" local fool. As noted earlier, Millard Fillmore was not the only mentally retarded individual in Job's Harbor. What distinguished him from other mentally retarded persons in Job's Harbor and, I suspect, what led to his eventual designation as "the" town fool, was that it was Millard Fillmore who made the most concerted attempt to participate actively in community life. Unlike the other mentally retarded adults who lived quietly at home with their immediate families, Millard Fillmore made a very real attempt to fulfill the expected adult male role. Had he been a good worker, in a society that values hard work highly, he might have fit in more successfully. As it was, his refusal to work steadily brought comment and disapproval from his neighbors. His attempts to participate in other social functions while deviating so markedly from the community work ethic underscored his intellectual deficits in the eyes of his neighbors.

While, as discussed earlier, few social sanctions could be imposed on Millard Fillmore directly, the social designation of "town fool" could be used by his fellow townspeople to provide him with a recognized role and frame his actions (or lack of action) in a more acceptable light. As the town fool, Millard Fillmore was perceived as serving a legitimate social function—he was a source of amusement. Laughter, rather than annoyance or anger, was assumed to be the appropriate response to his actions. But it would be misleading to assume that there was no undercurrent of social sanction involved. The reason why any one individual is considered as the "town fool" or the "village idiot" undoubtedly depends on a host of factors probably unique to that particular person, community, and society, but it is important to point out that these social roles are not automatically given to every mentally retarded individual in society. I suspect one crucial factor that will be found regularly where the "town fool" role occurs is that the individual so designated will have made more of an attempt than other retarded individuals in the community to participate in the wider society— and will have publicly proved him- or herself unsuccessful in doing so.

Millard Fillmore certainly seems to have played a more active role in small town life than he might have had he lived today. By blood and marriage he was connected to a significant proportion of the population, and from childhood on he was included in most social events. While often the butt of jokes or the subject of stories told around town, he was usually included in discussions, he was avidly sought out as a source of gossip, and he was usually greeted with kindness.

Yet while the prevailing ethic in town was that Millard Fillmore should be treated well, there was a striking discrepancy between the ideal and the real. As mentioned earlier, in much the same manner as modern day politicians and social administrators speak nostalgically about small town life, villagers talk in an idealized fashion about the world they once knew. "Everybody liked Millard Fillmore and was kind and decent to him," I was told. "Everybody made sure he got along okay." As one informant explained: "You know, today you take somebody like him, you'd take them and arrest them and put them away in some hospital somewheres. Back then, why we always took him in, fed him. Everybody did."

But most people also had limited patience with Millard Fillmore. Very few would invite him to spend the night in their house, although there were probably plenty of times when it was late and cold, and there was obviously no place else for him to go. Some were even as unkind to him as they were allowed to be, given the prevailing social constraints. Almost no one seemed bothered by how often he became the butt of jokes and pranks.

Where independence and self-sufficiency formed such an integral part of who you were and what you believed, there was a genuine hesitancy on the part of people, both individually and as a community, to offer anyone the option of being slightly more dependent than fellow townspeople. And, it must be stressed, there was just as much hesitancy on the part of needy individuals to request or accept what was believed to be, by all members of the society, "pure charity."

CONCLUSION

Obviously, we need to know a great deal more about the lives of mildly mentally retarded individuals in different types of communities in our own society, as well as more about their treatment cross-culturally. We know very little of mental retardation cross-culturally (Edgerton, 1970). While some very interesting work has been done on this subject concerning those who are severely or profoundly retarded (Gleason, 1982; Langness, 1982; Willis, 1973), we know virtually nothing about how or why people in various cultures are assigned to the group we would consider to be mildly mentally retarded. At what point is a person considered to be not simply unintelligent, but mentally retarded? As between 75% and 85% of all mentally retarded individuals are considered only mildly retarded (Edgerton, 1967; Scheiner & Abroms, 1980), this question is a significant one.[2]

Factors such as the need to master a complex technology and the expectation of becoming literate or memorizing complicated bodies of knowledge, whether social, religious, genealogical, and so on, all may serve as criteria for defining mental competence. It should be stressed here that I am not assuming that less technologically complex societies or societies with fewer deities or simple genealogical systems do not as readily distinguish individuals who are mildly retarded. I would, however, suggest that the more formal the educational systems and the more sophisticated the specialization required for subsistence activities, the more readily a person's intellectual capacity might determine most or all, and not just part, of his or her interactions with others—in other words, the more readily he or she will be seen as a retarded person first and a unique individual second.

Millard Fillmore, living in the fairly complex world of Job's Harbor, where adult citizenship, literacy, the expectations of marriage and family, and, most important, self-sufficiency were all inherently part of the expectations of adulthood, could not function "well enough." As we have seen, Millard Fillmore was a unique individual, but one attribute, that of mental retardation, transcended all others. Throughout his lifetime he was known, and today is remembered, principally as "the town fool."

Millard Fillmore Hathaway's life is just one among many. As an informant told me during the course of these interviews, "Every small town had someone like Millard Fillmore. We thought he was special because he was ours." There have been a number of large-scale sociological and psychological studies that have increased our knowledge of mentally retarded persons. I believe there is also a need for more studies that closely examine the lives of individual mentally retarded persons, for they have been and will continue to be a part of our society. It is only by studying their lives in fuller detail that we can begin to better articulate the needs, the problems, and the potentials for this large group of fellow human beings.

NOTES

1. I am grateful to those citizens of Job's Harbor who participated in this study and to the National Institute of Mental Health, whose Pre-Doctoral Dissertation Fellowship allowed me to undertake a large part of the field work reported here. Pseudonyms are used throughout this chapter.
2. Estimates vary on what percentage of those considered retarded are thought to be mildly retarded (see, for example, Edgerton, 1967; Scheiner & Abroms, 1980). While they may disagree on the exact numbers, almost all authors believe that at least three-quarters of all retarded individuals can be included in this group.

REFERENCES

Binet, A., & Simon, T. (1916). New methods for the diagnosis of the intellectual levels of subnormals. In A. Binet & T. Simon (Eds.), *The development of intelligence in children* (pp. 37–90). Baltimore: Williams & Wilkins.

Edgerton, R. B. (1967). *The cloak of competence: Stigma in the lives of the mentally retarded.* Berkeley: University of California Press.

Edgerton, R. B. (1970). Mental retardation in non-western societies: Towards a cross-cultural perspective on incompetence. In H. C. Haywood (Ed.), *Sociocultural aspects of mental retardation* (pp. 523–559). New York: Appleton-Century-Croft.

Gleason, J. J. (1982, October). *Culture: A view from the inside: Toward the ethnographic study of social interaction among the severely and profoundly mentally retarded.* Wenner-Gren Foundation Working Papers in Anthropology.

Gould, S. J. (1981). *The mismeasurement of man.* New York: Norton.

Groce, N. E. (1985). *Everyone here spoke sign language: Hereditary deafness on Martha's Vineyard.* Cambridge, MA: Harvard University Press.

Langness, L. L. (1982, July). *Mental retardation as an anthropological problem.* Wenner-Gren Foundation Working Papers in Anthropology.

Scheiner, A., & Abroms, I. (1980). *The practical management of the developmentally disabled child.* St. Louis: C. V. Mosby.

Willis, R. H. (1973). *The institutionalized severely retarded.* Springfield, IL: Charles C. Thomas.

Chapter 9

WHO IS BOBBY?

Ideology and Method in the Discovery of
a Down Syndrome Person's Competence

David A. Goode

It is true both that some men are wiser than others and
that no one thinks falsely.

—Protagoras

This chapter builds on the sociological analysis that emerged in the course
of ethnographic studies with deaf-blind children diagnosed as having ru-
bella syndrome.[1] This research revealed the difficulties people have in
understanding such children and how our most consistent response to them
has been one of "fault finding."[2] Clinical personnel and lay persons (except
parents) saw, experienced, and "explained" these children exclusively in
terms of "faults" and remedial actions to correct those faults.

A MATTER OF PERSPECTIVE:
ETIC AND EMIC VIEWS OF DISABILITY

My research challenged the deeply pejorative stance taken toward deaf-
blind children by demonstrating some of their true skills and competencies
that were not apparent from the perspective of an average person. This was
made possible through my attempts to experience the world from an alingual, deaf-blind perspective. I observed the details of these persons' daily
lives, simulated their organic deficits by means of artificial devices that
limited my hearing and sight, and thereby came to understand the sensibil-

---

An earlier version of this chapter was published in G. Kielhofner (Ed.). (1983). *Health
through occupation: Theory and practice in occupational therapy* (pp. 237–255). Philadelphia:
Davis.

ity and legitimacy of their subjective perspective and experience. While the prevailing clinical perspective on these children classified them among the lowest functioning human beings in our society, my work validated the idea that competence—indeed the whole identity of a deaf-blind child—had to do with the social context in which the child was experienced as well as the role and background of the person describing or assessing the child. Physicians and parents were in quite open disagreement about the capabilities and identities of particular children.

In anthropology, objective, analytic, or clinical approaches to understanding culture and human behavior are called "etic" perspectives. Etic perspectives are distinguished from the "emic," native, subjective, or insider point of view. Etic frameworks are external to the situation under analysis, and many etic or analytic models may be brought to bear on any situation. Ordinarily, the etic reality of the scientist is used as a superior criterion against which the native insider reality is judged. Emic or native viewpoints are discovered from within the situation under study. It is the perspective the person in the activities uses to produce the actions that the observer sees. As Evans-Pritchard (1937) noted, it is no accident that etic perspectives lead to fault finding, while emic perspectives permit others to gain a better sense of the rationality, purpose, and efficiency of native behaviors. Clinical frameworks tend to be exclusively etic and explicitly oriented to finding and eradicating flaws through therapy, treatment, or training of some sort. Their descriptions of behavior *inevitably* find no value in deviation from accepted behavioral norms. The emic perspective necessarily emphasizes, in contradistinction, the value and creativity of deviant behaviors.

For a variety of reasons, hospitals and clinics are likely to produce fault-finding images and identities of deviant clients based on etic criteria applied to the person's behavior. I found that the clinical model of deaf-blind children's behavior completely dominated intervention strategies, programs, and placements. More positive evaluations of these children, found almost exclusively in parental testimony, were ruled (often on an a priori basis) invalid or even delusional. As a result, intervention reduced quality of life for many of these children, as their own self-chosen behaviors, competencies, likes, and dislikes were ignored in planning programs for them. Instead, their lives were guided by a list of professionally located faults and technical solutions.

Having unearthed and clarified some of these issues, I was asked to do research on a small group of occupational therapists who were providing services to developmentally disabled adults living in community placements (Kielhofner & Takata, 1980). This group consisted of therapists who were moving away from the purely neurological, physiological, and psychoanalytical models of intervention associated with their profession toward an intervention paradigm that was humanistic and oriented to the everyday realities of their clients. Their intent was to focus their concern beyond etic descriptions of pathology and to examine and aid persons with differing competencies in their struggle to master everyday life. They wanted to see how clients spent their time, what skills and deficits they exhibited in their daily routines, and how they experienced and felt about their lives.

This approach was resonant with the perspective I had developed while working with deaf-blind people and their families. These therapists had already joined in collaborative work with an anthropologist and had begun to draw upon sociological principles to design effective intervention strategies with their clients. My role was to collect ethnographic observations and videotape their help-giving efforts. I set out to discover whether the arguments I had developed regarding deaf-blind children would also apply to adults who were biologically far less damaged. I focused on certain clients to whom the therapists were providing service. In case after case it became apparent that the fault-finding procedures I found in my earlier research with institutionalized deaf-blind children were precisely what these clients had also experienced. Our collaboration of social scientists and occupational therapists enabled the latter to establish an emic perspective as a central part of their evaluation and service delivery. This did not happen overnight, but required a long period of self-examination and self-discovery in addition to close attention to the details of the retarded persons' lives. Partly because I had experienced success with the strategy twice before and partly because there is a growing tendency for social scientists and therapists to realize the competence of the devalued by taking their perspective, I chose to illustrate some of these processes through the case study of a single man named Bobby. (All names used here are pseudonyms.)

WHO IS BOBBY?

Robert, or Bobby as he preferred to be called, was a 50-year-old man with Down Syndrome who had resided at the Sin San board and care facility for 7 years before our contact with him. He had been separated from his parents at a young age, lived with relatives for a short while, and was moved through varied living arrangements prior to his arrival at Sin San. Sin San—and other facilities like it—have been thoroughly described elsewhere (Bercovici, 1983). However, it should be noted that our ethnographic research led us to view such places as small-scale institutions within the community. This understanding of his environment was crucial to our appreciation of the adaptive competence of much of Bobby's behavior.

The Clinical Identity

I first came to know Bobby through his clinical records. He had a fairly substantial file that accompanied him wherever he moved and that summarized his "career" (Goffman, 1961) in human service contexts. His record was a kind of clinical biography that described his contacts with various helping professionals, their assessments and descriptions of him, as well as any remedial procedures offered to correct his deficiencies. These texts (for what they did or did not contain) were testaments to the clinical identity Bobby had been given. Nowhere was Bobby discussed in terms of his having any sort of competence and human value; instead an exclusively fault-finding perspective was employed. The descriptions pointed to a series of encounters in which clinical standards of normality had been used as criteria to identify the constitutional faults of the client. The unintended but functional effect of this predominantly diagnostic outlook was to portray Bobby as essentially incompetent and hopeless. Consider the following excerpts from Bobby's file:

> *Medical assessment*: "Down Syndrome . . . diabetes with peripheral vascular disease . . . edema of lower extremities."
>
> *Communication assessment*: "Speech or language therapy is not recommended as prognosis for improvement is poor . . . client can communicate basic needs but cannot express complex ideas and understands very little . . . difficult to communicate with."
>
> *Cognitive assessment*: A quick test of intelligence yielded a mental age of approximately 2.8 years. Clinician concludes that Bobby is "severely mentally retarded with severe brain damage."
>
> *Occupational therapy*: "Time and effort in this area are not suggested as prognosis for improvement is poor . . . maintain client in a protected environment as he can never function independently."

While these comments are out of context, they are not intended to exclude the "good" said about Bobby. There were no such comments. The contents of clinical files typically display only lists of the faults of chronically damaged persons, especially someone as "low functioning" as Bobby.

I had read many files like Bobby's before and had learned to regard them with some skepticism. Time and again I would read a file and then go and meet a child only to find that while the file did provide some valid technical data, it failed to provide anything that allowed me to understand the child or work with, teach, or relate to him or her. Thus, we took Bobby's file as an etic account of his life. We wanted to allow these clients to develop a more positive identity for us. We read their files expecting to find discrepancies between them and our own videotapes and fieldnotes. We even hoped for such differences.

Understanding Bobby

As noted above, getting to know these individuals in emic terms was an unfolding process. In Bobby's case videotaping would have an important role. Occupational therapists on the project who had been working with Bobby for some time described him as a clinically low functioning individual with remarkable native skills. I went to Sin San and met Bobby, and we began to see each other regularly. At that time, the members of the project and I experienced Bobby as a warm and friendly man whose presence (despite his sometimes poor self-care skills) was generally benign and positive. We all liked Bobby. He was bald and rotund with a simple perspective, which, even in the early part of our relationship, we learned to appreciate as expressing competent self-awareness and knowledge of his immediate surroundings. I selected Bobby as the client on whom I would concentrate my research efforts. It was clear that Bobby was retarded and in many ways incompetent. We had considerable difficulty understanding Bobby when he spoke, and we spoke simply to him because he could not comprehend complicated matters. However, we had yet to appreciate his full competence and cognizance.

Only on reviewing videotapes of our interactions with Bobby were his competence and abilities fully revealed to us. About 2 months after our first meeting, a series of events occurred that radically changed our appreciation of Bobby's competence and our relationship with him. Therapists and research staff had come to Sin San for the purpose of videotaping various clients, and we found ourselves in a room with three residents, including Bobby, who waited while we set up our equipment. When we finished, one of the therapists asked Bobby to leave because we were going to videotape the other two residents—twin sisters—and we wished to ensure the privacy of their remarks. Bobby insisted that he be allowed to remain during the taping. An altercation ensued, increasing in vehemence until the situation was finally resolved. The entire incident was captured by accident on tape.

The following edited transcription of this incident includes Bobby; Gary, an occupational therapist; Marty, a research assistant with the project; and Arlene and Alice, twin sisters who were going to be videotaped.

Marty: Does it bother you to leave now? (*Bobby is sitting and looking down, dejected. He looks up at Marty while she talks.*)
Bobby: [unhearable utterance] (*Bobby turns his head away while talking. Bobby looks at Marty while she speaks.*)

Marty: When we film you, no one else is gonna be there except you and
Bart [the facility cook] and all of us. I think it would make it a lot
easier for Arlene and Alice to talk about what it is they want to talk
about if they'd just be alone. OK. How do you feel about that?
(*During this explanation Bobby turns his head down, looking very un-
happy. He moves his hands to his mouth.*)

Bobby: Bart Daniel. [The meaning of this utterance is not apparent.]
(*Again Bobby turns toward Marty using hand gestures, voice, and inflec-
tion in his answer to her.*)

Marty: Is it OK if you leave now and we'll get to you next, OK?
(*Looking at Marty, Bobby quickly turns away and clearly displays his dis-
pleasure.*)

Gary: Well, uhh, the reason, the reason we're gonna do Arlene and Alice
is because they have . . . (*The names Arlene and Alice bring a raising
of the eyebrows and shrugging gesture on the part of Bobby.*)

Bobby: [interrupting] Bart say you talk to me! (*Bobby is adamant in tone.*)

Gary: What? We will, we will! We'll get time to talk to you. (*Gary is
startled, uses a defensive tone, and then reassures Bobby.*)

Bobby: An, Bart Daniels. (*Bobby points to the kitchen and looks at Gary. He
uses an assertive tone while shaking his head negatively.*)

Gary: We're gonna talk to Bart too. He said he was gonna be in the
movie with you. (*Bobby watches Gary, whose tone is reassuring.*)

Bobby: A body in the room, Bart, too. (*Again Bobby is assertive and shaking his head negatively. He is looking very bothered here.*) [At this point
it appears Bobby is trying to say everyone can stay in the room.]

Gary: Well, I, aah, I am sorry Bobby. I didn't understand you. What?
(*As Gary apologizes, Bobby looks away and puts his hand on his chin,
leaning.*)

Bobby: Bart Daniels is gonna to do another one? (*Very distressed here,
Bobby shakes his head negatively.*)

Marty: Bart Daniels is gonna to do another one? [Obviously she does
not understand what this utterance means.] (*Bobby listens to Marty's
repeat of his statement, nodding agreement.*)

Bobby: An Alice too. (*Still looking.*)

Arlene: Oh, he don't mean nothin! [referring to Bobby]

Gary: Okay, Bobby, we'll set this up . . . (*Bobby begins to look at Gary,
but turns away.*)

Marty: Since they [referring to Alice and Arlene] have to work in the
morning we thought we'd get them filmed first. And then, right
when we're finished, we'll come and film you and Bart in the
kitchen. (*Bobby, with hand on chin, is looking at the floor with an unchanging expression.*)

Gary: You know, Bobby, I'm sorry we hurt your feelings, but we didn't mean to. We didn't know it would make you feel bad if we did Arlene and Alice first.

Bobby: (*Bobby does an affrontive gesture—crossing the visual field with eyes turned down, indifferent to Gary's apology he stares off into space.*) [unintelligible utterance] . . . get somebody else.

Gary: Are you gonna be mad at us all day? (*Bobby sneaks a look at Gary and turns away quickly. There is silence for 18 seconds as he stares out of the window.*)

Bobby: I'll sit, I'll take a chair over there. (*Looks at Marty and gestures toward the couch near a window.*)

Gary: Oh, you said you'll sit back there?

Bobby: Yeah. (*Bobby looks at Gary and begins to grin when he hears Gary has understood him.*)

Marty: Oh, you said you'll sit back there, oh I see, Bobby. (*Bobby looks at Gary while Marty talks.*)

Gary: Bobby, I don't think that's fair, though, to Arlene and Alice in case they talk about things that are private. (*Bobby looks at Gary, his face turns to a frown, and he looks down and away.*)

Marty: [starts an explanation] We'll probably do a lot of films with everyone together, but this is a specific thing that is just for Alice and Arlene. (*Bobby looks at Marty and turns away.*)

Bobby: I would turn my head and tell nobody else. (*Bobby's voice is very shaky and filled with emotion. He's more upset than before.*) [Here Bobby clearly demonstrates he understands what privacy is all about.]

Marty: You won't tell anybody else! Well, I don't know that they just might feel up-tight. Well, I dunno. Why don't you ask them? (*Bobby still is looking out of the window. The "vibes" are heavy here.*)

Gary: Yeah, why don't you? Well . . . what?

Bobby: Well me and Jimmy . . . [unintelligible utterance] (*Bobby turns toward Arlene and Alice and camera follows to the sisters.*)

Gary: Well, what about you, Alice?

Alice: That's all right for him to be in here. (*Bobby smiles as Alice indicates his presence is fine with her.*)

Gary: You don't care?

Alice: Don't care, honey.

Marty: Yeah.

Gary: Well, maybe it's OK.

Marty: Sure.

Bobby: They don't care.

Gary: [relieved] OK, well, then I guess it's all taken care of. (*Bobby gets up.*)

Although this incident may seem unexceptional, it proved not to be so. At the time of the actual incident many of Bobby's utterances were not understood, but it was apparent that he had gotten his way. During the incident we were not cognizant of the mechanisms he employed, and we reasoned that if such mechanisms could be found, we could document competence inconsistent with Bobby's clinical picture.

The videotape revealed expressions of competence immediately. Bobby's superior knowledge of his social environment and his relationship to the twin sisters was the actual issue. Specifically, Bobby knew better than we the propriety of raising the issue of privacy with them. From his perspective, this issue was an imported (etic) concern of ours. It made no sense to insist on privacy, and his repeated, escalating protests reflected his frustration with our ignorance. Bobby had to rely on the more competent client (one of the sisters) to formulate this in a way we could understand, but once expressed, the instructional value of Bobby's protests was clear. For these former inmates who had no locks on their doors or any other personal space, privacy was not a reasonable concern. Bobby had understood this and used this as a basis for his strategy. Partially because he was right, he was successful, and it was we who would have to adjust our ideas about such matters within the board-and-care context. It is for this reason that the transcription of the tape is titled "Privacy Lost".

As I watched the videotape repeatedly, an even more radical appreciation of Bobby's abilities to understand and communicate emerged. At the time of the incident and during our initial viewings of the tape, it appeared that many of Bobby's utterances were unintelligible, if not unintelligent. But after watching the tape a number of times, many "unintelligible" utterances began to sound clear to us. While it was true that persons on the tape did not seem to understand Bobby, the same persons repeatedly watching the tape could hear words where formerly they heard mumblings. We discovered that normal persons had a paradoxical reaction to Bobby's talk. They denied understanding him, but often took in more information than they were aware of. For example, on the tape the occupational therapist reacted to Bobby's statement as if he did not understand it, but then proceeded to complete an answer to Bobby's question. We began to appreciate the degree to which Bobby's not making sense to us was as much our fault as it was his.

Prior to this discovery, we had thought that Bobby's utterances were nonsensical and we largely ignored them. When we mechanically altered Bobby's tonal qualities on the tape, many of these formerly senseless utterances became more audible. By means of mechanical readjustment they were "reperceived" as sensible (or sometimes potentially sensible) statements. Anyone who interacted with Bobby would perceive that his speech was apraxic. It was less obvious that his syntactically fractured talk had meaning, and especially that it was meaningfully related to the context of conversations. It had been our common assumption that Bobby did not understand much of what went on around him. But after watching the tape perhaps 30 times, a new definition of the situation emerged: Bobby's behavior seemed more like that of a foreign-speaking person than that of a retarded one. Apart from his difficulties in making himself understood, the transcript of that tape revealed that Bobby had followed the direction of the conversation and had produced semantically meaningful, if ill-formed, utterances. We began to appreciate that cognitively Bobby was far more complex than we had supposed. He was clearly above the 2.8 year mentality assigned to him in his clinical record. His appreciation of abstractions such as privacy, as both a local and larger cultural issue, and his 50 years of experience distinguished Bobby's perception of the world from that of a 3-year-old.

As we watched other tapes of Bobby, we heard how our participation with him determined, to a large degree, his competence. How we defined Bobby's participation, as in our abilities to understand his utterances, structured his potential competence with us. If this was true, we reasoned, perhaps a different communicational cohort—possibly his friends at the facility—could perceive more competence. We began to observe and tape Bobby in peer group interaction and were astonished at the extent to which our supposition was true. Bobby's friends reported that as far as they were concerned he had no communication problems and "talked fine." His more intimate friends claimed that Bobby talked as well as you or I, but that "we just didn't understand him." It did not take long for us to understand that familiarity and intimacy were the key determinants in viewing Bobby as competent to communicate and think. As we shall see when we discuss Bobby's relationship to the facility cook, Bart, these claims were not merely fictions of Bobby's friends' imaginations. Peer interaction tapes showed that Bobby behaved more competently with his friends than with project staff. As one project member put it, Bobby's competence did not travel well because it was linked to a particular cohort of intimates within a closed residential system.

Once the videotape had alerted us to the possible semantic content of Bobby's more problematic utterances, we began to understand his talk better. Furthermore, as we recognized the ecological specificity of his competence, we could make use of the local context to increase his competence in interaction. For instance, one occupational therapist found that conducting a conversation with Bobby in his room practically eliminated communication problems.

Bobby and Bart:
Emic and Etic Perspectives on Friendship

Our experience with the videotape discovery of Bobby's communicative and interactional competence and his superior native knowledge naturally led us to a systematic search for a whole range of socially adaptive skills that we had ignored in our etic interpretation of him. These competencies were not obvious and involved taking off "clinical blinders." Our growing emic conception of Bobby meant that virtually every "pathological" behavior we and others had identified in Bobby was open for review.

For example, we recorded another videotape showing an "interview" of Bobby by his friend and benefactor, Bart, the facility cook (see also Sutherland, 1980). The tape revealed a relationship in which Bobby was, in a clinical perspective, infantilized—treated as a child to the point where he called Bart, the younger of the two, his "daddy." Previously we saw Bobby as Bart's victim, since Bobby apparently lacked the communication and cognitive abilities to resist Bart's manipulations. Some of the scenes of infantilization on tape were striking. At one point Bart recited his pet name for Bobby, "Bobby-Baby-Boo-Boo-Bow-Bow-Porky-Pig-Oink-Oink," and followed this with a request that Bobby "bark" during the song "How Much Is That Doggy in the Window?" Paradoxically, Bart prided himself on being Bobby's best friend. Bobby called Bart his "daddy" and "best friend." Theirs was a contradictory relationship in which Bart clearly appeared to have the upper hand. For a while, everyone felt sorry for Bobby.

After our discovery of Bobby's competence in "Privacy Lost," we watched the scenes of infantilization with new interpretations of Bobby's behavior. It was not the case that Bobby was stupid and was manipulated by Bart. Instead we found ample evidence that Bobby was aware of and uncomfortable with his role and at times resisted being cast in this devalued and patronized position. Bobby allowed this in order to reap certain material and psychological benefits, which accrued from having the cook as friend and benefactor. Bart provided Bobby with special treats and evening snacks from the kitchen; he bought gifts and took Bobby for rides in his car. Furthermore, Bart was sincerely affectionate and employed his demeaning tactics in the belief that Bobby was not hurt by them. Bearing in mind the deprivations common to places like Sin San, the material and psychological advantages of having a normal friend who was also the cook become obvious. Moreover, competition for these scarce resources was fierce, and there were people at the facility with more skills than Bobby could bring into play. Yet it was Bobby who secured a normal member of the staff as his special friend. This was a source of pride for him, apart from the gifts, trips, and sandwiches. Given Bobby's situation at Sin San, he could have attained Bart's attentions in no other way than to act as his "pet." For Bobby, the role with all its costs was worth its benefits.

It is important to note that this emic account of Bobby's behavior was not simply a matter of wanting to find competence in his actions. Viewing the videotapes of him and Bart allowed us to switch frames of reference to a more adaptive theory of Bobby's relationship with Bart. This was not another etic version of Bobby's behavior but rather was an obvious (to Bobby at any rate) reality in his relationship to Bart. That is, Bobby was clearly aware of the costs and benefits of infantilization, although he had never been called upon to justify or explain his strategy to any of his friends.

The evidence that the adaptive version of Bobby's behavior was emic rests upon Bobby's own testimony. During the Bart–Bobby interview, I had become angry with Bobby because I felt he should not tolerate such treatment. Failing to appreciate the rationale behind Bobby's strategy, I pulled him into a room and shouted, "How could you do that (the barking and so on)?" I was so displeased that I threatened to leave because of his behavior. Bobby kept telling me to "calm down" and that "it was OK." It was not until I viewed the tape and found the key to his strategy that I was able to appreciate his instruction. I visited him again and we had a talk. I formulated for him as simply as I could my new adaptive theory of his behavior with Bart. He clearly followed each point, indicating that he agreed with my description of why he "put up with Bart." He told me that he "did not like Bart that much." When I said something to the effect that it was not up to me to decide for him what was worth suffering for, he was vigorous in his agreement. As far as he was concerned, it was up to Bobby to decide what was all right and what was not. And he was right.

In Bobby's eyes, in his experienced world, he was effectively mastering his situation through his relationship with Bart. The genetic, psychological, and social resources through which this mastery was achieved were admittedly uncommon, but, as with most humans, there is generally little one can do about such givens. Bobby's control of his situation was in terms of his life limitations.

Additional incidents on videotape and further discussions with and observations of Bobby corroborated this improved image of his competence. We ceased using a high-pitched, slow, and patronizing drawl with him. We had lost the clinical Bobby—the list of faults and hopelessness that constituted his formal identity—and we began to talk to him as a person like ourselves.

THE ROLES OF PROFESSIONAL IDEOLOGY AND VIDEOTAPE IN ACHIEVING EMIC ASSESSMENTS

Videotape played a dual role in our re-evaluation of Bobby's identity and our own attempts to help the residents at Sin San. As a method to generate alternative, more accurate, and, in some senses, "better" descriptions of behavior and interaction, videotape was a sine qua non. It was especially powerful in allowing us to understand both problematic and successful helping efforts. During the "Privacy Lost" incident, it was through repeated reviews of the videotape that we came to realize how our own humanistic stance, though benign in intent (i.e., maintaining privacy) was insufficient since it was not yet emically informed. Video provided an opportunity and occasion to understand what we had not perceived in the interaction by repeatedly standing "outside" of our own interaction with Bobby. Eventually we saw ourselves importing an issue of privacy where it did not belong, to our client's detriment. Tapes were an avenue through which we could explore the nature of our own participation with clients, and they seemed never to fail to deliver news in that regard. There was always something, professional or personal, to be learned by watching our actions on tape.

Viewing tapes of what we had done put us in a paradoxical position regarding the "actual" state of affairs as we experienced it. On the one hand, the tape was used to recapture much of the detail of what was said or done by Bobby or by us. We consulted videotapes to get a deeper and more accurate perception of what had been a lived reality for us. On the other hand, in producing alternative and better accounts of what actually happened we took by definition a very unnatural stance toward that reality. During viewing sessions it was not uncommon to hear things like, "I didn't realize that Bobby was making so much sense," or "It was I who didn't understand him; that never occurred to me." These are interesting observations and accurate—with respect to our viewings of the tape—but they were absolutely unrelated to our thoughts during the actual situation. The observations were, instead, extrinsic to the situation and a product of repeated viewings of tape and our efforts to understand what had happened. Having achieved these situationally extrinsic definitions of who Bobby actually was or what we had really done, and reflecting on our stance during the interaction, we all felt that we had been ignorant of who Bobby was as well as of the organization of our activities. Put as simply as possible, one cannot avoid the impression that persons generally do not know, other than in practical ways, what they are doing while they are doing it. Not that we do not have serious thoughts about what we were doing. Indeed, clinical rationales of action are often supported by voluminous articulations. But, these are, at best, partial understandings of our actions.

SOCIOGENIC IDENTITIES

In addition to relating the process by which we came to redefine Bobby's identity and our participation with him, I would like to offer a sociological explanation for these events. Such an exposition has to account for how it can be that the same person may have different identities and exhibit dissimilar behaviors depending on the interactional context (i.e., in the clinic or at home). Thus we have to address the social bases for differential identity and competence in a single individual. A shorthand way of saying this would be that we have to understand how persons' identities are sociogenic (literally, socially generated). The explication of this idea will run counter to most clinical conceptions of competence as a stable trait.

The idea of context-dependent identities and skills, while discontinuous with some psychodynamic notions of personal identity and behavior, is not odd or unexpected for the sociologist. The conception of context-specific identities has been part of modern sociology for over 50 years. In addition, the findings of social psychologists such as Asch (1956) and Zimbardo (1973) establish the primacy of situational factors in determining behavior.

Videotapes of Bobby in contexts other than those mentioned above reveal over and over again that Bobby's competence—indeed, the entire nature of his participation—seemed largely socially determined. Even with children such as the alingual, congenitally deaf-blind who have extremely limited behavioral repertoires, it is generally true that competence, participation, behavior, and cognition—that is, basic constituents of who a person is in any situation—are largely matters having to do with the social organization surrounding them (e.g., the clinic versus the home). An important part of the message of this chapter is that what is sociologically accepted with respect to "normal" persons is also true of disabled persons. Such a correlation allows us to consider the implications of this for the logic and practices of the helping professions that serve disabled persons and to discuss the significance of a conception of human identities as context specific for our understanding of human behavior in general.

Harold Garfinkel's (1967) conception of persons as "organizationally incarnate" is an inclusive account of the social production of identities. Garfinkel argues that it is the social organization surrounding people that gives them their identity and defines for them their participation, cognition, and so forth. Congruence or lack of congruence of identities in this approach is ultimately explained in terms of similarities or dissimilarities in social organization. Arguing in accordance with this position, physicians, occupational therapists, friends, and researchers tell different, partial, but organizationally sufficient truths about Bobby. These truths are for all practical purposes adequate to the work of doctoring (as defined by the physician) at a particular clinic, being a friend, being in a research relationship, and so forth. There is absolutely no empirical requirement that what persons say about Bobby or do with him be consistent within each setting. Thus, minimally, the professional or clinician should be aware of the realistic character of procedures and findings, and this awareness should affect practice with clients.

The implications of this theory for a conception of a person's competence are fairly clear. What most persons would call Bobby's competence (with emphasis on the possessive) is actually part of his socially produced, organizationally adequate identity. Any clinician's assessment of Bobby's competence reflects as much about the social organization of clinical work, the clinician's training, and a particular clinic's instruments and procedures, as it does about Bobby per se. Any researcher's belief about Bobby's competence reflects as much about the researcher, organization of the research, and so forth, as it does about Bobby. As our history with Bobby demonstrates, radically different conceptions of his competence arose from different kinds of social relations with him. In this sense it should be no surprise that Bobby's friends felt he had no language difficulties and spoke with him freely, while clinicians who were strangers to Bobby found him to have extremely marginal language skills.

Partly because they have done their professional best with "Bobby" (we'll use him in an exemplary way here), and partly because they believe in the validity of their tests and procedures, many clinicians find it difficult to accept that their clinically adequate procedures fail to detect Bobby's competence in other settings. Most often they are completely unaware of the problem, believing that their procedures capture Bobby's competence independent of any specific social context. They perceive their test results as indicating stable attributes of Bobby, and thus they fail to grasp the social relativity of their own assessments and procedures. In so doing they also fail to understand the relationship between Bobby's clinically determined competence and his competence as experienced by his daily associates. For professionals with an "everyday" orientation, such a gap in knowledge brings into question the efficacy and validity of many intervention procedures.

It was possible and valid to see Bobby as merely "a case" of Down Syndrome or as a person, if judged by normal standards, with a host of related problems. But it was equally valid and in most contexts more beneficial for Bobby to see him as a man with an unusual countenance and different ways of thinking and evaluating, trying to explore and master his everyday world. The humanistic basis of such a description, too often absent from clinical evaluations, directed our attention away from a client's deficits—from the ways he was different from us—and toward a person like ourselves who happened to have deficits in some areas and skills in others. Our experiences with Bobby showed that such a change was plausible and to the benefit of all concerned.

NOTES

Acknowledgments. Special thanks to Wolf Wolfensberger, Gary Kielhofner, Isidore Goode, Sylvia Bercovici, Herbert Grossman, Donald Sutherland, and Robert Edgerton for comments on earlier drafts. Pamela Aregood provided excellent secretarial support.

1. The research on the deaf-blind children cited in the text may be found in Jacobs (1980). This chapter is dedicated to the memory of Bobby, who died in 1979.
2. The concept of fault finding is taken from the work of Harold Garfinkel (personal communication, 1975). The general approach taken in this work stems largely from his influence. The discussion of emic and etic knowledge owes much to conversations with him and Melvin Pollner (personal communications, 1973-1978).

REFERENCES

Asch, S. E. (1956). Studies of independence and conformity: A minority of one against a unanimous majority. *Psychological Monographs, 70*(9, Serial No. 416).

Bercovici, S. (1983). *Barriers to normalization: The restrictive management of retarded persons.* Baltimore: University Park Press.

Evans-Pritchard, E. E. (1937). *Witchcraft, oracles and magic among the Azande.* Oxford: Oxford University Press.

Garfinkel, H. (1967). *Studies in ethnomethodology.* Englewood Cliffs, NJ: Prentice-Hall.

Goffman, E. (1961). *Asylums: Essays on the social situation of mental patients and other inmates.* Garden City, NY: Doubleday, Anchor Books.

Jacobs, J. (Ed.). (1980). *Mental retardation: A phenomenological approach.* Springfield, IL: Charles C. Thomas.

Kielhofner, G., & Takata, N. (1980). A study of mentally retarded persons: Applied research in occupational therapy. *American Journal of Occupational Therapy, 34*, 252-258.

Sutherland, D. (1980). Contest and competence: Some situations of mental retardation in a medicated ethnography of communication (Doctoral dissertation, University of California, Los Angeles, 1980). *Dissertation Abstracts International, 41*, 307A–308A.

Zimbardo, P. (1973, April 8). A Pirandellian prison. *New York Times Magazine*, pp. 38–53, 56–60.

Chapter 10

"TRY HARDER"

The Experience of Disability
and the Dilemma of Normalization

Marilynn J. Phillips

For persons with disabilities, the dilemma of "trying harder to succeed" involves, first and foremost, a determination of what is meant by success. Does success mean the pursuit of normalization, or even the illusion of normality, at all costs? Or does success mean, as one participant in my study quipped, "becoming a professional handicapper," that is, becoming an individual known primarily by his or her disability?[1] At what point can the disabled person shed the social stereotypes and be accepted as an individual who is also physiologically different? And at what point can those with disabilities relinquish the stereotypical handicapped roles, sometimes as secure as they are suffocating, in their pursuit of uniqueness and individuality (Gartner, 1982)?

Over an 18-month period, during my residence in a midwestern university town, I documented oral narratives from 22 females and 13 males with various physical disabilities (Phillips, 1984; Stahl, 1977). Informants ranged in age from 21 to early 60s. Two-thirds have been disabled since early childhood. All except two are Caucasian, these two being racially mixed but reared in predominantly Caucasian environments. Like many other disabled people (Fine & Asch, 1981) my informants have higher than average educational levels though lower than average socioeconomic levels in comparison with their able-bodied peers. (All informants cited are referred to by pseudonym and their identities disguised to preserve their privacy.)

For many of my informants, their own ambivalence about the cultural value of perseverance is further complicated by rehabilitation practitioners' objectives of normalization, particularly when informants perceive such objectives to be inconsistent with their personal expectations and goals. It is

---

An earlier version of this chapter appeared in *Social Science Journal, 22*(4), 45–57, 1985.

true that the explicit objective of the rehabilitation paradigm is that the client "attain his maximal potential for normal living" (Krusen, 1971), with an emphasis on "potentiation" and not necessarily on normalization. However, informants report that in their rehabilitation experiences it was normalization, and not necessarily potentiation, that was emphasized. Informants indicate that for the most part they respected their practitioners as individuals; yet, they also express their ambivalence toward what they perceive to be an implicit goal of the rehabilitation process, namely, normalization. I say "ambivalence" because informants did discuss their own desires to achieve normality, while claiming distrust for those practitioners who emphasize normalization.

A significant variable in informants' determination of success is an ideological shift—away from absolute belief in the rehabilitation paradigm and toward a perception of their own minority status, this latter consciousness apparently wrought by the disability rights movement. The factor of ideology appears to affect whether and to what degree informants defined success in terms of social or personal accomplishment. Their narratives identify five major kinds of success: acquiescence, normalization, adaptation, renegotiation, and inversion. The first two are invoked for social success, and the last three for personal success. No informant subscribed solely to one or another of these definitions; in fact, most vacillated among the five. Such vacillation suggests that theirs are not static, but dynamic approaches to definitions of success. That is, their definitions vary according to context-specific situations and the type of accomplishment (social or personal) desired. These definitions of success are part of a dynamic, and even transformational, process by which the individual attempts to assert control over his or her unique disability-related experiences (Phillips, 1988).

First to be considered are three ideological frameworks that provide the basis for the informants' ambivalence and influence their selection of a particular success definition: the cultural notion of perseverance, the rehabilitation model, and the social minority model. Following these are analyses of the five definitions of success given by informants in their oral narratives.

THE CULTURAL NOTION OF PERSEVERANCE

Americans are enjoined to succeed in all undertakings. As Ortner (1973) observes, the traditional Horatio Alger story remains a key scenario in American culture, promising even those of a lowly birth the opportunity, if they try hard enough, to achieve success. Although the more sophisticated twentieth-century, poor-boy-makes-good promise can be disputed, the popular media are replete with stories about Americans who persevere and who believe that hard work pays off. Surely a notion so ingrained in the American psyche influences the manner in which individuals with disabilities are expected to "overcome" all obstacles in their pursuit of a higher station—in their pursuit of normality (Gliedman & Roth, 1980).

From the perspective of the American ethos, "If you try hard enough, you will succeed," and even beyond its manifestations in the popular images of a Franklin Delano Roosevelt or a Helen Keller, there continue to be cultural exaltations of disabled persons who "try harder" in their pursuit of normalization (Alsop, 1982; Lash, 1980; Looker, 1933). Such lauding of the perseverance of disabled persons was demonstrated most recently in the extensive media coverage of spinal cord-injured Nan Davis's working-to-walk campaign. Indeed, slogans modeled on such an American ideal have facilitated fund raising for, among others, the Sister Kenny movement in the 1940s and the 1950s (Cohn, 1975; Kenny & Ostenso, 1943), for which the motto "They shall walk again" promised the American people that contributions would inspire "crippled" children to try harder. More modern campaigns, particularly the controversial Jerry Lewis Telethon for Muscular Dystrophy, assure the public that their financial contributions will permit medical researchers to work ever more diligently on finding cures, while those already "afflicted" will continue to persevere. Implicit in such pronouncements is a belief that perseverance will result in the *defeat* of disability (although "overcoming" a disability is a viable symbolic alternative). Additionally, though, such perseverance also assumes that the individual's goal is the resumption of physiological normality and, ideally, the return to societal responsibilities (Gliedman & Roth, 1980; Parsons, 1951/1967).

THE REHABILITATION MODEL

In American culture, it is primarily the rehabilitation process that assists the disabled individual to recoup those American virtues, independence and self-reliance, supposedly lost due to disablement. In cases of those disabled since birth or childhood, such attributes are assumed not even to have been instilled through "normal" socialization processes (Vash, 1981). This medical model approach is increasingly refuted by practitioners who recommend individualizing the rehabilitation process to identify specific needs and goals of each client, instead of subsuming the client to the social goals of normalization and physical restoration (DeLoach & Greer, 1981).

The problem of individualizing the rehabilitation process was addressed by some practitioners even before the advent of the disability rights movement. For example, in her classic work, Wright (1960, pp. 13–14) decries the "overriding potency" of "normal behavior" used as the standard by many rehabilitation practitioners. She concedes, however, that the standard of achieving normality might be abided when

1. Increasing the disabled person's awareness of physiological potential helps to avoid the internalization of the notion of spread
2. Permitting the individual to cling to the normal ideal serves as a transition to recognition of real limitations
3. Normalizing interactional mannerisms (social etiquette) enhances the disabled individual's sociability
4. Permitting the disabled individual to undergo even painful physiological restoration affects positively the psychological adjustment to the disability

Wright and others (Kerr, 1977) also caution practitioners to avoid the deification of normality and suggest instead that they guide the disabled individual, particularly the newly disabled individual, through the predictable phases of mourning, learning to subordinate physique, and containing disability effects. Although Wright allows that normalization might be abided, she counsels the practitioner nevertheless to try to effect changes in the disabled individual's belief systems, because, as a prerequisite to self-acceptance, the disabled individual must retreat from negative social images and accept the "difference as nondevaluating." Less than such acceptance (including denial), Wright believes, results in maladjustment. In addition, although Wright is cognizant of the many negative societal reactions to physical disability, she still contends that American cultural attitudes toward "atypical physique" are conflicting, that is, "viewing [it] on the one hand as a sign of inferiority, and on the other hand as neutral or even as an indication of virtue and goodness meriting special reverence." She concludes (Wright, 1960) with a telling question: "Why is it [then] that the person with a disability focuses on the personally more devastating side of the conflict?" (p. 106).

Thus, Wright clearly, though unintentionally, illustrates the cultural preconceptions toward disability that are ingrained even in advocate professionals. On the one hand, Wright vehemently rejects the notion that physically disabled persons collectively are psychologically different from their able-bodied peers. On the other hand, she suggests that disabled individuals are psychologically similar, perhaps even pathologically so, in that they often choose to focus on "the devastating side of disability" (p. 106) rather than on their superior status. Significantly, other scholars in the field of the psychology of disability make assumptions of maladjustment even as they argue for clients' rights to be treated like individuals. Notably an exception, DeLoach and Greer (1981) attribute more to the social dimension of adjustment and argue for the practitioner's responsibility to advocate social reform, and Vash (1981) concludes that activism is for the disabled individual the culmination to any personal "transcendence." Still, in effect these analyses of the social and psychological contexts for disabled persons are an accurate portrayal of the quixotic interpersonal environment in which disabled persons must self-determine their social and personal goals and, therefore, their own definitions of success.

Indeed, informants report that the rehabilitation model, even in its modern, meliorative orientation, still encourages both practitioner and client to "try harder" to effect personal adjustment *to* society. As Hey and Willoughby (1984) point out, such a posture of adjustment to society may reinforce among clients and society stereotypical notions about the helplessness of disabled persons, resulting in a perpetuation of their social and economic segregation. Moreover, as Hahn (1983) notes, out of an amalgam of admiration and sympathy and pity has grown a cultural paternalism that guides the development of a welfare-oriented, rather than a work-oriented, public policy for the disabled. Roth (1983), as well, cautions that "like motherhood and apple pie" (p. 59) disabled people often are free from overt attack, particularly since their physical characteristics may elicit sympathy; but covertly this "aura of paternalism" continues to "permeate relations between disabled and nondisabled segments of the population" (p. 59), perhaps reinforcing rather than eradicating the social and self-perceptions of disabled individuals' inferiority and consequently their predilection for failure.

THE SOCIAL MINORITY MODEL

What concerns the informants who are active in disability rights is that the rehabilitation model, even as liberalized by Wright and others, continues to focus on their victim status and their problems as stigmatized persons, rather than assisting disabled persons in redefining criteria by which success (or normality) is measured. As informant Jacob Lind retorts, "There is nothing *wrong* with me!"—a position in accordance with Goffman's (1963) contention that normality and stigma are not qualities inherent in persons but rather social perspectives.

Regional and national disability rights movements have engendered in persons with disabilities a belief in their social minority status and a rejection of their culturally assigned anomalous status. Indeed, the notion of "normal" is mocked by those who remind the able-bodied of their own vulnerability, taunting them with the label "t.a.b." (temporarily able-bodied); and many disabled persons seek to be regarded as members of a distinct group that functions to enhance the physiological diversity of the larger culture (McCay & Makowsky, 1969). In decades past, disabled role models included not only the famous among the perseverant, but also common men and women, and often children, whose perseverance against the odds was captured in inspirational stories of their lives (Killilea, 1952). In stark contrast, role models during the apex of the disability rights movement were abstractions of the "radical cripple," whose countenance and rhetoric generated a sense of extended community among diverse and divergent groups of disabled persons (Heumann, nd). Indeed, even those disabled perceived to have been smothered by social exclusion and segregation, such as those living in institutions, often heeded the rhetoric calling for independence and self-reliance. Since the 1980s, disabled role models may have become abstractions *not* of a personality type, but once again of traditional American ideals. That is, many disabled individuals, like their able-bodied peers, desire success, not necessarily within the social isolation of their group, but rather "in the real world."

In the past there were numerous success stories about those who overcame handicaps (Asch & Sachs, 1983). The newer notion of "real world" success appears to be different from what Roth (1983) describes as (earlier) acquiescent notions of overcoming and adjusting. The current variant, influenced greatly by the disability rights movement but also by traditional American virtues and values, is a composite of accommodation and potentiation: assimilation *sans* denial. Someone like informant Jacob Lind, who desires a hiatus from involvement in the disability rights movement in order to achieve success in the "real world," does not deny his disability, nor does he feel that he must adjust to society, abandon the cause, or reject his social minority status. Rather, he believes that he has a contract with society, an expectation that society will act responsibly by accommodating his physiological differences and needs (primarily through the removal of architectural barriers) and that he will act responsibly by striving to be self-reliant and independent. For Jacob, the social minority model is the means by which consciousness is raised for sociopolitical action not only for collective gains, but also for individual success. Although the disability rights movement professes an ideology of activism, as Roth (1983) notes, it also affirms an "overwhelmingly and classically liberal [ideology] . . . to be included in the social contract that has been part of this nation since its founding" (p. 61). The narratives of informants are replete with speculations about a new status quo, a new society, and a new social structure—a radical rhetoric. But by and large, these informants demonstrate the ideals of a liberal ideology in their pursuit of success. The conflict they feel, the dilemma that they have, is how to maintain a positive self-image and achieve personal success, while striving for a successful social image in a society that is reluctant to accommodate, for social, political, and economic reasons, their physiological differences (DeJong & Lifchez, 1963).

DEFINITIONS OF SUCCESS IN THE NARRATIVES

Many of my informants feel caught in a dilemma: It is reasonable that they desire to maximize and/or restore their physiological abilities, yet some feel ambivalent about capitulating to societal pressure to achieve form and function normality. To illustrate, some informants have elected *not* to spend time and energy learning how to walk again. Frank Congress, for example, rejects ambulation with the same intensity of conviction that popular media's Nan Davis exhibits in her working-to-walk campaign. Robert Bell admits that he "would like to be able to stand up long enough to lift his wheelchair over the curbs," but acknowledges that he is unwilling to expend his energy indefinitely in the pursuit of becoming ambulatory once again, especially in lieu of furthering his professional career. Jonathan Webb reveals that he "doesn't really mind" using a wheelchair the rest of his life, if "only [he] could use [his] arms again." In contrast, Bonnie Anderson indicates why she perseveres, through numerous surgical procedures and continuous physical therapy, to achieve ambulation: "Because they respect you more if you can 'stand up to' them!" But perhaps even Bonnie's extensive surgical experiences have resulted in more than physical restoration. As MacGregor (1974) infers, the process of restorative surgery itself can be a positive factor in the individual's self-esteem, providing for self and for others evidence of one's social success in maximizing form and function capabilities and one's personal success in determining the fate of his or her own body, a body perceived to be "out of control." As informants relate in their narratives, each disabled person individually must negotiate the parameters of these definitions of success.

Success-as-normalization is marked by affiliation with "normals," distinctiveness as a handicapped person (overcoming), and disaffiliation from those perceived to *acquiesce* to the "cripple role." Others define success as a continuous *adaptation* of the environment to individuals' physiological needs. Some recount other strategies, including *renegotiating* social definitions of normality, or *inverting* the social stereotypes associated with disability. The majority evidence a complex approach to their selecting appropriate strategies for social interaction and personal satisfaction. For example, one disabled individual alternately may invoke success-as-normalization and success-as-adaptation to achieve social goals, yet acquiesce to the "cripple role" in order to manage, or to manipulate, one discrete situation. It is notable that I have *not* found any direct correlation between approaches selected and personality or physiological types. It does appear, however, that the disability rights movement has influenced individuals to retreat from acquiescence and normalization, and instead to define success in terms of adaptation, renegotiation, and, perhaps indirectly, inversion. My informants describe myriad contexts in which they define success, each definition according to a specific social or personal accomplishment desired. Following are cases illustrating such context-specific approaches to their definition of success.

The Case of Jessica Howard

In an essay on the circular problems and double standards confronting ethnic minorities, Riesman (1955) makes an analogy to the "cripple [making use of] his misery . . . for fragmentary purposes." Inadvertently, Riesman affirms the then-prevalent cultural assumption of the "cripple role." Unfortunately, the stereotype of the disabled person as dependent, helpless, weak, and passive still is prevalent, particularly among the nondisabled public but also among persons with disabilities (Fine & Asch, 1981). To be associated with the "cripple role" is tantamount to being assigned permanent child status. However, among my informants, it is rarely financial or physiological dependency that defines such acquiescence. They, like Riesman, define the "cripple role" as the manipulation of disability to achieve success, however "fragmentary." Yet, unlike Riesman, the informants do *not* believe that the majority of disabled persons play such a role.

Not surprisingly, none of the informants defines his or her own behavior in terms of acquiescence, although some mention suspicious strategies used by others. And, on occasion, some reveal in amusement, or in guilt, a "cripple" behavior to which they capitulated in order to accomplish a short-range goal. Most of them adamantly resent society's perception of an individual's ability to be independent and productive solely in terms of physiological capacities. Certainly, several of my informants may be perceived as dependent and nonproductive, yet through their labor they, in fact, do contribute to the community.

Jessica Howard, who has multiple sclerosis (MS), relies on Social Security Disability Insurance benefits; she also works as a volunteer at a community outreach center. She reciprocates in this way in order to retain her independence to think and to choose for herself. Although Jessica may appear to acquiesce because she requires financial and physical assistance, she does take responsibility for her own destiny, a responsibility hard won after her last MS exacerbation. It was then, after being institutionalized because rehabilitation practitioners presumed her to be dependent and helpless, that Jessica reassessed her own definitions of normality. She determined that "health was not all there is to being alive" and that independence is taking responsibility for her own survival. Although Jessica physically may appear to be acquiescent, she defines success as a renegotiation of society's notions of independence and self-reliance, and indeed of normality itself.

The Cases of David Simmons and Rebecca Johnson

One problem with success-as-normalization is its ambivalent message which entreats disabled individuals not only to reform society but also to transform themselves by simultaneously rejecting and affirming the ideal of normality. Success-as-normalization requires the individual to transcend human frailties (including the cultural valuation of normal physique), ameliorate those social ills that beset disabled persons, and appear and behave as normally as possible without deifying normality. Adaptation, on the other hand, means the conversion of the environment to the specifications of diverse physiologies, as in the application of new technologies.

That success definitions are also related to personal and even ideological perspectives is illustrated in the cases of two individuals whose cerebral palsy greatly impedes their speech patterns. David Simmons is in his mid-20s and is active in social functions held by the regional Center for Independent Living. A chair user, David is also physically limited to the extent that he requires assistance with virtually all activities of daily living (ADL). In addition, he is unable to speak in a manner comprehensible to most individuals with whom he interacts. David has few options in meeting his desire to communicate with others. He might elect to continue speech therapy and struggle to pronounce, albeit slowly and laboriously, a few words at a time. Instead, he opts to use a communication board, a system replete with deficiencies in that his vocabulary is limited by the constraints of space, but a system that does increase the numbers of persons with whom he can, at least potentially, communicate.

Rebecca Johnson, on the other hand, rejects such devices. She, too, has cerebral palsy and is a chair user. She has more mobility than David, as she is able to use her feet to push around a manual wheelchair and her hand to operate a battery-run wheelchair. An attractive woman in her late 20s, who insists on being well-groomed and expertly made-up, Rebecca has extended her strong sense of public presentation (Goffman, 1959) to her attempt to speak normally. In spite of her efforts, those who know Rebecca still have some difficulty understanding her particular style of speech. Others find her way of speaking extremely difficult to comprehend, straining to listen to each syllable and then piecing together words they do understand with phrases that they do not. Because Rebecca has some control over her speech, she attempts to potentiate whatever ability she has. On the other hand, in her struggle for what appears to be normalization (an independence from nonconventional methods and devices), she restricts the number of those with whom she can interact. The key to the difference between the approaches selected by David and Rebecca is not either's resistance to "trying harder" to achieve success, but rather their individual definitions of success.

Regarding their use of wheelchairs, both David and Rebecca define success as adaptation, the conversion of environment or mechanical devices to accommodate unique physiological characteristics. Yet, each approaches success at communication from different perspectives and with different goals. David accommodates others as well as himself, for although communicating with the board takes time for both David and the reader, the reader's patience is not overly taxed. After observing David at length, however, I began to realize that he is assertive and in control of the communication process. First, he has immediate access to interactions with strangers. It is true that many may react negatively to his disability and his physique. Yet, because of the communication board, he is approachable to the extent that his "speech" is universalized and can be understood even by strangers. Second, he adapts these aids not only to his own physiological limitations, but also to others' limitations (tolerance and time). Perhaps his is not a radical approach, but he achieves success by accomplishing social interaction otherwise unavailable to him, as well as easing some of the personal isolation resulting from his physiological limitations.

In contrast, Rebecca appears to choose as close an approximation to normality as possible, even though the result is that she communicates with only a few. It is also plausible that Rebecca, a gregarious person, resists using any devices that might impede her expressive nonverbal communication, an important aspect of body image (form maximization) (Birdwhistle, 1970). What is notable about Rebecca is her activism; she has participated in picketing and campaigned for disability rights. What appears to be her desire to achieve normality may, in fact, be her renegotiation of the definition of what is normal speech. Her decision to speak, rather than to use aids or mechanical devices, is an assertion of her right to control the means by which she communicates with others. For some, Rebecca's stance is stubborn and self-defeating. Yet Rebecca is challenging the tradition of disabled persons' accommodating to the nondisabled world.

Defining Mobility as Personal or Social Success

Each of the informants approaches function restoration and maximization differently, as is illustrated in their choices of mobility devices. Increasingly, battery-run wheelchairs are used not only by those for whom manual wheelchairs are inoperable, but also by those for whom the operation of manual wheelchairs requires an extraordinary and sometimes wasteful output of energy (Lifchez & Winslow, 1979). For Jacob Lind, the motorized wheelchair allows mobility independence and is a symbol of his freedom: "[When I went to college] voc rehab provided me with a motorized wheelchair, and so I was experiencing things for the first time in my life, being alone, and being forced to deal with the outside world, and forcing *them* to deal with me. I loved it!" Jacob adapts technology and a new environment (architectural accessibility) to his physiological needs. He is also, however, renegotiating definitions of the "appropriate place" for persons with disabilities.

On the other hand, other informants consider the use of mechanical devices indicative of a loss of control over the disability. Len Richardson, who has multiple sclerosis, uses a wheelchair only at work to facilitate his mobility there, although he is ambulatory at home and outside. He expresses a reluctance to "capitulate" to a more permanent use of a wheelchair, although he is unable to walk more than 50 feet. Len feels that he must resist using devices that not only mark, but also may exacerbate the progressive nature of his disability. He believes he is able to monitor his physiological changes by alternating his modes of mobility. In addition, because of his ambulation (limited as it is), he feels less isolated in a society that remains wheelchair inaccessible.

In contrast, Frank Congress regards his sportschair as an asset to his mobility. Frank, who lost both legs in an industrial accident, at first accepted the notion that to look and to act "normal" he would have to wear artificial legs. As he began to determine his own mobility needs, he rejected the physiological normalization afforded by prostheses. He chooses instead to adapt a mechanical aid, a sports wheelchair, to his needs, including his participation in wheelchair basketball. Also, to invert (and spoof) some of the social stereotypes (Douglas, 1973) about appropriate disability-related behavior, Frank relishes dramatizing his freedom from prostheses—unabashedly performing handstands on his sportschair, leg stumps jutting skyward.

Some informants do continue to work toward physiological restoration. Bonnie Anderson uses a wheelchair, yet she continues to undergo corrective surgery so that one day she will be able to walk. Bonnie defines success pragmatically, hoping to increase her employment prospects by being ambulatory. Although she rigorously supports architectural accessibility, she also affirms both the personal and the political importance, for her, of the restorative process: She quite literally desires to "stand up to" the able-bodied. Bonnie's ideological stance is that persons with disabilities must renegotiate definitions of normality: "We have 'physical characteristics,' *not* disabilities." Still, she is pragmatic about restoring her function to as close to "normal" as is possible. Bonnie defines success as a personal evolution: first, a retreat from the deification of normality; second, an identification with the disabled collective (the social minority model); third, an acceptance of social responsibility to maximize physiological capabilities; and fourth, an assertion of the right to control all decisions regarding one's body and one's life goals.

CONCLUSION

Of the informants cited here, Bonnie Anderson is perhaps the most reflective about the transformational process resulting from her disability-related experiences. The concept of transformation does not necessarily imply a progression through predictable stages or phases, although Bonnie does describe hers as a personal evolution. Nor does transformation denote what Vash (1981) calls transcendence, a deification of disability, and a kind of inversion of the cultural obsession with normality. Transformation is akin to a new individualism arising from the achievements of the disability rights movement. Ironically, out of this collective movement and out of disability kinship emerges an assertion of uniqueness and the right to individuality. Primarily it involves the disregarding of deviant status and inferior roles associated with the acquiescent "cripple role." Of course, such disavowal of deviance is not a new concept but traditionally was associated with the normalization process (Davis, 1975). What is new is that the former ideal of normalization now is perceived to have been but a grand deception (e.g., Gallagher, 1985). Certainly, my informants express that as a result of the movement, they have a new belief in their ability to control their own destinies without capitulating totally to normalization. They have disregarded the old strategies of defining social or personal success solely in terms of acquiescence and normalization, and have embraced new strategies of adaptation and renegotiation, and even of inversion. Still, the new definitions are strongly influenced by the liberal ideologies of American notions of trying harder to achieve independence and self-reliance. Yet, they are not merely new packaging for old liberal philosophies. They are different conceptual frames, different perceptions of self and of society (Bateson, 1978).

The oral narratives of my informants reveal all these ideological underpinnings of their definitions of success. My findings indicate that for my informants defining success is a complex and dynamic process, which is specific to each context and each new situation. They resist acquiescence, but acknowledge the social benefits that may accrue from playing the "cripple role." They have ambivalent feelings about normalization, resenting socially imposed criteria; but they do identify personal criteria for the potentiation of their physiologies. These personal criteria may involve renegotiation of cultural notions of normality, although at times the physiological outcome may be the same. However, it is the process that is most meaningful to them, as it is based on the new ideological perspective of their social minority status: They believe, or portend to believe, in their difference, not deviance.

Perhaps the most significant social implication of these findings involves a reassessment of the rehabilitation process. Although for many disabled individuals the rehabilitation experience is relatively short, its effects on individuals may be far-reaching. Certainly there is a cultural perception that persons with disabilities perpetually engage in rehabilitation, "trying hard" to achieve normalization. Newly disabled individuals particularly are affected by what may become for them an unending pursuit of form and function restoration. If they do not succeed at defeating their disability, they may presume that they have failed. As Scott (1969) reports, the rehabilitation process may accommodate, rather than defuse, such perceptions.

One aspect of this problem that was expressed in my informants' narratives is an overemphasis on the value of prostheses and cosmeses. They claim that the message too often is normalization through technology, rather than the adaptation by the individual of those devices relevant not only to physiological needs but also, and perhaps more important, to ideological perspectives. The rehabilitation model may need to accommodate these new perspectives and these nontraditional strategies, including the rejection by disabled persons of notions of "disability-appropriate behavior" (Fordyce, 1971), another concept that is anathema to the new ideology. This involves not only individualizing rehabilitation but also a commitment to and respect for diverse definitions of success that may be inconsistent with the traditional goals of rehabilitation or with the cultural notions of the meaning of success for persons with disabilities.

NOTE

1. The term *handicapper* is used in Michigan, where I did my field work.

REFERENCES

Alsop, J. (1982, January). Roosevelt remembered. *Smithsonian Magazine*, 38–49.
Asch, A., & Sachs, L. H. (1983). Lives without, lives within: Autobiographies of blind women and men. *Journal of Visual Impairment and Blindness*, 77, 242–247.

Bateson, G. (1978). *Steps to an ecology of mind*. New York: Ballantine Books.

Birdwhistle, R. L. (1970). *Kinesics and context*. Philadelphia: University of Pennsylvania Press.

Cohn, V. (1975). *Sister Kenny*. Minneapolis: University of Minnesota Press.

Davis, F. (1975). Deviance disavowal: The management of strained interaction by the visibly disabled. *Social Problems, 22*, 548–557.

DeJong, G., & Lifchez, R. (1963). Physical disability and public policy. *Scientific American, 248*, 40–47.

DeLoach, C., & Greer, Bobby G. (1981). *Adjustment to severe physical disability*. New York: McGraw-Hill.

Douglas, M. (1973). *Natural symbols: Explorations in cosmology*. New York: Vintage.

Fine, M., & Asch, A. (1981). Disabled women: Sexism without the pedestal. *Journal of Sociology and Social Welfare, 8*, 233–248.

Fordyce, W. E. (1971). Psychological assessment and management. In F. Krusen, F. Kottke, & P. Ellwood (Eds.), *Handbook of physical medicine and rehabilitation* (pp. 168–195) (2nd ed.). Philadelphia: Saunders.

Gallagher, H. (1985). *FDR's splendid deception*. New York: Dodd, Mead.

Gartner, A. (1982). Images of the disabled; Disabling images. *Social Policy, 13*(2), 14–15.

Gliedman, J., & Roth, W. (1980). *The unexpected minority: Handicapped children in America*. New York: Harcourt Brace Jovanovich.

Goffman, E. (1959). *The presentation of self in everyday life*. Garden City, NY: Doubleday, Anchor Books.

Goffman, E. (1963). *Stigma: Essays on the social situation of mental patients and other inmates*. Englewood Cliffs, NJ: Prentice-Hall.

Goffman, E. (1967). *Interaction ritual*. Garden City, NY: Doubleday, Anchor Books.

Hahn, H. (1983). Paternalism and public policy. *Society, 20*, 36–46.

Heumann, J. (nd). Consumer perspective. In D. Olson & E. Henig (Eds.), *Proceedings of an International Symposium: What ever happened to the polio patient* (pp. 141–145). Chicago: The Education and Training Center, Rehabilitation Institute of Chicago.

Hey, S. C., & Willoughby, G. (1984). Emerging trends among rehabilitation workers for the blind. In S. Hey, G. Kiger, & J. Seidel (Eds.), *Social aspects of chronic illness, impairment and disability* (pp. 4–14). Salem, OR: Society for the Study of Chronic Illness, Impairment and Disability & Willamette University.

Kenny, Sister E., & Ostenso, M. (1943). *And they shall walk again*. New York: Dodd, Mead.

Kerr, N. (1977). Understanding the process of adjustment to disability. In J. Stubbins (Ed.), *Social and psychological aspects of disability: A handbook for practitioners* (pp. 317–324). Baltimore: University Park Press.

Killilea, M. (1952). *Karen*. Englewood Cliffs, NJ: Prentice-Hall.

Krusen, F. H. (1971). The scope of physical medicine and rehabilitation. In F. Krusen, F. Kottke, & P. Ellwood (Eds.), *Handbook of physical medicine and rehabilitation* (pp. 1–12) (2nd ed.). Philadelphia: Saunders.

Lash, J. P. (1980). *Helen and teacher*. New York: Delacorte Press.

Lifchez, R., & Winslow, R. (1979). *Design for independent living*. New York: Watson-Guptill.

Looker, E. (1933). *The American way: Franklin Roosevelt in action*. New York: John Day.

MacGregor, F. C. (1974). *Transformation and identity*. New York: Quadrangle.

McCay, V., & Makowsky, B. (1969). Deafness and minority group dynamics. *The Deaf American, 21*, 3-6.

Ortner, S. B. (1973). On key symbols. *American Anthropologist, 75*, 1338-1446.

Parsons, T. (1967). *The social system*. New York: Free Press. (Originally published in 1951)

Phillips, M. J. (1984). Oral narratives of the experience of disability in American culture (Doctoral dissertation, University of Pennsylvania, 1984). *Dissertation Abstracts International, 45*, 1488A.

Phillips, M. J. (1988). Disability and ethnicity in conflict: A study in transformation. In M. Fine & A. Asch (Eds.), *Women with disabilities: Essays in psychology, culture, and politics* (pp. 195-214). Philadelphia: Temple University Press.

Riesman, D. (1955). *Individualism reconsidered*. Garden City, NY: Doubleday, Anchor Books.

Roth, W. (1983). Handicap as a social construct. *Society, 20*, 56-61.

Scott, R. A. (1969). *The making of blind men*. New York: Russell Sage Foundation.

Stahl, S. K. D. (1977). The personal narrative as folklore. *Journal of the Folklore Institute, 14*, 9-30.

Vash, C. (1981). *The psychology of disability*. New York: Springer.

Wright, B. (1960). *Physical disability: A psychological approach*. New York: Harper & Row.

Part IV

DISABILITY AND CULTURE

We have tried throughout this book—both explicitly and by illustration—to make a two-part argument. First, qualitative methods in the social sciences, and the interpretivist paradigm in general, are much better suited than traditional quantitative research methods to revealing people's perspectives on the attitudes, events, and structures that give meaning to their daily lives. Second, people with disabilities, and individuals involved with them in various ways, have traditionally not had the opportunity or encouragement to share and reflect on their perspectives on the meaning of disability in their lives. In other—and fewer—words: Qualitative research allows disabled people to tell their stories for all of us to hear.

However, telling stories can be a complicated business. The stories we tell, for example, cannot help being influenced by the stories we hear. Moreover, the stories we hear most often are those that carry the cultural baggage of normative standards and values. This is simply another way of recognizing the unavoidable importance of a culture's myths, symbols, traditions, and stereotypes in the formulation of individual perspectives from within that culture. Even if one wants to oppose the hidden assumptions and persistent stereotypes of the dominant cultural perspective, that very opposition initially gains its definition by contrast with the larger set of values and views that it wishes to challenge. Thus, as African-Americans continue to expand an appreciation for their rich, distinctive, and non-European tradition, they also explore the intentional and unintentional ways that the dominant white culture has suppressed that alternative set of collective images and myths. Women in America today exhibit a broad range of perspectives on their lives and goals, from conservative traditionalist to radical feminist. But increasingly, any individual woman's perspective on her life now includes at least an implicit comparison with how close or far it is from the June Cleaver and Marilyn Monroe stereotypes of previous generations. If there is something that can be referred to as the "dominant American culture," then one of the ways it perpetuates itself is by bombarding us all, in a variety of ways, with symbolic messages about what is beautiful, what is ugly; what is worthy, what is worthless; what is enviable, what is pitiful; what is loveable, what is repulsive.

229

The chapters in this final part, then, examine some of the cultural myths and symbols about disability that both influence and reflect the variety of individual perspectives on this topic. These chapters analyze the stories we all hear, even when we do not know we are listening, about what the dominant culture says it is "supposed" to mean to be disabled. One of the selections (Chapter 13) analyzes how a collective counterpoint of values and attitudes can also maintain its own rhythm of unconditional acceptance amidst the more powerful stereotypes of "differentness" and rejection.

This area of qualitative research is often closer in spirit and content to the humanities than to social science. It involves the direct application of hermeneutics, or interpretive understanding, that originated as principles for biblical and literary criticism. In this case, however, the notion of literature is expanded to encompass all the media through which the cultural messages about disability are conveyed. This can include the traditional critiques of childhood fairy tales with their deformed ogres, ugly witches, and pitiful Tiny Tims (Biklen & Bogdan, 1977) and academic discussions of disability as a theme in literary classics (Kriegel, 1987). However, it also extends to include such important carriers of cultural mythology as popular films (Longmore, 1985), mass advertising (Hahn, 1987), journalism (Biklen, 1986), and live entertainment like the circus sideshow tradition (Bogdan, 1988; Fiedler, 1978). What all these examples share is a reliance on what might be called a "social hermeneutic" to interpret the meaning of the social documents and artifacts for the portrayal of disability as a cultural theme. This social hermeneutic borrows many of its terms and techniques from the humanities, while discussing issues more common to sociology and political theory. As a technique it lies at the interface of art and science. But perhaps that is where—at the end of the millennium—most of us with or without disabilities live our lives.

The three chapters presented in Part IV represent some of the range of subject matter opened up by this social hermeneutic approach. In Chapter 11 Zola, using a ubiquitous, and seemingly innocuous, category of mass entertainment (murder mysteries), takes the reader through a catalogue of disabling stereotypes presented there. Zola's analysis shows the value of popular culture as a repository of social imagery. It also shows how stereotypes persist in the guise of heroes as well as villains. In Chapter 12 Wickham-Searl examines the interaction of two cultural constructs: disability and gender. She analyzes the influence of having a disabled child on a group of mothers identified as leaders or activists. Finally, in Chapter 13 Bogdan and Taylor turn to the most fundamental aspect of cultural perspective—what is required to be human—to describe the persistent themes of acceptance of disability that have steadily resisted the more dominant themes of cultural isolation and intolerance. Their study provides an excellent reminder of how social hermeneutics can begin with critique, but must move on to define a positive vision of what it can mean to be disabled.

REFERENCES

Biklen, D. (1986). Framed: Journalism's treatment of disability. *Social Policy, 16* (3), 45–51.

Biklen, D., & Bogdan, R. (1977). Media portrayals of disabled people: A study in stereotypes. *Interracial Books for Children Bulletin, 8* (6 & 7).

Bogdan, R. (1988). *Freak show: Presenting human oddities for amusement and profit.* Chicago: University of Chicago Press.

Fiedler, L. (1978). *Freaks: Myths and images of the secret self.* New York: Simon & Schuster.

Hahn, H. (1987). Advertising the acceptably employable image: Disability and capitalism. *Policy Studies Journal, 15,* 551–570.

Kriegel, L. (1987). The cripple in literature. In A. Gartner & T. Joe (Eds.), *Images of the disabled, disabling images* (pp. 31–46). New York: Praeger.

Longmore, P. K. (1985). Screening stereotypes: Images of disabled people in television and motion pictures. *Social Policy, 16* (1), 31–37.

SUGGESTED READINGS

Biklen, D., & Bailey, L. (Eds.). (1981). *"Rudely stamp'd": Imaginal disability and prejudice.* Washington, DC: University Press of America.

This collection of articles is a good illustration of examinations of the theme of disability as both symbol and subject in a broad sampling of modern authors. Works by Joseph Heller, Dalton Trumbo, William Faulkner, and others are discussed in detail. Thematic surveys of disability imagery in entire bodies of literature such as children's literature are also included.

Bogdan, R. (1988). *Freak show: Presenting human oddities for amusement and profit.* Chicago: University of Chicago Press.

Through the use of historical analysis of photographs and documents, as well as life history interviews, Bogdan explores the sideshow tradition of displaying people with various physical disabilities in carnivals and circuses. The author shows the complexity of interaction between individual choices and social stereotypes. Can someone freely choose to be exploited? Can the symbolism of such displays exceed the intentions of the immediate participants? Bogdan's book addresses these questions in the context of telling a fascinating story of American folklore.

Bower, E. M. (Ed.). (1980). *The handicapped in literature: A psychosocial perspective.* Denver: Love Publishing.

This book contains a useful compendium of excerpts from modern writers (e.g., Conrad, McCullers, Vonnegut, Maugham) involving the portrayal or description of people with various disabilities (e.g., blindness, deafness, mild retardation, aphasia, multiple disabilities).

Fiedler, L. (1978). *Freaks: Myths and images of the secret self.* New York: Simon
& Schuster.
  Fiedler begins with the tradition of literary criticism and moves to consider
  the themes of disability in art and literature. More often, the movement
  occurs in the opposite direction: People with an interest and background in
  disability move to the methods of literary criticism to develop their analysis.
  In any case, Fiedler's book is a well-known and insightful analysis that
  jumps from art, to ancient myth, to literature, to popular entertainment to
  make psycho-analytic arguments about the sources of our symbols.
Fine, M., & Asch, A. (Eds.). (1988). *Women with disabilities: Essays in psychology, culture, and politics.* Philadelphia: Temple University Press.
  This is an excellent collection of articles, mainly interpretivist in perspective, that examine the various ways in which issues of gender and disability
  intermix within our culture. The articles focus on the experiences of women
  with disabilities and look at the effects of the dual membership in groups
  affected by discrimination, stereotypes, and stigma.
Gartner, A., & Joe, T. (Eds.). (1987). *Images of the disabled, disabling images.*
New York: Praeger.
  This is an excellent collection of recent articles in social hermeneutics. It
  contains the Kriegel, Longmore, and Biklen studies referred to earlier.
  Other contributions come from Harlan Hahn, Deborah Kent, and Lisa
  Walker, among others.
Gilman, S. L. (1982). *Seeing the insane.* New York: John Wiley.
  Gilman's work provides a wonderful collection of drawings, paintings, pho-
  tographs, sculptures, and manuscripts from medieval times up to the beginning of the twentieth century. The collection shows how "insanity" has
  been presented in both popular art and clinical treatments, through strik-
  ingly similar images. It is an excellent example of the interpretive analysis of
  historical documents.

Chapter 11

"ANY DISTINGUISHING FEATURES?"

The Portrayal of Disability in the Crime-Mystery Genre

Irving K. Zola

"He had a small dark mole beneath the left eye. The lobe of his right ear was appreciably less than the other. The nail of the middle finger of the right hand was corrugated from an injury at some time. . . ."
—From *Max Carrados Mysteries* (1927)

THE CULTURAL ANALYSIS OF DISABILITY

Social scientists, activists, and advocates have recently argued that the notion of disability is as much a socially and politically constructed phenomenon as it is the presence of any particular physical, psychological, biochemical, or physiological difference (DeJong, 1979; Hahn, 1985; Scotch, 1984; Zola, 1982). Since the general treatment of people with such differences has often been to isolate them from the rest of the population, frequently in inaccessible places—separate communities, hospitals, sanitoria, even prisons (Zola, 1982)—much of what the general public "knows" or thinks it knows comes from what it hears, sees, and reads from secondary sources—the arts, mass media, and other popular purveyors of cultural imagery.

The crime-mystery genre is, it is argued, a major perpetuator of such images. By examining the social history of this genre, we can discover in microcosm many of the central elements in the persistent cultural stereo-

---

An earlier version of this chapter appeared in *Policy Studies Journal*, *15*, 485–513, 1987. Reprinted by permission of the Policy Studies Organization and Irving K. Zola.

types of disability. This study also describes an empirical analysis of some 150 writings and delineates the nature and distribution of disabilities, the roles with which disability is associated, and some selected behaviors of the bearers of disabilities. Together with a growing number of similar examinations of disability imagery presented by other segments of popular culture (e.g., Biklen & Bailey, 1981; Hahn, 1988; Kent, 1988; Kriegel, 1987; Longmore, 1985), this research hopes to establish an analytic context from which to evaluate, understand, and perhaps change such images—images that often underlie key assumptions of public policy.

THE IMPORTANCE OF THE CRIME-MYSTERY GENRE

Although we are always cautioned not to confuse bestsellerdom with the important themes of our time or "good literature," there are several reasons for investigating the depictions of disability in crime-mystery writing. First, there is its enormous endurance and appeal. Criminal activity has been a staple of popular literature for at least 150 years (Keating, 1982; Panek, 1979; Symons, 1972; Watson, 1971; Winks, 1981). Beginning in the mid-1800s in the United Kingdom the Newgate Calendar—with its brief vivid depictions of crime, its villains, and their pursuers—became very popular, soon leading to more extended tales, called "the penny dreadfuls." The United States origin is credited to Edgar Allan Poe, who between 1841 and 1843 wrote three short stories "inventing" the first detective, Auguste Dupin. This popularity continued unabated so that in 1941, Haycraft wrote, "It is a matter of sober statistical record that one out of every four new works of fiction published in the English language belongs to this category" (p. viii). Some 45 years later a *New York Times* bestseller list contained the works of Robert Ludlum, John LeCarre, Robert Parker, Dick Francis, and Elmore Leonard.

Crime-mystery authors as a group must be among the most prolific in modern history. Edgar Wallace published at least 173 titles. George Simenon (Inspector Maigret) over 300, and when Erle Stanley Gardner (Perry Mason) died in 1969, 135 million of his books were in print. Moreover, in the 1990s all the editions of the long-dead Agatha Christie (Miss Marple, Inspector Poirot) and Rex Stout (Nero Wolfe) are still available.

While these numbers justify a look, the structure and content of crime-mystery writing need closer scrutiny. "Disablement" is a fact of life and central to many such tales. Though a death is the most frequent mystery to be solved, many characters are "at risk" and many more experience a variety of injuries and illnesses in the course of the story. Thus we can investigate not only their frequency and demographic distribution but the resulting behavior and reactions as well. Moreover, with the struggle of "good and evil" and the presence of heroes, villains, and victims at the heart of the genre, we can study the metaphorical significance of such portrayals (Longmore, 1985).

The focus on physical as well as psychological detail is a special boon, particularly when we recall Harlan Hahn's (1984) commentary that such data are often absent from even the autobiographies of people with disabilities. Thus the title of this chapter is not merely an attempt to be clever, for physical descriptions of people abound (though their specific distribution may not), as does the general attention to other details, including psychological states. Indeed, from Sherlock Holmes to the "police procedurals" (Dove, 1982), there is not only a never-ending piling up of information ("clues," or "red herrings") but a continual inquiry into how some people feel about others as well as themselves (usually part of the search for motives and "states of mind"). This look beneath the surface also allows for the possibility of dealing with hidden or invisible disabilities and their management (Goffman, 1963). For at the core of the mystery is the assumption that people's motives and appearances are not always what they seem.

As the reader may already have gathered, I am an avid fan of this genre and have been for over 30 years. Given its readability and brevity and my nighttime reading habits, I have probably gone through well over 1,000 mysteries. At the point when I realized that such writing was worth more systematic attention, I (and later my colleagues Joanne Seiden and Pat Putnam Alexander) began to note and code all instances of explicit or inferred "disablement." Thus, when characters are "sick," "wounded," "hurt," "impaired" or when someone else describes a character in these terms—that is, the answers to the not-so-rhetorical question, "Any distinguishing features?"—it was copied. A reliability check indicated that inference was at a minimum, with an interrater agreement of some 97%.

Systematic sampling proved more difficult than expected. Though in recent years there have been analyses of "disability in literature" and general bibliographies of health and illness, in no listing of works categorizing "handicaps" or "disability" were there any citations of popular mysteries (e.g., Trautmann & Pollard, 1982). There is, however, an extensive literature, bibliographies, and even plot outlines (Albert, 1985; Penzler, Steinbrunner, & Lachman, 1977; Reilly, 1980; Steinbrunner & Penzler, 1975) of mysteries, which provided a beginning list of books and stories where disability was at least mentioned. This has continually been added to by colleagues knowing of my interest. At this stage of the research I have tended to focus on series, which allow for comparisons across time. So far the list includes over 150 works by some 40 authors.

While I have coded and counted some 15 descriptive and behavioral dimensions, this chapter will omit tabular presentations; any tabulation is obviously affected by the number of books read, the pages in a book, the style of the author, whether the disability "belongs" to a running character, and so forth. Instead, I have tried to contextualize the numbers and will present the directionality of the statistics. Hence there are many methodological caveats. One, however, is inherent to the structure of the genre and is generally adhered to by all critics and analysts. I, too, will tell you much about the authors, the stories, and the characters, but I will not, as the ads so often caution, reveal the ending.

AN HISTORICAL OVERVIEW

That villainy has long been associated with abnormality—whether physical, psychological, or mental—is documented in nonfiction (Lombroso, 1911/1948) as well as fiction (Biklen & Bailey, 1981; Fiedler, 1978). Thus from the earliest crime-fiction writing as well as in illustrations and silent films, one could easily recognize the villain by his or her features. She or he was inevitably unkempt, ugly, slobbering, sneering, and often scarred and disfigured (e.g., the "Clubfoot" series by Williams, 1918, 1919, 1923, 1924, 1928, 1932, 1936, 1944). It is not without significance that until the finale of TV's *MASH*, the record for the most watched single episode of a TV series belonged to the final episode of *The Fugitive*. Here the wrongly accused hero finally caught the heretofore unseen killer of his wife, the curly headed man with one arm. Nearly 100 years later, the tradition endures, though often with more subtle descriptions.

If villainy is a major association in the cultural imagery of disability, being a victim runs a close second (International Center, 1981; Longmore, 1985). From the earliest popular mysteries (MacHarg & Balmer, 1916) through the contemporary police procedurals (McBain, 1956, 1966, 1977, 1985) some of the best known authors have found it convenient to have people with disabilities as victims or bystanders (e.g., Sayers, 1928, 1932) or just colorful additions to their landscapes. A documentation of their existence per se would add little to our general knowledge. What came initially as a surprise, however, was the long continuing history of people with disabilities in hero/protagonist roles.

It may well be that the power of this negative association so "blinded" compilers, critics, and chroniclers of mystery that they largely ignored the positive images of disability—not the saints or innocents but rather the run-of-the-mill detective heroes who "just happen" to have a disability of some sort. Thus though Hoppenstand and Browne in 1983 and Hoppenstand,

Roberts, and Browne in 1985 note this phenomenon, they do so derisively, labelling such people "defective detectives." As a result, they seem unaware of the continuing popularity of a number of "straight" detectives with disabilities and consequently think of the whole set of portrayals as mere gimmickry.

It might well be argued that the extreme reclusiveness—going out only at night—and misanthropy of Edgar Allan Poe's Auguste Dupin and the arrogance, outbreaks of violence, and continual reliance on a "seven percent solution" by Conan Doyle's Sherlock Holmes would make them both "certifiable." The early 1900s, however, saw the introduction of several detectives about whom such inference was hardly necessary. Thomas W. Hanshaw's Cleek, the Man of 40 Faces (1912–1914, 1918) was first a criminal and then turned his self-proclaimed disability, "a rubbery face" with which he could change his entire appearance, to the services of Scotland Yard. For two decades, however, Ernest Bramah's Max Carrados (1914, 1923, 1927, 1934) was the most dominant. Not surprisingly, his disability was blindness, perhaps the most commonly depicted disability in all literature, one that often endows the bearer with very special abilities.

In 1923, Jim Hanvey, described variously as gross and enormous with fishlike eyes, waddled forth as the foremost private investigator in the United States (Cohen, 1923, 1929, 1930). In 1932 and 1933 Ellery Queen, under the pseudonym of Barnaby Ross, produced four novels (1932a, 1932b, 1933a, 1933b) about Drury Lane, an actor turned detective *after* a hearing loss "forced" his retirement from the stage. Their popularity paled before that of two detectives, "born" several thousand miles apart but sharing a good deal in common—Rex Stout's Nero Wolfe (1934) and John Dickson Carr's Dr. Gideon Fell (1933). They were "gargantuan" in knowledge and in girth. Wolfe is described variously as being between one-sixth and one-seventh of a ton. Dr. Gideon Fell was so huge as to "be a danger" wherever he sat. While Nero Wolfe barely moved, leaving his house only several times during his 40-year history, Dr. Fell got around—but not without difficulty. He used a cane to assist mobility and was constantly described as "wheezing" under his load. In 1937 Baynard Kendrick introduced Captain Duncan Maclain, a hero blinded in World War I and created, according to the author, to counter the overweening superiority and "unreality" of figures like Max Carrados. Kendrick, in fact, claimed that everything done by Maclain could be and had been done by someone with blindness.

Between 1937 and 1940 the pulp magazines discovered the utility and appeal of such detectives (Hoppenstand & Browne, 1983; Hoppenstand, Roberts, & Browne, 1985, p. 7). The gimmick was popular, if not the character himself. Paul Ernst's Seekay had no face; he wore a bland mask of celluloid. John Kobler's Peter Quest had a form of glaucoma that often temporarily blinded him in crisis situations; Nat Schachner's Nicholas Street had amnesia; Edith and Eijer Jacobson's Nat Perry had hemophilia. World War II killed the pulp magazines as well as this form of genre (though Duncan Maclain, Nero Wolfe, and Gideon Fell continued unabated), perhaps because the gimmickry paled before the real "grotesque" deformities and disabilities produced by the war.

Starting in the 1950s minorities of all sorts were on the scene (DeJong, 1979; Zola, 1979), and characters with disabilities began to emerge in significant numbers. In 1952, Richard Deming (1952, 1953, 1954), a quite prolific writer, created "Manny" Moon, an honest, quick-witted detective with an artificial leg. But it was left to Ed McBain, generally credited with the popularization of "the police procedural" (Dove, 1982) in his 87th Precinct series, to create in 1956 the longest recurring character with a disability. Steve Carella, one of the team of detectives, had first a fiance and for the next 30 years a wife, named Teddy, who was deaf from birth.

In 1962 in the United Kingdom, Dick Francis began writing a "thriller a year," which always combined horseracing and sleuthing and very often the issue of disability or disabled characters as central to the plot. In 1964 Judson Philips introduced Peter Styles, an investigative reporter who had lost a leg in a bizarre accident. Two rather gimmicky disabilities in characters appeared in 1966, though neither has appeared very frequently. Ellery Queen (1966) introduced Tim Corrigan, a one-eyed police detective who wore a black patch but whose vision never seemed affected, and Lawrence Block (1966) brought out Evan Tanner, a super-spy whose sleep center had been destroyed (i.e., he had no necessity for sleep) by a piece of shrapnel. (In 1977 Block introduced a much more realistic detective, an ex-cop, Matt Scudder, who because of overwhelming guilt continually struggles with alcoholism.) In 1967 they were joined by Michael Collins's Dan Fortune, a private detective who had lost his arm in a teenage escapade. The pace slowed until the mid-1970s (although 1972 marks the single appearance of one of the best—Steward's Sampson Trehune, 1973, who uses sign language to communicate) when, as people with disabilities began to organize on their own behalf (Crewe & Zola, 1983; Scotch, 1984), all manner of series characters with all manner of disabilities appeared. In the 1990s not only do such characters continue to flourish but new ones seemingly appear every year.

DISABILITY DIMENSIONS—A REFLECTION ON GENDER

The presence and nature of disabilities in the crime-mystery genre, while relatively easy to recognize, are not so easy to diagnose. The reader invariably first "sees" the person's disability through the eyes of someone else and usually by its effect on function (the person "limps," "stumbles," or "stutters") or on appearance (missing parts, scars, or other disfigurements). In the vast majority of instances we may never even be told the underlying condition or diagnosis.

Similarly, the most common descriptive outcomes of all these injuries, assaults, and disablements are the effects on function and appearance. The "impacts" of these, however, are age- and gender-related and, indeed, reinforce traditional age and gender roles. If whatever occurs does so at a young age, it is thought to be determinative of the character's future development. If it occurs at an older age, it is taken as a sign of the aging process. If it is in a man, it is something he has to overcome. If it is in a woman, she must learn and show that it does not get in the way of her femininity.

A particularly clear example of gender relatedness deals with scarification or disfigurement. Numerically this is evident in both men and women, though proportionately more in women. But it is given a different meaning for each. Men's scars are all over their bodies, almost randomly distributed. Women's scars are more likely to be facial or on their sexual organs and thus more purposefully inflicted—for example, she was for some reason specifically slashed or cut on her face, breasts, or vagina. For men, these scars are often badges—sometimes proof of their villainy, sometimes of their heroics, sometimes both. Dueling scars were particularly prominent in an earlier era, often indicating a German spy. For some villains the mashed noses and ears are also occupationally related. They are former fighters, a career often deemed a precursor to being a bodyguard, an enforcer, or a thug.

For women, however, scars rarely have such positive connotations. At one time they were badges of dishonor (shown in branding of the scarlet letter). In this genre such scarring almost always seems to be perceived as a cause of concern about their acceptance, especially as a sexual partner. Ellen, Detective Kling's lover in several 87th Precinct novels, was cut facially in the course of duty—as a decoy in a rape case. From book to book, she thus needs reassurance that she is desirable and continually considers plastic surgery as a more permanent solution. In Dick Francis's *Odds Against* (1966) the woman's facial disfigurement has no possibility of such a miracle cure. While she is resolved to live a life alone, we are given considerable detail on how she "manages her spoiled identity," from the type of work she does to how she dresses. In summary, while men are "at risk" of disablement because of what they do, women, children, and older people are "at risk" because of who they are.

SOCIAL DEMOGRAPHICS—
REFLECTIONS ON REPRESENTATIVENESS

All in all, the range in most demographic categories is rather narrow. Even controlling for the over-preponderance of protagonists with disabilities, there is still a greater number of men with disabilities, regardless of role, reflecting perhaps the male-oriented slant of the entire crime-mystery genre. Even though there have long been female writers, until fairly recently they were as likely to be writing about male heroes as about females (Agatha Christie has her Hercule Poirot and Miss Marple, P. D. James her Adam Dalgliesh and Cordelia Grey, Catherine Macleod her Sarah Kelling and Professor Shandy). Only in the late 1970s and early 1980s, it seems, did female writers, such as Amanda Cross, Karin Berne, Sara Paretsky, and Sue Grafton, begin focusing exclusively on female protagonists (Bargainnier, 1981; Budd, 1986).

Their age occupies a rather narrow band, somewhere usually between 30 and 50. While this is almost exclusively true of the heroes/protagonists, it is less true of the villians, where there is a sprinkling of some older wheezing mafia overlords and some youngish teenage vandals. The age spread is greatest among victims and bystanders (although the middle-age range is still modal), with these the only roles where the very young are likely to appear.

In terms of roles, a person with a disability is most likely to be a victim, a bystander, or part of the hero's entourage. The structure of the genre plays to this. Almost by definition, except in the relatively infrequent team efforts—such as the police procedurals—there is likely to be only *one* hero. Nothing, however, in the structure limits the number of victims or bystanders, or even villains (the latter are often parts of gangs or "organizations"). Yet two numerical statements about heroes and villains can be made. Villains can still often be identified by their guilty looks and slightly off-center appearance. They are, more than one might expect, very short "with Napoleonic complexes," very large in size and girth, frequently "greasy" and "sleazy" in appearance. But the out-and-out monster and grossly disfigured villain of a previous era are on the wane. On the other hand, though their total numbers may be small, the hero/protagonist with a disability (long lasting, if not permanent) is on the increase in our readings; so far, there are dozens. Thus the fact of disability alone does not ensure that the individual is likely to be cast in a negative light.

A final and quite surprising finding is that the number of people with a disability in a single book is significant in and of itself. From my previous impression of the relative dearth of such people, I thought that their distribution would follow a regular progression, with zero being the most common, one the next, and so forth. The nature of my sampling (most writing was read because disability appeared in the story) precluded any zeroes from occurring except in the adjunct books of the authors—that is, where I examined their other works. The actual distribution was quite the opposite, with a single character being the least likely occurrence. By actual count, the mode was 4, the average 5—all in all, quite consistent.

One interpretation of this is that "misery likes or needs company." Without trying to impute motives to the author, I think it more likely that once the taboo about the existence of disability is broken, it becomes possible to write about disability as part of the human condition and remarkably prevalent, with virtually the entire population "at risk" (Goffman, 1963; Zola, 1983, 1987).

TIME, TASKS, AND BEHAVIOR: REFLECTIONS ON REALISM

The passage of time is something with which all media have a problem. Personalized in the face of aging, the visual media generally have few courses of action. To make a younger person look older, wrinkles can be added to the face and gray to the hair. To make an older person look younger, scenes are often shot slightly out-of-focus and at a distance. Another alternative is to use different actors for different age periods (e.g., Robert de Niro and Marlon Brando in *The Godfather*).

The print medium has an easier task; an author can simply state that time has passed and, without the constraint of space, add the necessary believable details. But the crime-mystery genre does not have this option. It is no accident that heroes/protagonists are often between the ages of 30 and 50, the height of physical and sexual energy. For a series, especially the long-lasting ones, this constitutes a dilemma. Some essentially suspend time. Neither Nero Wolfe nor Dr. Gideon Fell, already in their 50s when introduced, aged at all; nor for that matter did the already very old Miss Marple. The most common solution is to collapse time. There is often a vague indication as to when certain events took place (e.g., several years ago). Steve Carella appeared on the scene as an already experienced detective—at most, in his late 20s. Now, 35 years later, neither he nor any other character has aged much, though his "twins," born in the late 1950s were 10 years old in 1986.

The wish to slow down, if not deny, aging may very well originate in commercial considerations of simply using what worked before for a continuing character. Nonetheless, this fictional agelessness can also have important, though unintended, implications, particularly for the attempts to deepen the texturing of disability. The denial of aging is almost tantamount to the denial of disability (Zola, 1986). As every study shows, as people age they are likely to have one or more chronic conditions that will interfere with their full participation in society (Zola, 1987)—at least as long as society maintains its current attitudinal and architectural structure. In addition, aging itself may complicate a particular disability. Thus even though Peter Styles may seem to limp less as the series progresses, most people will not. The causes of the limp may predispose one toward other conditions. The continuing strain on the healthy leg must take its toll; arthritis, which seems almost pandemic, will eventually add to the difficulty. In addition, some disabilities, long after the original onset, may change for the worse. The so-called post-polio syndrome may indeed be the precursor for many other disabilities (Halstead & Wiechers, 1985; Lauri & Raymond, 1984; Zola, 1987).

Thus the structure of a series has both a plus and a minus effect on an important dimension of disability. That the protagonists or, for that matter, any recurring characters retain their disability is a reminder of an essential truth—its permanence. On the other hand, to keep the characters and their disabilities unchanging plays to the stereotypical notion that they, their disabilities, and any dealings with or adjustment to the disabilities are static, occurring in the past and frozen in the present and future.

Another critical and criticized dimension of time is the speed with which heroes/protagonists in particular seem to recover from their various woundings and beatings. They may be unsteady on their feet, but ultimately there is a job that must be done. So they wrap on extra bandages or, in some cases, rip off those that restrain them and go off to finish what they started. While that still occurs (Chesbro's Mongo, 1977, 1978a, 1978b, 1982, 1985, is most notable), there seems less of it. Since heroes/protagonists rarely get killed, it is no surprise that they manage to survive in the most general sense. But the current group of heroes as well as victims do not recover so quickly. Toby Peters's back aches continually (Kaminsky, 1978b) as do Inspector Rostnikov's legs (Kaminsky, 1978a, 1981). Joe Binney has to be nursed back to health, which we read about in some detail (Livingston, 1984). Carella (McBain, 1968) walks around for weeks with bandages, the result of a burn that hinders everything he does, almost getting him killed. Dick Francis is perhaps the most consistent in this regard. Whether having a temporary injury or a permanent one, as a critic put it, "his people really get hurt and recover only as fast as a physically fit and resilient man would in real life" (Reilly, 1980, p. 343).

For almost all characters with permanent disabilities, the disablement took place in the far distant past and we learn about how they deal with it only in flashbacks. It is only when we meet up with Ginny Fistoulari and Sid Halley that we encounter characters in the full throes of such "dealings." The first words in *The Man Who Risked His Partner* set the tone of Ginny's story: "Six months after that bomb took Ginny's hand off, she still hadn't gotten over it" (Stephens, 1984, p. 1). Nor does she until the concluding scenes. She is seen through the eyes of her alcoholic partner (Mick Axbrewder, the narrator and chief protagonist of this and the previous Reed Stephens, 1980, mystery) as needing help, which he grittily supplies. He feeds her, dresses her, drives her, and eventually pushes her to take risks and become her old tough self. She, in turn, paralleling the examples in Goffman's *Stigma* (1963), continually tries to hide her stump, accepts help grudgingly, and rejects the prosthetic limb that, while it might aid her independence, would also forever make her disabled. This attention to detail communicates the initial pervasiveness of her disability. Though she may eventually discard outside help, the necessary adaptations will always be a part of her life.

In all his books, Dick Francis emphasizes not only the temporal dimensions of the healing process but how they play out in daily behavior. Most novelists forget that someone who limps may also walk "laboriously," "strain in having to climb," "get tired out a little more quickly," or "simply take longer to get someplace." Sid Halley (Francis, 1962) indeed shows such enduring and changing aspects of a disability, including the dressing and maintenance routine of his prostheses. While, as usual, detailed physical description is absent, there is voluminous material about his inner struggles and the outside's prejudices. Like Ginny, he has people pushing him to take hold. Unlike her, he has many others who would just as soon keep him in his place. Sid Halley (Francis, 1980) in his second appearance (in fictional time, a few years later; in writing time, over 15 years) is still struggling, both physically and psychologically. In the first book, it was with his mangled hand. In the second, it's with his amputation and the prostheses. Ginny's story ends with insight and her having put it all behind her. (Since this is part of a series, we may learn later whether this is true.) For Sid Halley, while this second (and final) novel ends on a happy note, we know that the disability will always be with him, not "overcome" but "integrated."

PRELIMINARIES:
BEGINNING DESCRIPTIONS, ANALYSES, AND CONCLUSIONS

There has been a profound neglect of popular mass literature in general and the crime-mystery genre in particular in current attempts to understand media depictions of disability. It is a neglect perpetuated in bibliographical sources because of their definitions of what is "literature." Aside from the difficulty this creates for researchers, analysts, and teachers seeking material, it further contributes to the myth about media's "neglect" of disability and heavily "negative" use.

The crime-mystery genre, while certainly offering many negative and stereotypical images (particularly in terms of sex roles), is still a rich and dense one. And although there is within the genre a debate as to how "responsive to the outside world" it should be, many authors like the depth of details (i.e., reality) they can include. Thus without trying to tell writers what to write, many "errors" are ultimately "correctable." Presentations at writers' conventions, publishing in popular culture and mystery analysis magazines, and the services—as in TV and movies—of expert consultants should correct much misinformation and even add to the depth of the characterization.

Many years ago (publication dates are often deceptive—Zola, 1981, 1982), I wrote that one of the dilemmas that people with disability confront is that they are seen globally but not particularistically. It starts with children who are initially taught to recognize a person with a disability when they see one, but then to block out the specific details of the disability. The crime-mystery genre frequently does this with exquisite precision. Readers may think that a particular writer is giving them a picture, but it is really created in their own mind, often using their own stereotypes. This does not mean that protagonists with disabilities are necessarily shadow figures. More than 50 years ago, Baynard Kendrick's Captain Duncan Maclain (1937) shared many inner dialogues, surprisingly rich in psychological detail, about how he felt "being blind." It may be that in writing about such protagonists the author, while wanting to be "realistic," can be so more easily in psychological and behavioral detail—that is, of self and of others (Zola, 1987). But at the same time the image may be so idealized as to be incapable of being depicted physically.

There may be other writing conventions that preclude how much should be told about the hero/protagonist. Indeed, it is no accident that in most series one can only guess at the age of the main character. On the other hand, series as well as writers have loyal followers, and while the author may not wish to change one hair on the head of the protagonist, one of the most pleasant surprises of our research is the documentation of how many other characters with disabilities *do* appear. They come and go, are fully developed in one novel, and then play a secondary role in another. For instance, Mark Devlin, certainly one of the more aptly described wheelchair users, was Eleanor Gordon's lover and aide in sleuthing in Karin Berne's *Bare Acquaintances* (1985) and a mere bystander in *Shock Value* (1986).

Whatever the faults of existing descriptions, they are clearly—in number and in sheer detail—more frequent and less stereotypical (with the notable exception of age and sex roles) than in previous literature. If this trend continues, readers can expect future descriptions to include even more realism and accuracy. The direction that such future accounts might take is shown in a recent commentary by Fred Hafferty. Written in response to my requested evaluation of Joe Binney, "the deaf detective" (Livingston, 1982, 1984), Hafferty, a social scientist, an expert consultant, and a person with a hearing impairment, acknowledged the frequent mention and accuracy of much of Binney's behavior in regard to his deafness. His inability to carry on telephone conversations, his speech peculiarities, his requests to others to look him in the face or talk more slowly so that he can lip read are very accurate. In this way, the reader is reminded—by behavior, not labelling—that Joe has a hearing loss. On the other hand, Hafferty (personal communication, May, 1986) notes:

> At one point in the book, Joe explains to another character about what it is like to lip read. He mentions correctly that you pick up only about half of what the other person is saying. You have to fill the other half with contextualized guesswork. Not totally deaf people, like myself, do the same thing. The problem is you make lots of mistakes. You "hear" things that weren't said. Sometimes you respond inappropriately. Now this really throws some social interactions for a tizzy. Does Joe make any mistakes? Does Joe ever respond inappropriately? Nope. Actually there was only one time when he even thought that he might have lip read incorrectly. One of the eventual bad guys told a junior banker that if he didn't get a loan from him he would get it from the "white hats." Joe didn't understand the reference and wondered if in fact he had said something else. Actually, the bad guy did say "white hats" and it turned out to be an important clue (a reference to The Purple Gang of Detroit). The point to all of these ramblings is that never do we see Joe making a mistake, and believe me we all make them. In the same vein, never do we see (or hear) Joe utilizing ambiguous responses in those all too frequent situations where we (us hard of hearing folks) don't quite catch what is going on but have been asked a question. Laughing at someone else's joke you didn't hear, or responding to questions with a "unhuh," "umm" or some equivalent device is a stock in trade. We're experts in getting people to repeat themselves without having to ask them to repeat themselves. Do we see/hear Joe doing any of this stuff? Noooooooooo!!!

In short, all this literature offers a promising beginning, but it still has a long way to go.

Finally the crime-mystery genre with its emphasis on heroes—even vulnerable ones—overcoming all the barriers is woefully short of solid structural and social analysis. (A few critics claim otherwise, and I have discussed the issue and them more fully in Zola, 1987.) This specific lack of structural analysis stems directly from the down-playing of physical detail. For example, when characters trip, fall, miss, misperceive, or miscommunicate, they usually blame themselves and their missing appendage, function, or sense. They may, as a result, feel that it is time to get that long-rejected seeing eye dog, braille recorder, hearing aid, cane, or other assistive or prosthetic device. They rarely curse the geographical, architectural, or manufactured environment (or alert the reader that anyone should). The one exception so far is Karin Berne's *Bare Acquaintances* (1985). Eleanor Gordon, the protagonist, describes her first impression of Mark Devlin's home.

> I gazed around appreciatively . . . a nice collection of contemporary art. It fit Mark as much as the house did. Clean, smooth lines, no kitsch, no frill. From the outside, it was California ultramodern, with chalet-style redwood beams sloping from roof to ground. A sweeping canopy stretched from high above the front door to the other side of the circular driveway, but when Mark got out of the car to get his wheelchair from the trunk, I realized the overhang was not merely for effect. It was an umbrella.
>
> The house had been designed for Mark's convenience, from the seat and grab-rails in the shower to the extra-wide hallways and doors. The carpet was low pile for easy maneuvering, the light switches at a handy height, and all the entrances had ramps instead of steps. The main part of the house—living room, dining room, and den—was combined into one large area, separated by the arrangement of furniture rather than walls. A double couch and several oversize armchairs provided seating around the fireplace, with a spacious corner where Mark could get to the shelves of law books and pull right up to his antique roll-top desk. It was all very practical and imaginative, but it also demonstrated that Mark had not only money, but taste. (pp. 102–103)

The last words are particularly instructive, for they may unwittingly reinforce that the solution to such problems of accessibility is "private" and thus "possible" only when one has the necessary personal resources. It is Mark's problem and so is the solution—not society's. Hopefully it will not be long before such heroes and protagonists will go public in all senses of that word. Soon, some protagonist with a limp, a "touch" of emphysema or arthritis, or a missing limb will confront a long flight of stairs without a bannister and will mutter, "God dammit, how I hate stairs!"

REFERENCES

Albert, W. (1985). *Detective and mystery fiction: An international bibliography of secondary sources.* Madison, WI: Brownstone Books.

Bargainnier, E. F. (1981). *10 women of mystery.* Bowling Green, OH: Bowling Green State University Popular Press.

Berne, K. (1985). *Bare acquaintances.* New York: Popular Library.

Berne, K. (1986). *Shock value.* New York: Popular Library.

Biklen, D., & Bailey, L. (Eds.). (1981). *"Rudely stamp'd": Imaginal disability and prejudice.* Washington, DC: University Press of America.

Block, L. (1966). *The cancelled Czech.* New York: Fawcett.

Block, L. (1977). *Time to murder and create.* New York: Dell.

Bramah, E. (1923). *The eyes of Max Carrados.* London: Grant Richards.

Bramah, E. (1934). *The bravo of London.* London: Cassell.

Budd, E. (1986). *13 mistresses of murder.* New York: Ungar.

Carr, J. D. (1933). *Hag's nook.* New York: Harper.

Chesbro, G. (1977). *Shadow of a broken man.* New York: Signet.

Chesbro, G. (1978a). *An affair of sorcerers.* New York: Simon & Schuster.

Chesbro, G. (1978b). *City of whispering stone.* New York: Signet.

Chesbro, G. (1982). *Turn loose the dragon.* New York: Ballantine.

Chesbro, G. (1985). *The beast of Valhalla.* New York: Atheneum.

Cohen, O. R. (1923). *Jim Hanvey, detective.* New York: Dodd, Mead.

Cohen, O. R. (1929). *The May Day mystery.* New York: Appleton.

Cohen, O. R. (1930). *The backstage mystery.* New York: Appleton.

Collins, M. (1967). *Act of fear.* New York: Dodd, Mead.

Crewe, N., & Zola, I. K. (Eds.). (1983). *Independent living for physically disabled people.* San Francisco: Jossey Bass.

DeJong, G. (1979). Independent living: From social movement to analytic paradigm. *Archives of Physical Medicine and Rehabilitation, 60,* 435-446.

Deming, R. (1952). *The gallows in my garden.* New York: Rinehart.

Deming, R. (1953). *Tweak the devil's nose.* New York: Rinehart.

Deming, R. (1954). *Whistle past the graveyard.* New York: Rinehart.

Dove, G. N. (1982). *The police procedural.* Bowling Green, OH: Bowling Green State University Popular Press.

Fiedler, L. (1978). *Freaks: Myths and images of the secret self.* New York: Simon & Schuster.

Francis, D. (1962). *Dead cert.* New York: Holt Rinehart.

Francis, D. (1966). *Odds against.* New York: Harper & Row.

Francis, D. (1980). *Whip hand.* New York: Harper & Row.

Goffman, E. (1963). *Stigma: Notes on the management of spoiled identity.* Englewood Cliffs, NJ: Prentice-Hall.

Hahn, H. (1984). *The good parts: Interpersonal relations in the autobiographies of physically disabled persons.* New York: Wenner-Gren Foundation Working Papers in Anthropology.

Hahn, H. (1985). Disability policy and the problem of discrimination. *American Behavioral Scientist, 28*, 293–318.

Hahn, H. (1988). Can disability be beautiful? *Social Policy, 18*(3), 26–31.

Halstead, L. S., & Wiechers, D. (1985). *Late effects of poliomyelitis.* New York: Symposia Foundation.

Hanshaw, T. W. (1912–1914). *Cleek of Scotland Yard.* New York: Doubleday, Page.

Hanshaw, T. W. (1918). *Cleek, master detective.* New York: Doubleday, Page.

Haycraft, H. (1941). *Murder for pleasure.* Cheshire, CT: Biblio and Tannen Booksellers & Publishers.

Hoppenstand, G., & Browne, R. B. (1983). *The defective detective in the pulps.* Bowling Green, OH: Bowling Green State University Popular Press.

Hoppenstand, G., Roberts, G. G., & Browne, R. B. (1985). *More tales of the defective detective in the pulps.* Bowling Green, OH: Bowling Green State University Popular Press.

International Center for the Disabled in collaboration with the United Nations (Sponsors). (1981, October 27). Pity and fear: Myths and images of the disabled in literature, old and new. *Proceedings of a literary symposium.* New York: Authors.

Kaminsky, S. M. (1978a). *Death of a dissident.* New York: Charter Books.

Kaminsky, S. M. (1978b). *Murder on the yellow brick road.* New York: St. Martin's Press.

Kaminsky, S. M. (1981). *Black knight in Red Square.* New York: Charter Books.

Keating, H. R. F. (1982). *Whodunit? A guide to crime, suspense and spy fiction.* New York: Van Nostrand.

Kendrick, B. (1937). *The last express.* New York: Doubleday.

Kent, D. (1988). In search of a heroine: Images of women with disabilities in fiction and drama. In M. Fine & A. Asch (Eds.), *Women with disabilities: Essays in psychology, culture, and politics* (pp. 90–110). Philadelphia: Temple University Press.

Kriegel, L. (1987). The cripple in literature. In A. Gartner & T. Joe (Eds.), *Images of the disabled, disabling images* (pp. 31–46). New York: Praeger.

Lauri, G., & Raymond, J. (Eds.). (1984). *Proceedings of the Rehabilitation Gazette's 2nd International Post-Polio Conference and Symposium on Living Independently with Severe Disability.* St. Louis, MO: Gazette International Networking Institute.

Livingston, J. (1982). *A piece of silence.* New York: Signet.

Livingston, J. (1984). *Die against Macready.* New York: Signet.

Lombroso, C. (1948). *Crime: Its causes and remedies.* Montclair, NJ: Patterson Smith. (Originally published in 1911)

Longmore, P. K. (1985). Screening stereotypes: Images of disabled people in television and motion pictures. *Social Policy, 16*(1), 31–37.

MacHarg, W., & Balmer, E. (1916). *The blind man's eyes.* New York: A. L. Burt.

McBain, E. (1956). *Cop hater.* New York: Permabooks.

McBain, E. (1966). *Eighty million eyes.* New York: Delacorte.

McBain, E. (1968). *Fuzz.* New York: Doubleday.

McBain, E. (1977). *Long time no see.* New York: Random House.

McBain, E. (1985). *Eight black horses.* New York: Avon.

Panek, L. (1979). *Watteau's shepherds: The detective novel in Britain, 1914–1940.* Bowling Green, OH: Bowling Green State University Popular Press.

Penzler, O., Steinbrunner, C., & Lachman, M. (1977). *Detectionary—A biographical dictionary of leading characters in mystery fiction.* Woodstock, NY: Overlook Press.

Philips, J. (1964). *The laughter trap.* New York: Dodd, Mead.

Queen, E. (1966). *Where is Bianca?* New York: Popular Library.

Reilly, J. M. (Ed.). (1980). *20th century crime and mystery writers.* New York: St. Martin's Press.

Ross, B. (1932a). *The tragedy of X.* New York: Viking.

Ross, B. (1932b). *The tragedy of Y.* New York: Viking.

Ross, B. (1933a). *Drury Lane's last case.* New York: Viking.

Ross, B. (1933b). *The tragedy of Z.* New York: Viking.

Sayers, D. L. (1928). *The unpleasantness at the Bellona Club.* New York: Harper & Row.

Sayers, D. L. (1932). *Have his carcase.* New York: Harper & Row.

Scotch, R. (1984). *From goodwill to civil rights: Transforming federal disability policy.* Philadelphia: Temple University Press.

Steinbrunner, C., & Penzler, O. (Eds.). (1975). *Encyclopedia of mystery and detection.* New York: McGraw-Hill.

Stephens, R. (1980). *The man who killed his brother.* New York: Ballantine.

Stephens, R. (1984). *The man who risked his partner.* New York: Ballantine.

Steward, D. (1973). *The acupuncture murders.* New York: Harper & Row.

Stout, R. (1934). *Fer-de-Lance.* New York: Farrar & Reinhart.

Symons, J. (1972). *Mortal consequences—A history from the detective story to the crime novel.* New York: Harper & Row.

Trautmann, J., & Pollard, C. (1982). *Literature and medicine: An annotated bibliography* (rev. ed.). Pittsburgh: University of Pittsburgh Press.

Watson, C. (1971). *Snobbery with violence—Crime stories and their audience.* London: Eyre & Spottiswoode.

Williams, V. (1918). *The man with the clubfoot.* London: Jenkins.

Williams, V. (1919). *The secret hand.* London: Jenkins.

Williams, V. (1923). *Return of clubfoot.* London: Jenkins.

Williams, V. (1924). *Clubfoot the avenger.* London: Jenkins.

Williams, V. (1928). *The crouching beast.* London: Hodder & Stoughton.

Williams, V. (1932). *The gold comfit.* London: Hodder & Stoughton.

Williams, V. (1936). *The spider's touch.* London: Hodder & Stoughton.

Williams, V. (1944). *Courier to Marakesh.* London: Hodder & Stoughton.

Winks, R. W. (1981). *Modus operandi: An excursion into detective fiction.* Boston: David R. Godine.

Zola, I. K. (1979). Helping one another: A speculative history of the self help movement. *Archives of Physical Medicine and Rehabilitation, 60,* 452–456.

Zola, I. K. (1981). Communication barriers between the 'ablebodies' and the 'handicapped'. *Archives of Physical Medicine and Rehabilitation, 62,* 356–359.

Zola, I. K. (1982). *Missing pieces: A chronicle of living with a disability*. Philadelphia: Temple University Press.

Zola, I. K. (1983). The mirage of health revisited: On the omnipresence of illness. In I. K. Zola, *Socio-medical inquiries: Recollections, reflections, and reconsiderations* (pp. 135–150). Philadelphia: Temple University Press.

Zola, I. K. (1986, May). *Toward a unifying agenda: Some major issues cross-cutting policies and problems concerning aging and disability*. Paper presented at PEW Health Policy Fellows Conference, The Challenge of Long Term Care and Disability: Policies, Programs, and Perceptions, Philadelphia.

Zola, I. K. (1987, June). *How is your sex life, Ellery Queen? The portrayal of disability in the crime-mystery genre II*. Paper presented at the meeting of the Society for Disability Studies, El Paso, TX.

Chapter 12

MOTHERS WITH A MISSION

Parnel Wickham-Searl

Families of persons with special needs have been scrutinized for decades by researchers concerned to identify and analyze problems that are thought to impede the healthy development of children. Much of the time parents have been held accountable for the problems experienced by their children with handicaps (Ferguson & Ferguson, 1987). Traditionally, the prevailing approach to families with disabled members has emanated from the fields of medicine and psychology, education, and social welfare. Relying on the methods of the physical sciences, professionals from these fields have examined family members as physicians would examine sick patients. As a result, most professionals assume that families are engaged in never-ending struggles to relieve devastating personal and social problems that accompany the presence of a person with special needs in a family. Thus parents and other family members are viewed by most professionals in terms of their weaknesses and deficits rather than for their resources and strengths (Lipsky, 1985).

Increasingly, though, these assumptions of pathology are being challenged. As the deficit models that underlie much of current professional research and practice are being questioned, alternative theories that affirm competencies within families are taking their place (Wikler, Wasow, & Hatfield, 1983). These theories derive from a social science perspective that relies on information provided by the parents themselves (Turnbull & Turnbull, 1985). Such individual interpretations of personal circumstances contrast sharply with the explicit, ostensibly objective perspectives provided by professionals. The shift from the highly objective, scientific approach to families of disabled persons to a subjective, interpretivist approach is regarded by Skrtic (1986) as a shift in paradigms of thought. No longer content to rely exclusively on the theories and constructions of professionals in medicine and psychology, the studies of families and disability have adopted ideas and methodologies from diverse fields of social science and humanities. Most notably, those who attempt to understand the experiences of parents of children with handicaps are now turning more frequently to the parents themselves for their own interpretations of their situations. Instead of assuming a problem orientation at the outset, these researchers depend on the parents to define their personal conditions and social interactions in order to create meaning in the social world around them (Berger & Luckmann, 1967).

The research reported here reflects this transition from a paradigm that represents the scientific, clinical approach to studying parents to a more subjective, interpretive approach. Drawing from the parents' own perspectives, the study explores some of the ways in which they have assigned meaning to their own and their family's experience of living with a child with a disability. No claim is made that the parents who were selected to be interviewed for the study are representative of all or even most families who have children with handicapping conditions. On the contrary, the parents were selected because their experiences are probably unique (Filstead, 1970). Each of them, all women, has transcended her personal experience as the mother of a child with special needs to assume a public role in disability-related work. The overall purpose for this research was to explore some of the strengths that certain parents bring to or derive from their responsibilities of caring for a disabled child.

Originally, the research intended simply to inquire about the factors that enabled the women not only to manage satisfactorily at home, but, in addition, to take on public work associated with disabilities. As the study progressed, however, and the interviews with the women were analyzed, the focus of the study began to organize around three central themes that were especially meaningful to the women (Bogdan & Biklen, 1982).

The principal theme portrays the experiences of the mothers as they adopted new roles in public life as a type of personal journey. The transition from a private life of parenting a child with a handicap to a public role in disability work resembles an unanticipated adventure that the women undertook. The second theme has to do with the work that the women take on. Reacting to personal interactions with professionals and service systems that they perceived as largely unhelpful, the women committed themselves to changing the social conditions that threaten the well-being of parents and persons with disabilities. The third theme examines the personal growth reported by the women and analyzes the conditions that promoted their development. First, though, let me describe the research method that was used to collect and analyze the information from the parents, and then discuss the information that was obtained in terms of the three prevailing themes.

METHODS

The study used qualitative methods in order to capture fully the perspective of the women who were interviewed. Like personal written narratives, the data for the study reflect the thoughts, feelings, and interpretations of experiences from the women themselves. The research is descriptive in nature, in that it seeks simply to present the women's perspectives of themselves and their work, rather than viewing the women's experiences through a preconceived, theoretical lens. Such an approach allowed me to understand the issues in terms expressed by the women and to appreciate the relative importance of some factors over others from the women's points of view. At the outset, I understood that these parents might attribute meaning to some ideas or situations in ways that differed from my own perspective. Thus the intention was to understand the meanings that these women ascribe to their world, their family, and themselves (Blumer, 1969).

The methodological approach to this study represents a form of analytic induction, as described by Bogdan and Biklen (1982). Since the original purpose of the research was to explore some of the strengths that are reported by parents who have children with disabilities, the research process attempted to obtain the perspectives of a select group of mothers who could contribute information about the topic. As the interviews progressed, theories concerning the parents' experiences began to emerge. While the ideas represented in this study are exploratory only, they do provide important insights into the capabilities of women who successfully care for a disabled child at home and at the same time are engaged in valued disability-related public work.

Interest in the study evolved from my personal acquaintance with scores of women who, as parents of children with special needs, are recognized as contributors in the field of disabilities. To complement this personal knowledge, I conducted in-depth, open-ended interviews with 12 women who are recognized for their accomplishments in disability-related work. Since the purpose of the research was to explore some of the strengths that are reported by parents who have children with disabilities, I selected individuals who are recognized both as parents and as contributors in disability work to participate. And because my purpose was to describe the experiences and perspectives of these individual women, no effort was made to obtain comprehensive information from large numbers of persons. Indeed, the research was intended to understand thoroughly the experiences of these few women. Initially, I expected to find commonalities among the women's experience that could inform theory. However, as the interviews proceeded, differences among experiences became as important as similarities.

Clearly, men, too, have made the transition from private to public roles in the area of disabilities. However, the study focused on women because I felt that the nature of the women's values, personal goals, and work might be fundamentally different from that of men (Belenky, Clinchy, Goldberger, & Tarule, 1986). Because no men were interviewed, the presence and the extent of that difference cannot be known. Furthermore, the women who participated in the study rarely referred to men other than their husbands or fathers. Part of the importance of their experience to the women themselves seems to derive from their social interactions with other women who share a common experience and a common desire to change themselves and the world about them.

I used a process of purposeful nomination to choose the sample of 12 women. This process ensured that all the participants were perceived by others first as successfully parenting a child with a handicapping condition and second as performing a significant public role in the area of disabilities. Each of the women has acquired a role in either a voluntary capacity or a paid position in a nonprofit organization. All live in urban or suburban communities in New York state. Nominations of persons to be interviewed were sought from program directors, agency administrators, university faculty members, and other parents.

I made an initial telephone call to each woman to request her participation, to explain the study, and to arrange a meeting. No one declined to participate. Semi-structured interviews were held with the women, aided by an interview guide of 10 questions (Jahoda, Deutsch, & Cook, 1951). Some of the questions sought background information as a context to understand the women's experience. Other questions concerned the women's interpretations of their experiences. Questions that asked for background information included descriptions of the child with a disability and information about personal characteristics and history, such as age, level of education, parents, and work experience. Questions about perceptions of present experiences included current home and work responsibilities, enabling factors, barriers to work, and personal changes.

While the interviews were organized around specific questions, not every woman was asked every question. More often than not, responses to some questions arose in discussions of other questions. Thus I tried to establish a flexibility that permitted the women to respond in a manner that eased recall and communication. Interviews were tape-recorded and transcribed. I also took notes during the interviews, which I then incorporated into the transcripts for analysis.

THE WOMEN

The 12 women interviewed for this study are recognized leaders in parent organizations, disability advocacy groups, and service provider organizations. Four of the women volunteered many hours a week in parent-to-parent activities, board of directors responsibilities, and various ad hoc committees concerning disabilities. In addition, one of those women worked as a volunteer teacher's aide in a school classroom. Four other women held paid positions in not-for-profit organizations that provide parent-to-parent information, referral and support, and direct family support services, including respite. Three women were employed in a university-sponsored project concerned with public policy analysis and disability rights advocacy. The final participant worked for pay as a teacher's assistant in a public school setting for children with special needs. Of the eight who held paid positions, all worked full-time except for one woman, who was about to begin full-time work within a few months.

The women ranged in age from 36 to 54, they were all white, and they would all probably be considered middle class. They all resided in metropolitan or suburban areas in New York state. Two of the women were single; the rest were married. Educational history for the participants divided fairly evenly. Four of the women had stopped with a high school diploma. Five had completed college, and three had master's degrees. All of the post graduate degrees were in education. Four of the women were actively pursuing additional degrees.

The women reported that their children who have special needs would most likely be considered severely handicapped. The disabilities range from undefined developmental disabilities to mental retardation, emotional disturbance, autism, seizure disorders, sensory impairments, learning disabilities, and physical handicaps. Several of the children have more than one handicapping condition. In all but two situations, the children were identified as needing special care right from birth or shortly thereafter. Only one child was not recognized as having exceptional needs until the primary school years. Ten of the children were boys, and of the three girls, one was deceased. One of the women had two children with disabilities. In three cases, the child with a disability was an only child. In two families, the child with a disability was adopted, although the parents were not aware of the handicaps at the time of adoption. In both of these families, other children were adopted as well. The children's ages ranged from 5 to 32.

THE JOURNEY

The experiences described by the women I interviewed suggest a series of adventures that thoroughly changed their lives. Their lives might be thought of as a journey along an unknown path that began with the birth of their disabled children. One notable pair of parents, Suzanne and Robert Massie (1975), have presented their own personal adventures with their family, which includes a son with hemophilia. They have entitled their narrative *Journey*, in recognition of the unfamiliar and unpredictable events of parenting a child with a handicapping condition. Like the Massies, the women in this study described the occurrences of parenthood that precipitated their personal travels and discussed the feelings and activities that propelled them in their work.

Mothers First

The journeys of the women who were interviewed for the study began with the responsibilities of motherhood shortly after the birth of their children or, in the case of two, when their children were adopted. Almost all related the circumstances of their children's birth or early diagnosis. Some described a special kind of bonding that occurred with their infants who were handicapped. One mother talked about the emotions that she felt upon learning that her adoptive daughter was disabled.

> She got more and more difficult and finally I took her to several doctors trying to find out what was wrong. I thought she had allergies, and we tried all sorts of things, and I kept taking her back to my doctors. Finally we were referred to the ARC [Association for Retarded Citizens] and they came out and tested her and she was developmentally delayed. And so then we really realized what we were dealing with, you know, a child with disabilities. By then we were very emotionally attached to her, and so we just started pursuing whatever avenues we could to find help for her.

Like other families who have children with severe and multiple handicaps (Featherstone, 1980; Greenfeld, 1972; Park, 1972), the daily responsibilities of parenting were intense and exhausting for these mothers. For most, there were constant demands: feeding a child who had difficulty eating; managing behaviors that were hard to control and harder yet to live with. For many, the duties remained strenuous, even as their children grew older. Although many of the women had professional careers before the birth of their children, the obligations of their family prevented their return to work. While they expected to stay home with their disabled children, the decision to do so was still sometimes difficult. Some had to give up occupations in which they were already engaged.

One mother, who had intended to go back to work after the birth of her son, realized that it would be necessary for her to stay home instead. "Because our baby-sitter quit on us, we decided it was too hard for both my husband and me to work, and we felt we had to meet Corky's needs, so I made the decision at that point in time to stay at home." Another woman describes a similar experience.

> After I moved here I just really felt that Justin needed me to be home, plus I couldn't find sitters on an everyday basis to go back to work. It really affected him very negatively because he needed to know where I was going to be that day, who was going to come, who was going to take care of him. That was really important.

Whether the women considered their time at home with their children an obligation or an opportunity, none seemed to question the need for it. On the contrary, it appears possible that without the experience of mothering a child with special needs, these women may not have had the desire or the interest to take on additional responsibilities.

Initiations

As one of their major responsibilities of motherhood, the women became initiated into the world of professionals in health, social service, and educational systems. Many began a search for services that remained elusive for years. Starting when their children were infants, the women's acquaintance with professionals began first with physicians and progressed to education personnel. One woman succinctly described the tortuous route she took for professional advice. "When Billy was diagnosed, we had gone to a million doctors and then we went to Chicago, and then Chicago referred us to the ARC here. Dr. Stoddard was the physician on staff then. He referred us to the Center."

Most of the women described negative experiences with professionals that triggered their later activism. Without exception, the women criticized the decisions or the attitudes of many of these professionals. The examples they provided appear as pivotal experiences in their emerging public roles. Some of the criticisms focused on professional attitudes.

> At that time the school district was very difficult to deal with. They put every obstacle that they could to serving Justin. They said that they weren't going to have at that time a Committee on the Handicapped meeting because how could they get all those important people together to meet over every single kid, and they actually said these things. At a public meeting they said that you parents that have trainables are lucky that we do anything. After all, they're taking money away from our normal kids. It really shocked me.

Even those professionals who were respected by parents failed to perceive the stresses and demands of children with severe handicaps within the family.

> This is my favorite story, and I love my pediatrician, so I have to tell you. My daughter was born at 30 weeks gestation. She spent 7 weeks in the intensive care unit. She was on a ventilator. We went through all this and we finally got to the point where one Thursday night they called and said, "It's time to take Melissa home." And that's the way she was discharged. One day's notice, and her discharge papers said "see your pediatrician in a month." My pediatrician's advice was to treat her like a normal kid. I have since laughed with him over this. I said, "Don't send home a kid like this to a family and tell them, treat her like a normal child. Don't ever do that again." I think he meant it with all good intent.

This mother told her story with a note of affection for the pediatrician. But another mother was not so generous. She criticized not only the attitudes of her child's teacher, but the methods used to control behavior in the classroom.

> He (my child) looks very typical but he acts out a lot. At the time, he repeated, he had echolalia. And the teacher would say, "You sit down and be quiet." And then Michael would say, "You sit down and be quiet," so she would slap him across the face. At first the teacher was supportive, but what she wanted to hear was that this was a bad kid and how do I change him. So it ended up that they built a time-out room for him against my wishes. In fact I called a meeting and told them I didn't want it built and they said they were going to build it but they wouldn't use it until I approved. And it was between the inside and outside doors of the school, and the two walls were cement. It was in the corner of the room, and two walls were plywood with a doorway. And he was dragged there and they hired someone special to come in during the time that was difficult for him just to drag him out. And I mean drag. He was literally dragged down the hall by his feet, dragging his head across the floor. He was six-and-a-half at the time.

For many, these introductions to "professional" practices opened into a world few of the women were aware of before the birth of their children with disabilities. They tended to be the catalytic experiences that prompted the women to take action, not only to ensure that their own children were treated properly and that their personal feelings and ideas were respected, but to see that other parents might benefit from their experience. Their missions took on two forms in this germinating period: First, to help other parents to avoid some of the problems that they had experienced; and second, to change the attitudes and practices of professionals who either failed to give adequate advice or who delivered destructive intervention. In general, the mothers' interactions with professionals served as points of departure in the transition from their private family-centered world to a public life.

Transitions

Most of the women traveled similar routes to their public roles. Only one person was employed in work related to disabilities before the birth of her child with handicaps. Two activities seemed to introduce the women to public service. Some parents took on public speaking engagements before audiences composed mainly of other parents of children with disabilities. Others received telephone calls from parents who were looking for advice and assistance from another parent with a similar experience. Many of the women who were interviewed seemed to start either as volunteers with these parent-to-parent responsibilities or as public speakers, or both. In both situations, the purpose was to assist parents over some of the hurdles that they might encounter with physicians, therapists, social workers, or teachers. The benefits accrued to both sides of the relationship, for the volunteer parent also gained. "We're always available when anybody needs us to speak at the seminars they have. That's always enjoyable because you seem to learn more yourself. I don't think you ever stop learning about disabilities and the way people feel about them."

Speaking at meetings and receiving telephone calls from other parents were one of the common early steps that these parents experienced in the formative period of their journeys. Occasionally a parent would be invited to speak to a class of special education teachers or other professionals in training, but more frequently the audience consisted of other parents and the professionals who organized the event. Sometimes, but not always, a parent with a child with special needs would contact a "veteran" parent for advice and support. The initiating parent was usually encountering a new experience when she called, and she needed someone to talk to who could provide her with information, advice, and emotional support.

Another activity undertaken by some of the women early in their public lives involved organizing work in parent-to-parent groups. One mother who was interviewed described her beginning efforts to initiate a support group for parents whose newborn infants were hospitalized in intensive care units.

When my child was born 5 years ago there wasn't really anything as
far as parent-to-parent support. So a group of us got together and
we went to the March of Dimes and they became our parent organization. That was really my first involvement as far as any organization is concerned.

As this woman was starting the parent-to-parent group, she was drawn into
other community groups that concerned persons with disabilities. She became a member of the state Perinatal Association and served on the Execu-
tive Council of the local chapter of the March of Dimes.

A similar project that was organized with the assistance of one of the
women grew out of a parent-to-parent support group. She described an
informal kind of respite with other members of the group.

The parents in our group became our best friends. We still go on
parent weekends with the parents we knew from the Center. The
way we started was a couple of parents and we went on vacation.
We rented a 15-passenger van, and we went away for the weekend.
We all organized it. We just said, "Let's go away, let's do something.
Let's all go away together for the weekend." So we went away, and
then it just started; every single year we went away for one weekend
in June and just got away from it all. Those people are our best
friends.

As they become known for their abilities to speak publicly, to organize, and to advise, the women were invited to serve on various boards of
directors, task forces, advisory groups, and committees. Mostly these organizations were committed to working on problems that coincided with
the women's own personal interests and experiences. And again, while the
women felt that their contributions to the organizations were worthwhile,
they also derived benefits for themselves and their children.

I always feel like everything that I'm doing is also benefitting
Corky. Because I feel like the more that I learn the more that I find
out about who's involved with people with special needs, the better
I am going to be able to get services for Corky, or find the right
people to see for diagnosis, or just sort of see what's out there for
the long term as well.

Because their public work produces personal advantages, it may be thought
of as an extension of the private responsibilities of mothering a child with a
handicapping condition. The two roles, public and private, have never been

completely separate for the women; indeed, they tend to complement one another.

Further openings occurred for those women who live in areas where professionals valued their contributions. Three of the women interviewed for this project were employed as part-time or full-time staff members in funded projects sponsored by nonprofit organizations or a university. The nonprofit organizations provide parent-to-parent support as well as an array of direct family support services, including respite. The university sponsors public policy research that concerns families and individuals with disabilities. All but one of the parents currently employed were hired on the basis of their previous voluntary community service in disabilities. One woman's professional experience included work in the area of disabilities that predated her personal experience as the mother of a child with a handicap.

Barriers

Although the transition to public life appeared inevitable, in retrospect the way had not always opened easily for these women. Those with younger children tended to have more obstacles to overcome in their volunteer or paid jobs than those whose children were older. They all cited child care as a primary difficulty. Some relied on relatives to care for their disabled youngster while they were at meetings or at work. Many who volunteered attended meetings mostly in the evenings when husbands were home to help care for the children. One woman described a playgroup of typical children that included her son, who had a handicap. In addition to the daytime activities for her son, the other mothers in the group would also help out with baby-sitting when necessary.

Several of the women asserted that they were able to do their work because of three factors: Their families, including husbands, were supportive; they had adequate child care when they needed it; and their family was sufficiently well off financially that they were not compelled to work. The importance of these three factors was illustrated by one woman who had none of them. Living singly, she had had very little outside care for her son when he still lived at home, and she was always short of money. Even after her son moved to a new home provided by a service organization, this woman still found it difficult to make ends meet on the salary she earned at the nonprofit organization where she worked. For her, love for the job was not enough. She expressed her resentment that her work was not valued enough by society to allow her to earn a respectable living.

I wonder if part of the reason that we're so grossly underpaid is because we're women. I don't think . . . [our work is] valued, and I think people undervalue our expertise, especially because many of us are parents. A lot of what we've acquired has been through practical experience and not formal education, and I think that that kind of knowledge can be undervalued.

This woman looked beyond personal satisfaction to monetary compensation to determine the worth of her contributions. For her, volunteering was out of the question. She needed a steady paycheck, and she measured her own value—at least partially—in terms of the payment she received.

In contrast to this perspective, however, many of the other women appear to be thoroughly content with their volunteer status. They derive a personal satisfaction from their work. As one woman says:

> I have done volunteer work all these years, and I didn't get paid a penny, and it cost me a lot of money for gas. My husband used to say I put more miles on the car in a week than he did and I wasn't making anything. But I valued what I did then, and it's real nice to do something and get paid for it. To me that's kind of like a bonus because I love what I do. I don't know how to explain it otherwise. I think the pay is a bonus. I know if I didn't get paid I would still be doing volunteer work in this field.

Such a commitment suggests not only complete satisfaction with the work, but an inevitability in the women's journeys as well. None of them was considering a different path in the future. All would probably agree that they had learned too much and the work was too important for them to think about doing anything else. Besides, their work responsibilities were linked so closely to their family obligations that the two appeared to be indistinguishable at times.

THE MISSIONS

As the mothers became more confident and began to question the guidance and control of professionals, they took on a role that Darling (1979) refers to as "parental entrepreneurship." The entrepreneurial role of parents involves an effort to locate assistance from professionals in terms that the families can apply to their situation at home. Not content to adopt solutions that corresponded with the professionals' definition of what the family's problems might be, many parents in my study eagerly sought assistance that addressed the issues that they personally had identified. When such assistance was either not available or not forthcoming, some of these parents eventually created the solutions themselves in the form of a program, such as a respite service organized by a group of parents who had personally experienced the need for such a service. This creative form of entrepreneurship Darling (1979) describes as "crusadership," for the role takes on the qualities of a mission that emerges from the interactions of parents within an association who share experiences and a vision for change in the systems that provide services to families with disabled children.

Crusadership

The notion of crusade suggests a total, direct, and active commitment to a religious cause and implies a journey with a specific objective. The journey for many parents of children with special needs might refer to the process of change that they experience as their knowledge about their child, professionals, service systems, and themselves expands, and as they encounter and adapt to new situations. A crusade is a journey, but a special journey with a mission. In their book, *Journey*, Robert and Suzanne Massie (1975) write about their experience as parents in terms of a battle.

> This book is the story of one of these battles. The disease we have fought is hemophilia. The details of this struggle are personal, but the story itself is not unique. Every family with a handicapped or chronically ill child shares the same problems: lack of money, isolation from the community of the healthy, prejudice, misunderstanding in the schools, loneliness, boredom, depression. (p. xi)

The mission undertaken by the Massies, which by their own account completely changed their lives, involved a search for adequate and affordable medical care, appropriate educational services, and tolerance and understanding among strangers as well as friends.

Other parents carry on similar crusades against systems that have failed to deliver the necessary programs required for children with special needs: Schools that isolate children with handicaps and deny the importance of social learning; health personnel who see only the problems of children with handicaps and overlook their accomplishments; communities that pity and ignore children who are different (Darling, 1979; Greenfeld, 1972, 1978; Schaefer, 1982). While the missions of parents may vary, they arise from common experiences of disappointment and frustration with individuals and agencies that fail to recognize the needs of families and the contribution that parents bring to identify and solve problems.

Crusadership suggests an intensity of effort and single-minded purpose. The objectives of parents who become crusaders are entirely straightforward. Those who write personal narratives put their efforts into informing others about the issues involved in raising a child with special needs (Featherstone, 1980). Other parents devote their energies to organizing parent-to-parent support groups or promoting advocacy organizations for specific concerns. Some parents will initiate services that they themselves needed but were unable to locate. And still others return to school for formal training to allow them to contribute alongside other professionals. While the method is a little different for each type of endeavor, the anticipated results are very similar. The parents who engage in these crusades are committed to changing the world in a way that reflects how the parents themselves have experienced life with a child with a handicap.

Focus and Intensity

In most cases, professionals become the chief target of parents in their crusades, since professionals are the people with whom parents interact most frequently with concerns about their children, and many professional practices represent specific problems reported by parents. At the root of much of the friction between professionals and parents of children with handicaps are differing perceptions of how choices for treatment and programs should be made and who should make them. Based on their years of formal training and experience in the field, professionals most often claim title to the expert role, which permits them to assert authority over the decision-making process as it concerns children with handicaps and their families. However, as pointed out by Gliedman and Roth (1980), the notion of professional expertise is flawed. While certainly professional expertise is legitimized with credentials and formal preparation, professionals do not always apply their expertise to the advantage of their clients. Through perpetuation of the "deviancy model," which asserts that parents themselves become part of the problem to be addressed, professionals may thwart parents' attempts to find solutions to problems encountered with their children at home.

Flowing from their personal experiences with professional service systems, the missions of the women I interviewed generated intensity and commitment. One woman described the purpose of her work in helping other parents in terms of empowerment.

> I think I'm empowering parents, giving them the knowledge. A lot of times they'll call up and they'll say, "Well, Community Services said they couldn't do this and that," and I'll tell them what to do,

the people to contact, and how to phrase things to get services. So I think a lot of it is empowerment and advocacy. And I think that when there are serious school problems, the most knowledgeable parents need the support of somebody else with them, even if you're just there as a witness to what's going on.

Another thought about her mission in more general terms. "I feel that if I can help someone, direct them a little bit, or just listen to them, just try and help them feel what they're going through or try to give them a direction to go in, I feel that that's what I'm here to do. I feel like this is my job now." The sense of destiny expressed by this woman captures the feelings of many of these mothers who may not have experienced a vocational commitment earlier. Their passion is found in the words of another woman.

> I love what I do. I love my job. Now I hear people say they don't like their jobs, and I love mine. I wish that someone else could do all the paperwork and go to all the meetings and I could do all the hands-on service. I love meeting with families and supporting them, even on the phone. I like being with people. I like getting to know people with disabilities and understanding them.

The responsibilities of providing parent-to-parent support and the responsibilities of motherhood are closely linked. One mother considered some of the similarities of the two roles and perceived a potential conflict between mothering and empowering other parents.

> I think mothers and maternal passions always want to encourage people to do for themselves, and I see that as my role as a mother. But there's a danger to wanting to "mother," which is not the same as [being] maternalistic. I think the way I differentiate, and I have no idea how sound this is scientifically, maternalism is kind of "doing for."

This woman was concerned that she, in her role of assisting other parents, could become too controlling, too directing. She felt that truly to empower the other parents with whom she works, she needed to give them the tools and the encouragement to go ahead and make wise decisions, as a parent would with children.

This same woman, while still actively engaged in parent-to-parent work, had recently taken on even more responsible work on a state-level commission. As her responsibilities grew, her mission shifted focus, depending on her personal situation at home and the people she met in the course of her work. Initially, she engaged in parent-to-parent work within a hospital setting for families with children in intensive care. As she came to understand the systems, and as the needs of her family changed, she became a strong advocate for home care for seriously ill children. Understanding that case management is one of the critical services that families depend on and that often has detrimental effects on families, she became intensely committed to a system of case management and client advocacy that was removed from other service-providing functions. Further, she took on the cause for mainstreaming children with disabilities in public schools and other institutions as her own child became eligible for educational services. As this mother assumed state-level responsibilities, she recognized the achievement with the simple statement, "I think [about] the fact that a parent has this position, [and] I feel very sensitive about doing it. It's a great challenge."

Another woman spoke of an experience she had with the local school district when it refused to consider a neighborhood school placement for her son. Excluded from programs because of his disruptive behavior, he was considered for only the most restrictive educational placement. When she protested the recommended move to a residential school in another city, this mother, with the aid of understanding professionals, "got a new program started in the city for Matt." As she recalled,

> That worked out quite well, and I can remember saying to [my friend], you know, someday I'm going to do something so other parents don't have to go through what I went through. So it was always there, that that was something that I wanted to do. And then when I got to know more parents and a member of the board, and found out all about this, oh, it's just exactly perfect for me.

At the time of the interview, this mother was employed full-time in a nonprofit organization that provided family support services. Her job title was Family Guide, and her job was to serve as a personal resource for family members who called the agency for information and support.

Another woman worked as a volunteer on numerous boards of directors, task forces, and committees. She described her personal commitment to mainstreaming in schools and her efforts to see that all children with disabilities, including her own son, had opportunities to attend school with typical children.

> As my son is getting to the age where he can go to public school, I would like him to be in an integrated setting. I feel that I'm going to have to work very hard for that. Kelsey was at the SCD school

where he went for the infant stimulation program. I sat in on a committee of people that were looking at how they could get their kids
integrated and not have a segregated setting for kids with special
needs. What it was, there were some people at the SCD who felt that
the segregated programs that they had for kids with special needs
were not the way it should be. So they were looking at the way that
they could change it from a segregated program.

This mother recognized the distance she had to travel to accomplish her
goal of an integrated school setting for her son. She had already managed to
navigate the problems of her child's preschool years and was about to
confront the issues that were arising as her son entered public school. Like
the others, this woman's mission shifted focus as her child grew, but
maintained a steady course devoted to the welfare of other children with
disabilities and their families.

PERSONAL JOURNEYS

As the women assumed outward, public identities that complemented their
private roles as mothers of children with special needs, they also experienced extensive inner, personal changes. One way to understand the
changes is to refer to concepts of personal, adult development. In part,
people are shaped by their social environment, by the conditions in which
they live, and by the individuals with whom they interact. At the same
time, however, people contribute unique personal characteristics that influence their environment. According to developmental theorists, it is the
interactive process between social forces and individual attributes that produces personal change. Erik Erikson (1980) refers to a series of crises that
must be resolved adequately in order for a person to progress in his or her
development. The crises occur as individuals meet new and increasingly
complex problems in their environment. As a person confronts new situations that require resolution, he or she develops new capabilities to meet the
ever-changing conditions of the social environment. One of the notable
contributions of Erikson is his ability to view human development as a
natural, healthy process, rather than assuming pathology in the human
condition (Sprinthall & Sprinthall, 1987).

Growth and Maturity

The women of this study probably have been challenged by more
intense—or, at least, more enduring—crises than many other women are

and may have been more successful at resolving the problems they face than others may be. Their personal development has taken many forms. First, they attested that they have become much more knowledgeable about disability and dealing with professionals. They learned about other people and about social systems, they learned new skills, and they learned about themselves. The mothers described this learning process as a vital element of their personal change. Some of the learning occurred as a result of the women's experiences with their children with handicaps. One mother described her newly found appreciation for her son's development.

> I think I appreciate little things, where I didn't before. When you have a child who doesn't do as much, the first time they do something, you're just so thrilled. Even when my son first pulled the toilet paper all through the house, I was so thrilled because he had never done it before.

This same mother talked about her own developing patience as she attempted to understand her son. "I think I'm more patient. That's the biggest thing. I wasn't a very patient person before. I've had to be *so* patient with Brian."

Another woman described her interest in learning new skills that might help her child at home.

> I like to learn how to deal with things. Last week I had to have the psychologist out to my house three times because Karen's been doing a lot of screaming and tantrumming, probably between 1 and 4 hours a day. This summer the techniques I'm using aren't working, so I'm looking for new ideas. I'm always open to finding new ways.

Not only have these women developed new capabilities at home, but they have gained new insights into other people and the service systems as well. One woman talked about the understandings she gained from working with other parents.

> The first thing that comes to mind is divorcing the personal situation and looking at things from a global perspective. Not making assumptions about other people and circumstances, that is a real important skill. In this job in particular, you learn that families can be very different, circumstances can be very different, past experience can have a big impact.

Another woman found that many preconceived ideas about other parents changed as she became acquainted with them.

> I certainly have a different perspective on middle class families who have more financial means and have disabled children. I used to have the perspective that, well, they can buy anything that they want, and that's certainly true. But what's not available they can't buy. They still lack services and they still face a lot of stress.

This same woman went on to describe what she learned about the broader field of disabilities. "I've certainly gained in my knowledge. Not just about families but about the field, about educational issues, about residential issues. I've learned a lot about systems, and how they work, and how they don't work."

New personal knowledge was mentioned by most of the women. One spoke of her increased need for other people. "I really am seeking out more and more people in a wider spectrum. I feel like now there's almost a need to know more people because I need more supports. I need to know there are people out there that I can turn to. I think [my husband and I] both felt a little more self-sufficient before." Another described her growing self-confidence. "My confidence in public speaking and doing that kind of thing before small groups and large groups has really grown. I knew that would be part of [my work], but it was a lot more scary than I thought when I first started. I took a while before it felt really comfortable."

One mother discussed her emerging sense of power that she attributed to personal resiliency. "I think I'm a better person. I think I've grown. I think I've become strong—a lot stronger. A *lot* stronger. I'm always open to finding new ways. I guess that's why I'm strong. I don't get defeated easy. I keep coming back." One woman summarizes well the feelings of maturity expressed by most of the other women who were interviewed for the study.

> I'm old beyond my years. I feel like I've arrived. I don't know exactly how to express it. I have a niche. I like it, it works, it feels good. I don't know if many people can say that. There's a sense of self-satisfaction. It's like somebody wrote the job and it was just for me and it feels good and it works and gosh, I couldn't think of a better way to spend the day.

Redefining "Expertise"

Like this woman, many of the others gradually came to realize along the way that they were indeed making important contributions in their work, both volunteer and paid. With experience, they began to recognize that their own perspectives on issues concerned with disabilities were important and were different from those of professionals. They, too, were becoming experts and were gaining public recognition for their public roles. While they most likely would not deny the expertise of professionals, they perceived themselves, too, as experts, based on their personal experience of raising a child with special needs. They claimed that they knew their children better than professionals who saw the children infrequently. Such parents struggle against the commonly accepted notion of professional dominance legitimized by formally recognized expertise. Gliedman and Roth (1980) have described these conflicting interpretations of expertise.

> To be acknowledged to be an expert, one must obtain formal credentials and formal licenses. With few exceptions, neither laymen nor professionals respect the self-taught expert without proper credentials. . . . To be taken seriously, the parents' claim to expertise about their own child must be backed by a socially recognized formal credential that "proves" that they are experts about children in general. (p. 145)

The prevailing definitions of expertise are controlled by the professionals, who, because they are recognized publicly to assert authority, may tend to exclude their clients or patients from taking part in the decisions that affect them. In order for parents to have a meaningful role in their interactions with professionals, many feel that they too must acquire some form of legitimation, or public recognition of their expertise. Sometimes this recognition comes from formal training and certification in a particular professional field. Other times parents strive for recognition through effectively carrying out a public role over a period of time in which they come to be perceived by others, although not always by professionals, as an expert in their work.

Thus the mother who "taught" her pediatrician a "few things" about preparing parents for the homecoming of a hospitalized child exemplifies the type of expertise that evolves for some individuals out of their own, usually difficult experiences. She described her own personal transition to the expert role.

> People would say, you really helped me with that, you really made it easier, now I want to do it too. I think that was something that allowed me to feel confident. I think it was also professionals, certain professionals, listening to you and taking what you have to say as something that was valuable. I guess it was going on the speaker circuit, you know, all of a sudden I was a real viable commodity, to

have me do "the parent perspective," or something, and being able to deliver that message. I think by having other people start to value your opinion, your concerns, helps, it certainly builds on itself, and you begin to feel confident and competent. I think it's a self-esteem issue.

Not everyone, however, is concerned about the professional aspects of their work. They feel intuitively that their work is important and that they as individuals are valued, in spite of their lack of formal education. One mother described her feelings this way when she discussed her work coordinating a respite program.

I didn't go to college. I would have liked to but wasn't able to. We didn't have the money and my parents never supported my efforts to go, and at that time I just didn't know how to go about it on my own. And so I feel I'm lucky to be able to do what I'm doing and to be paid for it. I feel it's a real honorable job.

The route to publicly recognized expertise as the parent of a child with disabilities was complicated for many of the parents who participated in this study, because some of them had prepared previously for a teaching career. Already having a professional identity in one field, they found they had to start over in the area of disabilities. One woman described the conflicts brought about by the change from one professional role to another.

As a professional, as a teacher, I thought that, of course, I never knew all the answers, but I had the background as a basic training that made me feel like, OK, I know I have somewhere to start from. Whereas when you come into the field of disabilities because I have a kid who's disabled, I think, I'm sort of picking things up piecemeal and that to me makes it very hard to be secure.

Some of the skills brought from another profession were useful to the women in their new work in disabilities, as reported by one mother. "I think certain skills I brought from my other life are very helpful: . . . speaking skills or communication abilities. Some of the abilities to be assertive but not aggressive. Some of that is learned, and some of that I brought from a previous life." Another professional woman described the newfound abilities she learned as the mother of a child who is handicapped.

I would consider teaching a kind of service field, just as this [work] is, and I certainly was involved emotionally with the kids but not to the degree that things are now. I feel like in all the things I do there is that personal attachment to them that I didn't have before. Interestingly, enough, I think that if I was back teaching now I would be looking at things differently because of my own child.

Sources of Support

From this mother's report as well as from many others, it is evident that the women attributed much of their own learning to their children who are handicapped. In addition, all relied on other adults to provide support and encouragement in their work efforts and in their personal development. Most found this nurturing in their homes, with their husbands, with parents or in-laws, and with older children. Some, including one woman in particular, had to go outside the home to find adults who could provide sustenance. Husbands, as well as the children, could be too needy themselves to be able to help. One mother talked about the many friends and colleagues who helped her through the difficult times. "I've met some really special people who've really enriched my life a lot, who I wouldn't have known otherwise. That's where I feel kind of blessed. My son has a disability, but I've been able to meet these people. I've become really close with some people." She went on to list some of the types of people who had been most helpful to her. They included other parents, the other people in her office with whom she worked, and a few professionals who had been especially helpful. Others also listed special professionals who had become friends. One mother said: "The professionals I've met—because they allowed me to feel good about what I had chosen to do—have a role here as to why I continue." Thus not every professional with whom the mothers interacted failed to provide necessary assistance. Indeed, some provided the crucial nurturance that enabled the parents to develop their capabilities, both personally and publicly.

Without exception the women attributed many of their accomplishments to the favorable circumstances in which they lived: sufficient financial means, stable and helpful families, adequate education, as well as numerous friends, relatives, and acquaintances. The presence of all these conditions seemed to permit the women the time, energy, support, and probably some of the abilities to carry out their missions both at home and in their work.

CONCLUSION

Several conclusions can be drawn from the information provided by the parents who were interviewed for this study. First, it is apparent that the experience of parenting a child with handicaps can enable a mother to develop capabilities that previously were unknown to her. The mothers' personal growth resembles a journey in unfamiliar territory that extends the women's roles of mothering to publicly acknowledged leadership positions in disability-related work. In spite of the difficulties of parenting a child with a handicapping condition, these women are able to overcome some of their personal problems to assist other parents, either individually or within service systems. And indeed, the women seem to be compelled to travel this road. None question the necessity or the wisdom of their endeavors. On the contrary, they approach their work with the energy and commitment of crusaders.

The second conclusion to be drawn is that these parents tend to be highly critical of professional attitudes and practices. The failure of many physicians and educators in particular to address needs as perceived by the parents themselves has forced these women to defy entrenched practices. Service systems, too, have failed these families. Inadequate health and educational services have resulted in parents searching for necessary programs while at the same time fending off proffered services that fail to correspond with need. In a related, and third, conclusion, the women develop a perception of expertise that challenges traditional professional habits and views. With personal growth comes a confidence in their own abilities as experts in disability-related matters and an assurance that their work is important and meaningful.

The final conclusion concerns the factors that allow the women to pursue their work. Like many others, their path is made easier by the fact that many of them are not obligated to work for a living. For the most part they are provided for, and as a result are free to take on work for which there is little or no remuneration. All of the women are educated, many of them college graduates, some of them educational professionals. Their self-confidence and articulateness are evidence of prior learning experiences. But perhaps most important are the husbands, other family members, friends, and some professionals who have provided the support and encouragement that help to propel the women in their missions. And in the last analysis, the mothers rely on their children for the insights and knowledge that allow them to succeed in their work. For it is the children themselves that the women credit as teachers and leaders in the crusade.

REFERENCES

Belenky, M. F., Clinchy, B. M., Goldberger, N. R., & Tarule, J. M. (1986). *Women's ways of knowing: The development of self, voice, and mind.* New York: Basic Books.

Berger, P., & Luckmann, T. (1967). *The social construction of reality.* Garden City, NY: Doubleday.

Blumer, H. (1969). *Symbolic interactionism: Perspective and method.* Englewood Cliffs, NJ: Prentice-Hall.

Bogdan, R. C., & Biklen, S. K. (1982). *Qualitative research for education: An introduction to theory and methods.* Boston: Allyn & Bacon.

Darling, R. B. (1979). *Families against society: A study of reactions to children with birth defects.* Beverly Hills, CA: Sage.

Erikson, E. (1980). *Identity and the life cycle.* New York: W. W. Norton.

Featherstone, H. (1980). *A difference in the family: Life with a disabled child.* New York: Basic Books.

Ferguson, P. M., & Ferguson, D. L. (1987). Parents and professionals. In P. Knoblock (Ed.), *Understanding exceptional children and youth* (pp. 346–391). Boston: Little, Brown.

Filstead, W. (Ed.). (1970). *Qualitative methodology.* Chicago: Markham.

Gliedman, J., & Roth, W. (1980). *The unexpected minority: Handicapped children in America.* New York: Harcourt Brace Jovanovich.

Greenfeld, J. (1972). *A child called Noah.* New York: Holt, Rinehart and Winston.

Greenfeld, J. (1978). *A place for Noah.* New York: Holt, Rinehart and Winston.

Jahoda, M., Deutsch, M., & Cook, S. (1951). *Research methods in social relations.* New York: Dryden.

Lipsky, D. K. (1985). A parental perspective on stress and coping. *American Journal of Orthopsychiatry, 55,* 614–617.

Massie, R., & Massie, S. (1975). *Journey.* New York: Knopf.

Park, C. C. (1972). *The siege: The first eight years of an autistic child.* Boston: Little, Brown.

Schaefer, N. (1982). *Does she know she's there?* Toronto: Fitzhenry & Whiteside.

Skrtic, T. M. (1986). The crisis in special education knowledge: A perspective on perspective. *Focus on Exceptional Children, 18*(7), 1–16.

Sprinthall, N. A., & Sprinthall, R. C. (1987). *Educational psychology* (4th ed.). New York: Random House.

Turnbull, H. R. III, & Turnbull, A. P. (1985). *Parents speak out: Then and now* (2nd ed.). Columbus, OH: Charles E. Merrill.

Wikler, L., Wasow, M., & Hatfield, E. (1983). Seeking strengths in families of developmentally disabled children. *Social Work, 28,* 313–315.

Chapter 13

THE SOCIAL CONSTRUCTION
OF HUMANNESS
Relationships with
Severely Disabled People

Robert Bogdan & Steven J. Taylor

While no one can dispute the fact that people with obvious disabilities often have been cast into deviant roles in society, an exclusive focus on rejection has led many sociologists to ignore or explain away instances in which rejection and exclusion do not occur. Symbolic interactionism and labelling theory, though not by nature deterministic, often have been presented in terms of the inevitability of labelling, stereotyping, stigmatization, rejection, and exclusion of people defined as deviant, including those with recognizable disabilities. According to Goffman (1963), people with demonstrable stigma are seen as "not quite human" and "reduced in our minds from a whole and usual person to a tainted, discounted one" (p. 5). Scott (1969) emphasizes how blindness is "a trait that discredits a man by spoiling both his identity and his respectability" (p. 24). The rejection and exclusion of deviant groups are so taken for granted that instances in which nondeviant persons do not stigmatize and reject deviant ones are often described in terms such as "denial" and "cult of the stigmatized" (Davis, 1961; Goffman, 1963).

This chapter is directed toward understanding the perspectives of non-disabled people who do not stigmatize, stereotype, and reject those with obvious disabilities. We look at how nondisabled people who are in caring and accepting relationships with severely disabled people (people with severe and profound mental retardation or multiple disabilities) define those people. Although the disabled people in these relationships sometimes drool, soil themselves, do not talk or walk—traits that most would consider

---

highly undesirable—they are accepted by the nondisabled people as valued and loved human beings. They have moral careers that humanize rather than dehumanize (Goffman, 1961; Vail, 1966).

The position taken in this chapter is that the definition of a person is not determined by either the characteristics of the person or the abstract social or cultural meanings attached to the group of which the person is a part, but rather the nature of the relationship between the definer and the defined. In taking this position we call for a less deterministic approach to the study of deviance and suggest that people with what are conventionally thought of as extremely negatively valued characteristics can have moral careers that lead to inclusion. In a more abstract sense, this chapter suggests that the sociology of exclusion is only part of the story and that a sociology of acceptance needs to be added (Bogdan & Taylor, 1987; Taylor & Bogdan, 1989).

In the first section of the chapter, we describe our research methodology and the data on which our analysis is based. In the following section, we discuss accepting relationships between people with severe disabilities and nondisabled people. We then turn to a discussion of the nondisabled people's definitions of their disabled partners, specifically the perspectives that sustain their belief in the humanness of the disabled people. In the conclusion, we briefly present our views on how the relationships and perspectives described in this study should be interpreted.

THE DATA

The theory presented in this chapter is grounded in over 15 years of qualitative research (Taylor & Bogdan, 1984) among people defined as mentally retarded as well as staff, family members, and others who work with or relate to people so defined. Our earliest research was conducted at so-called state schools and hospitals or developmental centers for people labelled as mentally retarded; in other words, "total institutions" (Goffman, 1961). Ironically, in this research, we studied the dehumanizing aspects of institutions and specifically how staff come to define the mentally retarded persons under their care as less than human (Bogdan, Taylor, deGrandpre, & Haynes, 1974; Taylor, 1977/1978, 1987; Taylor & Bogdan, 1980). Similarly, through life histories of ex-residents of institutions, we looked at the life experiences and perspectives of people who had been subjected to the label of mental retardation (Bogdan & Taylor, 1982). This research supported the literature on stigma, stereotyping, and societal rejection of people with obvious differences.

In more recent years, we have studied people with disabilities in a broad range of school (Bogdan, 1983; Taylor, 1982) and community settings (Bogdan & Taylor, 1987; Taylor, Biklen, & Knoll, 1987). For the past 4 years, as part of a team of researchers, we have been conducting site visits to agencies and programs that support people with severe disabilities in the community. To date, we have visited over 20 places located throughout the country and we continue to make visits. Each of these places is selected because it has a reputation among leaders in the field of severe disabilities for providing innovative and exemplary services. We have been especially interested in visiting agencies that support children with severe disabilities in natural, foster, and adoptive families, and adults in their own homes or in small community settings. The visits last for 2 to 4 days and involve interviews with agency administrators and staff, family members, and, if possible, the people with disabilities themselves, and observations of homes and community settings. Our design calls for us to focus on at least two people with disabilities at each site. However, at most sites, we end up studying the situations of six to eight individuals. During the visits, we are usually escorted by a "tour guide," typically an agency administrator or social worker, although this is not always the case. At several sites, we have been provided with the names and addresses of people served by the agency and visited them on our own.

Our methodological approach falls within the tradition of qualitative research (Taylor & Bogdan, 1984). First of all, our interviews are open-ended and designed to encourage people to talk about what is important to them. Second, based on visits, we prepare detailed fieldnotes, recording interviews and observations. To date, we have recorded roughly 1,000 pages of fieldnotes. Finally, our analysis is inductive. For example, the perspectives and definitions described in this chapter emerged as themes in the data.

Over the course of our visits, we have probably learned something about the lives and situations of over 100 people with disabilities or at least about the perspectives of the many nondisabled people who are involved with them. This chapter focuses on the nondisabled people involved with a smaller number of people with disabilities. In the first place, we are concerned here with nondisabled people who are involved with people who have been labelled by professionals as severely disabled, especially people who cannot talk, and whose humanness (for example, the ability to think), as described later in this chapter, is often considered problematic. In the second place, we report on nondisabled people who have formed humanizing definitions and constructions of these severely disabled people. Not all the family members, staff members, and others whom we have met and interviewed hold the perspectives described in this chapter. People who are

involved with people with severe disabilities have a broad range of definitions of those people, from clinical perspectives (Goode, 1984) to dehumanizing perspectives (Taylor, 1977/1978; Vail, 1966) to the humanizing
perspectives described here.

The research methodology on which the chapter is based has several
obvious limitations. For one, we spent relatively little time with each of the
people included in this study. In contrast to other interviewing studies we
have conducted, in which we spent from 25 to 50 hours or more interviewing people, the interviews in this study lasted from approximately 1 to
3 hours. This does not afford the opportunity to develop any level of
rapport with people, to double check stories, or to probe areas in depth.
However, we have spent enough time in institutions, schools, and service
settings and interviewing people with disabilities and their families to know
when people are merely reiterating formal policy or the official line.

Further, most of our data are generated from interviews and consist of
verbal accounts. While we occasionally observed interactions between disabled and nondisabled people, this study is based primarily on what people
said to us and not what we observed them do.

Thus, this is a study of how nondisabled people present their disabled
partners to outsiders. Depending on one's theoretical perspective, this study
can be viewed in terms of either "accounts"—how people "do" humanness
in interaction with an outsider—or "social meanings"—how people define
others in their lives as revealed by what they say in interviews. Based on our
own theoretical framework, symbolic interactionism (Blumer, 1969; Mead,
1934), we are inclined to view this study in the latter way. In other words,
how nondisabled people present their disabled partners in interview situations in some way reflects how they view their partners.

ACCEPTING RELATIONSHIPS

The nondisabled people described in this chapter have developed accepting
relationships with people with severe and multiple disabilities. An accepting
relationship is defined here as one between a person with a deviant attribute—for our interests, a severe and obvious disability—and another person
that is long-standing and characterized by closeness and affection. In the
relationship, the deviant attribute, the disability, does not have a stigmatizing or morally discrediting character. The humanness of the person with the
disability is maintained. These relationships are based *not* on a denial of the
difference, but rather on the absence of impugning the other's moral character because of it.

It is when these relationships are compared with staff-to-client relationships in formal organizations designed to deal with deviant populations (Higgins, 1980; Mercer, 1973; Scheff, 1966; Schneider & Conrad, 1983; Scott, 1969) that they become especially interesting sociologically and important in human terms. People with the same characteristics can be defined and interacted with in one way in one situation and in a radically different way in another. As Goode (1983, 1984) points out, identities are socially produced and depend on the context in which people are viewed. The same group of people who are viewed as "not like you and me"—essentially as nonpersons—by institutional attendants (Taylor, 1977/1978, 1987) are viewed as people "like us" by the nondisabled people in this study. Notwithstanding cultural definitions of mental retardation and the treatment of people with mental retardation in institutional settings, nondisabled people can and do form accepting relationships with people with the most severe disabilities and construct positive definitions of their humanness. While we do not claim that accepting relationships of the kind described in this study are common or representative, we do claim that such alliances exist, need to be understood and accounted for, and call into question deterministic notions of labelling, stigma, and rejection.

DEFINING HUMANNESS

Twenty-year-old Jean cannot walk or talk. Her clinical records describe her as having cerebral palsy and being profoundly retarded. Her thin, short—4-feet-long, 40-pound—body, atrophied legs, and disproportionately large head make her a very unusual sight. Her behavior is equally strange. She drools, rolls her head, and makes seemingly incomprehensible high-pitched sounds. This is the way an outsider would describe her, the way we as sociologists encountering her for the first time described her.

Some scholars and professionals would argue that Jean and others like her lack the characteristics of a human being (see Frohock, 1986, for a discussion). Jean and the other severely and profoundly retarded people in our study have often been the target of the indictment "vegetable." People like those in our study have been routinely excluded from the mainstream of our society and subjected to the worst kinds of treatment in institutional settings (Blatt, 1970, 1973; Blatt & Kaplan, 1966; Blatt, Ozolins, & McNally, 1979; Taylor, 1987).

To Mike and Penny Brown (these and the other names in the chapter are pseudonyms), Jean's surrogate parents for the past 6 years, she is their loving and lovable daughter, fully part of the family and fully human. Their sentiments are similar to those expressed by the other nondisabled people in our study when discussing their disabled partners. In the remainder of this chapter, we describe the perspectives of nondisabled people that underlie their relationships with disabled people and sustain their belief in the others' essential humanness. While these nondisabled people seldom use the word "humanness" in describing their partners, we use it because it captures their taken for granted view.[1] The nondisabled view the disabled people as full-fledged human beings. This stands in contrast to the dehumanizing perspectives often held by institutional staff and others, in which people with severe disabilities are viewed as nonpersons or subhuman (Bogdan et al., 1974; Taylor, 1987). We look at four dimensions:

1. Attributing thinking to the other
2. Seeing individuality in the other
3. Viewing the other as reciprocating
4. Defining social place for the other

These perspectives enable the nondisabled people to define the disabled as people "like us" despite their significant behavioral and/or physical differences.

Our analysis has parallels to and builds on a small number of interactionist and ethnomethodological studies of how people "do" normalcy or deviance (Becker, 1963; Goode, 1983, 1984, 1986, 1990; Gubrium, 1986; Lynch, 1983; Pollner & McDonald-Wikler, 1985). In contrast to some of these studies, we focus not on interactional practices that produce normalcy or humanness, but on the perspectives (Becker, Geer, Hughes, & Strauss, 1961) associated with defining the other as human. Thus, we are interested in people's mental constructions of the severely disabled person. This is partially a matter of the nature of our data and partially a matter of theoretical framework.

Attributing Thinking to the Other

The ability to think—to reason, understand, and remember—is a characteristic that is commonly thought of as defining humanness. Intelligence is what separates people from animals. Many of the disabled people in the relationships we studied are unable to talk and have been diagnosed as severely or profoundly retarded. A few accomplish minimal communication through communication boards—boards with pictures or symbols on them that the person can point to as a method of communicating. In conventional psychological testing, many have extremely low IQs (below 20), so low in some cases that they are considered untestable. Many give few or no obvious signs of experiencing the stimuli presented to them. Most people would say that they lack the ability to think.

At first glance the assumption that people with severe and profound mental retardation and multiple disabilities cannot think makes sense. Upon closer examination the question of whether or not these severely disabled people think is much more complex. The nondisabled people in this study believe and cite evidence that their disabled partners can and do think. Some people state emphatically that they know exactly what the disabled person thinks. Others report that although it is impossible to tell for sure what is going on in the other person's mind, they give the person the benefit of the doubt.

What a person thinks is always subjective and never totally accessible to others (Schutz, 1967, Ch. 3). We know what other people think or experience through their ability to produce symbols, using speech, writing, gestures, or body language, that are meaningful to us. The severely disabled people in this study are extremely limited in their ability to move or make sounds and hence to produce symbols. Yet the inability to produce standard symbols does not prevent their nondisabled partners from attributing thinking to them.

According to the nondisabled people, thinking is different from communicating thought. From their perspective a person can have full thinking capacity, be "intelligent," and reflective but be locked in a body that is incapable of or severely limited in communication.

They hold the view that their severely disabled partners are more intelligent than they appear. Their physiology keeps them from revealing their intelligence more fully. As Gubrium (1986) writes of people with Alzheimer's disease, "Yet, while the victim's outward gestures and expressions may hardly provide a clue to an underlying humanity, the question remains whether the disease has stolen it all or only the capacity to express it, leaving an unmanifested, hidden mind" (p. 40).

For some people, attributing thinking to a person with severe disabilities is a matter of reading into the gestures or movements he or she can make. In a case study of communication between a deaf-blind child with severe mental retardation and her parents, Goode (1990) describes how the mother, in particular, made use of nonlanguage resources and gestures to figure out what the young girl was thinking. Similarly, Gubrium (1986) reports how family members or caregivers of people diagnosed as having Alzheimer's disease "sharpen their perception so that whatever clues there are to the patient's inner intentions can be captured" (p. 45).

In this study, the nondisabled people emphasize the significance of minor sounds and movements in attributing intelligence and understanding to the disabled people. For example, one 3-year-old boy we observed is completely paralyzed. The only movements Mike makes, which are involuntary according to professionals, are slight in-and-out movements with his tongue and slow back-and-forth rolling of his blind eyes. Mike's foster parents have been told by doctors and social workers that the boy is not able to understand or communicate, that he has no intelligence. But the parents see in his movements signs that refute the diagnosis. They describe how when certain people come into his room slight alterations in the speed of the tongue movements can be observed. They also claim that the boy, on occasion, moves his eyes toward the person in the room who is talking, an indication to them that he can hear and recognize people.

These people claim not only that their disabled partners can think, but that they can understand their partners and know *what* they are thinking. With the limited menu of gestures and sounds that many severely disabled people have, one might think that it would be extremely difficult for a partner to believe that he or she knew what was on the other's mind. For these people, this is not the case. While all the nondisabled people acknowledged sometimes having difficulty in knowing what their partners think, they maintain that they are able to understand them. They say that they can read gestures and decipher signs of the inner state of the other that strangers cannot see. For instance, some claim that they can understand their partners by reading their eyes.

For other people, intuition is the source of understanding people with severe disabilities and what they think. As the parent of a profoundly retarded young woman explained when asked how she knows her daughter understands: "It's just something inside me. . . . I really believe that deep in my soul." Goode (1990) reports that parents and others in intimate relationships with people with severe disabilities often "just know" what the person is thinking or feeling.

Finally, some nondisabled people understand their severely disabled partners by putting themselves in their position or "taking the role of the other." That is, they imagine what they would feel in the same situations. One foster mother says that she makes decisions about how to treat her foster daughter by pretending she is the daughter and experiencing her actions. She reports experiencing vicariously the pleasure of being taken care of by looking at what she is doing for her foster child from the child's perspective. While people acknowledge the likelihood that their assessments of the other's inner life often may be flawed, they believe that the process brings them closer to their partners and leads them to a better understanding of what they are experiencing.

The nondisabled people's belief in the ability of their severely retarded friends and loved ones to think often runs counter to professional and clinical assessments (Goode, 1983; Pollner & McDonald-Wikler, 1985). In some cases doctors have told them that their partners are brain dead. The nondisabled people report that they have often been bombarded with specialists' judgments that, in their eyes, underestimate their partners' capabilities. They argue that specialists are not privy to the long, day-by-day, hour-by-hour observation of the person. Behaviors that they cite as indicating understanding do not occur with such frequency that the professional is likely to see them. Further, unlike the nondisabled partners in the relationships, professionals are not intimately familiar with their clients and therefore are not attuned to the subtleties of their sounds and gestures.

What also bolsters the belief that the professionals are wrong in their assessments of intelligence are numerous examples of past professional judgments that were wrong. Some have watched their disabled companions live through predictions of early death. Others have cared for their disabled partners at home in spite of advice that such living arrangements would not be possible and that the disabled people would be destined to live their lives in an institution.

As a foster parent of a person who was profoundly retarded told us: "They [the physicians] said she'd have to be in an institution. I said to myself, 'That's all I need to hear. We'll see about that.' I knew I could take care of Amy and I have." In one family in which there are one profoundly retarded and two severely retarded adolescents the parents told us that their foster children had been excluded from school because professionals had judged them incapable of attending. Immediately after they were released from an institution and came to live with the family they began attending regular school.

Regarding whether or not people with severe disabilities, including those diagnosed as having severe and profound mental retardation, can understand and think as other people, professional assessments stake no greater claim to truth than the assessments of the nondisabled people reported in this study. Critiquing Pollner and McDonald-Wikler's (1985) account of a family's "delusional" beliefs in the competence of a severely retarded child—what they refer to as the "social construction of unreality"—Goode (1990) points out that clinical and medical bodies of knowledge cannot be used to provide a standard by which to judge the legitimacy of family belief systems. Clinical perspectives are based on different ways of knowing and seeing than the perspectives of people involved in intimate relationships with people and disabilities. Further, clinical diagnoses are often proven wrong based on their own criteria. For example, case histories have come to light of people diagnosed at an early age as having no mental capacity who later were found to have normal intelligence when provided with communication devices (Crossley & McDonald, 1980; Hay, 1982).

Seeing Individuality in the Other

Sitting in the living room of a foster home for a severely retarded young woman who had spent the majority of her life in an institution, the father described her as having very pretty hair and a great sense of humor and as being a very appreciative person. When this young woman arrived home from school she was dressed in a new stylish outfit complete with Reebok running shoes. He told us how Monica loved to get dressed in new clothes and how the color she had on was her favorite. He told us how her hairstyle had changed since she came to live with his family, from an institutional bowl cut to its present high fashion style. Monica had a communication board on her lap. She moved her hand, placing it in the vicinity of the picture of a radio. He said: "OK, I have to start dinner and then I'll get the radio. We are having your favorite, chicken." As an aside he said, "Monica loves to listen to music and she gets very excited when she can smell something that she likes cooking."

We have discussed how the nondisabled people in our study construct humanness by attributing thinking to their severely disabled companions. But being a person involves something more than thinking. A person is like all other people but also unique; at least in this culture humanness implies individuality. For the people we have been studying an important aspect of constructing humanness is seeing the others as distinct, unique individuals with particular and specific characteristics that set them apart from others. As illustrated in the story of Monica's foster father, nondisabled people in caring relationships with disabled persons see the others as having distinct personalities, particular likes and dislikes, normal feelings and motives, a distinct background—in short, a clear identity—and manage their appearances to conform to their own views of them.

Personality

The nondisabled people used a variety of words to describe the distinctive qualities of their severely disabled partners. The adjectives silly, fun, shy, live wire, bright, appreciative, nice, likeable, calm, active, kind, gentle, wonderful, amusing, pleasant, and good company fall under the broad category of "personality." Most of the words are resoundingly positive. Occasionally one might hear phrases like: "He's a handful," or "She gave me a lot of trouble yesterday," indicating a more critical evaluation of the partner. But even here, the tone is accepting and the comments never indicting.

Many nondisabled people have nicknames for their disabled partners. Often the nicknames are given because they capture something unique about the person's personality. One man who has developed a close relationship with an elderly disabled man who had spent over 50 years of his life in an institution calls the older man "Mr. Rudy." Mr. Rudy is blind, unable to talk, and walks only by leaning on a wall. The nondisabled man is not able to explain how he came up with the nickname but believes that Mr. Rudy seems to go with the man's personality. He says that Mr. Rudy has been through a lot in his life, but "he made it and still has it together." For him, the name Mr. Rudy for the elderly man conveys a sense of dignity.

None of these people use phrases like "profoundly retarded" or "developmentally disabled" to refer to their friend or loved one. Some feel that clinical designations are too impersonal and do not tell much about the character and personality of the labelled person. A few indicate that they believe that clinical labels define a person in terms of deficits rather than positive characteristics, a vantage point they prefer not to see their companions from. The label can strip the person of his or her unique personality. By using a rich repertoire of adjectives and defining the person in specific personal terms, these people maintain the humanness of their severely disabled partners.

Likes and dislikes

Another dimension of individuality involves being discriminating—having tastes and preferences. As illustrated in the remarks Monica's father made in describing her, the nondisabled people in this study know their partners' specific likes and dislikes and discuss them willingly. While people with severe disabilities may be extremely limited in their activities and hence have few areas in which they can express preferences, the nondisabled people present them as having definite likes and dislikes regarding the things they do experience (Goode, 1990). Music, food, colors, and individual people are commonly cited as areas where people with severe disabilities have preferences. Monica loves to listen to music, has a favorite color, and prefers to eat chicken. In one home with three disabled young people, nondisabled family members explain that one person prefers classical music, a second likes rock, and a third does not like music. In another case, a woman who has a caring relationship with a 43-year-old severely retarded woman described the woman as enjoying camping, sailing, and canoeing.

By viewing the disabled person as having likes and dislikes, the nondisabled person not only confirms his or her individuality, but often reinforces the bonds between them as well. Comments such as, "She likes to eat everything we do!" and "He loves the banana bread I make" indicate that the disabled and nondisabled people share things in common.

Feelings and motives

In everyday interaction, we attribute feelings and motives to other people's words and acts. Rather than defining the actions of the disabled people as symptomatic of an underlying pathological state (Taylor, 1977/1978), the nondisabled people in our study define them in terms of normal motives and feelings. A foster mother tells the following story about her foster child, Mike:

> Wednesday night he started to cry continuously. I got real upset and called my husband and told him to come right back. As soon as he got here he talked to Mike like only he can: "Hey, Bubba, what's wrong with you." Mike stopped crying and I held him but then he started up again. My husband told me to give him back and he sat in the rocker and talked with Mike and he stopped again. But the minute he got ready to lay him down he started up again. . . . so he (Mike) has got to know something. How would he know to cry again, that we were going to lay him down?

As the above quotation illustrates, Mike's foster mother, as do the others we have studied, takes outward signs—crying, laughing, sighing—as indicators that the severely disabled person has the same feelings and motives as other people. When crying, laughing, and sighing are observed in conjunction with particular events, the events are said to have provoked them, thus revealing to the interpreters that the person is in touch with his or her surroundings and is expressing human emotion.

Life histories

One aspect of seeing another person as an individual is constructing a biography of the person that explains who he or she is today. In interviews, nondisabled people tell stories of the background experiences of the disabled people. The individuality and the humanness of the disabled people are communicated through biographies that are often unique and detailed. Life histories are sometimes told in two parts. The first has to do with the disabled person's experiences prior to the formation of the relationship. Especially when the person has been institutionalized, the nondisabled person describes the suffering and deprivation the disabled person has experienced. In recounting these experiences, the nondisabled person often puts him- or herself in the disabled person's position and imagines what it would have felt like. In some cases, the people with disabilities are presented as survivors or even heroes for having undergone their experiences. The second part of the life history relates to improvement in the lives of the disabled people, especially when they are living with the nondisabled person telling the story. For example, the nondisabled partners often point to changes in weight, behavior, skills, personality, and appearance.

Managing appearances

The nondisabled people in this study not only see individuality in the disabled people, but actively create it by managing the appearances of the disabled people to downplay their visible differences and to accentuate their individual identities. They present a normal version of the person's self to outsiders and to themselves. By paying attention to clothing style and color and being attentive to other aspects of the person's appearance (cleanliness, hairstyle, nails, make-up for women, beards for men), they help construct an identity consistent with their definitions of the person. In the case of Monica described earlier, for example, her foster parents selected clothes and a hairstyle that made her look attractive. The management of the disabled person's appearance often conforms to gender stereotypes. Many foster parents of young girls dress them in frilly, feminine dresses, complete with bows in their hair. Thus, the person not only has an identity as an "individual" in an abstract sense, but as a "little girl," "teenage boy," "middle-aged woman," "elderly man," and so on.

To an outsider, many of the disabled people in this study have obvious physical abnormalities, including large heads, frail bodies, bent limbs, and curved spines. However, the nondisabled people seldom mention these characteristics except when a particular condition is causing the disabled person difficulties or when they are recounting an outsider's negative reactions to the person's abnormalities.

The nondisabled people often express pride in the disabled person's appearance. For disabled people who have been institutionalized, many people comment on the significant changes in their looks since leaving an institution. The change is from institutional clothing, unstyled haircuts, dirty skin, and sloppiness to a physical self closer to that of other people. The transformation is symbolic of the disabled person's metamorphosis from dehumanized institutional inmate to family member or friend.

In dramatic contrast to total institutions that strip people of their identities (Goffman, 1961), the nondisabled people in this study see and assist in the accomplishment of individual identities for the people with disabilities with whom they are involved. Personality, likes and dislikes, feelings and motives, a biography, and appearance are all individualized aspects of a person. By highlighting the severely disabled person's personal attributes and contributing to creating them, the nondisabled people in our study maintain the humanness of their partners.

Viewing the Other as Reciprocating

For somebody to be thought of as a full human participant in a relationship, the person has to be seen as contributing something to the partnership. Exchange theorists (Blau, 1964) have pointed to the tendency for close relationships to be reciprocal, with both parties defining the relationship as one in which they receive as much as they give. According to exchange theorists, people with equal resources (some combination of social worth, talent, material resources, and so on) tend to form enduring relationships. When one person does not have as much to offer, the relationship suffers from disequilibrium and this is experienced as stressful for the parties. Under these conditions the weaker partner is diminished in the other's eyes. Such formulations narrowly define the nature of the commodities exchanged and exclude the type of alliances discussed in this chapter.

From the outside it might appear that the relationships in our study are one-sided (the nondisabled person giving all and receiving nothing) and, using the logic of exchange theory, doomed to stress and disintegration. After all, severely disabled people appear to have so few resources, so little of social value, talent, and material resources to exchange. This is not the way the nondisabled people in our study see their relationships or the people with disabilities. They define the person with a disability as reciprocating or giving something back, however abstract the benefit.

Joe Bain, who, along with his wife and two children, shares his home with three severely disabled young adults, tells why he has the disabled people living with them: ". . . I am not doing what I'm doing for their benefit. They may benefit from it but I like it. It's fun, I see them as just people I enjoy to be with."

While not all the people in this study are so exuberant, most mention deriving pleasure from their relationships because they like the disabled people and enjoy being with them. For some the disabled person is an important source of companionship. One person says that she does not know what she would do if she did not have her disabled loved one to take care of and to keep her company. A number of people mention how disabled people expand their lives by causing them to meet new people and learn about aspects of their communities they had not been in touch with previously.

Companionship and new social relations are perhaps the most concrete of the benefits people talk about. Some nondisabled people are philosophical about what the person with a disability gives them. A few believe that the relationships with severely disabled people have made them better people. A mother of a 6-year-old boy who is severely retarded and has hydrocephaly says, "He has taught me to accept people for how they are. No matter how limited you are, that everyone has within them a quality that makes them special." Another parent, this time a father whose son is severely retarded and has spina bifida, states, "He made all of our children and ourselves much more caring, much more at ease with all handicapped people."

As discussed in earlier sections, the nondisabled people feel that they know their severely disabled partners intimately. They understand them and know their particular likes and dislikes. Intimately knowing the individual disabled person gives the nondisabled person a feeling of being special. According to one person who has a caring relationship with a profoundly retarded child, "I think we have a very special relationship in that very often we're together alone. I feel like I'm the one person who knows him better than anyone else. I feel like I can tell if he's sick or what he needs better than anybody else."

Another benefit that some nondisabled people report as receiving from their relationships is a sense of accomplishment in contributing to the disabled people's well-being and personal growth. As discussed in the case of personal appearance, the nondisabled people see positive changes occurring in their disabled loved ones or friends. Often the progress would be considered minor by outsiders, something they would not notice or understand, but for the nondisabled person in the relationship it is significant. For example, one person who is in a relationship with a nonverbal, severely retarded woman describes how she had told the woman, Susan, to brush her teeth. Commenting that when Susan came out of the bathroom she was holding a toothbrush and toothpaste with the cap stuck, she explains, "That is asking for help; that is communication. She never would have done that 5 years ago; she wouldn't have even gone for the toothbrush and toothpaste!" Regarding a severely disabled woman, another woman says, "She laughs, she didn't do that before. People might think it's minor, but with Jane progress is slow."

Defining Social Place for the Other

Discussions of humanness often point to the social nature of humans as being a defining characteristic. People are social beings. Humans belong to groups and are part of social networks, organizations, and institutions. Within these social groups, individuals are given a particular social place. The concept of role is often used to describe a person's social place. But social place is not merely a matter of playing a social role. It is also a matter of being defined as being an integral part of the group or social unit. There is a personal dimension to roles. Roles are particularized for each social unit and personalized by each occupant. Through fulfilling particular social roles, social actors are defined as being part of humanity.

The nondisabled people described in this study define their disabled partners as full and important members of their social units and hence create a social place for them. First of all, they incorporate the disabled people in their definitions of their groups or social networks. While some of the relationships discussed in this chapter involve two people, one disabled and one not, most involve the place of people with disabilities within families. In families, in particular, the disabled person is likely to be viewed as a central member. Thus, the person does not simply play the role of a son or daughter, but is seen as "my son" or "my daughter." A foster parent of several children with severe disabilities, who could not have children of his own, says, "This gives us our family." In a foster family, the mother describes how her natural son sees the foster child: "He's the little brother he never had." In many cases, the family would not seem like the same family without the disabled person.

Second, the nondisabled people define a part for the disabled people in the rituals and routines of the social unit. In any group, members develop intertwined patterns of living. For instance, in a family, members coordinate getting up, taking showers, getting breakfast, accompanying each other on important occasions, preparing for holidays, going on vacation, having birthday parties, and so on. The inclusion of a severely disabled person in a family's or primary group's routines and rituals, in its private times and public displays, acknowledges to the members that he or she is one of them. The person fills a particular social place. As a foster parent of two people with severe disabilities explains, "We bring them to all family gatherings. My sister said we could hire a baby-sitter and leave all of the foster children home. We said that where we go, they go. . . . The family accepts them as part of the family."

When, because of hospitalization or other reasons, people with disabilities are missing from the social unit, other members talk about how they are missed and how things are not the same without them. The person's absence interferes with normal family routines.

Primary groups belong to larger networks of human relations. When severely disabled people are integrated into primary groups and have their humanness declared there, they have a vehicle to be included in the social web that defines community membership. The mother of a 6-year-old profoundly retarded girl who spent most of her life in an institution said, "We take her to church, the grocery store, and everywhere we go."

CONCLUSION

The humanizing sentiments underlying the relationships described in this chapter are not unique to unions between nondisabled and severely disabled people. They are the same sentiments described in the phenomenological literature as sustaining the perception of the social world as intersubjective (Husserl, 1962; Psathas, 1973; Schutz, 1967). As Jehensen (1973) writes, "As an actor on the social scene, I can recognize my fellow-man not as 'something,' but as 'someone,' a 'someone like me'" (p. 221). So too do the nondisabled people in this study recognize people with severe disabilities as "someone like me"; that is, as having the essential qualities to be defined as a fellow human being. Disability is viewed as secondary to the person's humanness. What makes the perspectives described in this chapter striking is that they are directed toward people who have often been denied their humanity and in some instances defined as nonpersons (Fletcher, 1979).

An understanding of how nondisabled people construct the humanness of severely disabled people can inform ethical debates surrounding the treatment of infants, children, and adults with severe disabilities (Association for Persons with Severe Handicaps, 1984). Whether or not people with severe disabilities will be treated as human beings, or persons, is not a matter of their physical or mental condition. It is a matter of definition. We can show that they are human by proving that we are capable of showing humanity to them. It is easy to dismiss the perspectives described in this chapter. One might argue that the nondisabled people are deceiving or deluding themselves when they attribute human characteristics to people with severe and profound mental retardation and other disabilities. For example, some might consider the belief that people with severe or profound retardation can and do think to be outlandish. Yet it is just as likely that those who dehumanize people with severe disabilities, dispute their human agency, and define them as nonpersons are deceiving themselves. After all, no one can ever prove that anyone else is "someone like me" or that the assumption of common experience is anything but an illusion. What others are depends on our relationships with them and what we choose to make of them.

NOTES

Acknowledgments. This chapter was prepared as part of the Research and Training Center on Community Integration, funded by the National Institute on Disability and Rehabilitation Research, U.S. Department of Education (Cooperative Agreement No. G0085C03503 with the Center on Human Policy, Syracuse

University). The opinions expressed herein are solely those of the authors, and no official endorsement by the U.S. Department of Education should be inferred.

1. Whether or not people with severe disabilities "really are" human is not a matter of social definition. This is a moral and philosophical question and not a sociological one.

REFERENCES

Association for Persons with Severe Handicaps. (1984). *Legal, economic, psychological, and moral considerations on the practice of withholding medical treatment from infants with congenital defects.* Seattle, WA: Author.

Becker, H. S. (1963). *Outsiders: Studies in the sociology of deviance.* New York: Free Press.

Becker, H. S., Geer, B., Hughes, E. C., & Strauss, A. A. (1961). *Boys in white: Student culture in medical school.* Chicago: University of Chicago Press.

Blatt, B. (1970). *Exodus from pandemonium.* Boston: Allyn & Bacon.

Blatt, B. (1973). *Souls in extremis.* Boston: Allyn & Bacon.

Blatt, B., & Kaplan, F. (1966). *Christmas in purgatory.* Boston: Allyn & Bacon.

Blatt, B., Ozolins, A., & McNally, J. (1979). *The family papers.* New York: Longman.

Blau, P. (1964). *Exchange and power in social life.* New York: John Wiley.

Blumer, H. (1969). *Symbolic interactionism.* Englewood Cliffs, NJ: Prentice-Hall.

Bogdan, R. (1983). "Does mainstreaming work?" is a silly question. *Phi Delta Kappan, 64,* 427–428.

Bogdan, R., & Taylor, S. J. (1982). *Inside out: The social meaning of mental retardation.* Toronto: University of Toronto Press.

Bogdan, R., & Taylor, S. J. (1987). Toward a sociology of acceptance: The other side of the study of deviance. *Social Policy, 18*(2), 34–39.

Bogdan, R., & Taylor, S. J., deGrandpre, B., & Haynes, S. (1974). "Let them eat programs": Attendants' perspectives and programming on wards in state schools. *Journal of Health and Social Behavior, 15,* 142–151.

Crossley, R., & McDonald, A. (1980). *Annie's coming out.* New York: Penguin.

Davis, F. (1961). Deviance disavowal: The management of strained interaction by the visibly handicapped. *Social Problems, 9,* 120–132.

Fletcher, J. F. (1979). *Humanhood: Essays in biomedical ethics.* Buffalo, NY: Prometheus Books.

Frohock, F. M. (1986). *Special care: Medical decisions at the beginning of life.* Chicago: University of Chicago Press.

Goffman, E. (1961). *Asylums: Essays on the social situation of mental patients and other inmates.* Garden City, NY: Doubleday, Anchor Books.

Goffman, E. (1963). *Stigma: Notes on the management of spoiled identity.* Englewood Cliffs, NJ: Prentice-Hall.

Goode, D. A. (1983). Who is Bobby? Ideology and method in the discovery of a Down syndrome person's competence. In G. Kielhofner (Ed.), *Health through occupation* (pp. 237–255). Philadelphia: Davis. [See Chapter 9 of this book.]

Goode, D. A. (1984). Socially produced identities, intimacy and the problem of competence among the retarded. In S. Tomlinson & L. Barton (Eds.), *Special education and social interests* (pp. 228–248). London: Croom-Helm.

Goode, D. A. (1986). Kids, culture and innocents. *Human Studies, 9*, 83–106.

Goode, D. A. (1990). On understanding without words: Communication between a deaf-blind child and her parents. *Human Studies, 13*, 1–37.

Gubrium, J. F. (1986). The social preservation of mind: The Alzheimer's disease experience. *Symbolic Interaction, 9*, 37–51.

Hay, D. (1982). My story. *Mental Retardation, 32*, 11–16.

Higgins, P. C. (1980). *Outsiders in a hearing world: A sociology of deafness.* Beverly Hills, CA: Sage.

Husserl, E. (1962). *Ideas.* New York: Collier.

Jehensen, R. (1973). A phenomenological approach to the study of the formal organization. In G. Psathas (Ed.), *Phenomenological sociology* (pp. 219–250). New York: John Wiley.

Lynch, M. (1983). Accommodation practices: Vernacular treatments of madness. *Social Problems, 31*, 152–164.

Mead, G. H. (1934). *Mind, self and society.* Chicago: University of Chicago Press.

Mercer, J. (1973). *Labeling the mentally retarded.* Berkeley: University of California Press.

Pollner, M., & McDonald-Wikler, L. (1985). The social construction of unreality: A case study of a family's attribution of competence to a severely retarded child. *Family Process, 24*, 241–254.

Psathas, G. (Ed.). (1973). *Phenomenological sociology.* New York: John Wiley.

Scheff, T. (1966). *Being mentally ill.* Chicago: Aldine.

Schneider, J. W., & Conrad, P. (1983). *Having epilepsy: The experience and control of illness.* Philadelphia: Temple University Press.

Schutz, A. (1967). *The phenomenology of the social world.* Evanston, IL: Northwestern University Press.

Scott, R. (1969). *The making of blind men.* New York: Russell Sage Foundation.

Taylor, S. J. (1978). The custodians: Attendants and their work at state institutions for the mentally retarded (Doctoral dissertation, Syracuse University, 1977). *Dissertation Abstracts International, 39*, 1145A–1146A.

Taylor, S. J. (1982). From segregation to integration. *Journal of the Association for the Severely Handicapped, 7*(3), 42–49.

Taylor, S. J. (1987). Observing abuse: Professional ethics and personal morality in field research. *Qualitative Sociology, 10*, 288–302.

Taylor, S. J., Biklen, D., & Knoll, J. (Eds.). (1987). *Community integration for people with severe disabilities.* New York: Teachers College Press.

Taylor, S. J., & Bogdan, R. (1980). Defending illusions: The institution's struggle for survival. *Human Organization, 39*, 209–218. [See Chapter 4 of this book.]

Taylor, S. J., & Bogdan, R. (1984). *Introduction to qualitative research methods: The search for meanings* (2nd ed.). New York: John Wiley.

Taylor, S. J., & Bogdan, R. (1989). On accepting relationships between people with mental retardation and non-disabled people: Towards an understanding of acceptance. *Disability, Handicap & Society, 4*(2), 21–36.

Vail, D. (1966). *Dehumanization and the institutional career.* Springfield, IL: Charles C. Thomas.

CONCLUSION
The Future of Interpretivism in Disability Studies

Philip M. Ferguson, Dianne L. Ferguson,
& Steven J. Taylor

We began this book with a description of its contents as a collection of "research stories." We want to return to this characterization in these concluding remarks. We will not try somehow to summarize the selections: The diversity and range of the contributions would quickly overwhelm us should we even attempt it. Instead, we want to build upon the collective illustration of interpretivist research provided here to speculate about the future of such an approach in disability studies. It is a fairly safe prediction that over the next 10 years interpretivism will gain a greatly increased prominence within disability research. The more interesting question is whether and how that newfound prominence will really change things. What special promise might interpretivism hold for our future understanding of people with disabilities? What new and different stories will this research tell? Will their telling make a difference?

It is our belief that interpretivism is more than merely one more way to study disability. We do not go so far as to say that it is the only proper way. The eclectic spirit of postmodernism makes such purist claims increasingly difficult to accept (Bernstein, 1988; Rorty, 1979; Smith, 1989). For us, it is parity, not purity, that interpretivism should seek in its epistemological debate with objectivism. The two paradigms seem ultimately equal in their inability to provide some transcendent foundation for knowledge that is both consistent and universal. However, from our point of view within the interpretivist perspective, it is precisely this recognition of the inescapable contextuality of our knowledge and beliefs that will increasingly allow the practical and moral strengths of interpretivism to emerge. Once free of the continual burden of justifying themselves to others, interpretivist scholars in disability studies can concentrate on fulfilling the promise of their paradigm to improve people's lives. There are at least three areas to watch for that improvement.

TELLING DIFFERENT STORIES:
DISABILITY AND SOCIAL CONSTRUCTION

The first, and perhaps most fundamental, promise of interpretivism for special education and related fields has to do with what we understand about disability itself. Interpretivism encourages us to re-examine the basic questions we ask as researchers and practitioners. As the chapters in this book demonstrate, instead of asking about the "nature" or "essence" of disability, interpretivists are more likely to ask: "What is the experience of disability?" As the philosopher Wittgenstein put it in his famous phrase: "Don't ask for the meaning, ask for the use." That is, ask for the context, the construction through which physical reality takes shape. Interpretivism maintains that disability is not a fact or an entity, whose nature is just waiting to be discovered. Disability is rather an experience waiting to be described, or, more precisely, a social construction of multiple experiences waiting to be recognized.

One familiar example of this approach is our society's approach to mild mental retardation. Over the years the "official" definitions of this condition have changed in terms of the range and sufficiency of IQ scores that qualify someone as mentally retarded. For example, in 1973, the entire category of "borderline retardation" was dropped from the *Manual of Terminology* of the American Association on Mental Deficiency (as the major professional organization in the field was known then). What changed, of course, in this revised definition was not some set of brute *facts* that dramatically "cured" thousands of individuals previously diagnosed as mentally retarded (Blatt, Bogdan, Biklen, & Taylor, 1977). What changed was simply the socially agreed upon rules used to identify some people as mentally retarded and others as not. Interpretivism teaches us not to ask about the meaning of mental retardation, but to ask how the term is used by those who apply the label to others.

The difference is important. The interpretivist perspective teaches us that the social construction of disability, in this case, is more than just the social rule. It is also the actions of applying the rule. The definition is important only in the context of who is using it, and upon whom it is being used. Similarly, when—say at the end of an assessment report—a school psychologist speaks (or writes) words such as, "This child has an IQ of 62," he or she also does something more than just utter some words. The statement by that person, in that context, *makes* the child mentally retarded. In a very real social sense, the child was not so until those words were uttered. As a consequence, the child's experience of life, and of schooling, changes. What it means to be "a student" is different from what it means to be "a mentally retarded student," even when the child can read or not read exactly the same words, remember or forget exactly the same math facts, and survive daily on the same mean streets outside of school.

It is that new life story that the interpretivist paradigm teaches us to value and discover. Sometimes, in fact, our field has responded to these realizations about the power and meaning of social constructions. Consider, for example, the shift in preferred usage from "mongolism" to "Down syndrome." These words, both official labels at different times, ostensibly refer to exactly the same condition, yet connote vastly different social constructions about the significance of that physical beginning.

TELLING STORIES DIFFERENTLY: DISABILITY AND SOCIAL TEXT

The interpretivist paradigm not only urges us to ask different questions, it also prompts us to ask questions differently. To illustrate this implication we can look at the category of profound, rather than mild, mental retardation. Despite the evidence of several chapters in this book, this extreme type of disability may still seem particularly hard for interpretivism to explore extensively. Surely the vulnerability of a social constructivist approach to understanding the experience of disability emerges at precisely those points where culture seems beside the point; where physiology has gone so far awry that it appears to overwhelm the social context.

As we mentioned in our introduction, and as the individual chapters have variously demonstrated, a central tenet of interpretivism is that reality is created and social. In other words, the paradigm assumes that we humans are active participants in the social interpretation of our world, rather than mere reactors to our confrontations with an unchanging world of facts that are "out there" in the "real world." The challenge of profound retardation for interpretivism is precisely how close it seems to come to the absence of active participation. It is not just that the passivity is often enforced by limbs that do not move or environmental barriers that trap the individual physically. One reason for the relative scarcity of interpretivist research with profoundly retarded and multiply handicapped individuals is the difficulty in conceiving the social world of someone whose experience of concepts and communication is so uncertain for us. The relativity of language seems a woefully inadequate explanation.

Our response to this apparent limitation is to emphasize the "social" part of social construction. Interpretivism is not dependent on a kind of romanticist subjectivism as the approach to inquiry. A slight shift in our basic metaphor—from "story" to "text"—may help explain the difference. Interpretivism, or at least the version of it that we endorse, can be understood as analogous to the literary interpretation of a particular text. For social science, the social setting or process becomes the "text." Just as with literary criticism, part of determining the meaning of a "social text" is finding out what the authors of that text intended it to mean. That is never enough, however. The meaning of a social text belongs as well to the text itself, as a whole, and must be determined anew by all those who "read" it. Our point is that the promise of interpretivism is not merely the detailed description of a single perspective, but the appreciation of that perspective as part of a larger story as well. Clifford Geertz (1979) has referred to this process of social interpretation as a kind of "dialectical tacking" (p. 239) between part and the whole, using each to explicate the other. Severely or profoundly retarded people do not need to have any communicative skills to have participated as co-authors, if you will, of the various social texts to which they belong. Even if some of them do not noticeably interpret the experience for themselves in any strong sense of human agency by telling their own stories, the social text remains—containing their contribution—for others to interpret. People do not have to talk to tell their stories, and those stories can have meanings that their authors will never know.

It is with these examples, when we start stretching the notion of human agency, that the interpretivist paradigm allows us to ask questions differently. We do not mean to overstate the situation: The interpretivist paradigm is at its best with people who can tell their own stories, in their own words. Nonetheless, there are stories to be discovered within the text for those who learn to ask questions differently. Sometimes the way to ask questions differently is not to ask questions at all, but simply to look; to see the experience (Biklen & Moseley, 1988). Sometimes asking questions differently means not to ask questions of ourselves—reflective questions—but to listen to the questions others are asking; or to admit different information as answers to our questions. We are learning, for example, to approach the puzzling behavior of some people as personal answers to some unheard questions. Teachers then try to discover the questions we should be asking in a kind of special education version of the game show *Jeopardy*.

One final aspect of telling stories differently is that we have an obligation to gain as many listeners as possible. Interpretivist research emphasizes good writing as inherent in good research. The effective and flexible presentation of findings is not an afterthought to be considered once the real research has been completed, but is an essential phase of accurate storytelling (Richardson, 1990). The most familiar model of research presentation in special education and rehabilitation journals adopts a kind of formulaic prose that seems to view words as a sort of verbal conveyor belt designed to deliver information efficiently and predictably. Of course, conducting research within the interpretivist paradigm does not guarantee well-written results. However, as many of the chapters here have demonstrated, the paradigm does allow the researcher to drop the pretense of the invisible author and replace it with a more active and flexible narrative voice. Establishing an authorial style becomes part of the interpretation, even if that means occasionally drawing attention to the writing itself. Telling stories differently, then, should also mean telling them better.

TELLING STORIES TOGETHER: INTERPRETIVISM AND COLLABORATIVE RESEARCH

A third area of influence that interpretivism should exert in the near future of disability studies is in our understanding of the multiple roles available to all the participants in the research process. As several of the chapters here demonstrate, collaborative forms of inquiry, such as action research, challenge the traditional separation of researcher and "subject." However, as we have just discussed, emphasizing the perspective of the research participants does not mean that interpretivism intends simply to capture the "insider" view of things. Research should not be a war where two sides fight over control of information. Collaboration does not mean surrender; neither "side" should be a captive of the other.

Both insider and outsider roles remain important for interpretivist research. In fact, one of the contributions of interpretivism is to recognize those roles as ultimately inescapable. As soon as we, as researchers, become involved with helping other people tell their stories we inevitably become involved in telling *our* stories of *their* stories; we present our interpretations of their interpretations. Not only are there multiple perspectives, then, but there are multiple *layers* of perspective as soon as one enters the reflective process of research (Giddens, 1976; Smith, 1989).

There are three points that interpretivism makes for the importance of collaborative research as a response to this inevitability of multiple perspectives. First, collaboration should not become a futile attempt to escape any point of view, but should aim to discover the value of them all. Second, collaboration recognizes that both an inner and an outer layer of interpretation exist—to some extent—in any research. Third, and most promising, interpretivism implies that both layers are available—again, to a varied extent—to both outsiders and insiders. That is, insiders (disabled people, teachers, family members, service providers) can become researchers, and researchers can become participants (as in "participant observation"). The greatest value of interpretivist collaboration is to allow each individual to assume multiple roles within the research as much as it allows multiple individuals to assume each role (Adler & Adler, 1987).

   None of this discussion assumes that interpretivist research has already worked out all the methodological details for design, application, presentation, and appropriate collaboration. Part of what makes the future of this research exciting is the prospect of discovering, applying, and revising guidelines for making methodological decisions about whose perspectives to emphasize, how to present those perspectives with the least distortion and richest context, and how and with whom to collaborate. Promising new methods of data collection are emerging (Miles, 1990). New approaches to issues of sampling and generalizability are being proposed (Schofield, 1990). Variations in field work relationships are being evaluated (Adler & Adler, 1987). Proposals for new criteria for evaluation of interpretivist research are addressing the unique potential of the paradigm rather than trying to measure success solely by objectivist standards (Lather, 1986, 1990; Lincoln & Guba, 1986, 1990; Wolcott, 1990). Both the curse and the blessing for interpretivist researchers is that they will live in interesting times.

DISABILITY, INTERPRETIVISM, AND THE PURSUIT OF SOCIAL JUSTICE

Finally, we want to conclude by returning to the promise of interpretivism on behalf of the "underdog" in society. What can we hope for interpretivism to contribute in the pursuit of social justice for people with disabilities and their families? For us that must always be the pragmatic test of a paradigm's assumptions: How does it help make life better for devalued individuals and groups? With interpretivism, this returns us to where we began in our introduction: What is the value of telling stories? In one respect, we hope that the book itself has gone at least part of the way to answering that question. If the chapters included here do not demonstrate that value, then nothing we add in this conclusion can convince the reader. We can perhaps make more explicit our own understanding of two ways in which this final promise of interpretivism can be realized. First, the stories being told can have a reformative effect by virtue of their content. The telling of their experiences by people who lived for years in the large, segregated institutions has been one of the most powerful arguments for deinstitutionalization during the past 20 years in our country. Parents' descriptions of their experiences and perspectives about raising their children with severe disabilities in the community, in the local school, and with other children have been one of the primary forces toward integrated, inclusive education. The very emphasis of interpretivism on the micro-level description exalts the specific, the contextual, the local, the individual—in short, all that can be so easily flattened out in the more abstract structural analyses of world systems and ideologies. Ironically, perhaps, it is this commitment to completeness of description within interpretivism that allows it to create the firmest foundation for social change. Like the bumper sticker says, think globally, act locally. It begins with the individual.

This reformative effect of stories is related to a second, empowering effect of simply getting to tell one's stories. Interpretivism empowers devalued groups within our society by giving them a voice. Indeed, interpretivism can even empower groups such as teachers and other practitioners by legitimizing their credibility and the authenticity of their perspective through collaborative research. Certain individuals within our society have almost always gotten to tell their stories more often, to more people, and with less questioning than have other individuals. Able-bodied, white males come to mind as one such group of individuals whose own stories—and their stories about others—get a lot of telling. That imbalance allows an impression of unanimity about things that quickly transforms a social construction into a biological destiny. Interpretivism empowers by challenging that monologue. Equally important, interpretivism empowers by connecting people together to hear each other's stories. In advocacy circles, this is called networking. Interpretivism pursues social justice one story at a time.

So, let us tell our stories and recognize them as legitimate. Let us listen to the stories of others, and appeciate them as additions, not as contradictions. Most important, as we interpret the future and reflect on the past, let us proclaim the value of those whose stories have so often gone untold.

REFERENCES

Adler, P. A., & Adler, P. (1987). *Membership roles in field research* (Qualitative Research Methods Series, Vol. 6). Newbury Park, CA: Sage.

Bernstein, R. J. (1988). *Beyond objectivism and relativism: Science, hermeneutics, and praxis.* Philadelphia: University of Pennsylvania Press.

Biklen, S. K., & Moseley, C. R. (1988). "Are you retarded?" "No, I'm Catholic.": Qualitative methods in the study of people with severe handicaps. *Journal of the Association for Persons with Severe Handicaps, 13,* 155–162.

Blatt, B., Bogdan, R., Biklen, D., & Taylor, S. J. (1977). From institution to community: A conversion model. In E. Sontag, J. Smith, & N. Certo (Eds.), *Educational programming for the severely and profoundly handicapped* (pp. 40–52). Washington, DC: Council for Exceptional Children.

Geertz, C. (1979). From the native's point of view: On the nature of anthropologi-
    cal understanding. In P. Rabinow & W. M. Sullivan (Eds.), *Interpretive social
    science: A reader* (pp. 225–241). Berkeley: University of California Press.
Giddens, A. (1976). *New rules of sociological method.* New York: Basic Books.
Lather, P. A. (1986). Issues of validity in openly ideological research: Between a
    rock and a soft place. *Interchange, 17*(4), 63–84.
Lather, P. A. (1990). Reinscribing otherwise: The play of values in the practices of
    the human sciences. In E. G. Guba (Ed.), *The paradigm dialog* (pp. 315–332).
    Newbury Park, CA: Sage.
Lincoln, Y. S., & Guba, E. G. (1986). But is it rigorous? Trustworthiness and
    authenticity in naturalistic evaluation. In D. D. Williams (Ed.), *Naturalistic
    evaluation* (pp. 73–84). San Francisco: Jossey-Bass.
Lincoln, Y. S., & Guba, E. G. (1990). Judging the quality of case study reports.
    International Journal of Qualitative Studies in Education, 3, 53–59.
Miles, M. B. (1990). New methods for data collection and analysis: Vignettes and
    prestructured cases. *International Journal of Qualitative Studies in Education, 3,*
    37–51.
Richardson, L. (1990). *Writing strategies: Reaching diverse audiences* (Qualitative Re-
    search Methods Series, Vol. 21). Newbury Park, CA: Sage.
Rorty, R. (1979). *Philosophy and the mirror of nature.* Princeton, NJ: Princeton
    University Press.
Schofield, J. W. (1990). Increasing the generalizability of qualitative research. In
    E. W. Eisner & A. Peshkin (Eds.), *Qualitative inquiry in education: The continu-
    ing debate* (pp. 201–232). New York: Teachers College Press.
Smith, J. K. (1989). *The nature of social and educational inquiry: Empiricism versus
    interpretation.* Norwood, NJ: Ablex.
Wolcott, H. F. (1990). On seeking—and rejecting—validity in qualitative research.
    In E. W. Eisner & A. Peshkin (Eds.), *Qualitative inquiry in education: The
    continuing debate* (pp. 121–152). New York: Teachers College Press.

ABOUT THE EDITORS AND CONTRIBUTORS

Philip M. Ferguson is a Research Associate with the Specialized Training Program, Center on Human Development, University of Oregon. Most of his research focuses on people with severe developmental disabilities and their families. He is also interested in the historical development of social policy in the area of mental retardation.

Dianne L. Ferguson is an Associate Professor in the Division of Special Education and Rehabilitation where she is co-coordinator of the teacher training program of the Specialized Training Program, Center on Human Development, University of Oregon. Her interests include the areas of teacher preparation in special education and supporting families of people with disabilities. Much of her work with teachers has looked at using collaborative research methods to improve the education of students with the most severe disabilities. She is the author of *Curriculum Decision Making for Students with Severe Handicaps: Policy and Practice*.

Steven J. Taylor is an Associate Professor of Education and Director of the Center on Human Policy at Syracuse University. Together with Robert Bogdan, Dr. Taylor is the author of *Introduction to Qualitative Research Methods: The Search for Meanings* and *Inside Out: The Social Meaning of Retardation*. He has written extensively on the integration of people with disabilities into all areas of society, and has a particular interest in the analysis of social policies that try to support such integration.

Robert Bogdan is a Professor at Syracuse University in the Department of Sociology and the Division of Special Education and Rehabilitation. His research has looked at a variety of topics within the broad category of the social construction of disability. In addition to the books written with Steven J. Taylor, he has also written (with Sari K. Biklen) a popular text on interpretivist methods, *Qualitative Research for Education: An Introduction to Theory and Methods*. His most recent book (*Freak Show*) examines the history of the circus side show tradition in America and the lives of the people who worked in such shows.

Mary Alice Brown has been a doctoral student in the Department of Sociology at Syracuse University.

Christy Davis is a Resource Teacher at Powell Middle School in Powell, Wyoming. Her professional interests involve the provision of support to students with mild disabilities in integrated education settings.

Susan B. Foster is a Research Associate with the Office of Postsecondary Career Studies and Institutional Research at the National Technical Institute for the Deaf, a college of Rochester Institute of Technology. Most of her research focuses on the education and employment of people who are deaf. She is also interested in general issues of social policy and the integration of disabled people. She is the author of *The Politics of Caring*, and editor (with Gerard G. Walter) of *Deaf Students in Postsecondary Education.*

David A. Goode is an Associate Professor of Sociology and Coordinator of the Developmental Disabilities Program at the College of Staten Island, City University of New York. Dr. Goode has an interest in phenomenological studies of persons with severe disabilities as well as research and policy in quality of life issues. He has published extensively and lectured internationally.

Nora Groce is a Medical Anthropologist with the School of Public Health at Yale University. Her research focuses on cross-cultural studies of disability and society. In addition to numerous articles in this broad area, she is also the author of *Everyone Here Spoke Sign Language: Hereditary Deafness on Martha's Vineyard* (1985). This book explored a historical example of the incorporation of a specific disability within the life and culture of a small, island community.

Paul C. Higgins is a Professor of Sociology at the University of South Carolina, Columbia. He primarily explores how disabled and nondisabled people live and act together—and apart. Among his books are *Outsiders in a Hearing World*, *The Rehabilitation Detectives*, and *The Challenge of Educating Together Deaf and Hearing Youth.*

Susan Janko is Coordinator of Evaluation and Community Outreach for the Child Development and Mental Retardation Center at the University of Washington. Her research and professional interests are primarily in the areas of intervention and social policy related to children and families at risk.

Marilynn J. Phillips is Associate Professor in the Department of English and Language Arts at Morgan State University in Baltimore, Maryland. Her research uses her training as a folklorist to collect and study oral narratives of the experience of disability, and the portrayal of disability in the media. She is currently working on a book that will focus on the oral narratives of former "poster children," and the social presentation of such children in the media.

Bonnie Todis is a Research Associate and Project Coordinator at the Oregon Research Institute in Eugene, Oregon. Her current research is using both qualitative and quantitative methods to investigate factors that help children with physical disabilities develop high self-esteem. In addition to her research on the social support systems of elderly people with disabilities, she has also published qualitative studies of families who have adopted children with disabilities.

Parnel Wickham-Searl is an Assistant Professor and Coordinator of Special Education at Dowling College, in Oakdale, New York. In her research, she integrates an interest in women's issues with the study of families and disability.

Irving K. Zola is a Professor of Sociology at Brandeis University and the editor/publisher of the *Disability Studies Quarterly*. He is a founding member of both the Boston Self-Help Center (a counseling and advocacy organization for individuals with disabilities), and the Society for Disability Studies (a multi-disciplinary organization established to promote humanistic and social scientific research on disability and chronic illness). Dr. Zola is the author, co-author, or editor of numerous books such as *Missing Pieces*, *Ordinary Lives*, *Independent Living for People with Physical Disabilities*, and *Socio-Medical Inquiries*.

INDEX